Handcrafted CABINETRY

Professional Designs ◆ Practical Techniques

Handcrafted
CABINETRY

Robert A. Yoder, Editor

Reader's Digest

Pleasantville, New York

The writers and editors who compiled this book have tried to make all of the contents as accurate and as correct as possible. Plans, illustrations, photographs, and text have all been carefully checked and cross-checked. However, due to the variability of local conditions, construction materials, personal skill, and so on, neither the writers nor The Reader's Digest Association, Inc., assume any responsibility for any injuries suffered or for damages or other losses incurred that result from the material presented herein. All instructions and plans should be carefully studied and clearly understood before beginning construction.

The designs for the projects in this book are the copyrighted property of the craftsmen who designed and built them. Readers are encouraged to reproduce these projects for their personal use or for gifts. However, reproduction for sale or profit is forbidden by law.

Printed in the United States of America on acid-free ∞, recycled ♻ paper

On the cover (clockwise from left): "Three-Drawer Side Table" (page 104) by Ben Erickson, "Eastern Shore of Virginia Corner Cabinet" (page 61) and "Philadelphia Highboy" (page 352) by Lonnie Bird, "Jewelry Box" (page 331) by Ben Erickson, and "Hall Table" (page 87) by Robert A. Yoder.

Editor: **Robert A. Yoder**
Contributing Writers: **Paul Anthony, Kenneth S. Burton Jr., Bill Hylton, Bob Moran, Tony O'Malley, David Page, Rick Peters, Andy Rae, Phil Totten, Robert A. Yoder**
Cover and Interior Book Designer: **Christopher Rhoads**
Design Coordinators: **Carol Angstadt, Randall Sauchuck**
Layout Designer: **Dale Mack**
Illustrator: **Frank Rohrbach**
Project Photographers: **John Hamel**, except for the following: **Mark Darley**, pages 118, 279, 280, and 296; **Keith Harrelson**, pages 26 and 282; **Mitch Mandel**, pages 2 and 288; **Steve Payne**, pages 41 and 286; **Robert P. Ruschak**, pages 150 and 281
Step-by-Step Photographer: **Mitch Mandel**
Cover Photographer: **John Hamel**
Cover Photo Stylist: **Marianne Grape Laubach**
Photography Editor: **James A. Gallucci**
Copy Editors: **Barbara McIntosh Webb, Nancy N. Bailey, Candace Levy**
Manufacturing Coordinator: **Mark Krahforst**
Indexer: **Nan N. Badgett**
Editorial Assistance: **Susan L. Nickol**

Library of Congress Cataloging-in-Publication Data

Handcrafted cabinetry : professional designs, practical techniques / Robert A. Yoder, editor.
    p.   cm.
includes index.
ISBN 0–76210–173–3 (hardcover)
1. Cabinetwork. I. Yoder, Rob.
TT197.H33 1999
684.1'6—dc21   98–40259

2 4 6 8 10 9 7 5 3 1   hardcover

Contents

About the Cabinet Designers

Lonnie Bird teaches furniture making at Ohio's University of Rio Grande. He also operates a woodworking shop in Gallipolis, Ohio, where he builds reproductions of eighteenth-century American furniture. Lonnie is a contributing editor to *American Woodworker* magazine, in which he writes about basic techniques such as gluing up and dimensioning stock as well as about advanced techniques such as using a shaper and making mitered sticking.

Glenn Bostock's career in woodworking began at age 10, when his father began to teach him woodworking. At age 23 he went into business with his wife, Cheryl, building fine furniture. Glenn works mainly in teak and domestic hardwoods. The Bostock Company, located in Horsham, Pennsylvania, focuses primarily on commercial woodworking and some residential applications.

In addition to operating a woodworking business and studio in New Tripoli, Pennsylvania, **Kenneth S. Burton Jr.** teaches woodworking at the Yestermorrow School in Warren, Vermont. Ken has a Master of Fine Arts degree in furniture design from the Rochester Institute of Technology.

Ben Erickson, the owner of Erickson Woodworks in Eutaw, Alabama, designs and builds cabinets, furniture, and millwork. Ben has been a contributor to several books, including *Cabinetry* and *The Woodworker's Problem Solver,* and he has written technical articles for *Fine Woodworking* magazine. *American Woodworker* magazine featured his design for a coffee table. Warner Books will publish Ben's forthcoming novel, which includes a chapter about woodworking.

Mitch Mandel is an accomplished woodworker. He has built nearly all of the furniture in his home in Schnecksville, Pennsylvania. Mitch has shot thousands of photographs for woodworking books, including all of the covers for the best-selling series *The Workshop Companion.* Mitch occasionally contributes to *American Woodworker* magazine, which has featured his walnut drop-leaf dining table on its cover.

Cabinetmaker **Voicu Marian** came to the United States in 1977 from Romania, where he learned woodworking at an early age in his uncle's shop. Voicu set up his woodworking shop in Alliance, Ohio, and has been building his own designs as well as commissioned pieces ever since. In 1989 he won Best of Show for a hall table with a mirror in Across the Boards at Ohio's Canton Art Museum. In 1997 he won honorable mention for a tie cabinet at the AMERICAN WOODWORKER Show™. Voicu's furniture designs have appeared in *Fine Woodworking, Woodwork,* and *American Woodworker* magazines.

Jim Michaud is a cabinetmaker and contractor specializing in kitchen renovations in the Boston North Shore area. He is also a writer and editor and has contributed to *American Woodworker* magazine and to *Shop Tips.*

Tony O'Malley was the editor of *The Woodworkers Problem Solver.* He has worked as a professional woodworker in Philadelphia. Tony continues to make fine furniture on a commission basis in his workshop in Emmaus, Pennsylvania.

Jim Probst is proud to say that Probst Furniture Makers of Hamlin, West Virginia, has been a successful business for over 15 years with customers throughout the world. Jim describes himself as a self-taught woodworker, influenced by the Shaker style of furniture, although presently most of the furniture he builds is in the Mission style. Jim works in domestic hardwoods, primarily cherry, but also in walnut and maple. His sideboard appeared in the West Virginia Juried Exhibition in Charleston, West Virginia, in 1997–1998.

Andy Rae is an award-winning designer and furniture maker from Lenhartsville, Pennsylvania. Andy is a juried member of the Professional Guild of Upper New Jersey and a juried member of New Jersey Designer Craftsmen.

Robert J. Treanor's main interests are in Shaker, Windsor, and Early American furniture. A freelance writer, he has written more than 35 articles on furniture and woodworking for *American Woodworker, Fine Woodworking,* and other magazines. Robert builds fine furniture in his workshop in San Francisco, California.

Robert A. Yoder is a designer and builder of fine furniture, in particular tables, cabinets, and built-ins, as well as musical instruments, including guitars, harps, and dulcimers. Rob, an editor of woodworking books, edited *Martin Guitars* and *Cabinetry* (which has sold over 700,000 copies). Rob received honorable mention for the design and construction of a walnut hall table at the 1996 AMERICAN WOODWORKER Show™.

Introduction

There is just something so *real* about woodworking. Something so very practical, rewarding, and very, very valuable. Something tangible that will still be here when our hands have gone to dust.

I've been working wood now for about 20 years, and I continually find the process highly satisfying. The smoothing, cutting, and shaping of the raw materials. The care with which they are fitted, sanded, and finished. As I write this, I can instantly recall the satisfying sour smell of fresh-cut oak, the sweet smell of walnut and butternut, and the pungent, nose-tickling smell of poplar. I can even recall how each wood smells when scorched by a saw blade in need of sharpening.

I love the thrill of planing a rough-cut board to reveal the sensuous swirling of grain hidden inside. I relish the challenge of searching for the perfect board, the perfect grain pattern, the perfect match with the perfect project. We are blessed to be woodworkers.

The woodworkers whose designs you'll find in *Handcrafted Cabinetry* love the craft, too. Their love is obvious. Just look at the cabinets in the "Gallery of Fine Cabinetry" on page 279, and you won't have any doubt. Some of the projects are simple, elegant, and practical; others are incredibly detailed and complex. But all were made by fine artisans who have a deep and abiding commitment to their art.

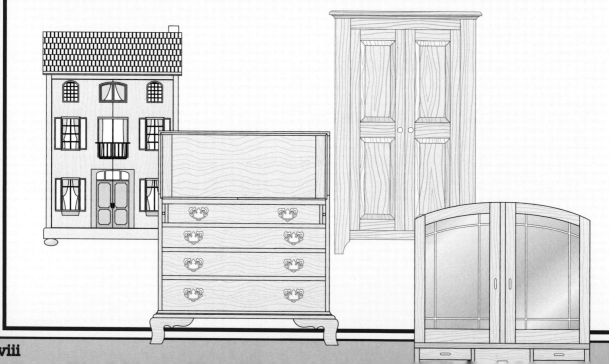

After you select projects that appeal to you, read the directions, and check the drawings and materials lists against the reality of the wood you will cut, prepare, join, and finish. Then, add your own personal touches to the designs.

The designs in *Handcrafted Cabinetry* are the intellectual and artistic property as well as the bread and butter of the woodworkers who dreamed them up. Of course, you can make exact duplicates, but there is no need for most woodworkers to copy the designs of others because we have the skills to customize the projects to fit our unique needs. You can build the "Platform Bed" in any size you need, lower or raise the height of the "Eastern Shore of Virginia Corner Cupboard" to fit in your house, or customize the home office cabinets or built-in shelving to fit any room of your house.

I encourage you to put your own mark on these projects. If you take the time to finely craft your woodworking projects, they will be around a lot longer than any of us. We woodworkers have the opportunity to leave a legacy of excellence as our fine furniture passes from generation to generation.

So, flip through these pages and find something you would like to make. Bend the design to fit your needs. Then head to your workshop, take some time to smell the wood chips, and make something real.

Robert A. Yoder

Robert A. Yoder
Editor

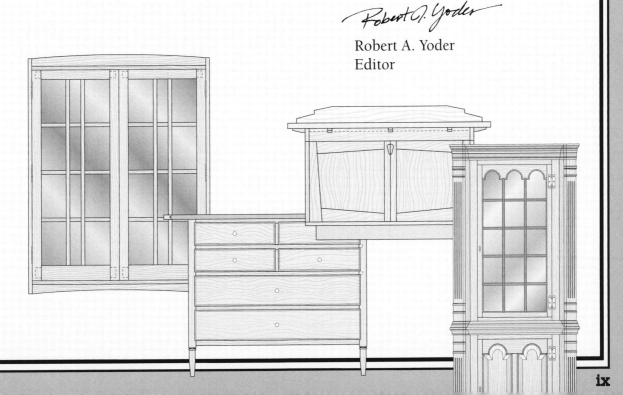

Dining Room and Kitchen

Step-Back Cupboard

by Mitch Mandel

The step-back cupboard, or hutch, is a versatile furniture form that combines display shelves on top with a storage cabinet below. It functions perfectly in a dining room, holding china, glassware, and the like; but it can also serve nicely in a den, a family room, or even a large entrance hall.

When designing this step-back cupboard for my dining room, I incorporated features from several pieces I had seen in magazines, books, and antique stores over the years. And I chose construction methods that made it easy to build with skills and tools I possess— dadoes and rabbets for the cases, biscuit joinery for attaching the face-frame pieces to the case, mortise-and-tenon joints for the doors, and table saw–cut cove molding for the crown.

Don't let the imposing size of a hutch dissuade you from building one. (The cost of materials—now that's another matter: This project required about 150 board feet of solid cherry, including waste factor, and a half-sheet

of ¼-inch cherry plywood.) Like all complex furniture projects, this one should be tackled as a series of smaller assemblies. Build the cases first, then make the doors and drawers, and then add the base and crown molding.

Exploded View

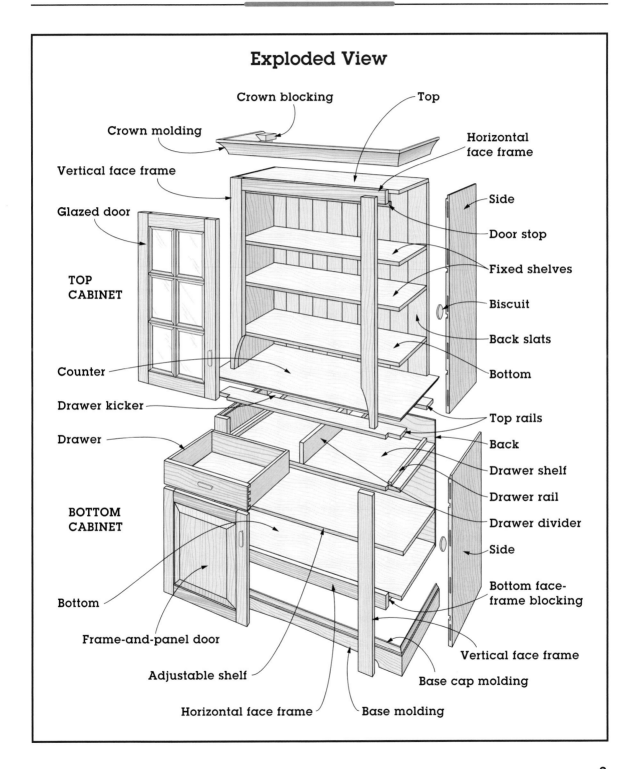

Crown blocking

Top

Crown molding

Horizontal face frame

Vertical face frame

Side

Glazed door

Door stop

Fixed shelves

TOP CABINET

Biscuit

Back slats

Counter

Bottom

Drawer kicker

Top rails

Drawer

Back

Drawer shelf

Drawer rail

BOTTOM CABINET

Drawer divider

Side

Bottom

Bottom face-frame blocking

Frame-and-panel door

Vertical face frame

Adjustable shelf

Base cap molding

Horizontal face frame

Base molding

Build the Cases

1 **Glue up the wider case parts, and cut the stock to size.** Select the best material from your stock for the most visible parts of the project—the case sides, the bottom case counter, the doors, and the face-frame parts. When gluing up panels for the sides, try to choose boards of similar widths, with grain and color that match well. For example, I used a 7-inch-wide × 8-foot-long board, crosscut in half and glued into a wide panel, for each of the top case sides.

Note that the counter and base molding are ⅞ inch thick; they just looked too skinny drawn at ¾ inch thick. These are the kind of small but important details that separate a custom-built piece of furniture from a manufactured one.

When the glue is dry, rip all the case parts to width, then crosscut them to length.

2 **Cut the dado and rabbet joints.** Lay out the dadoes for the upper case shelves and lower case drawer shelf and bottom according to the dimensions shown in *Side View—Cross Section* and *Case Joinery Detail*. I used a T-square fence to guide the router when making dado and rabbet cuts, as shown in the photo below. Unlike a plain straightedge

Quick tip

The bottom case parts may be too wide to crosscut on your table saw. They were too big for mine—so I cut them slightly long with a circular saw and then trimmed the ends with a router and flush-trimming bit riding against a straightedge.

A T-square fence saves time and adds greater accuracy than a plain straight fence when routing dadoes.

Materials List

Part	Dimensions	Part	Dimensions
Bottom Case		Horizontal muntins (4)	$\frac{3}{4}" \times 1" \times 14\frac{3}{4}"$
Sides (2)	$\frac{3}{4}" \times 17\frac{1}{4}" \times 35\frac{1}{4}"$	Vertical muntins (6)	$\frac{3}{4}" \times 1" \times 10\frac{1}{4}"$
Bottom	$\frac{3}{4}" \times 17" \times 47\frac{1}{4}"$	Glazing strip stock	$\frac{1}{4}" \times \frac{3}{8}" \times 40'$
Drawer shelf	$\frac{3}{4}" \times 17" \times 47\frac{1}{4}"$	Drawer fronts (2)	$\frac{3}{4}" \times 4\frac{7}{16}" \times 20\frac{9}{16}"$
Drawer divider	$\frac{3}{4}" \times 17" \times 4\frac{1}{2}"$	Drawer box sides (4)	$\frac{1}{2}" \times 4\frac{7}{16}" \times 16\frac{1}{4}"$
Top rails (2)	$\frac{3}{4}" \times 3\frac{1}{2}" \times 47\frac{1}{4}"$	Drawer backs (2)	$\frac{1}{2}" \times 3\frac{13}{16}" \times 20\frac{1}{16}"$
Drawer kickers (2)	$\frac{3}{4}" \times 3\frac{1}{2}" \times 10\frac{3}{4}"$	Drawer bottoms (2)	$\frac{1}{4}" \times 16\frac{1}{4}" \times 20\frac{1}{8}"$
Drawer rails (2)	$\frac{3}{4}" \times \frac{3}{4}" \times 16\frac{1}{4}"$	Handle stock	$\frac{3}{4}" \times 1" \times 20"$
Adjustable shelf	$\frac{3}{4}" \times 16\frac{1}{8}" \times 46\frac{7}{16}"$	Front crown molding	$\frac{3}{4}" \times 5" \times 55"$
Shelf edge	$\frac{3}{4}" \times 2" \times 46\frac{7}{16}"$	Side crown molding (2)	$\frac{3}{4}" \times 5" \times 20"$
Counter	$\frac{7}{8}" \times 19" \times 50"$	Front crown blocking	$1\frac{1}{2}" \times 3\frac{1}{2}" \times 48"$
Vertical face frames (2)	$\frac{3}{4}" \times 3" \times 35\frac{1}{4}"$	Side crown blocking (2)	$1\frac{1}{2}" \times 3\frac{1}{2}" \times 16"$
Horizontal face frame	$\frac{3}{4}" \times 3" \times 42"$	Front base molding	$\frac{7}{8}" \times 4\frac{5}{8}" \times 50"$
Bottom face-frame blocking	$\frac{3}{4}" \times \frac{3}{4}" \times 46\frac{1}{2}"$	Side base molding (2)	$\frac{7}{8}" \times 4\frac{5}{8}" \times 19"$
Back	$\frac{1}{4}" \times 29\frac{1}{4}" \times 47\frac{1}{2}"$	Front base cap molding	$\frac{3}{4}" \times \frac{3}{4}" \times 50"$
		Side base cap molding (2)	$\frac{3}{4}" \times \frac{3}{4}" \times 19"$
Top Case			
Sides	$\frac{3}{4}" \times 12\frac{3}{4}" \times 45\frac{1}{4}"$	**Hardware**	
Top and bottom (2)	$\frac{3}{4}" \times 12" \times 43\frac{1}{4}"$	#8 × 2" drywall screws (as needed)	
Fixed shelves (2)	$\frac{3}{4}" \times 11\frac{7}{8}" \times 43\frac{1}{4}"$	#8 × 1¼" drywall wood screws (as needed)	
Back slats (10)	$\frac{3}{4}" \times 4\frac{5}{8}" \times 45\frac{1}{4}"$	#6 × 1¼" roundhead wood screws (12)	
Vertical face frames (2)	$\frac{3}{4}" \times 3" \times 45\frac{1}{4}"$	#6 × ¾" flathead wood screws	
Horizontal face frame	$\frac{3}{4}" \times 2\frac{1}{2}" \times 38"$	4d finish nails (as needed)	
Door stop	$\frac{1}{2}" \times 1\frac{1}{2}" \times 42\frac{1}{2}"$	2½" × 1½" brass butt hinges (8)	
		Brass roller catches (2). Available from Woodworker's	
Doors, Drawers, and Trim		Supply, Inc., 1108 North Glenn Road, Casper, WY	
Bottom door stiles (4)	$\frac{3}{4}" \times 2\frac{1}{2}" \times 23\frac{1}{8}"$	82601; (800) 645-9292; part #8000-501	
Bottom door rails (4)	$\frac{3}{4}" \times 2\frac{1}{2}" \times 18\frac{1}{2}"$	#20 biscuits (as needed)	
Bottom door panels (2)	$\frac{3}{4}" \times 16\frac{5}{8}" \times 18\frac{1}{4}"$	Glass, ⅛" thick, cut to fit	
Top door stiles (4)	$\frac{3}{4}" \times 2\frac{1}{2}" \times 35\frac{1}{2}"$	Shelf support pins (4)	
Top door rails (4)	$\frac{3}{4}" \times 2\frac{1}{2}" \times 16\frac{1}{2}"$		

fence, the T-square eliminates the process of squaring the fence to the workpiece, and it also makes locating the fence foolproof.

Next, cut rabbets in the case sides for the tops. The bottom case has a modified web frame for its top, as shown in *Top View—Cross Section*. Two rails run side to side and are joined

Front View   Side View—Cross Section

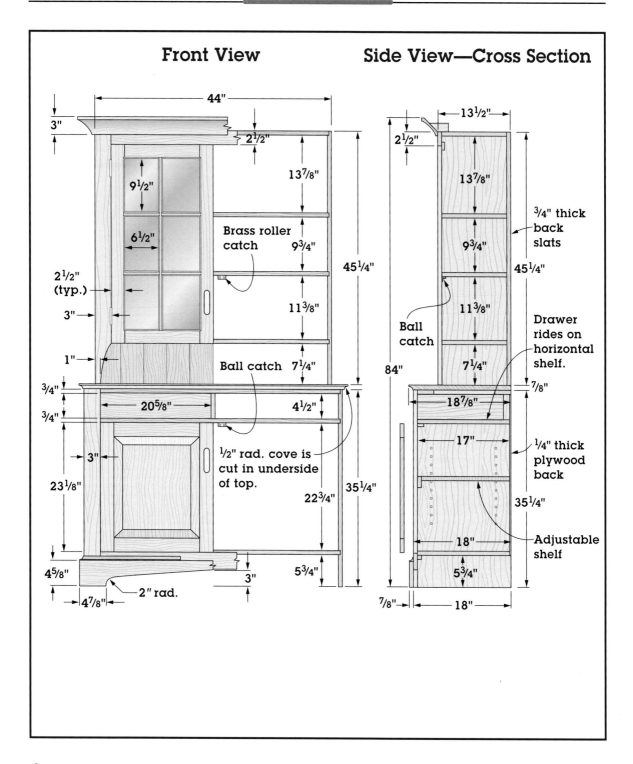

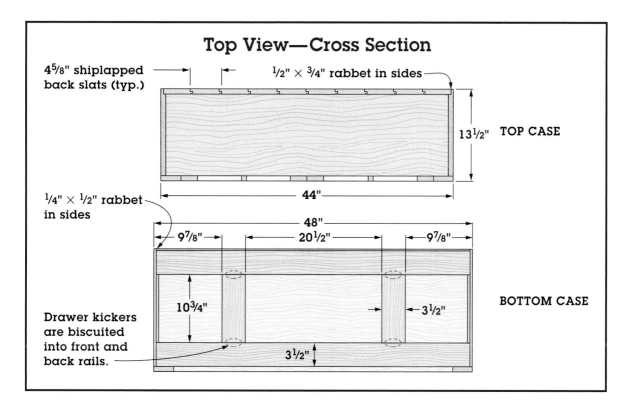

Top View—Cross Section

$4^5/8$" shiplapped back slats (typ.)

$1/2$" × $3/4$" rabbet in sides

$13^1/2$" TOP CASE

44"

TOP CASE

$1/4$" × $1/2$" rabbet in sides

48"

$9^7/8$" $20^1/2$" $9^7/8$"

BOTTOM CASE

$10^3/4$"

$3^1/2$"

Drawer kickers are biscuited into front and back rails.

$3^1/2$"

to two drawer kickers running front to back. I cut the rabbets across the full width of the sides, just like on the top case sides, but these rabbets could also be stopped for the rails.

Also, cut the rabbets in the back edge of each case side for the backs. Note that the backs are different thicknesses, and so the rabbets are different sizes, as shown in *Top View—Cross Section.*

The drawer divider is not dadoed into the horizontal members above and below it. I used biscuit joints here because it was easier, and I didn't want to see an exposed dado joint. You could instead simply butt-join and screw these parts together.

③ Notch the bottom case horizontals. On the bottom case, the drawer shelf and the front top rail don't get trimmed with a face-frame piece; instead they get notched to receive the vertical face frame, as shown in *Notch Detail.* I cut the notches with a handsaw. The short crosscut forms the visible

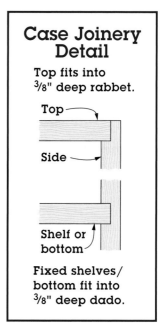

Case Joinery Detail

Top fits into $3/8$" deep rabbet.

Top

Side

Shelf or bottom

Fixed shelves/ bottom fit into $3/8$" deep dado.

Notch Detail

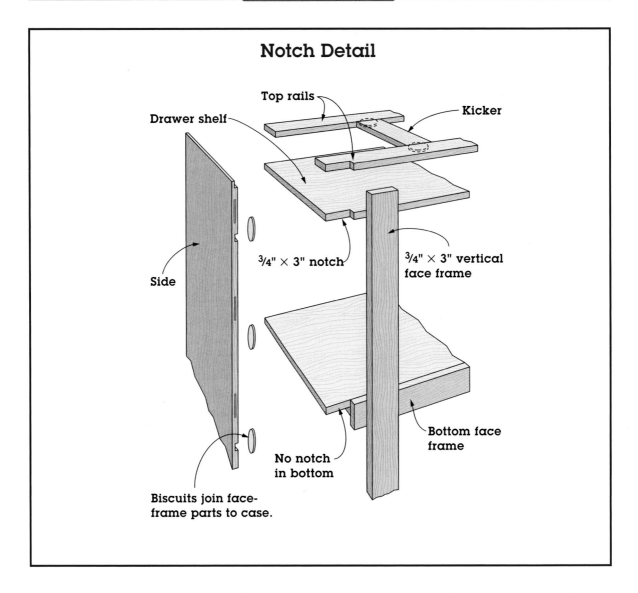

Top rails

Kicker

Drawer shelf

Side

¾" × 3" notch

¾" × 3" vertical
face frame

No notch
in bottom

Bottom face
frame

Biscuits join face-
frame parts to case.

joint that needs to be crisp, so I scored the cut with a utility knife before sawing it. The rip cut forms the seat for the vertical face frame and should match its thickness.

4 **Assemble the cases.** Fit the drawer kickers between the top rails with biscuits (or a tongue-and-groove joint if you don't have a biscuit joiner), but glue only the front joints. This allows the back joints to open and close slightly when the solid top, which is screwed to the rails, expands and contracts, as shown in *Notch Detail* and Top View—*Cross Section*. Put the cases together without glue first to check that the parts fit correctly. Cut the plywood back for the bottom case at this point. Then assemble the cases with glue.

Secure the top rails of the bottom case with a couple of 4d finish nails in predrilled holes. As you attach the back, make sure the case is square by measuring across the diagonals, and sight across the front of the case to make sure it is not twisted.

Drill two rows of shelf-support holes in each bottom case side for the adjustable shelf.

5 **Cut and attach the face-frame parts.** The face-frame parts are not assembled before they are attached to the case. Instead, you will screw the frame parts together from behind with pocket screws after they have been attached to the case.

Cut the vertical face-frame parts to length. Lay out the curve on the top case's vertical face-frame pieces, tape them together, and cut both curves at the same time on the band saw. Clean up the saw marks using files and sandpaper.

Attach the vertical face-frame pieces to the case using biscuits; if you don't have access to a biscuit joiner, secure them instead with glue and a couple of finish nails.

If you are using a biscuit joiner, line up the vertical face-frame pieces with the case sides and lay out the position of the biscuits. Then use the biscuit joiner to cut the matching biscuit slots in the parts, and glue the vertical face-frame pieces to the case sides. Now the two horizontal face-frame pieces can be crosscut to fit between the verticals. Drill the pocket screw holes, as shown in the photos on page 10, then glue and screw these face-frame pieces onto the case with #8 × 1¼-inch drywall screws.

6 **Shape and attach the counter.** Rout a cove into the bottom edge of the counter using a ½-inch-radius bit with a bearing guide. Screw through the top rails into the counter from below with #8 × 1¼-inch drywall screws to attach the counter to the case.

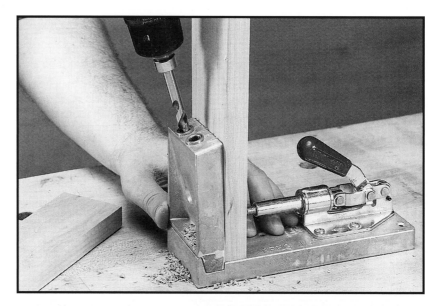

A pocket-hole jig allows you to drill angled screw holes at the ends of the horizontal face-frame piece easily. Simply clamp the frame piece upright in the jig and drill the holes with the stepped drill bit provided with the jig.

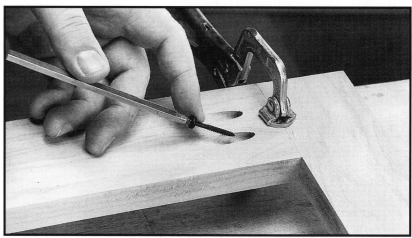

The countersunk holes created with the pocket-hole jig allow you to attach two adjoining frame rails with screws easily. The actual face-frame verticals should already be attached to the case.

7 **Shape and attach the top-case back boards.** The back of the top case is made of shiplapped boards, each screwed to the top and all the shelves. Cut the back boards to width, but leave them long for now. Rout or saw rabbets on both faces of all but two of the back boards: one on the face, the other on the back. The outside back boards get rabbeted on one edge only. Then rout a bead into the face rabbet of each back board, as shown in *Back Board Detail*. Screw the back boards one at a time to the top and fixed shelves with #8 × 1¼-inch drywall screws.

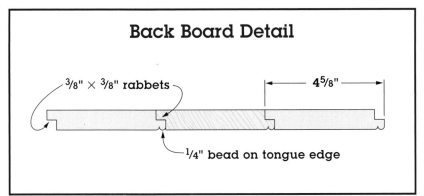

Back Board Detail

$3/8" \times 3/8"$ rabbets

$4^{5}/8"$

$1/4"$ bead on tongue edge

Make the Raised-Panel Doors

Note that the mortise-and-tenon joints for the glazed doors are identical to those in the raised-panel doors except that the tenons are not haunched. Cut the parts for these doors, and cut the joints for both at the same time if you wish. Once the mortises and tenons are cut, separate the top door parts from the bottom door parts, and build each pair of doors separately.

1 **Rout the mortises.** Use a plunge router with an edge guide to rout the mortises. The mortises should be centered in the stock thickness, but always position the router's edge guide against the same face (all front faces, for example) of each stile just in case the stock thickness varies slightly. Rout the mortises in several steps, taking about $1/4$ inch of wood each time. If you don't have a plunge router, drill a series of holes and chop out the waste with a chisel.

2 **Cut the tenons.** You can cut the tenons with the rails held either upright in a tenoning jig or flat on the table saw with a dado blade.

Before cutting the tenon shoulders, note that the outside shoulder on each bottom door is offset—or haunched—as shown in *Raised-Panel Door*. Be sure to lay out and cut the haunched shoulders on these tenons first. Use the miter gauge

Quick tip

If you don't have a beading bit on hand for the bead in the back slats, you could add a small chamfer to both edges of the joint. The purpose of the bead or chamfer is to conceal gaps that result if the seams between the slats open up slightly when the wood contracts.

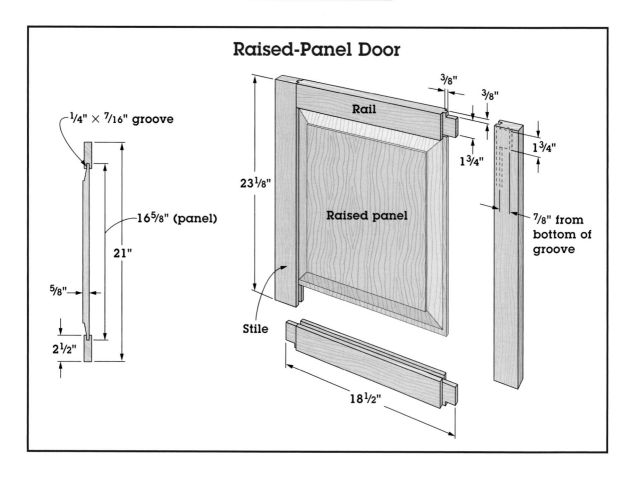

Raised-Panel Door

to guide the rail, and use the rip fence as a depth stop. Then move the fence ⁷⁄₁₆ inch farther away from the blade and cut the other three tenon shoulders.

3 **Cut the panel groove.** The panel groove is ¼ inch wide and ⁷⁄₁₆ inch deep (to match the haunch) and centered in the stock thickness. Cut the groove on the table saw, either with a series of saw cuts or with a single dado-blade cut.

4 **Raise the panels.** Raise the panels, as shown in "Routing Raised Panels" on page 14. I used a horizontal panel-raising bit to raise my panels. The main advantage over other approaches is that it forms a flat tongue on the edge of the panel that fits snugly in the groove.

5 **Assemble the doors.** Sand the panel bevels fully; then assemble the doors, gluing the tenons into their mortises. Make sure the doors are flat and square when clamped. Avoid getting glue into the panel grooves because the panels must be able to expand and contract freely.

Make the Glazed Doors

The glazed doors start out just like the raised-panel doors, with basic mortise-and-tenon joints. Note, however, that the tenons are not haunched. I made these doors using a rail-and-stile router-bit set, which is often called a cope-and-stick set. These cutters are available in two configurations—one has two separate bits, and one (like the one I used) has a single arbor with reversible cutters, as shown in the photo at right. One bit or one setup cuts the profile on the edges of all the parts, including the rabbet for the glass. This is often called the sticking cut. The second bit or setup cuts a counterprofile on the ends of the muntins; this second profile mates with the profile of the first cutter. This is called the cope cut. To help visualize the profile shaping, see *Routing Door Profiles* on page 18.

When making cope-and-stick doors, it's a good idea to go through the whole sequence of setups for both cuts on scrap stock before working on your real door parts.

1 **Rout the mortises; cut the tenons.** Rout the mortises and cut the tenons as you did in Steps 1 and 2 on page 11, but do not leave a haunch on the tenons.

2 **Rout the door frame profile.** Once the door frame parts are mortised and tenoned, set up a rail-and-stile router bit in a router table to cut the profile along the edges of the frame parts. As shown in *Routing Door Profiles,* the bit cuts the front edge profile and the back rabbet for the glass at the same time. Cut the profile along the inside edges of all the door frame parts.

I used this bit to cut the profile in my stiles and rails. As shown, the bit cuts the cope at the ends of rails or muntins. When the two wing cutters are added, it cuts the edge profile in the rails and stiles.

Routing Raised Panels

There was a time when only two types of woodworkers could create fancy, raised panels—professional woodworkers with big dollar shapers and specialized cutters, or old-time wood joiners with specialized hand planes and scrapers. These were the masters of the craft, leaving the amateur to make do with flat panels or slab doors. Then, along came the router to save the day for the amateur woodworker and hobbyist. Now you can create perfect raised panels by fastening your router in a router table to essentially create a minishaper.

There are two distinct kinds of bits made for routing raised panels on the router table, as shown in the photo at right. Both types are available in a variety of raised panel profiles to suit your fancy. Both types have their pros and cons, and when using either type of bit, there are a few cautions to keep in mind:

- Use these bits in a router table for adequate stability and safety.
- To prevent kickback and to keep your hands a safe distance from the cutter, use hold-downs and featherboards whenever possible.
- Always position the cutter under the workpiece, never between the workpiece and the table or fence.
- Take a series of light cuts, and make the final pass about $\frac{1}{16}$ inch deep.
- Always rout the ends of the panels first, then the edges.

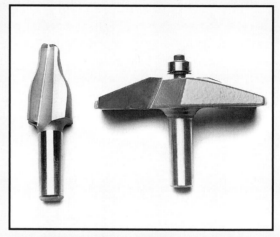

Two types of panel-raising bits are available—vertical *(left)* and horizontal *(right)*.

HORIZONTAL PANEL-RAISING BITS

These bits are very large cutters that do their work with the panel lying flat on the router table, as shown in the top photo on the opposite page. Because of their large size, these bits require a powerful router—2 horsepower at least, 3 horsepower recommended—with speed control. Most bit manufacturers recommend speeds of 10,000 to 12,000 rpm instead of the typical 20,000 rpm of most routers.

These bits are certainly kin to their big brother shaper cutters—they look similar when set up, and they cut in the same way. They are also the more expensive choice of the router bit pair.

Horizontal bits are convenient because the panel is easy to move across the

Horizontal panel-raising bits allow the workpiece to rest flat on the table. They also have ball-bearing guides, so they work on curved panels as well as straight ones.

table. They also typically have a ball-bearing guide, so they're ideal for raising curved panels. These bits look a bit threatening whizzing round and round only inches from your fingers, but if you use them properly with push sticks and paddles, you can produce a great-looking panel and keep all of your digits, too.

The best thing about horizontal panel-raising bits is the smooth cut they produce. The long, sweeping motion of the cutting wings slices away the wood without leaving ridges or milling marks like those left by a thickness planer or vertical panel-raising bit. To get the best cut possible, the cut should be made a little bit at a time, raising the bit slightly with each pass. This is heavy-duty cut-

ting and, if you try to bite off too much at once, the panel may splinter or decide to fly across the shop.

VERTICAL PANEL-RAISING BITS

These bits are smaller and less expensive than horizontal bits, and they can be run at normal high speeds. They can also be used with a less powerful router. Vertical panel-raising bits seem a bit safer because less of the cutting edge is exposed. However, the panel must be oriented vertically, and this requires a tall auxiliary fence, as shown in the photo below. These bits also require a featherboard to help keep the panel stable as the cut is made, and they won't work on curved panels.

As mentioned earlier, vertical panel-raising bits do leave more milling marks then horizontal panel-raising bits, so you will need to do a bit more sanding.

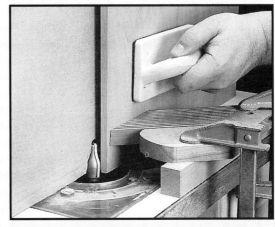

Vertical panel-raising bits require a tall fence and a featherboard to ensure that the panel is stable as it's cut.

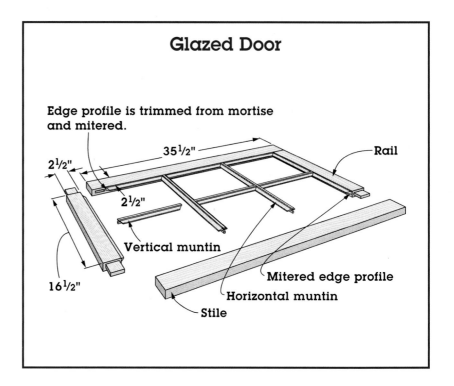

Glazed Door

Edge profile is trimmed from mortise
and mitered.

35$\frac{1}{2}$"

2$\frac{1}{2}$"

Rail

2$\frac{1}{2}$"

Vertical muntin

Mitered edge profile

16$\frac{1}{2}$"

Horizontal muntin

Stile

③ Miter the profile. To join the outer door frame, you need to miter the profile on the ends of the rails and also at the base of the mortise on the stiles, as shown in *Glazed Door.* Cut the miters on the table saw, as shown in the photos on the opposite page, then remove the excess material adjacent to the mortises on the stiles. I used the band saw to saw off most of the waste, then I trimmed cleanly to the shoulder line with a chisel. If necessary, trim the miters to fit using a mitered guide block that can be clamped to the door parts.

④ Shape the muntins. The muntins get profiled on both edges, which is a challenge on such small stock—$\frac{3}{4}$ inch × 1 inch. So start with longer and wider pieces of stock, as shown in Step 3 of *Routing Door Profiles* (three pieces of stock about 2$\frac{1}{4}$ inches wide × 36 inches long should do), profile both edges, and then rip the muntin stock to width.

With the blade set at 45 degrees, set the fence to locate the miters on the stiles. The blade should just reach the base of the edge profile. Reset the fence to miter the profile at the ends of the rails.

Profiling the second edge of the muntins is more difficult—the piece is not only small, it's tippy now that one edge is profiled. The solution is to create a chute that captures the workpiece so it stays tight to the router table and fence as it's pushed past the cutter, as shown in Step 4 of *Routing Door Profiles*. The chute is formed by two elements: the standard router table fence and a counterprofiled capture fence. With these parts in place, you can safely shape the second edge of the muntins.

To make the counterprofiled capture fence, you have to change the router setup to make the cope cut or simply use a scrap piece left over from the shaping of the door rails and stiles.

When everything is set up, make the cut on the router table, following the steps shown in *Routing Door Profiles*.

5 **Shape the glazing strips.** The glazing strips have the same profile as the rest of the door parts, only they're cut from ¼-inch-thick stock. The safest way to get these skinny parts is to shape both edges of longer and wider pieces, then rip the profiled strips from the pieces. With most cutters, you can make the strip profile cuts with the router bit in the same position it was in for the frame profile cut. Rout each edge of the 1¾-inch-wide pieces, then rip the ⅜-inch-wide glazing strip from each edge. (See Step 2 of *Routing Door Profiles*.)

Routing Door Profiles

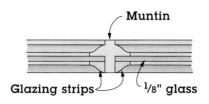

Muntin

Glazing strips — ⅛" glass

MUNTIN CROSS SECTION

Step 3. Shape 1st edge of muntins (both edges of wider piece, then rip individual muntins).

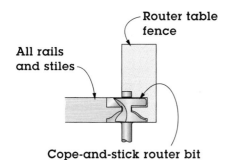

Router table fence

All rails and stiles

Cope-and-stick router bit is set for sticking cut.

Step 1. Rout the door frame profile.

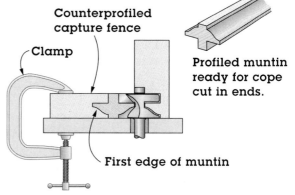

Counterprofiled capture fence

Clamp

Profiled muntin ready for cope cut in ends.

First edge of muntin

Step 4. Rout 2nd edge of muntins, with 1st edge supported by counterprofiled capture fence.

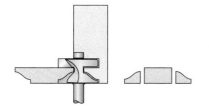

Step 2. Rout the glazing strips, then rip from wider stock (⅜" × 1¾").

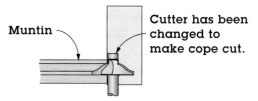

Muntin

Cutter has been changed to make cope cut.

Step 5. Rout the cope cut in the ends of the muntins.

6 **Preassemble the doors, and cut the muntins to size.** You need to preassemble the door frames in order to position the horizontal muntins in front of the shelves and also to determine the length of the vertical muntins.

To do this, lay the assembled door frames right on the case, with the case lying flat on its back. Position the horizontal muntins over the shelves, and mark their locations on the stiles. Then cut the vertical muntins to length.

7 **Cope the muntins, and assemble the doors.**
Change the router setup to make the cope in the ends of all the muntins. Again, you'll need to use a counterprofiled piece to support the stock—only this time it will move with the stock, as shown in the photo at right.

Now the doors (at long last!) are ready to be assembled. The muntin intersections are very fragile, with minimal glue surfaces and no practical way to apply clamp pressure directly to the joints. The trick is to use the door frame as a clamp for the four muntin intersections.

Glue the muntins together in one step, lining them up with the marks on the door frame to be sure everything is square, then glue the frames together around the assembled muntins.

Use a square backer board to guide the muntin past the cutter when cutting the cope. The edge of the backer board is counterprofiled to fit into the edge of the muntin.

Make the Drawers

1 **Cut the parts to size.** Check the size of the drawer openings, and adjust the size of the parts if necessary.

2 **Cut the joints and assemble the drawers.** Cut dovetails on the front ends of the sides and corresponding half-blind dovetail sockets on the ends of the drawer fronts, as shown in *Drawer Construction*. If you have a dovetail-cutting jig, you can use it to cut these dovetails, or see "Cutting Dovetails" on page 164 for details on cutting these joints by hand.

Cut rabbets on the back ends of the sides and a groove around the inside bottom edge of the sides, backs, and fronts for the drawer bottom, as shown in *Drawer Construction*. Make the rabbets and grooves with a dado blade in the table saw. Check that the parts fit, then glue the drawers together.

Note that the drawer back is narrower than the sides so the bottom can be slid into place after finishing. Screw the bottom to the back with #6 × ¾-inch flathead wood screws.

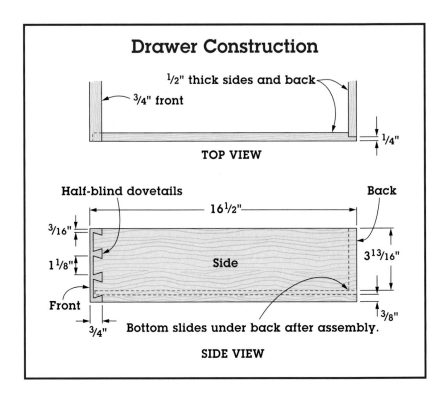

Drawer Construction

TOP VIEW

½" thick sides and back

¾" front

¼"

Half-blind dovetails

Back

16½"

3/16"

1⅛"

Side

3 13/16"

Front

¾"

3/8"

Bottom slides under back after assembly.

SIDE VIEW

Fit the Doors, Handles, and Hardware

1 **Hang the doors.** Trim the doors to fit their openings before hinging them. I gave the door stiles a light trim with a single pass over the jointer. Then I crosscut the doors so there is about $\frac{1}{16}$-inch gap at the top and bottom.

Mortise and mount the hinges on the doors first. To cut the hinge mortises, first put them in position on the edge of the door and scribe around them with a marking knife.

Then, position each door in its opening with shims underneath. Transfer the hinge locations to the face frames.

After the hinge mortises have been laid out, use a small laminate trimmer with a straight bit to cut away most of the mortise to the depth of the hinge leaf. This method gives the mortise a flat, consistent bottom.

Finally, square the corners of each mortise with a chisel.

2 **Install the door catches.** I used brass roller catches to hold the doors closed. First screw the catch to the underside of the second fixed shelf in the top cabinet and to the drawer shelf in the bottom cabinet. Then insert the mating hardware into the catch to transfer its location to the door. Screw the hardware to the door.

3 **Make the handles.** Making your own handles may seem like a detail hardly worth the trouble, but it's a feature that can give your work a distinctive look. And these handles, shown in *Making Handles*, are really simple to make. I started with a single length of walnut scrap, then routed a cove into three of the four faces of the stock, as shown. Next, I cut the handles to length, and rounded over the corners on a belt sander held stationary in the bench vise. I made a small template to locate the two screw holes for each handle and drilled ⅛-inch holes in the doors and drawer fronts. I used the same template to drill pilot holes in the handles themselves. I mounted the handles (after finishing) with #6 × 1¼-inch roundhead wood screws through the back of the door stiles and drawer front.

Quick tip

When routing small parts, always use featherboards to keep the small stock in its proper place. Clamp one featherboard to the fence to push the stock against the router table, and clamp a second to the router table to push the stock against the fence. Keep your hands away from the cutter by using push sticks.

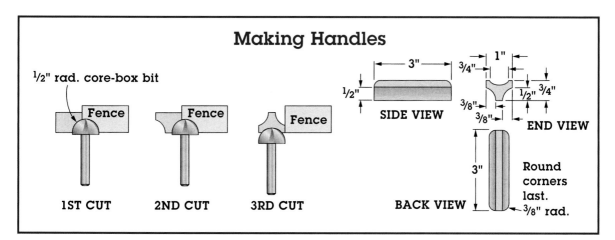

Making Handles

½" rad. core-box bit

Fence — 1ST CUT

Fence — 2ND CUT

Fence — 3RD CUT

SIDE VIEW — 3" · ½"

END VIEW — 1" · ¾" · ½" · ¾" · ⅜" · ⅜"

BACK VIEW — 3" · Round corners last. ⅜" rad.

Make and Apply the Trim

1 **Shape the base molding.** The base molding is just square stock with a separate base cap on top. Draw the

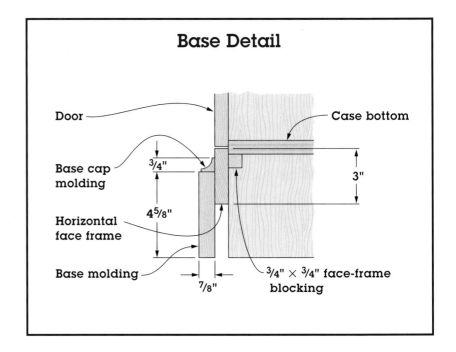

Base Detail

Door

Case bottom

Base cap
molding

3/4"

3"

Horizontal
face frame

4⁵⁄₈"

Base molding

7/8"

3/4" × 3/4" face-frame
blocking

arch shape on the front of the base molding, as shown in *Front View*. Cut the shape on the band saw or with a saber saw, then sand the curve smooth.

2 **Shape the base cap molding.** Rout a cove into a piece of stock for the base cap molding. For small shaped parts like this, I prefer to shape a wider piece—about 2 inches—then rip the narrow piece from it. It's safer, plus you end up with a smoother cut because the workpiece is easier to feed steadily.

3 **Cut and attach the base and base cap moldings.** When fitting mitered moldings, it's best to cut the miters first, then cut any square ends. So cut both mitered ends of the front first, then the mitered end of each side, and last the back end of each side. Follow the same sequence for the base cap molding.

With the bottom case sitting on a level surface, glue the front base molding onto the horizontal face frame, as shown in *Base Detail*. The side base molding can't be glued to the case sides— it would prevent the side from expanding and contracting due to changes in humidity. Instead, glue the miters only, and secure the back end of the side with a screw in an enlarged hole in the case side. (I used a #8 × 1¼-inch flathead wood screw in a ¼-inch hole.)

Glue on the front base cap, tacking it down with 4d finish nails. Nail the side base cap pieces onto the base but not onto the cabinet sides.

4 **Shape the crown molding.** Large cove moldings can be easily cut on the table saw by passing the stock over the blade at an angle in a series of light passes. For more information on this procedure, see "Cove Cutting on the Table Saw" on page 24.

When the cove is cut, bevel the edges on the table saw, as shown in *Crown Molding Detail*.

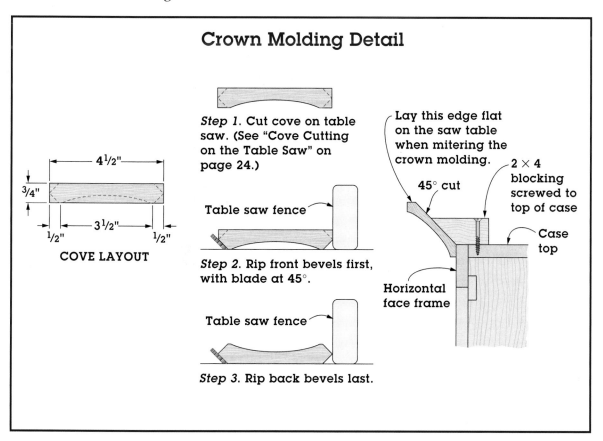

Crown Molding Detail

Step 1. Cut cove on table saw. (See "Cove Cutting on the Table Saw" on page 24.)

Table saw fence

Step 2. Rip front bevels first, with blade at 45°.

Table saw fence

Step 3. Rip back bevels last.

4½"

¾"

3½"

½"   ½"

COVE LAYOUT

Lay this edge flat on the saw table when mitering the crown molding.

45° cut

2 × 4 blocking screwed to top of case

Case top

Horizontal face frame

Cove Cutting on the Table Saw

Large cove moldings can be cut on the table saw by passing the stock over the blade at an angle in a series of light passes. A straight-edged board clamped to the saw serves as the fence.

1 Lay out the cove and set the fence angle. Lay out the desired cove on the end of a piece of sample stock. The angle is determined by the width of the cove. The simplest way to gauge the fence angle is to raise the blade to the height needed to cut the full cove. Then place the sample stock piece flat on the saw table right in front of the blade with the marked end facing the blade. Sighting along the table saw top, angle the sample stock until the curve of the blade coincides with or obstructs the curve of the cove, as shown in the top right photo. This is a "ballpark" approach to the fence angle; but a few degrees in either direction will yield a similar cove on your stock. Clamp a wooden fence to the table saw right alongside the sample stock passing in front of the blade.

2 Cut the cove. When the fence has been clamped in place, lower the blade to $\frac{1}{16}$ inch high and pass the sample stock over the blade, making a series of very light cuts until you reach the full depth of the cove, as shown in the bottom right photo. If the finished cove

With your eye at the level of the saw table, angle the sample cove stock until the cove aligns with the blade.

Clamp a fence at an angle to the blade, and make a series of very light cuts until the cove shape is complete.

is too wide, reduce the angle between the fence and blade, and if it's too narrow, increase the angle. Once the fence angle is right, lower the blade again and cut the cove in the crown molding stock.

When the cove has been cut in your good stock, scrape and sand the cove to remove the milling marks.

5 **Cut and fit the crown blocking.** The crown molding overlaps the top horizontal face frame and the sides of the cabinet by about ⅝ inch. To provide more of a seat for it, rip a length of 2 × 4 at 45 degrees, and screw it to the top of the case, as shown in *Crown Molding Detail*.

6 **Miter and attach the crown molding.** Miter the corners of the crown molding to fit around the top of the upper case. You can cut the miters on a table saw with a 10-inch blade, but an electric miter saw does the job more easily.

When cutting the miters, position the stock upside down on its topmost edge, as defined in *Crown Molding Detail*. Cut the front molding first, using the case itself to locate the cut marks. Then cut the miters on the side pieces.

Finish the Cabinet

1 **Sand the cabinet, and apply a finish.** Remove the doors, drawers, and hardware. Sand all the parts progressively to 180 grit. Apply a finish of your choice. I brushed on two coats of Waterlox, an oil-based varnish.

2 **Install the glass.** Lay the finished doors face down on a blanket, and position the glass panels. Miter the glazing strips to fit around the glass. Then, apply a light bead of silicone caulk around the perimeter, and set the mitered glazing strips in place. Let the silicone set up for a day, then re-hang the glazed doors.

3 **Attach the shelf edge, and install the adjustable shelf.** Glue and clamp the shelf edge to the front edge of the adjustable shelf, as shown in *Side View—Cross Section*. When the glue is dry, trim the shelf to fit in its opening and install it on shelf support pins. If necessary, bevel the ends of the shelf edge to ease installation.

Classic Huntboard

by Ben Erickson

This classic southern huntboard design is adapted from a Carlyle Lynch drawing of an antique. A huntboard was traditionally used for serving food after the hunt. Today it's perfect as an accent piece in the front hall or as a sideboard in the dining room.

I made my version from walnut, selecting showy grain for the doors and drawer fronts and a more subdued, but interesting, grain for the top. The plain, straight-grained wood used for the rest of the piece keeps it from appearing overly busy. I accented the doors and drawers with maple string inlay that is bisected by inset brass keyhole escutcheons. String inlay also accents the top. Bullnose cock beading protrudes ⅛ inch from the edges of the doors and drawers, giving the piece a classic, sophisticated appearance.

Building this huntboard is a great exercise in mortise-and-tenon joinery, although, in my version, I substituted biscuits for some of the original joinery.

Exploded View

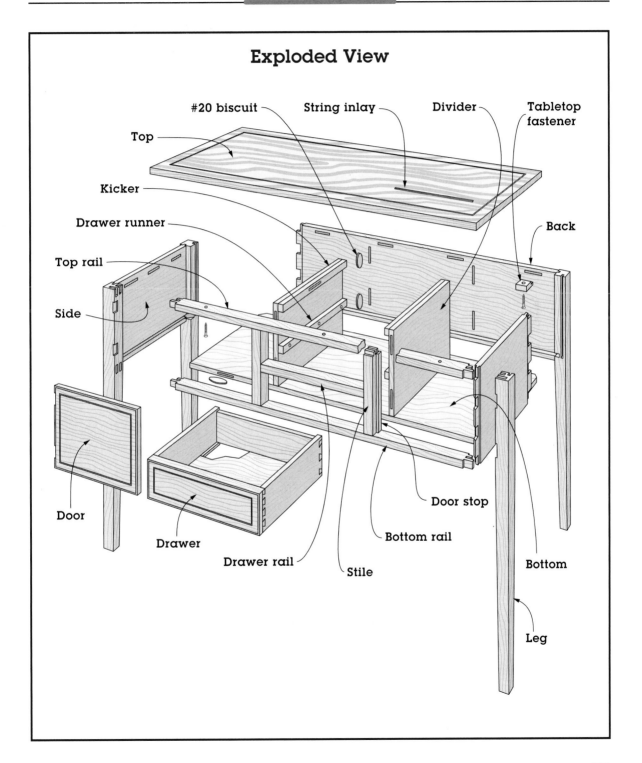

#20 biscuit

String inlay

Divider

Tabletop fastener

Top

Kicker

Drawer runner

Back

Top rail

Side

Door

Drawer

Drawer rail

Stile

Door stop

Bottom rail

Bottom

Leg

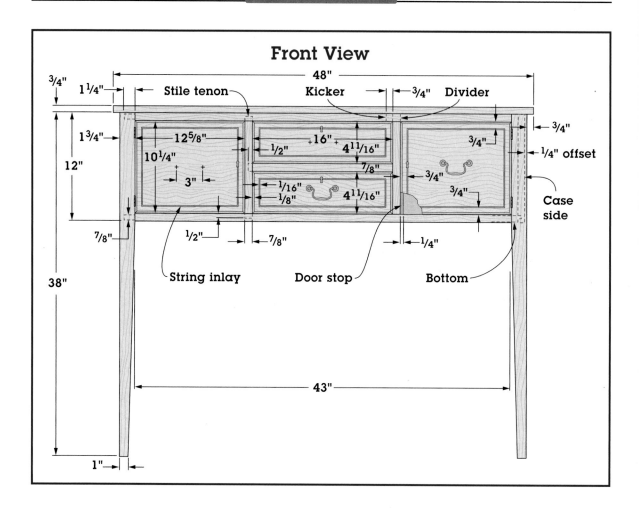

Front View

Make the Top

1 **Mill wood for the top.** Glue up the 18 × 48-inch top from two or three boards that have been planed to the thickness given in the Materials List. Orient the grain to obscure the glue joints, and then situate four or five bar clamps along the length of the glue-up, both above and below the stock. Make sure the edges of the boards remain aligned as you tighten the clamps.

2 **Cut and sand the top.** After the glue has dried, cut the top to the size given in the Materials List, and

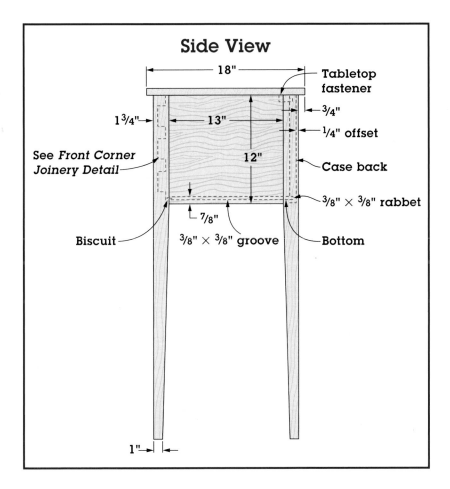

Side View

18"

Tabletop
fastener

3/4"

1 3/4" 13"

1/4" offset

*See Front Corner
Joinery Detail*

12"

Case back

3/8" × 3/8" rabbet

7/8"

Biscuit   3/8" × 3/8" groove

Bottom

1"

sand the edges to a slight roundover (1/16- to 1/8-inch radius).
You will install the string inlay at the same time that you do
the doors and drawer fronts.

Build the Case

The antique huntboard case was joined with pegged mortise-
and-tenon joints. In my adaptation, I retained most of the
mortise-and-tenon joinery, but modern glues eliminate the need
for pegs. I also substituted biscuit joints for the connections between the dividers and the case and between the bottom rail and
the bottom. If you decide to use tenons, make sure you add the

extra length needed to the dividers. I used clear walnut throughout, but you could use a secondary wood such as poplar, maple, or 3/4-inch hardwood plywood for the bottom and interior dividers. Use a hardwood like maple for the drawer runners.

1 **Cut the pieces to size.** Joint, plane, and cut the pieces for the case to the sizes given in the Materials List, edge-joining boards if necessary to make the sides, back, and bottom.

2 **Mortise the legs.** Before tapering the legs, cut their haunched mortises. Lay them out according to *Corner Detail* and *Front Corner Joinery Detail*. Note that the double mortises in the front legs are open at the top and that the top and bottom rails are flush to the leg. The mortises in the back legs meet each other at full depth, which allows a bit of space between the ends of the tenons.

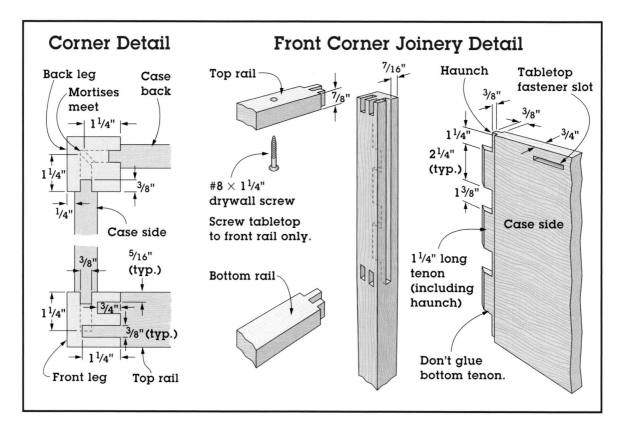

Corner Detail

Back leg
Mortises meet
Case back
1 1/4"
1 1/4"
3/8"
1/4"
Case side

3/8"
5/16" (typ.)
1 1/4"
3/4"
3/8" (typ.)
1 1/4"
Front leg
Top rail

Front Corner Joinery Detail

Top rail
7/8"
7/16"
Haunch
Tabletop fastener slot
3/8"
3/8"
1 1/4"
3/4"
2 1/4" (typ.)
1 3/8"
Case side

#8 × 1 1/4" drywall screw
Screw tabletop to front rail only.

Bottom rail

1 1/4" long tenon (including haunch)

Don't glue bottom tenon.

Materials List

Part	Dimension	Part	Dimension
Top		Cock beading,	
Top	$\frac{3}{4}$" × 18" × 48"	drawer sides (4)	$\frac{1}{8}$" × $\frac{1}{2}$" × $4\frac{11}{16}$"
Tabletop fasteners (12)	$\frac{3}{4}$" × $1\frac{1}{2}$" × 2"	Door stops (2)	$\frac{1}{4}$" × $\frac{3}{8}$" × $10\frac{1}{4}$"
		String inlay	$\frac{1}{16}$" × $\frac{1}{8}$" × 25'
Case			
Legs (4)	$1\frac{3}{4}$" × $1\frac{3}{4}$" × 38"		
Back	$\frac{3}{4}$" × 12" × $45\frac{1}{2}$"	**Hardware**	
Sides (2)	$\frac{3}{4}$" × 12" × $15\frac{1}{2}$"	#8 × $1\frac{1}{2}$" drywall screws (2)	
Top and bottom rails (2)	$\frac{7}{8}$" × $1\frac{3}{4}$" × $45\frac{1}{2}$"	#8 × $1\frac{1}{4}$" drywall screws (as needed)	
Drawer rail	$\frac{7}{8}$" × $1\frac{3}{4}$" × 17"	#6 × $\frac{3}{4}$" flathead wood screws (as needed)	
Stiles (2)	$\frac{7}{8}$" × $1\frac{3}{4}$" × $11\frac{1}{4}$"	$\frac{11}{16}$" × $\frac{3}{8}$" brass inset keyhole escutcheons (4).	
Dividers (2)	$\frac{3}{4}$" × $11\frac{1}{8}$" × $13\frac{3}{4}$"	Available from Woodcraft Supply, P.O. Box 1686,	
Drawer runners/kickers (4)	$\frac{3}{4}$" × $\frac{7}{8}$" × $13\frac{3}{4}$"	Parkersburg, WV 26102-1686; (800) 225-1153;	
Bottom	$\frac{3}{4}$" × $14\frac{1}{8}$" × $45\frac{1}{4}$"	part #02U01	
		Brass door locks (2). Available from Crown City	
Doors and Drawers		Hardware Co., 1047 No. Allen Avenue, Pasadena,	
Doors (2)	$\frac{3}{4}$" × 10" × $12\frac{3}{8}$"	CA 91104; (626) 794-0234; part #191Q (1 left	
Drawer fronts (2)	1" × $4\frac{7}{16}$" × 16"	hand, 1 right hand)	
Drawer backs (2)	$\frac{1}{2}$" × $3\frac{11}{16}$" × 16"	Brass drawer locks (2). Available from East Coast	
Drawer sides (4)	$\frac{1}{2}$" × $4\frac{11}{16}$" × 15"	Refinisher's Warehouse, 13 Amy Elsey Drive,	
Drawer bottoms (2)	$\frac{1}{4}$" × $14\frac{5}{8}$" × $15\frac{1}{2}$"	Charleston, SC 29407-1702; (800) 636-8555;	
Cock beading, door top		part #S4G	
and bottom (4)	$\frac{1}{8}$" × $\frac{7}{8}$" × $12\frac{5}{8}$"	$\frac{7}{8}$" × $1\frac{1}{2}$" brass door hinges (2 pairs). Available	
Cock beading,		from Woodcraft Supply; part #16Q22	
door sides (4)	$\frac{1}{8}$" × $\frac{7}{8}$" × $10\frac{1}{4}$"	Brass door and drawer pulls, 3" centers (4). Avail-	
Cock beading, drawer top		able from East Coast Refinisher's Warehouse;	
and bottom (4)	$\frac{1}{8}$" × $1\frac{1}{8}$" × 16"	part #B8B	

I cut the mortises using a hollow chisel mortiser, but you could rout them with a plunge router. If routing, cut away the stock little by little until you reach the final depth.

3 **Cut the mortises in the rails and stiles.** Lay out the stopped mortises in the rails and stiles, as shown in *Front View* and *Top View,* and cut them out.

If you don't own a biscuit joiner, you should also rout or chisel mortises in the stiles and case back for the dividers. These mortises only need to be $\frac{1}{4}$ to $\frac{3}{8}$ inch deep.

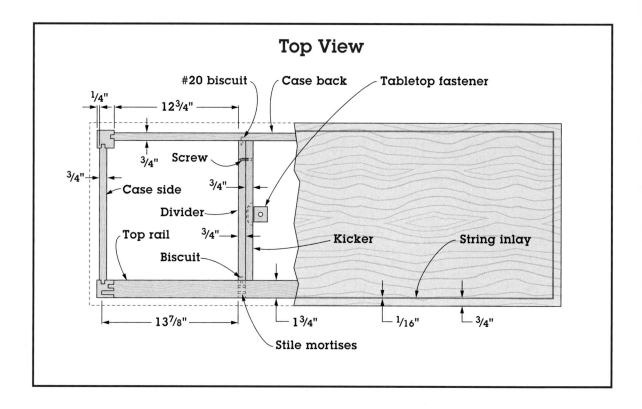

Top View

#20 biscuit · Case back · Tabletop fastener

1/4"

12 3/4"

Screw

3/4"

Case side

3/4"

Divider

Top rail

3/4"

Biscuit

13 7/8"

1 3/4"

1/16"

3/4"

Stile mortises

Kicker

String inlay

4 **Cut the rail and stile tenons.** Lay out the double tenons on the rails and stiles, and cut them to fit snugly in their mortises. I cut the tenon cheeks on my table saw, using a tenoning jig, as shown in the photo on the opposite page. I removed the waste between the tenons by making several passes, and cut the tenon shoulders on my radial arm saw.

5 **Cut the side and back tenons.** Lay out and cut the tenons on the case sides and back. The side and back panels are too big for my tenoning jig to handle, so I cut the tenon cheeks on the table saw by guiding the stock against a high auxiliary fence attached to the table saw fence. To cut the haunches, I used my band saw, but a jigsaw could also be used. Miter the ends of the rear tenons, as shown in *Corner Detail,* so they won't obstruct each other inside the rear legs.

If you don't have a biscuit joiner, you should also cut tenons in the ends of the dividers. These tenons only need to be

¼ to ⅜ inch deep (corresponding to their mortises). Remember to add the extra length for the tenons to the divider stock before you cut it to length.

6 **Taper the legs.** When your joints fit well, taper the legs on their inside edges to 1 inch at the bottom. Cut the taper on the table saw with the help of the jig shown in *Table Saw Tapering Jig*. Adjust the table saw fence so that the blade will start to cut the taper just below where the legs meet the bottom edge of the case sides, as shown in *Side View*. Use push sticks to hold down the jig and the leg as you cut the taper.

7 **Cut the tabletop fastener slots.** I use my biscuit joiner to cut stopped slots around the inside case edge for tabletop fasteners, as shown in *Exploded View*. A continuous slot is traditional, but I think stopped slots make a stronger edge. I don't slot the top rail, but instead use #8 × 1¼-inch drywall screws to attach the top there. If you don't have a biscuit joiner, you can use a ¼-inch-diameter straight bit in a router, and guide the cut with the router fence. The fasteners on the sides and back will allow the top to move seasonally.

8 **Cut the bottom grooves.** On the table saw, rip ⅜ × ⅜-inch grooves ⅞ inch up from the bottom of the case sides and back to hold the case bottom.

9 **Rabbet the bottom.** Rout a ⅜ × ⅜-inch rabbet in the ends and back edge of the case bottom with ⅜-inch rabbeting bit. Make sure the bottom fits easily in its grooves.

10 **Cut the leg notches.** The back legs must be notched to accept the back corners of the case bottom, as shown in *Exploded View*. Test fit the case sides and back to the legs, then transfer the top edge of the bottom groove onto the legs. Draw a mark ¾ inch down from the first line, and then make a 45 degree cut at each mark across the corner with a dovetail saw, as shown in the photo on page 34. Chisel away the waste. With the case still test fit, cut off the rear corners of the case bottom and check its fit in the notches.

Holding the rails upright in a tenoning jig allows you to cut the double tenons easily. First, cut the tenon cheeks, and then cut away the waste between the tenons, as shown here.

Quick tip

To prevent splitting the sides and back, the wood must be allowed to expand and contract seasonally across its width. I allow for that movement in the bottom leg mortise. If I'm building during the humid summertime, I'll cut the bottom tenon for a snug fit across its width. If I'm working in winter, I'll make the tenon 1/16 inch narrower to allow future side expansion. When assembling the case, I don't glue in the bottom tenon.

Cut across the inside corner of each leg to accept the case bottom. Remove the waste between the cuts to create the notch.

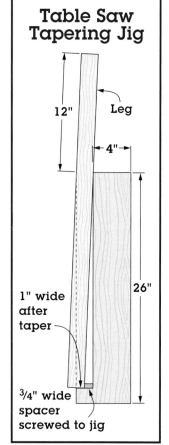

Table Saw Tapering Jig

12"

Leg

4"

26"

1" wide after taper

3/4" wide spacer screwed to jig

11 **Cut the biscuit joints.** Mark out and cut the biscuit slots in the rails, stiles, dividers, bottom, and back, positioned as shown in *Exploded View* and *Top View*. If you don't have a biscuit joiner, you can use splines or dowels instead.

12 **Test fit the rest of the case.** In preparation for the glue-up, assemble the entire case without glue to check the fit of all the pieces. Now is the time to trim the solid wood bottom to allow for seasonal movement. Its side edges can bottom out in the side grooves, but its rear edge should be allowed to move in the rear groove. If building in the driest season, rip about 1/4 inch off the front edge of the bottom. Also, lay out, drill, and cut slotted screw holes for attaching the bottom to the dividers. The slotted holes allow for movement.

13 **Glue up the case.** Begin assembly by gluing up the rails and stiles, clamping everything squarely. Then, glue the legs to the rails and allow the glue to dry. Next, glue the bottom and dividers to the rails and stiles. (Test fit the case sides into the front legs to help you align the bottom on the rail.) Don't glue the bottom to the dividers; instead, drive #8 × 1¼-inch drywall screws through the slotted holes.
   Glue the back to the rear legs and allow the glue to dry. Then, glue the front and back assemblies to the sides and dividers. Remember to glue only the top two tenons in the rear

legs. If you are using solid wood for the bottom, don't glue it into its grooves. Finally, secure the drawer runners and kickers to the dividers with #8 × 1¼-inch drywall screws.

Make the Doors and Drawers

I made all of the doors and drawer fronts from one, 10-inch-wide walnut board, selected for its showy grain. I marked and cut the pieces carefully to ensure continuation of the grain across the length of the front. The drawers are constructed traditionally, with half-blind dovetails in the front and through dovetails in the back. I used maple for the drawer back and sides for durability. The drawer bottoms are hardwood plywood.

Because the doors and drawers are solid wood, you have to allow for seasonal wood movement. In dry weather, I allow roughly a ¹⁄₁₆-inch gap above and below each door and drawer front. When humid, I allow only ¹⁄₃₂ inch.

1 **Make the doors and drawers.** Cut out the doors and drawer fronts to the sizes given in the Materials List. Adjust the widths as necessary to allow for wood movement. Then build the drawers. Cut the dovetails using a fine saw and chisels (or you can use a dovetail jig and router if you are so equipped). If you cut the pins first, remember to allow for the top and bottom cock beading when laying out the tails, as shown in *Drawer Side View*. Assemble the drawers, fit them to their openings, then cut ⅛ × ⅜-inch rabbets in the sides of the drawers, as shown in *Drawer Cock Beading*.

2 **Install the string inlay.** Rout ¹⁄₁₆ × ¹⁄₁₆-inch grooves for the string inlay in the top, doors, and drawer fronts. The groove is set in ¾ inch from each edge of the top. On the doors and drawer fronts, it's set in ⅝ inch from each edge, not counting the cock beading. Make the string inlay and install it in its grooves. (For string inlay instruction, see "Jewelry Box" on page 331.)

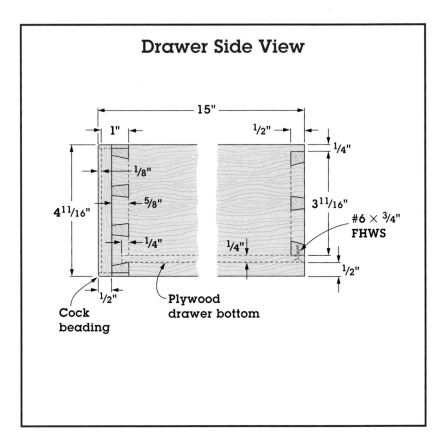

Drawer Side View

15"

1"

1/2"

1/4"

1/8"

5/8"

3¹¹/₁₆"

4¹¹/₁₆"

#6 × 3/4"
FHWS

1/4"

1/4"

1/2"

1/2"

**Cock
beading**

Plywood
drawer bottom

Rout the bullnose for the
cock beading in wider
stock on the router table.
Bury the bit in a cutout
in the fence, as shown,
and guide the stock
against the fence. Rip
the cock beading to its
final thickness on the
table saw.

3 **Make and install the cock beading.** Sand the
drawer fronts and doors. The bullnose on the front
edge of the cock beading can be made in several different
ways. You can rip the material to size, and then sand or plane
the bullnose by hand, or you can rout the bullnose.

If you decide to use the router, rout the bead first in the edge
of wider stock. Put a 1/8-inch-diameter beading bit in a table-
mounted router and guide the stock against a fence as you
rout, as shown in the photo at left. When the bead has been
routed in the wider stock, rip the cock beading to its final
thickness on the table saw.

Fit and attach it to the drawers, as shown in *Drawer Cock
Beading*. Finally, fit and attach the cock beading to the edges of
the doors. I use epoxy on the door end-grain joints for extra
strength.

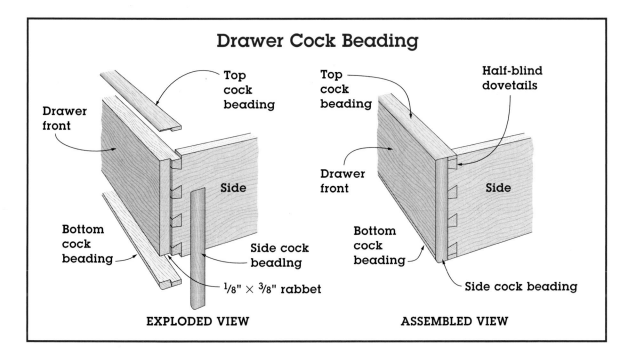

Drawer Cock Beading

Top cock beading

Drawer front

Side

Bottom cock beading

Side cock beading

$1/8" \times 3/8"$ rabbet

EXPLODED VIEW

Top cock beading

Half-blind dovetails

Drawer front

Side

Bottom cock beading

Side cock beading

ASSEMBLED VIEW

Install the Hardware

I installed half-mortise locks in the drawers and doors. The locks have a $3/4$-inch keyhole setback, which centers their key-hole escutcheons nicely on the string inlay. I used inset key-hole escutcheons. Although these are harder to install than surface-mounted escutcheons, I think they're much classier. Inset escutcheons are installed before mortising for the locks. You may want to practice lock and escutcheon installation in scrap first, since it can be a bit tricky.

1 **Install the keyhole escutcheons.** For each es-cutcheon, begin by drilling a hole to accept its circular head, as shown in *Front View*. Use a spur point bit to prevent tear-out, and drill only to the depth equal to the thickness of the escutcheon.

Now, lay the escutcheon in place and scribe its outline onto the workpiece. (If the escutcheon is tapered, the smaller side should be down.) Alternatively, to transfer the outline, you can lay carbon paper under the lower section of the escutcheon and press it down with a bolt chucked in a stopped drill press, as shown in the photo below left.

Carefully chisel out the waste to the same depth as the hole you drilled. Test fit the escutcheon in its hole without pressing it all the way in. When you've gotten a good fit, mix a little walnut sanding dust with epoxy and line the hole with the mix, which will fill any slight imperfections. Then clamp the escutcheon flush into its hole using waxed paper between the clamp and the escutcheon. Sand the escutcheon flush after the epoxy dries.

2 **Cut the lock mortises.** On the drill press, drill a hole all the way through the round escutcheon head and door or drawer front. Use a bit that matches the inside diameter of the escutcheon. Next, use a ruler and square to lay out the mortise for the lock body on the inside of the door or

To mark the position of the escutcheon, first chuck a bolt in the drill press. Then, put the escutcheon in place on the door or drawer front with carbon paper underneath it. Press the escutcheon down gently with the bolt to transfer the outline.

Scribe around the lock's flange with a marking knife, and then chisel a recess for it. The flange should be flush with the surface of the wood edge.

drawer front so that the lock pin will be centered on the hole you just drilled. Chisel out the mortise or rout it carefully with a router and a ¼-inch-diameter straight bit. (A trim router works well for this delicate routing.)

Place the lock in the mortise, aligning the pin with the hole, and scribe the outline of the lock's top flange onto the edge of the door or top edge of the drawer front. Cut the recess to the depth of the flange, as shown in the photo on the opposite page.

Using a coping saw, cut out the remainder of the keyhole waste, being careful not to score the escutcheon. Hold the lock in place and check the key operation. Adjust the lock position if necessary.

I like to mortise the lock's back flange flush with the wood surface, which looks much nicer than leaving it proud. If you do this, you'll have to widen the mortise for the edge flange. When you're done, install all of the locks temporarily with steel screws that match the size of the brass screws supplied with the lock. When the piece has been finished, you can re-place the steel screws with the soft brass ones.

3 **Hang the doors.** The door hinges are mortised into the legs only to avoid cutting into the door's cock beading. Fit the doors in their openings, and mark the hinge mortises on the legs. When installed, the hinges should align with the string inlay in the door, as shown in *Front View*. Make them deep enough to accept the full depth of the hinges, minus ¼₆₄ inch for door clearance. Cut the mortises, and install the hinges temporarily with steel screws that match the brass ones supplied with the hinges.

4 **Cut the lock bolt mortises.** To locate the position of a lock bolt mortise, close the door or drawer with the lock bolt raised, touching the bolt to the stile or rail. Then transfer the bolt's position across the edge of the stile or rail. Measure the distance from the face of the bolt to the face of the door or drawer front (not to the edge of the cock beading). Transfer this measurement onto the stile or rail, and lay out the mortise. Drill a series of holes within the layout lines.

Finally, if the lock comes with a catch plate, position the catch plate over the mortise, scribe around it, and then cut out a recess for mounting it flush.

5 **Drill holes for the pulls, and install the stops.** Drill the screw holes for the pulls, centering them on the middle of the doors and drawers, as shown in *Front View*. Install stops to keep the doors and drawer fronts flush to the case front. For adjustable drawer stops, I simply install screws into the case back at the rear of the drawer sides. For door stops, I lock one of the doors, then glue and brad a $\frac{1}{4} \times \frac{3}{8}$-inch wood strip onto the stile right behind the door, as shown in *Exploded View*.

Finish the Huntboard

1 **Finish the wood.** Remove the locks, hinges, and pulls, and sand the wood progressively from 150 to 220 grit. Clean off any dust, and apply your favorite finish. I used tung oil varnish, topping it with paste wax. Be sure to wax the drawer sides and runners so they'll slide easily.

2 **Attach the top.** Make wooden tabletop fasteners, as shown in *Tabletop Fastener Detail*, and install the top. I screw the top to the front rail, but attach the tabletop fasteners everywhere else, allowing the top to expand and contract about $\frac{5}{16}$ inch.

3 **Do the final assembly.** Rehang the doors and reinstall the locks, this time using the brass screws supplied with the hinges. Attach the pulls to the doors and drawers. Have dinner.

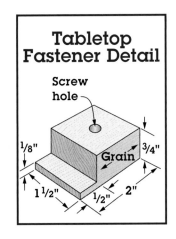

Tabletop Fastener Detail

Screw hole

Grain

1/8"

3/4"

1 1/2"

1/2"

2"

Cherry Sideboard

by Jim Probst

This sideboard combines two classic woodworking techniques: post-and-rail construction and frame-and-panel construction. The posts, or legs, are joined by rails forming a framework, much like a face frame, at the front, back, and sides. Except for the drawer compartment at front and center, each opening in the framework is filled by a framed panel.

On that tried-and-true aesthetic foundation, there's no need for much additional ornamentation. But a little contrast can go a long way toward distinguishing a piece of furniture. The curved bottom rails help "lift" the piece visually up off the floor. And the protruding ebonized strips inlaid into the cherry drawer fronts add a dash of art deco or oriental style. But at the same time, the solid, square-edged top keeps the piece very much down-to-earth.

The process of building the sideboard starts with the post-and-rail framework. Once this structural "skeleton" is test assembled, you can determine the exact dimensions for the back frame-and-panel assemblies, the end panels, and the plywood shelf cases. Then the entire cabinet gets glued up in a sequence of smaller assemblies before the whole thing comes together. The doors and drawers are added last.

Exploded View

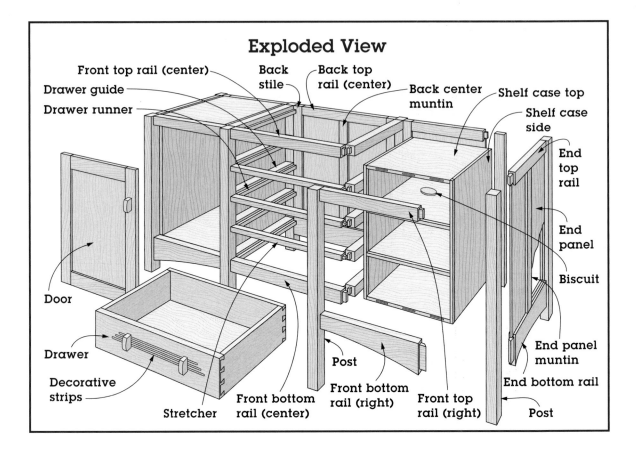

Front top rail (center)
Drawer guide
Drawer runner
Back stile
Back top rail (center)
Back center muntin
Shelf case top
Shelf case side
End top rail
End panel
Biscuit
Door
End panel muntin
Drawer
End bottom rail
Decorative strips
Post
Stretcher
Front bottom rail (center)
Front bottom rail (right)
Front top rail (right)
Post

Build the Post-and-Rail Framework

The post-and-rail structure of this sideboard is not complicated, but there are a lot of parts to make and join. To keep the parts organized, mark each one carefully, and always mark the same side—either the face or the back.

To further simplify things, I've made the joinery as consistent as possible throughout—for example, all the tenons are ⅜ inch thick and all the grooves are ⅜ inch wide so they can be cut on a router table with the same bit. In a nutshell, you want to cut the mortises and grooves in all the posts, and then cut and tenon the rails that connect the posts, including the back rail-and-stile assemblies.

Materials List

Part	Dimension	Part	Dimension
Shelf Case		End panels (4)	$\frac{3}{8}$" × $7\frac{3}{8}$" × $24\frac{1}{2}$"
Sides (4)	$\frac{3}{4}$" × $15\frac{1}{8}$" × 26"	Drawer guides (10)	$1\frac{3}{8}$" × $1\frac{1}{2}$" × $16\frac{1}{4}$"
Top/bottom (4)	$\frac{3}{4}$" × $15\frac{1}{4}$" × $15\frac{1}{2}$"	Drawer runners (10)	$\frac{1}{2}$" × 1" × $15\frac{1}{4}$"
Shelves (4)	$\frac{3}{4}$" × $15\frac{1}{8}$" × $15\frac{7}{16}$"	Top	1" × 22" × 66"
Edge-banding strips (4)	$\frac{1}{8}$" × $\frac{3}{4}$" × 26"		
Shelf edging strips (4)	$\frac{1}{8}$" × $\frac{3}{4}$" × $15\frac{1}{2}$"	**Doors**	
		Stiles (4)	$\frac{7}{8}$" × 2" × 24"
Cabinet Frame		Top rails (2)	$\frac{7}{8}$" × $2\frac{1}{4}$" × $14\frac{1}{2}$"
Posts (8)	$1\frac{3}{8}$" × $1\frac{3}{8}$" × 31"	Bottom rails (2)	$\frac{7}{8}$" × $2\frac{1}{2}$" × $14\frac{1}{2}$"
Front top rails, left and right (2)	1" × $1\frac{1}{2}$" × $17\frac{1}{2}$"	Panels (2)	$\frac{3}{8}$" × $12\frac{1}{2}$" × $19\frac{3}{4}$"
Front bottom rails, left and right (2)	1" × 4" × $17\frac{1}{2}$"	**Drawers**	
Front top rail, center	1" × $1\frac{1}{2}$" × $26\frac{1}{4}$"	Fronts (4)	$\frac{7}{8}$" × $5\frac{1}{4}$" × $24\frac{3}{8}$"
Front bottom rail, center	1" × 2" × $26\frac{1}{4}$"	Sides (8)	$\frac{5}{8}$" × $5\frac{1}{4}$" × $16\frac{1}{4}$"
Stretchers (3)	1" × 1" × $25\frac{1}{2}$"	Backs (4)	$\frac{5}{8}$" × $5\frac{1}{4}$" × $24\frac{3}{8}$"
Back stiles (6)	$\frac{7}{8}$" × $2\frac{1}{4}$" × $27\frac{1}{2}$"	Bottoms (4)	$\frac{1}{2}$" × $15\frac{7}{8}$" × $23\frac{5}{8}$"
Back top rails, left and right (2)	$\frac{7}{8}$" × $1\frac{1}{2}$" × $13\frac{3}{4}$"	Decorative strips (18')	$\frac{1}{4}$" × $\frac{5}{16}$"
Back bottom rails, left and right (2)	$\frac{7}{8}$" × 4" × $13\frac{3}{4}$"	Pulls (10)	$\frac{5}{8}$" × $\frac{7}{8}$" × 2"
Back top rail, center	$\frac{7}{8}$" × $1\frac{1}{2}$" × $22\frac{1}{4}$"	Dowels (20)	$\frac{1}{4}$" × 1"
Back bottom rail, center	$\frac{7}{8}$" × 4" × $22\frac{1}{4}$"		
Back center muntin	$\frac{7}{8}$" × $1\frac{1}{2}$" × 23"	**Hardware**	
Back panels, left and right (2)	$\frac{3}{8}$" × $12\frac{1}{2}$" × $22\frac{1}{2}$"	#8 × $1\frac{1}{4}$" drywall screws (as needed)	
Back center panels (2)	$\frac{3}{8}$" × 10" × $22\frac{1}{2}$"	#8 × $1\frac{1}{4}$" roundhead wood screws with washers (8)	
End top rails (2)	1" × $1\frac{1}{2}$" × 17"	#20 biscuits (as needed)	
End bottom rails (2)	1" × 4" × 17"	L-style offset knife hinges (4). Available from Rockler Woodworking and Hardware, 4365 Willow Drive, Medina, MN 55340; (800) 279-4441; part #26278	
End panel muntins (2)	1" × $1\frac{1}{2}$" × 25"	$2\frac{1}{2}$" × $1\frac{1}{2}$" butt hinges (4) (optional)	
		Magnetic door catches (2)	
		Shelf support pins (16)	

1 **Mill the posts.** Because the posts are the main structural element of the credenza, it's important to start with posts that are straight and dead square. Plane the stock for the posts to about $1\frac{1}{2}$ inches thick. Then, joint an edge on each board. Rip one post at a time (also at about $1\frac{1}{2}$ inches)

(continued on page 46)

Front View

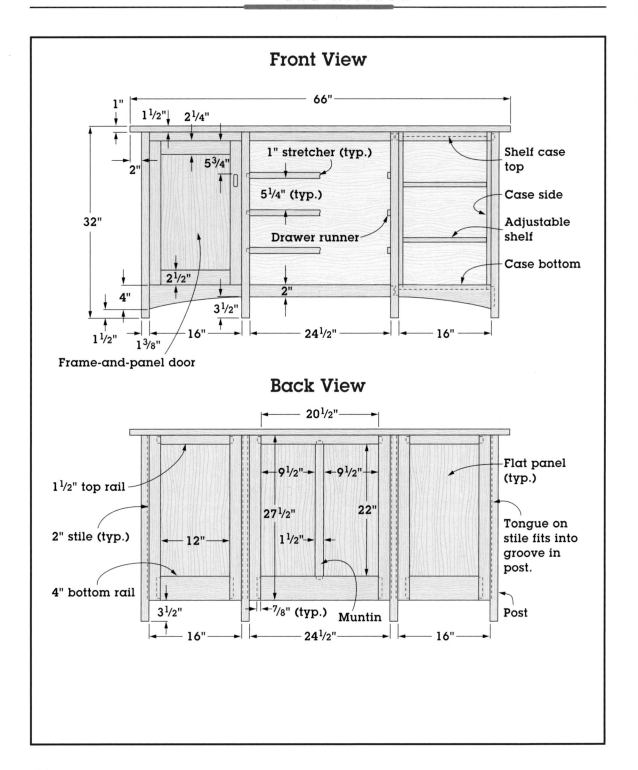

1"

1 1/2"   2 1/4"

66"

2"

5 3/4"

1" stretcher (typ.)

5 1/4" (typ.)

Drawer runner

Shelf case top

Case side

Adjustable shelf

Case bottom

32"

2 1/2"

2"

4"

3 1/2"

1 1/2"

16"

1 3/8"

24 1/2"

16"

Frame-and-panel door

Back View

20 1/2"

1 1/2" top rail

9 1/2"   9 1/2"

Flat panel (typ.)

2" stile (typ.)

12"

27 1/2"

1 1/2"

22"

Tongue on stile fits into groove in post.

4" bottom rail

3 1/2"

7/8" (typ.)

Muntin

Post

16"

24 1/2"

16"

End View

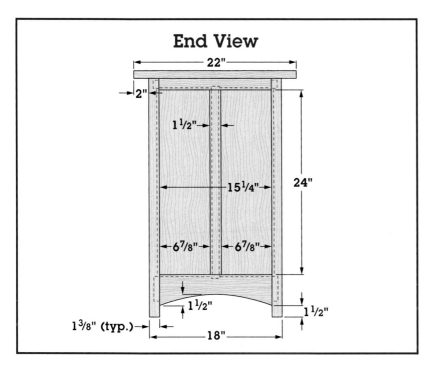

Top View—Cross Section

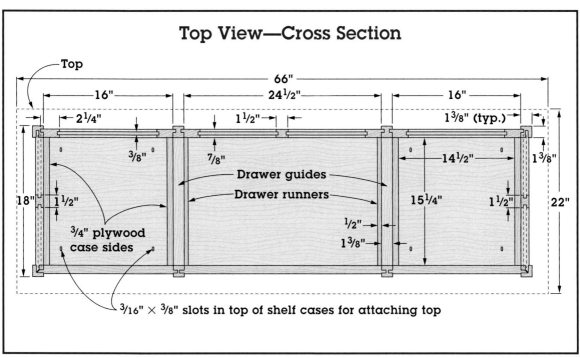

Top

66"

16"   24¹/₂"   16"

2¹/₄"   1¹/₂"   1³/₈" (typ.)

3/8"   7/8"   14¹/₂"   1³/₈"

Drawer guides

Drawer runners

18"   1¹/₂"   15¹/₄"   1¹/₂"   22"

1/2"

³/₄" plywood
case sides   1³/₈"

³/₁₆" × ³/₈" slots in top of shelf cases for attaching top

and rejoint the edge of the board before ripping the next post from it. This gives you posts with three planed sides that should be dead square. If any of the posts bow when they are sawed off the board, the extra stock thickness allows you to rejoint them straight before final planing to $1\frac{3}{8}$ inches thick.

Next, plane the sawed edge of each post, then plane either face adjacent to the one just planed. This makes the posts square. Finally, lower the planer setting and pass each post through twice—one cut on any two adjacent faces—until you reach the final thickness.

2 **Cut the remaining frame parts.** Cut all the rails, stiles, and muntins to the sizes given in the Materials List. Hold off cutting the $\frac{3}{8}$-inch-thick panels until the frames they fit within can be assembled for test fitting.

3 **Mortise the posts.** All the mortises in the posts are $\frac{3}{8}$ inch wide and centered in the stock. And the mortises are fairly shallow—$\frac{7}{8}$ inch is the deepest. For both reasons, the mortises are easily plunge-cut on a router table. The fence setting stays the same for all the mortises, and only the bit height gets adjusted between cuts.

Lay out all the mortises on the posts, as shown in *Mortise and Groove Layout*. Set the router table with a $\frac{3}{8}$-inch bit, and set the fence to center the mortises in the stock. Mark on the router table the ends of the bit, which will guide the starting and stopping of the cuts, as shown in the photo on page 48. Cut each mortise in several passes, raising the bit about $\frac{1}{4}$ inch on each pass until a depth of $\frac{7}{8}$ inch is reached.

Cut all the $\frac{7}{8}$-inch-deep corner mortises in the posts, then cut $\frac{5}{8}$-inch-deep mortises on the inner posts. Next, cut $\frac{1}{2}$-inch mortises on the inside faces of the four inner posts that receive the drawer guides. Also, cut all the $\frac{7}{8}$-inch-deep mortises in the back rails and stiles, as shown in *Back Frame-and-Panel Construction*.

4 **Rout the panel grooves.** All but the two front inner posts get grooved to receive panels. The end rails and muntins and the back muntin also get grooved. All these

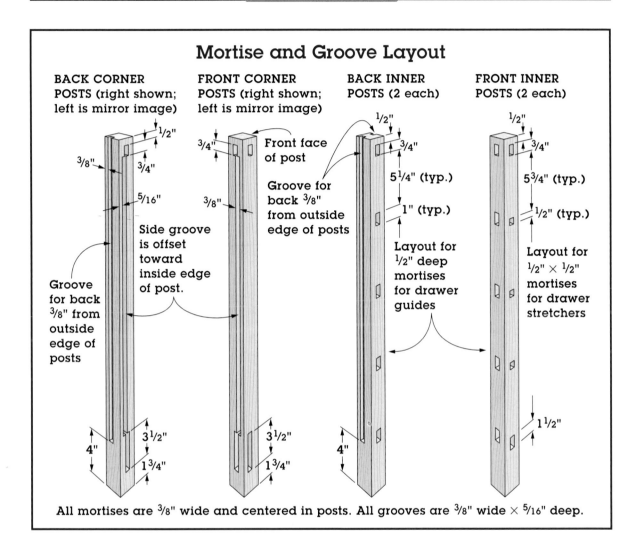

Mortise and Groove Layout

BACK CORNER POSTS (right shown; left is mirror image)

FRONT CORNER POSTS (right shown; left is mirror image)

BACK INNER POSTS (2 each)

FRONT INNER POSTS (2 each)

1/2"

3/8"

3/4"

5/16"

Groove for back 3/8" from outside edge of posts

Side groove is offset toward inside edge of post.

4"

3 1/2"

1 3/4"

3/4"

Front face of post

Groove for back 3/8" from outside edge of posts

3/8"

3 1/2"

1 3/4"

1/2"

3/4"

5 1/4" (typ.)

1" (typ.)

Layout for 1/2" deep mortises for drawer guides

4"

1/2"

3/4"

5 3/4" (typ.)

1/2" (typ.)

Layout for 1/2" × 1/2" mortises for drawer stretchers

1 1/2"

All mortises are 3/8" wide and centered in posts. All grooves are 3/8" wide × 5/16" deep.

grooves are ⅜ inch wide and 5/16 inch deep. However, all the grooves are not identically positioned on the parts.

First rout the grooves in the back posts for the back panel assemblies. These grooves are located ⅜ inch from the outside face of the posts, as shown in *Mortise and Groove Layout*. They start 4 inches from the bottom and run all the way out the top of the posts.

The grooves in the corner posts for the end panels run between the top and bottom mortises. They are offset toward the inside of the stock, 5/16 inch from the inside edge.

With the ends of each mortise marked on the outside face of the stock, hold the post against the fence while lowering it onto the bit so the forward mortise mark aligns with the forward bit mark. Advance the stock until the rear mortise mark aligns with the opposite bit mark, then carefully raise the stock off the bit.

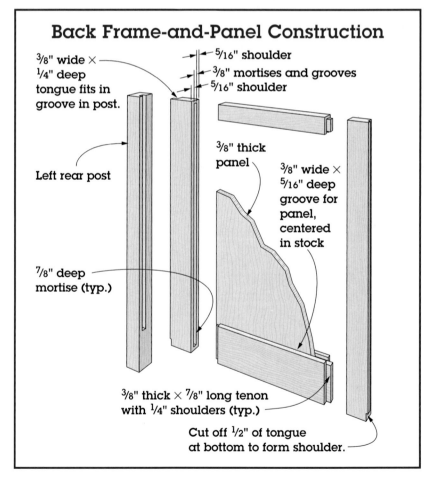

Back Frame-and-Panel Construction

3/8" wide × 1/4" deep tongue fits in groove in post.

5/16" shoulder
3/8" mortises and grooves
5/16" shoulder

3/8" thick panel

3/8" wide × 5/16" deep groove for panel, centered in stock

Left rear post

7/8" deep mortise (typ.)

3/8" thick × 7/8" long tenon with 1/4" shoulders (typ.)

Cut off 1/2" of tongue at bottom to form shoulder.

The groove in the corner posts for the end panels must be offset inward so it aligns with the grooves in the thinner rail stock.

With this same fence setting, rout the grooves in the end rails and end muntins, as well as the rails, stiles, and muntins for the back frame-and-panel assemblies. Note that the grooves in the back stiles go from mortise to mortise, leaving a ¼-inch shoulder at each end. All these grooves are centered in the 1-inch-thick stock, ⁵⁄₁₆ inch from both faces, as shown in *Back Frame-and-Panel Construction* and in the photo above.

5 **Cut the muntin mortises.** Lay out and cut the mortises in the end rails and the center back rails for the muntins. The mortises fall within the grooves and are just ³⁄₁₆ inch deeper than the groove to accommodate the ½-inch-long stub tenons on the ends of the muntins.

6 **Cut all the tenons.** Like the mortises and grooves, there are several tenon variations, but they too can be cut in groups. All tenons are ⅜ inch thick, and all have ¼-inch shoulders on the ends, as shown in *Tenon Detail*. The length and the offset vary.

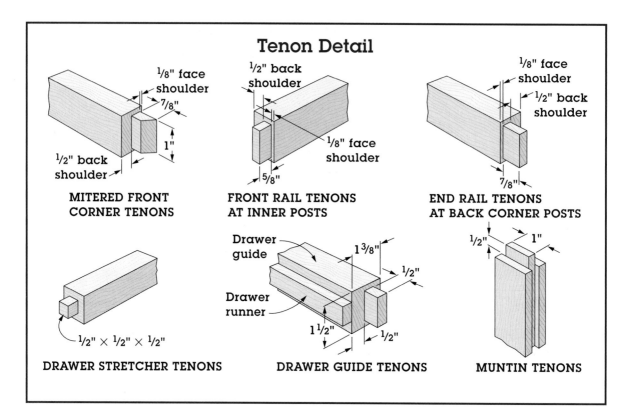

Tenon Detail

MITERED FRONT CORNER TENONS
- 1/8" face shoulder
- 7/8"
- 1"
- 1/2" back shoulder

FRONT RAIL TENONS AT INNER POSTS
- 1/2" back shoulder
- 1/8" face shoulder
- 5/8"

END RAIL TENONS AT BACK CORNER POSTS
- 1/8" face shoulder
- 1/2" back shoulder
- 7/8"

DRAWER STRETCHER TENONS
- 1/2" × 1/2" × 1/2"

DRAWER GUIDE TENONS
- Drawer guide
- Drawer runner
- 1 3/8"
- 1/2"
- 1/2"
- 1 1/2"

MUNTIN TENONS
- 1/2"
- 1"

Because the longest tenon is 7/8 inch, I decided to forego making cheek cuts, conventionally done with the stock held vertically in a tenoning jig. Instead, I made all the tenons by passing the stock one, two, or three times over a dado blade in the table saw, guiding the stock with the miter gauge. With this approach, only the fence setting and the blade height need to be adjusted to get the different tenon shoulders. The trick is to make *all* the cuts necessary for each length tenon, adjusting the *blade height* as needed, before changing the fence setting for the next set of tenons. This way, all four shoulders on each tenon will be in the same plane.

Start with the ten main frame rails. These tenons are offset from the center of the stock, with a 1/8-inch shoulder at the front and a 1/2-inch shoulder at the back. Cut all the 7/8-inch-long tenons first, adjusting the blade height between sets of cuts to get the different shoulders. Then, cut the 5/8-inch-long tenons on the front rails that join the inner posts.

The cheeks on short tenons can be easily cut by making a couple of passes over a dado blade. Adjust the blade height to cut the short edge shoulders, again making two passes.

Next, cut all the $\frac{1}{2}$-inch-long stub tenons on the stretchers, guides, and muntins, as shown in the photo above. These tenons are centered in the stock. Finally, cut all the $\frac{7}{8}$-inch-long tenons on the back rails, which are also centered in the stock.

7 **Miter the front corner tenons.** Because their mortises intersect, the front corner tenons need to be mitered. This is done easily on the table saw with the blade angled to 45 degrees, using the miter gauge to guide the stock. A portable miter saw also will work fine.

8 **Shape the bottom rails.** Lay out a smooth curve on each of the two bottom front rails and the two bottom end rails, according to the dimensions shown in *Front View.* Cut them on the band saw or with a saber saw, and then smooth the curves with a sanding block.

9 **Attach the drawer runners.** The drawer runners are centered on the drawer guides and flush with the tenon shoulders at their ends. Predrill countersunk holes in the runners for #8 × $1\frac{1}{4}$-inch drywall screws. Apply glue to the back of a runner, center it on the guide, and hold it there with spring clamps. Drill $\frac{3}{32}$-inch holes into the drawer guide, and screw the runner on, as shown in the photo on page 52.

Glue and screw the
drawer runners to
the guides.

10 Rabbet the back stiles. The back outside corner of the six rear stiles gets rabbeted to form a ⅜-inch-thick × ¼-inch-long tongue, as shown in *Back Frame-and-Panel Construction*. I cut the rabbets on the table saw with a dado blade. With a handsaw, remove ½ inch of the tongue at the bottom to form a shoulder.

11 Test fit the entire framework. At this stage, you can assemble the entire cabinet structure to make sure all the parts fit correctly. Assemble the three small back frames. Knock together the front and back post-and-rail frames. Then bring the front and back assemblies together with the end rails and the drawer guides. Apply clamps if necessary to pull all the joints together completely. Then you can determine the final size of the back and end panels, as well as the size of the plywood shelf case parts.

12 Cut the panels. Measure each panel opening and add ½ inch to each dimension. This allows ⅛ inch total "breathing room" in each direction. This allowance is crucial across the width to accommodate expansion. I allow the same amount on the length just for consistency of measurements and so the panels don't bottom out in their grooves.

Glue up narrower panels on edge to get the necessary width, then plane the glued-up panels to a finished thickness that matches the groove. Sand all the panels before assembling the frames.

Build the
Plywood Shelf Cases

1 **Cut the plywood parts to size.** Cut the ¾-inch-thick plywood for the sides, top, bottom, and shelves. Glue the ⅛-inch-thick, solid edge banding to the front edge of the sides and shelves but not to the top or bottom. (The width of the sides is ⅛ inch less than the top and bottom but should be equal once the edge banding is applied to the sides.) Trim the edge banding flush with the surfaces of the case parts with a block plane.

2 **Drill the shelf support holes.** Make a hole-drilling template from ¼-inch plywood or Masonite, as shown in *Plywood Shelf Cases*. For this cabinet, I used a template with a single row of holes, as shown in the drawing on page 54. Use a depth stop on your drill to limit the hole depth. Clamp the template to the inner (show) face of the side, aligning it with the bottom corner, and drill each row of holes.

3 **Cut the biscuit joints.** Lay out and cut biscuit slots in the case parts. Then sand the case parts before assembling them.

4 **Assemble the plywood cases.** Glue and clamp the plywood cases together. Check the diagonal measurements of the cases to make sure they are square. Make sure the shelves fit the cases.

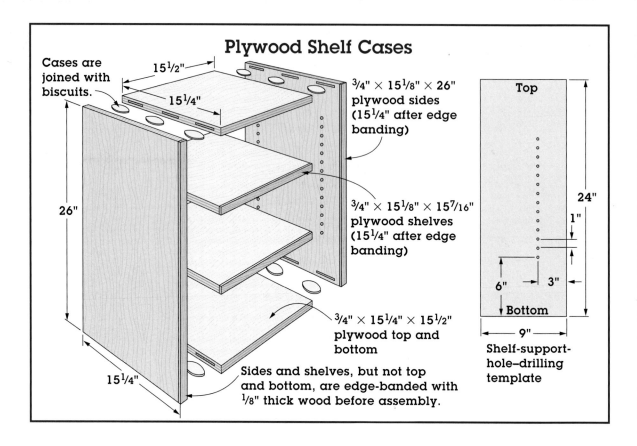

Plywood Shelf Cases

Cases are joined with biscuits.

15¹⁄₂"

15¹⁄₄"

³⁄₄" × 15¹⁄₈" × 26" plywood sides (15¹⁄₄" after edge banding)

26"

³⁄₄" × 15¹⁄₈" × 15⁷⁄₁₆" plywood shelves (15¹⁄₄" after edge banding)

15¹⁄₄"

³⁄₄" × 15¹⁄₄" × 15¹⁄₂" plywood top and bottom

Sides and shelves, but not top and bottom, are edge-banded with ¹⁄₈" thick wood before assembly.

Top

24"

1"

6"   3"

Bottom

9"

Shelf-support-hole–drilling template

Glue the Cabinet Together

1 **Glue up the front frame.** First glue and clamp together each side portion of the front frame, checking the diagonal measurements to make sure each assembly is square. Then glue and clamp the center rails between the two side assemblies to complete the front frame.

2 **Glue up the back frame.** First, test assemble the three individual frame-and-panel assemblies to be sure the panels fit correctly. Then, glue each frame-and-panel assembly together. Do not glue the panels in place—they must be allowed to "float." *Note:* Because the edges of the stiles are already rabbeted, cut strips of scrap wood to fill the rabbets so the clamp pressure will be even on the stile edges.

Sand the faces of the back frame-and-panel assemblies, then glue them between the posts. Follow the same sequence as with the front frame—smaller side assemblies first, then the center section between the sides.

3 **Biscuit join the shelf cases to the front frame.** Cut biscuit slots in the front edge of the shelf case tops and bottoms, then cut corresponding slots in the top and bottom rails. The top surface of plywood case parts are flush with the top edge of the rails, so use the biscuit joiner fence on the top of each part.

Glue and clamp the cases to the front frame. Because the top of the shelf cases are flush with the top of the top rails, this is best done with the box and subassemblies upside down so everything can rest on a flat surface.

4 **Partially assemble the end panels.** Glue the end muntins between the end rails and slide the panels in place. (Again, do not glue the panels.) Check the diagonal measurement of this subassembly, from tenon shoulder to tenon shoulder, to make sure it is square.

5 **Complete the assembly.** The last assembly step is a big one and warrants an extra set of hands. Lay the front frame assembly with the attached cases face down. Glue in the end assemblies and all the drawer guides into the front frame. Finally, position the back frame in place and work all the tenons into their mortises. Tap all the joints home, then rotate the cabinet 90 degrees into an upright position. Apply two clamps front to back on each post, one at each rail.

Make and Hang the Doors

The doors are made much like the back frame-and-panel assemblies except that the tenons are deeper so the joints will withstand the greater stresses the doors will receive.

Quick tip

In my shop, we have a set of four 6-foot-long bar clamps that make this assembly easier to handle. If you have long clamps, consider this assembling approach:

Start by gluing and clamping the drawer guides to their posts, then assemble the center back frame-and-panel section, stretchers, and the top and bottom rails (center) to create the drawer case.

Next, assemble the end frames. When the glue is dry, glue the end frame panels, left and right back frame panels, and left and right rails to the drawer case, pulling together end to end with your long clamps.

Finally build the shelf cases and slip them into place from the bottom of the assembly. Secure the shelf with #8 × 1¼-inch drywall screws.

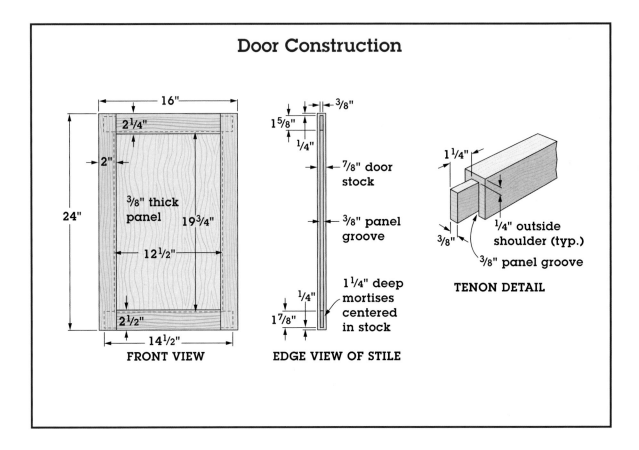

Door Construction

FRONT VIEW

16"

2¼"

2"

³⁄₈" thick panel

24"

19³⁄₄"

12½"

2½"

14½"

EDGE VIEW OF STILE

1⁵⁄₈"

¼"

³⁄₈"

⁷⁄₈" door stock

³⁄₈" panel groove

1¼" deep mortises centered in stock

¼"

1⁷⁄₈"

TENON DETAIL

1¼"

³⁄₈"

¼" outside shoulder (typ.)

³⁄₈" panel groove

Quick tip

To transfer hinge locations from the door to the frame accurately, position each door in its opening using thin wood shims. With the shims, you can create an even gap all the way around the door, so that it will open easily.

1 Cut the door joinery, and assemble the doors. Cut the door mortises, grooves, and tenons, as described already for the other parts, and as shown in *Door Construction*. The grooves are slightly deeper (³⁄₈ inch), and the tenons are longer (1¼ inch). Test fit the frames and cut panels to fit. Then glue the doors together.

2 Trim the doors to fit. Trim the doors so there is a consistent gap (between ¹⁄₁₆ and ⅛ inch) around each one.

3 Hang the doors. I chose offset knife hinges for this cabinet, though butt hinges would work as well. Cut the mortises in the doors first, and mount the hinges to the doors. Shim each door in its opening, transfer the hinge locations to the case, then cut the case mortises.

Mount the door catches. Attach magnetic door catches of your choice.

Make the Drawers and Pulls

1 **Size the drawer parts, and cut the joinery.** Measure the drawer openings, and then cut the drawer parts to size, adjusting the dimensions given in the Materials List as necessary. Lay out and cut the half-blind dovetails at the front corners and the through dovetails at the back corners of the drawer parts, as shown in *Drawer Construction*. See "Cutting Dovetails" on page 164 for detailed instructions. Also, cut the ¼-inch groove for the bottom in the sides and front.

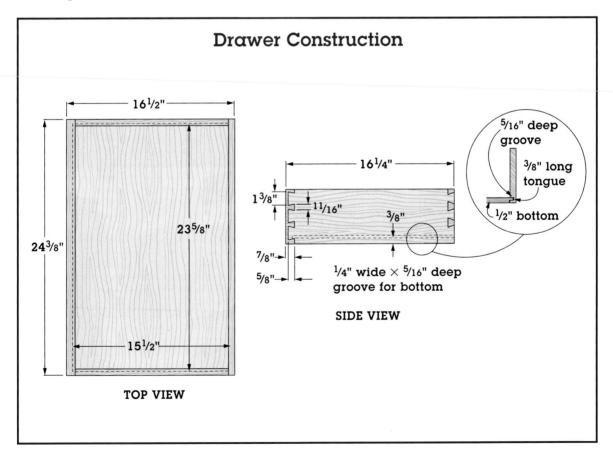

Drawer Construction

16½"

23⅝"

24⅜"

15½"

TOP VIEW

16¼"

1⅜"

1¹¹/₁₆"

⅜"

7/8"

5/8"

¼" wide × 5/16" deep groove for bottom

SIDE VIEW

5/16" deep groove

3/8" long tongue

½" bottom

Pull and Inlay Detail

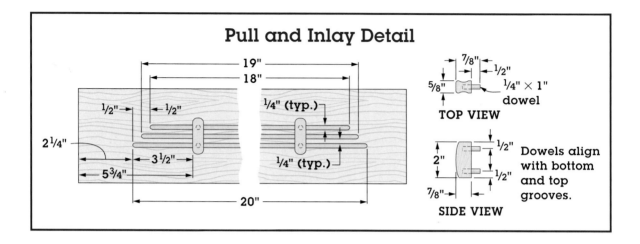

2 **Cut and fit the bottom.** Test fit the drawers. Glue up a panel for each of the drawer bottoms, and cut it to size. Rabbet the edge of the bottom to form a ¼-inch tongue, as shown in *Drawer Construction*.

3 **Cut the inlay grooves in the fronts.** On each drawer front, lay out the three stopped grooves that receive the decorative inlay strips, as shown in *Pull and Inlay Detail*. Use a plunge router with an edge guide to rout the grooves, as

Use a plunge router equipped with an edge guide to rout the stopped grooves. Use the layout itself to visually start and stop the cuts. Rout the middle groove on all the fronts, then adjust the fence and rout all the outside grooves.

shown in the photo on the opposite page. First, rout all the middle grooves, which are centered in the width of the drawer fronts. Then, adjust the edge guide and rout the other two grooves, which are equidistant from the edge.

4 **Taper the ends of the grooves.** The inlay is parallel with the drawer front except at the ends where it's raised up. To do this, you need to chisel a ramp at the ends of the grooves, as shown in the photo at left on page 60.

5 **Make the pulls.** Cut a wide cove into both faces of a single length of stock to form the pull shape, as shown in *Pull and Inlay Detail.* Then crosscut the individual pulls from the longer piece. On the drill press, drill two $1/2$-inch-deep × $1/4$-inch-diameter holes for the dowel tenons. Create the slight arch on the outside face of each pull with a belt sander or block plane. Cut the dowels to length and glue them into the pulls. Next, sand and stain the pulls. I used jet black India ink to give them the look of ebony, but any very dark stain will have a similar effect. When the pulls have been stained, locate and drill the holes for the pulls on the drawer fronts and on the doors. After finish sanding the drawer fronts and doors, glue on the pulls.

6 **Glue the inlay in place.** Cut to length the long strips that fit between the pulls, slightly round their pro-truding front edge with sandpaper, and then stain them with India ink. Glue them into their grooves with epoxy.

Cut the short strips of inlay to length and round one end with a sanding block. These strips should be a bit longer than the groove, so they can ride up out of the groove at the end. When the strips have been cut to length, stain them with India ink.

Glue the short strips into their grooves with the rounded ends extending up the ramps that you chiseled in the grooves. Clamp them in place, as shown in the photo at right on page 60.

7 **Assemble the drawers.** Once the inlay on the drawer fronts is complete, glue and clamp the drawers together.

Chisel a small ramp at the ends of the grooves for the inlay strips to ride up on. Angle the ramps at around 45 degrees, and extend them ¼ to ⅜ inch beyond the layout lines.

Position the short inlay strips into the grooves so that their rounded ends extend up the ramp at the end of each groove. Clamp the strips at the center of their length to slightly bend them down into their grooves.

Make the Top, and Finish the Sideboard

1 Glue up the top, and cut it to size. Edge-glue enough boards for the top. The glued-up top should be over-sized slightly for final trimming. Rip the glued-up top to width, then crosscut it to length.

To fasten the top to the cabinet, drill overlapping holes in the top of each shelving case to create slots for #8 × 1¼-inch round-head wood screws with washers. The slots should run perpendicular to the grain of the top. This way, the screws will slide back and forth with the top as it expands and contracts with the seasonal changes in humidity. Position the top on the cabinet, and screw it in place.

2 Finish the sideboard. To bring out the wood grain, sand the sideboard to 220 grit and then rub on a wiping varnish. Use steel wool between coats for a glass-smooth finish.

Eastern Shore of Virginia Corner Cabinet

by Lonnie Bird

If you've been looking for a special piece of furniture for the dining room, perhaps this is it. This walnut corner cabinet dates from 1745 and was originally built by an unknown cabinetmaker from the Eastern Shore region in Virginia. The original cabinet now sits in the Metropolitan Museum of Art in New York.

The joiner who built the original corner cabinet broke the piece into two halves, dividing it in the middle at the large horizontal waist molding between the two pairs of doors. If you would like to section the corner cabinet, the details show how the center waist molding would break. You must also cut the spine, back boards, canted sides, and face-frame boards to proper lengths, and add another shelf to serve as the bottom of the top section. However, since the cabinet is of manageable proportions, I chose to leave it as one piece when I built it, as shown in the plans.

Exploded View

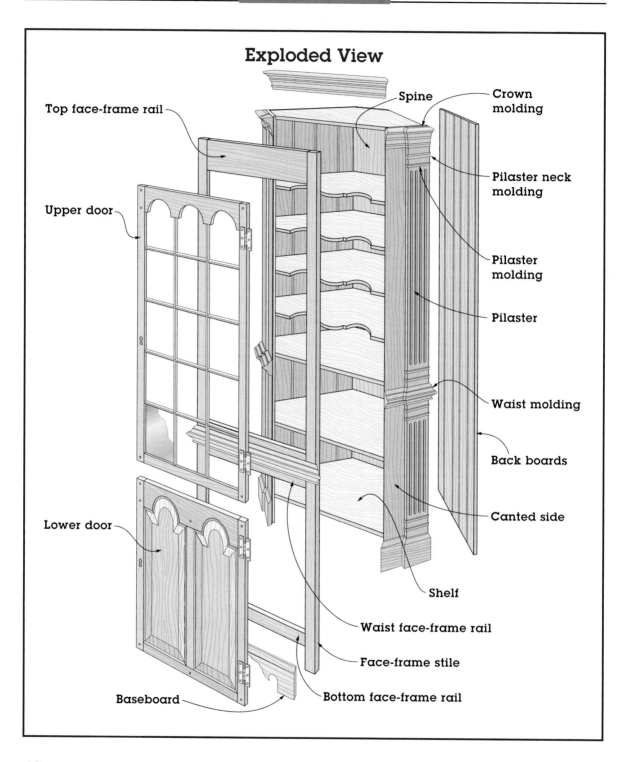

Spine

Crown molding

Top face-frame rail

Pilaster neck molding

Upper door

Pilaster molding

Pilaster

Waist molding

Back boards

Canted side

Lower door

Shelf

Waist face-frame rail

Face-frame stile

Baseboard

Bottom face-frame rail

Materials List

Part	Dimension	Part	Dimension
Case		Door panels (2)	$\frac{9}{16}$" × $9\frac{1}{4}$" × $21\frac{5}{8}$"
Face-frame stiles (2)	$\frac{7}{8}$" × $2\frac{1}{4}$" × $87\frac{1}{2}$"	Dowel pegs (7) (optional)	$\frac{5}{16}$" × $\frac{5}{16}$" × $1\frac{1}{4}$"
Top face-frame rail	$\frac{7}{8}$" × $5\frac{3}{4}$" × $24\frac{1}{2}$"		
Waist face-frame rail	$\frac{7}{8}$" × $6\frac{1}{2}$" × $24\frac{1}{2}$"	**Upper Door**	
Bottom face-frame rail	$\frac{7}{8}$" × $3\frac{1}{4}$" × $24\frac{1}{2}$"	Stiles (2)	$\frac{7}{8}$" × $1\frac{3}{4}$" × $44\frac{1}{2}$"
Canted sides (2)	$\frac{7}{8}$" × $7\frac{1}{4}$" × $87\frac{1}{2}$"	Top rail	$\frac{7}{8}$" × 4" × $21\frac{1}{2}$"
Spine	$\frac{7}{8}$" × 8" × $87\frac{1}{2}$"	Bottom rail	$\frac{7}{8}$" × $1\frac{3}{4}$" × $21\frac{5}{8}$"
Shelves (8)	$\frac{3}{4}$" × $18\frac{1}{2}$" × $35\frac{1}{2}$"	Vertical muntins (2)	$\frac{7}{8}$" × $\frac{7}{8}$" × $40\frac{1}{8}$"
Back boards	$\frac{1}{2}$" × random width × 84"	Horizontal muntins (4)	$\frac{7}{8}$" × $\frac{7}{8}$" × $20\frac{3}{8}$"
		Dowel pegs (5) (optional)	$\frac{5}{16}$" × $\frac{5}{16}$" × $1\frac{1}{4}$"
Pilasters (2)	$\frac{3}{4}$" × $4\frac{3}{4}$" × $87\frac{1}{2}$"		
Baseboard	$\frac{3}{4}$" × 5" × 50"		
Moldings		**Hardware**	
Waist molding	$1\frac{3}{4}$" × 4" × 50"	#10 × 2" flathead wood screws (as needed)	
Crown molding	$1\frac{3}{4}$" × $4\frac{1}{2}$" × 50"	#10 × $1\frac{1}{2}$" flathead wood screws (as needed)	
Pilaster neck molding	$\frac{1}{2}$" × 1" × 12"	6d cut nails (as needed)	
Pilaster molding	$\frac{3}{8}$" × $\frac{5}{8}$" × 84"	$1\frac{1}{4}$" × $1\frac{1}{2}$" cabinet locks (2). Available from Ball and Ball, 463 W. Lincoln Highway, Exton, PA 19341; (610) 363-7330; part #TCB-010	
Lower Door		Escutcheons (2). Available from Ball and Ball; part #L94-045	
Stiles (2)	$\frac{7}{8}$" × $1\frac{7}{8}$" × $24\frac{1}{2}$"	4" brass H-hinges (2 pairs). Available from Ball and Ball; part #H19-078	
Top rail	$\frac{7}{8}$" × $4\frac{1}{2}$" × $21\frac{1}{2}$"	Glass, $\frac{1}{8}$" thick, cut to fit upper door	
Bottom rail	$\frac{7}{8}$" × $1\frac{7}{8}$" × $21\frac{1}{2}$"		
Mullion	$\frac{7}{8}$" × $1\frac{3}{4}$" × $20\frac{7}{8}$"		

Build the Face Frame

It may seem a bit odd to begin a case piece by building the face frame, but it is the best starting point for this particular project. After the face frame is assembled, you add the canted sides, the shelves, and the back to complete the case.

The face frame consists simply of the vertical and horizontal members (stiles and rails) that delineate the openings for the upper and lower doors. The two stiles extend the height of the cabinet, with top, waist, and bottom rails running between them, as shown in *Face Frame.*

Front View

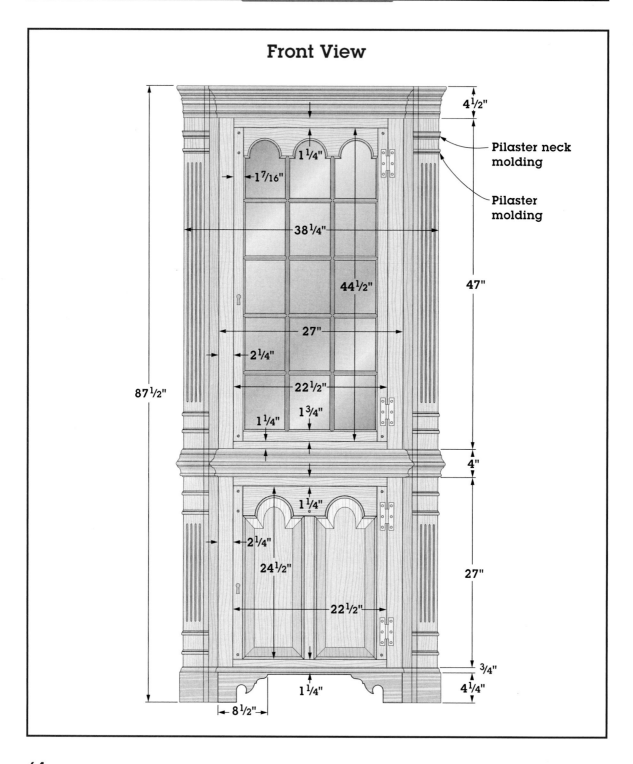

Pilaster neck molding

Pilaster molding

$4^1/2$"

$1^1/4$"

$1^7/{16}$"

$38^1/4$"

$44^1/2$"

47"

27"

$2^1/4$"

$22^1/2$"

$1^1/4$"

$1^3/4$"

$87^1/2$"

4"

$1^1/4$"

$2^1/4$"

$24^1/2$"

27"

$22^1/2$"

$3/4$"

$4^1/4$"

$1^1/4$"

$8^1/2$"

Section Views

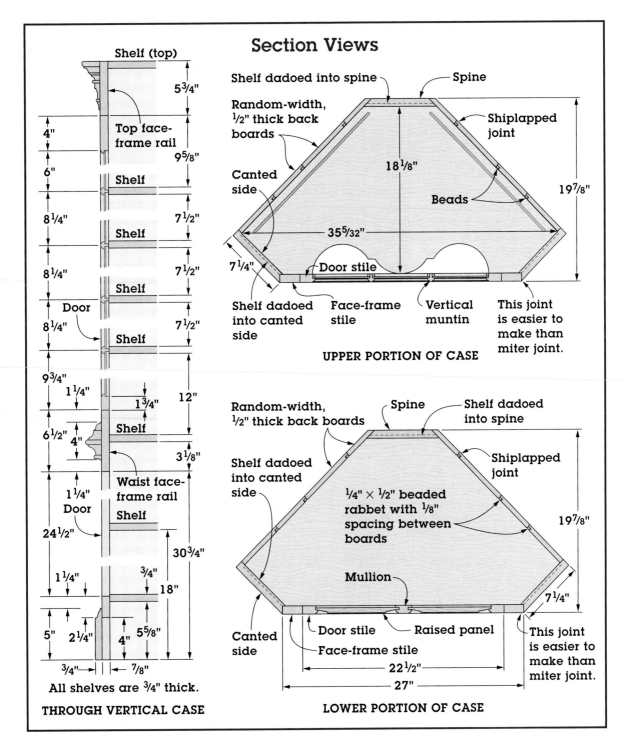

Shelf (top)

5$\frac{3}{4}$"

4"

Top face-frame rail

9$\frac{5}{8}$"

6"

Shelf

8$\frac{1}{4}$"

7$\frac{1}{2}$"

Shelf

8$\frac{1}{4}$"

7$\frac{1}{2}$"

Shelf

Door

8$\frac{1}{4}$"

7$\frac{1}{2}$"

Shelf

9$\frac{3}{4}$"

1$\frac{1}{4}$"

1$\frac{3}{4}$"

12"

Shelf

6$\frac{1}{2}$"

4"

3$\frac{1}{8}$"

Waist face-frame rail

1$\frac{1}{4}$"

Door

Shelf

24$\frac{1}{2}$"

30$\frac{3}{4}$"

1$\frac{1}{4}$"

$\frac{3}{4}$"

18"

5"

2$\frac{1}{4}$"

4"

5$\frac{5}{8}$"

$\frac{3}{4}$"

$\frac{7}{8}$"

All shelves are $\frac{3}{4}$" thick.

THROUGH VERTICAL CASE

UPPER PORTION OF CASE

Shelf dadoed into spine

Spine

Random-width, $\frac{1}{2}$" thick back boards

Shiplapped joint

Canted side

18$\frac{1}{8}$"

Beads

19$\frac{7}{8}$"

35$\frac{5}{32}$"

7$\frac{1}{4}$"

Door stile

Shelf dadoed into canted side

Face-frame stile

Vertical muntin

This joint is easier to make than miter joint.

LOWER PORTION OF CASE

Random-width, $\frac{1}{2}$" thick back boards

Spine

Shelf dadoed into spine

Shelf dadoed into canted side

Shiplapped joint

$\frac{1}{4}$" × $\frac{1}{2}$" beaded rabbet with $\frac{1}{8}$" spacing between boards

19$\frac{7}{8}$"

Mullion

7$\frac{1}{4}$"

Canted side

Door stile

Raised panel

This joint is easier to make than miter joint.

Face-frame stile

22$\frac{1}{2}$"

27"

65

1 Select the stock, and mill the parts to size. Cut the wood for the face frame to the sizes given in the Materials List. Walnut was the primary wood used in both the original corner cabinet and my reproduction. But other cabinet-grade hardwoods such as mahogany or cherry could be used. If you paint the piece—and many eighteenth-century pieces were painted—you could use poplar or even yellow pine.

To save time later, you can mill the stock for the canted sides, pilasters, baseboard, and shelves now. Bear in mind that because of their width, the shelves will probably have to be edge-glued together from narrower boards.

2 Cut the joints between the face-frame rails and stiles. The three rails are joined to the stiles with mortise-and-tenon joints. Because of the great width of the tenons on the top and waist rails, it's a good idea to divide them, as indicated in *Face Frame*. This will help prevent seasonal wood movement from breaking the joints.

Cut ⅜-inch-wide × 1-inch-deep mortises in the stiles with a hollow chisel mortiser, or rout them with a plunge router. If routing, position the mortises and guide the cuts with the router's edge guide. Using a chisel, square the ends of the mortises.

When the mortises are complete, cut tenons to fit them. Cut the tenons with a tenoning jig on the table saw if you have one, or cut them flat on the saw table with a dado blade. Set the tenon length with the table saw fence, and guide the stock with a miter gauge.

Form double tenons from each wide tenon on the top and waist rails. Use a saw and chisel to remove the waste between the tenons.

3 Glue together the face frame. Scrape and sand the pieces of the face frame. Glue and clamp the tenons into the mortises. Check carefully that the frame is square by measuring across diagonal corners of the frame. If the diagonal measurements are equal, the frame is square. If the measurements aren't equal, adjust the clamps and frame until they are.

Face Frame

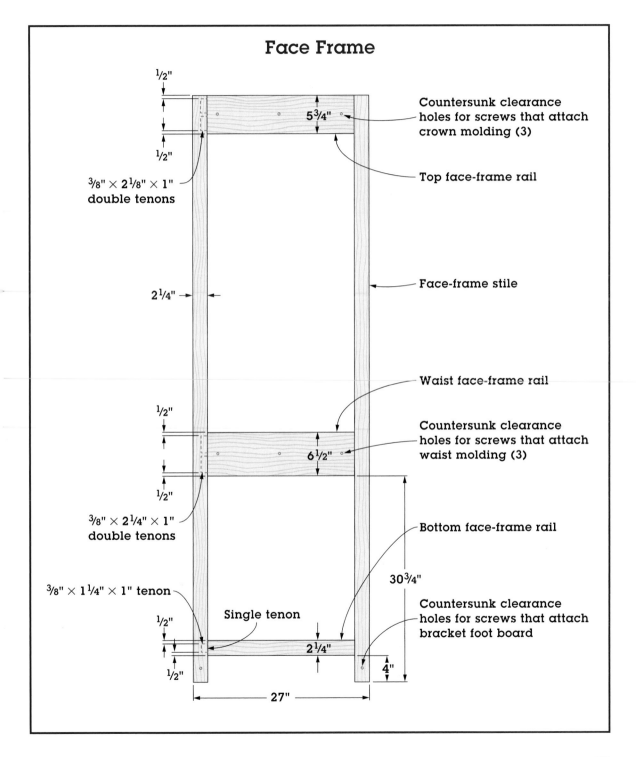

1/2"

1/2"

5 3/4"

Countersunk clearance
holes for screws that attach
crown molding (3)

Top face-frame rail

3/8" × 2 1/8" × 1"
double tenons

Face-frame stile

2 1/4"

Waist face-frame rail

1/2"

6 1/2"

Countersunk clearance
holes for screws that attach
waist molding (3)

1/2"

3/8" × 2 1/4" × 1"
double tenons

Bottom face-frame rail

30 3/4"

3/8" × 1 1/4" × 1" tenon

Single tenon

1/2"

2 1/4"

Countersunk clearance
holes for screws that attach
bracket foot board

1/2"

4"

27"

Complete the Case

The case consists of the canted sides, the bottom shelf, the top shelf, several fixed shelves, back boards, and a piece I'll call the spine. Helping to align and hold these parts together is the face frame, which you have already constructed.

1 **Cut the joint on the canted sides for the face frame.** The original cabinet seems to have a straightforward miter between the face frame and the canted side. This joint is difficult to glue, though, so I devised a different joint that's both easy to cut and simpler to control during glue-up, as shown in *Canted–Side-to-Stile Joint*.

The joint requires two rip cuts to be made into one edge of the side. The table-saw blade must be tilted to 45 degrees for both cuts. It's a really good idea to make test cuts on samples of the working stock to check out your cut depths before cutting the actual sides.

2 **Dado the spine and the canted sides for the fixed shelves.** The fixed shelves fit into ⅜-inch-deep × ¾-inch-wide dadoes cut into the spine and canted sides. Lay

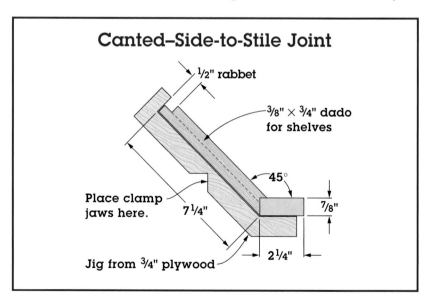

Canted–Side-to-Stile Joint

½" rabbet

⅜" × ¾" dado for shelves

45°

Place clamp jaws here.

7¼"

7/8"

Jig from ¾" plywood

2¼"

the pieces side by side on your bench, and mark them to-gether so each dado lines up accurately with the dadoes in the other two pieces. Cut the dadoes on the table saw.

3 **Rabbet the canted sides for the back boards.** The outside edge of each canted side is rabbeted to accept the first of the shiplapped boards that make up the cabinet back, as shown in *Canted–Side-to-Stile Joint*. Cut the ½-inch-deep rabbet with a dado cutter in the table saw, running the boards along the rip fence.

4 **Prepare the shelves.** The shelves, including the top and bottom—eight pieces in all—are all the same size and shape. The four shelves used in the upper section of the cabinet are distinguished from the others by their scroll-cut front edges and their plate grooves.

If you haven't already done so, begin by gluing up stock for each shelf.

When the clamps are off and the blanks have been sanded flat and smooth, cut the basic shape for each shelf on the table saw or band saw, following *Shelf Pattern Detail*. Clean up the band-sawed edges on the jointer or with a hand plane.

Select four of the shelves for the upper section of the cabinet. Enlarge the scroll-cutting pattern from *Shelf Pattern Detail*, and transfer the layout to the front edges of these four shelves. Cut to the layout lines on the band saw, then file, sand, and scrape the edges smooth.

Finally, rout ¼-inch-wide plate grooves in each of these shelves. Position the groove 1½ inches from the edge to which the back boards are attached, as shown in *Shelf Pattern Detail*. Use a core-box or roundnose bit in your router for this.

5 **Prepare the back boards.** The back is formed of ½-inch-thick boards of varying widths, joined edge to edge with unglued shiplapped joints and nailed to the shelves. The shiplaps prevent seasonal contraction of the boards from opening gaps between the boards that would expose the wall behind the cabinet.

Quick tip

Use a pattern and your router when you need to produce many parts that are identical. The pattern can be made of ¼-inch or ½-inch plywood or medium-density fiber-board (MDF), or even hardboard. Lay out and make the pattern very carefully.

When the pattern is done, trace around it on the stock for the parts, and rough cut them on the band saw. One by one, clamp the pattern to all the roughed-out parts, trimming them to final size with a flush-trimming bit in your router. The pilot bearing runs along the edge of the pattern, and the bit's cutting flutes trim the wood part flush with it.

Shelf Pattern Detail

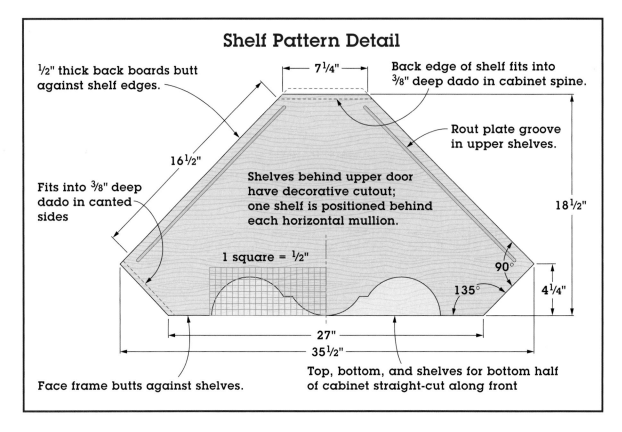

½" thick back boards butt against shelf edges.

7¼"

Back edge of shelf fits into ⅜" deep dado in cabinet spine.

Rout plate groove in upper shelves.

16½"

Fits into ⅜" deep dado in canted sides

Shelves behind upper door have decorative cutout; one shelf is positioned behind each horizontal mullion.

18½"

1 square = ½"

90°

135°

4¼"

27"

35½"

Face frame butts against shelves.

Top, bottom, and shelves for bottom half of cabinet straight-cut along front

The use of random-width boards for the back has its roots in history and practicality. Eighteenth-century woodworkers typically used whatever-width boards they had for a case back rather than ripping each one to the same width. This saved both work and wood.

One edge of each board has a ¼-inch bead cut on it. This bead dresses up the appearance of the boards, which can be seen through the glazed upper door. It also helps to mask the seams between boards, which open and close seasonally.

After the boards are milled to the desired thickness and the edges are jointed, rout the bead on one edge of each. I used a ¼-inch edge-beading bit in a table-mounted router to cut this profile.

To form the shiplapped joints, cut ¼-inch-deep × ½-inch-wide rabbets in the long edges of the boards with a dado cutter in your table saw. Be sure to alternate the faces of the boards as you rabbet them. On one edge of each board, the rabbet is cut into the face, while on the other edge of that board, the rabbet is cut into the back, as shown in *Section Views/Upper Portion of Case.*

6 **Assemble the case.** Begin this process by gluing the canted sides to the face frame. To clamp this sub-assembly, you'll need the help of the glue-up blocks shown in *Canted-Side-to-Stile Joint.* Make at least six of these blocks. They can be cut from scraps of ¾-inch plywood on the band saw.

When the glue has set, remove the clamps. Glue the shelves (including the top and bottom shelves) into the dadoes in the canted sides. Pull the shelves snugly into the dadoes with clamps, then drill and countersink pilot holes for #10 × 2-inch flathead wood screws through the center of the dadoes. Position them so the screw heads will be covered by the applied pilasters.

Glue and screw the spine to the fixed shelves, using #10 × 2-inch flathead wood screws. Take care to keep the cabinet body as square as possible. Check to make sure it is not twisted.

Allow these glue joints to dry, then nail the back boards to the fixed shelves with 6d nails. Don't jam the shiplapped joints tightly together; instead, leave a little room for seasonal expansion and contraction. As you nail the boards to the shelves, continue to check that the corner cabinet remains square.

Trim the Case

The case is embellished with several prominent moldings, a baseboard cut out at the front to resemble bracket feet, and pilasters that extend from the base to the crown on either side of the doors. The crown molding and baseboard mark the top and bottom of the case, and the waist molding divides it into upper and lower sections.

1 **Make the pilasters.** The pilasters are nothing more than 4¾-inch-wide strips of wood with eight stopped flutes cut into them. They are attached to the canted sides, and all the moldings are applied over them.

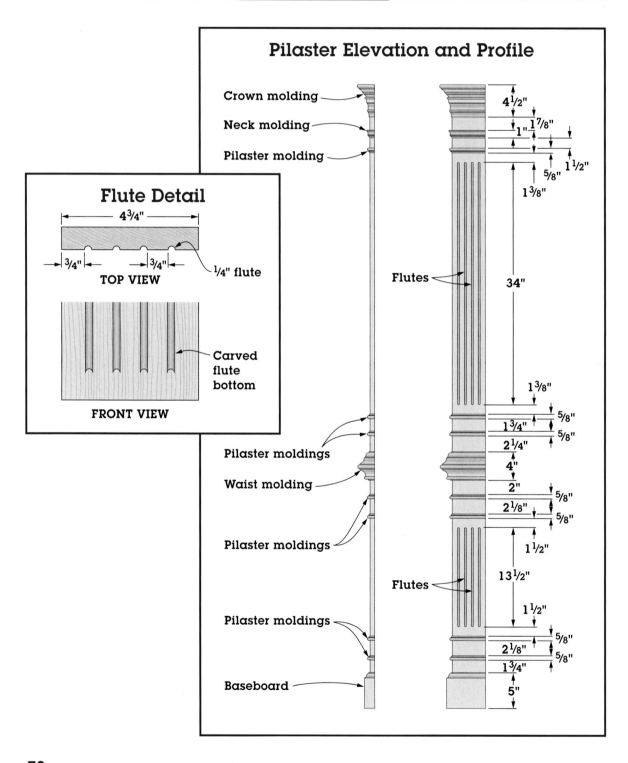

Pilaster Elevation and Profile

Crown molding

Neck molding

Pilaster molding

$4\frac{1}{2}$"

1" $1\frac{7}{8}$"

$1\frac{1}{2}$"

$\frac{5}{8}$"

$1\frac{3}{8}$"

Flutes

34"

$1\frac{3}{8}$"

$\frac{5}{8}$"

$1\frac{3}{4}$"

$\frac{5}{8}$"

$2\frac{1}{4}$"

4"

2"

$\frac{5}{8}$"

$2\frac{1}{8}$"

$\frac{5}{8}$"

Pilaster moldings

Waist molding

Pilaster moldings

$1\frac{1}{2}$"

Flutes

$13\frac{1}{2}$"

$1\frac{1}{2}$"

$\frac{5}{8}$"

Pilaster moldings

$2\frac{1}{8}$"

$\frac{5}{8}$"

$1\frac{3}{4}$"

Baseboard

5"

Flute Detail

$4\frac{3}{4}$"

$\frac{3}{4}$" $\frac{3}{4}$"

$\frac{1}{4}$" flute

TOP VIEW

Carved
flute
bottom

FRONT VIEW

Lay out the flutes on the two pilasters, clearly marking the stop lines. Clamp one pilaster to your bench, and rout the flutes with a ¼-inch core-box or roundnose bit. Use an edge guide on the router to guide the cuts. See *Flute Detail* and *Pilaster Elevation and Profile* for the spacing of the flutes.

While the top of the flute is rounded, the bottom of the flute is inverted, as shown in *Flute Detail*. To get this result, you must shape the bottom of each flute with a carving gouge.

2 **Attach the pilasters to the cabinet.** Sand the pilasters. Wrap sandpaper around a ¼-inch-diameter dowel to sand the flutes. Glue and clamp the pilasters to the canted sides, as shown in *Front View.*

3 **Make and attach the baseboard.** Cut the stock for the baseboard to the size given in the Materials List, then rout an ogee profile on it.

This stock must be cut to fit across the pilasters, canted sides, and cabinet face, as shown in *Front View.* All the joints between the pieces of the base must be mitered. (The baseboard and all moldings are cut off flush with the outside edge of the pilasters.) Before gluing the pieces into place, set all of them in place without glue to be sure of the layout and fit.

The shape of the bracket foot cutout is shown in *Bracket Foot Detail.* Enlarge the pattern, and transfer it to each side of the front baseboard. Cut out the bracket feet with a jigsaw. Smooth all sawed edges with a sanding drum chucked into your drill press. Finally, glue and clamp the mitered bracket feet and baseboards in place on the cabinet.

The stile of the face frame extends down behind each bracket foot. To strengthen the assembly, drive a #10 × 1½-inch flathead wood screw through each stile into the bracket foot.

4 **Cut the waist molding profiles.** The 4-inch-wide waist molding is a complex profile. To reproduce it in the home shop, you need to break it into a series of simple profiles that can be routed on separate strips. These are then glued up to form the molding. *Waist Molding* shows both the

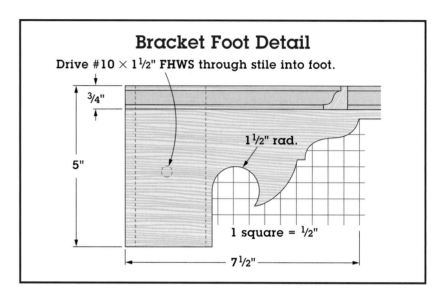

Bracket Foot Detail

Drive #10 × 1½" FHWS through stile into foot.

3/4"

5"

1½" rad.

1 square = ½"

7½"

profiles to be cut on the separate strips and the final, combined molding. The approximate stock length needed for the molding is given in the Materials List.

Ovolo: Begin at the top of the waist molding, and rout the ovolo. Start with a ¾ × ⅞-inch strip. Cut the quarter-round profile with a ½-inch beading bit or a roundover bit with the bearing removed. With either setup, you can create the two steps, or fillets, on either end of the curved shape. Since the desired bead is actually taller (⅝ inch) than it is wide (½ inch), you need to make a pass with a straight bit to trim the ⅛ × ⅛-inch second step, as shown in the drawing.

Cove and fillets: Two slightly different versions of this profile are needed for the waist molding. Both are cut in the same way. I'd suggest laying out the profile section on the end of the blanks. Cut the fillets on both, then do the coves. You'll need to adjust the setup used for the first cove before cutting the second.

Cut the fillets while the stock is still square. You can do it on the table saw or on the router table.

The cove profiles are best cut on the table saw. Refer to "Cove Cutting on the Table Saw" on page 24 for details on setting up the saw and making the cove cuts.

Torus: Rout this shape in two passes with a ¼-inch roundover bit or in one pass with a ½-inch bullnose bit. In

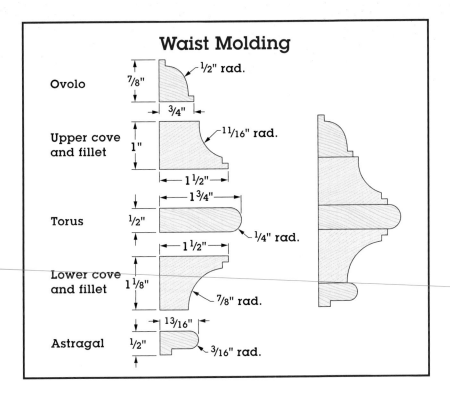

Waist Molding

Ovolo

7/8"

1/2" rad.

3/4"

Upper cove and fillet

1"

1 1/16" rad.

1 1/2"

Torus

1/2"

1 3/4"

1/4" rad.

Lower cove and fillet

1 1/8"

1 1/2"

7/8" rad.

Astragal

1/2"

13/16"

3/16" rad.

either case, do the job on the router table, guiding the workpiece past the bit along the fence (don't depend on the pilot bearing, in other words).

Astragal: The bottom strip is an astragal with a sort of heel. Start with a 1/2 × 3/4-inch strip. Cut a 1/8 × 1/2-inch rabbet in the bottom edge on the table saw. Then rout the bullnose with a 3/16-inch roundover bit or a 3/8-inch bullnose bit in a table-mounted router, as shown in the photo at right.

5 **Glue up and install the waist molding.** Sand each of the individual molding strips to remove milling marks, then glue and clamp them together to create the waist molding. When the glue is dry, make one light pass over the jointer on the back surface to even up the surfaces for gluing onto the cabinet.

Attach the waist molding much as you attached the bracket foot board. Miter the ends of the center piece to fit across the face of the cabinet and across the canted sides. An inside miter steps the molding around the pilaster. Cut it off flush with the

Cutting the bottom half of the waist molding's astragal with a roundover bit isn't as easy as cutting the top half. Because of the heel on the bottom surface of the astragal strip, you'll need to raise the bit and attach a support strip to the router table.

outside edge of the pilaster. Fit all of the pieces and miters to the corner cupboard without glue. When the fit is satisfactory, glue and clamp the waist molding to the cabinet.

Drill and countersink clearance and pilot holes to screw the waist molding to the cabinet from behind the canted sides and waist face-frame rail with #10 × 1½-inch flathead wood screws.

6 **Cut the crown molding profiles.** Like the waist molding, the crown molding is best reproduced by cutting and assembling individual molding strips. I have broken down the complex profile into eight simpler strips.

Bullnose: Start the crown molding with the top bullnose. This is not a true ¼-inch-radius half-round, though you could make it that if you wish. *Crown Molding* shows a ³⁄₁₆-inch-radius roundover on the top edge and a ½-inch-radius roundover on the bottom edge. To reproduce this combination, you need to make the cuts on a router table, with the fence guiding the workpiece.

You also can make the bullnose quickly by clamping the ½ × 1¾-inch blank to your bench and hand planing the profile on the top and bottom corners of the front edge. Sand away the small "facets" left by the plane.

Quarter round: While you have the ³⁄₁₆-inch roundover bit in the router, cut the small quarter-round bead that goes between the two coves.

Coves: The coves in the crown molding on the original cabinet, looked at in profile, are not true arcs of a circle. However, they are very close, and if you treat them as such, they are a whole lot easier to reproduce.

Cut the large cove with a ½-inch-radius cove bit in your table-mounted router. Cut the small cove with a ³⁄₈-inch-radius cove bit.

Astragals: There are two astragals in the crown molding. You can make both easily with a ⅛-inch roundover bit in your router or by clamping the molding piece to your bench and hand planing the radius.

Large conge: Draw the profile of this piece of molding on the end grain of the blank. With a 1-inch-diameter core-box or roundnose bit in your router, rout the shallow cove in the face of the piece. This is best done on the router table. Use the layout on the end of the blank to set the bit height.

Cut the $\frac{1}{8} \times \frac{1}{8}$-inch step next. Make this cut on the table saw. Again, use the layout to set the blade height and rip fence position.

Make the last cut on the table saw. Set the blade height and fence position using the layout on the molding blank. Make sure the waste falls to the outside of the blade, so it doesn't kick back the instant it is cut free of the blank.

Small conge: This strip is similar to the large conge molding, and it is produced the same way the large one was. Draw the profile on the end of the piece to help with machinery setups.

Rout the shallow cove with a 1-inch- or $1\frac{1}{8}$-inch-diameter core-box or roundnose bit. Trim the waste below the cove with a rip blade on the table saw.

Finally, make the small bottom quarter round by cutting a $\frac{1}{16} \times \frac{1}{8}$-inch step in the blank, then rounding over the edge with a small block plane and sandpaper.

7 **Glue up and install the crown molding.** When you have all the individual strips cut, sand them, then glue and clamp them together in the order shown in *Crown Molding*. Joint the back lightly one time to flatten it.

Attach the molding to the cabinet just as you did the waist molding. Miter the molding to fit across the face of the corner cabinet and around the canted sides. Miter it again to step out and around the pilasters. Drive #10 × $1\frac{1}{2}$-inch flathead wood screws through the canted sides and top face-frame rail, as you did to mount the waist molding.

8 **Cut and assemble the pilaster neck molding.** The neck molding is made in two pieces, as shown in *Pilaster Moldings*. The molding strips themselves are very slender, so it is a good idea to make the profile cuts on the edges of more substantial pieces of stock, then rip them off.

Crown Molding

Bullnose

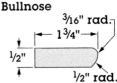

Large cove

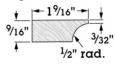

Quarter round

Small cove

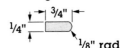

Astragal

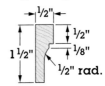

Large conge

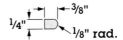

Astragal

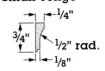

Small conge

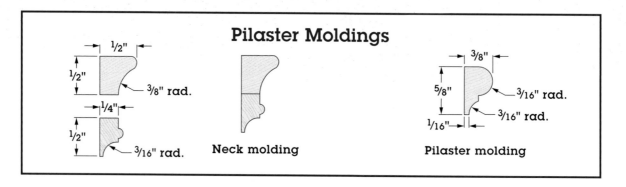

Pilaster Moldings

1/2"
1/2"
3/8" rad.

1/4"
1/2"
3/16" rad.

Neck molding

3/8"
5/8"
3/16" rad.
1/16"
3/16" rad.

Pilaster molding

Cut the top section first, using a ⅜-inch-radius cove bit in your table-mounted router. While the finished strip should be ½ inch square, make the cove cut on a strip ½ × 2 inches. You can round the top edge with a 1/16-inch roundover bit or by hand with a block plane and sandpaper. Rip the molding from the working stock, then use the stock for the second part of the neck molding.

The second piece has a full bead and a small cove. The best bet is to cut the cove first. Use a 3/16-inch-radius cove bit in your table-mounted router.

Turn the workpiece over, and cut the bead with a ⅛-inch-diameter edge-beading bit in a table-mounted router. Rip the profile from the stock.

Glue the two pieces together to make the neck molding.

9 **Cut the pilaster molding.** This one-piece molding has a bullnose profile paired with a small cove. Both profiles are cut on the router table, with the workpiece guided by the fence. As with the neck molding, the profiles should be cut on fairly wide strips of the requisite thickness (⅝ inch), then ripped free. Lay out the desired profile on the end of the blank to help with setups.

Cut the cove first. Use a ⅜-inch-diameter core-box or round-nose bit.

The bullnose shape can be cut either with a 3/16-inch-radius roundover bit or, better yet, with a ⅜-inch-diameter bullnose bit. With the latter bit, the bullnose profile can be completed in a single pass, with the workpiece resting on the router table with the cove up. With the roundover bit, the profile must be cut in two passes, and the bit must be extended quite a bit.

10 **Install all the pilaster moldings.** The neck moldings are positioned near the top of the pilasters right beneath the crown molding. The other molding repeats around each pilaster seven times, spaced in pairs above and below each set of flutes (the uppermost molding pairs with the neck molding). In an interesting design twist, the molding paired with the neck molding and sitting just below it is applied upside down relative to the other six moldings.

Sand the moldings and miter them to fit the pilasters as you have the other moldings. The molding spacings are shown in *Pilaster Elevation and Profile.* Glue and clamp them in place.

Make the Lower Door

The cabinet has a 15-light door on the upper section and a raised panel door on the lower section. The doors are mounted on surface hinges, two per door. Mortise locks are used to keep the doors closed.

While both doors are built in essentially the same way, it is a whole lot easier to understand the construction if they are handled separately. I will explain how to construct the lower door first, then the upper door. If you want to make both at the same time, which is what I did, you can do that.

1 **Mill the parts to size.** Begin by preparing stock for both doors, including stiles, rails, mullion, muntins, and panels. Cut the parts to sizes given in the Materials List. Check actual door openings to make certain these dimensions fit. Edge-glue boards, if necessary, to make the panels.

2 **Cut the joinery on the lower door parts.** As shown in *Lower Door Joinery Detail,* the lower door is composed of two stiles, two rails, a mullion, and two arch-topped, raised panels. The wide top rail has semicircular cutouts to accommodate the panels. All the frame members have an integral molding of a quarter-round profile. The frame is joined with mortise-and-tenon joints, and the quarter-round profile is mitered at the inside corners.

To begin, lay out and cut the ⅜-inch-wide × 1⅜-inch-deep mortise in the stiles, as shown in *Lower Door Joinery Detail*. At the same time, cut mortises centered on the top and bottom rails for the mullion. Cut all these mortises just as you did the ones in the cabinet's face-frame stiles. (Later on, when you trim the profile to accommodate the rails, the final mortise depth will be reduced to 1 inch.)

3 **Cut the arches in the top rail.** You can make the two semicircular cutouts in the top rail in several ways.

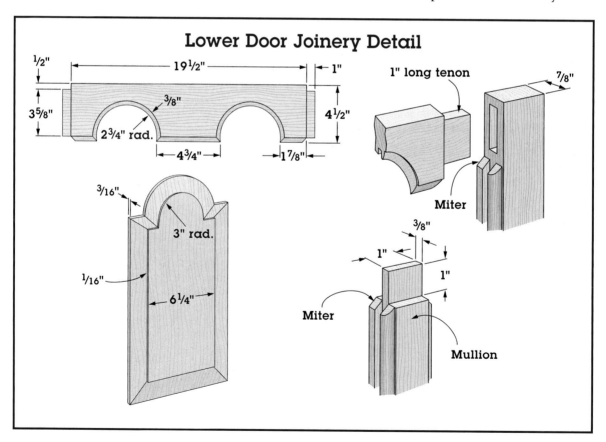

Lower Door Joinery Detail

The most straightforward way is to lay out the semicircles and cut out the shapes on the band saw or with a jigsaw.

Another way is to make a template from ¼-inch hardwood plywood. Smooth the template carefully to shape, and use it to lay out the door arches. Cut out the arches on the band saw or with a jigsaw, staying ¹⁄₁₆ inch back from the layout line. Clamp the template to the rail, and trim the rail flush with the template edge, using a router and flush-trimming bit. The bit's pilot bearing should reference the template's edge, of course.

4 **Cut the sticking profiles and panel grooves.** A profile cut on the interior edges of a frame is often called the sticking. Here, the sticking profile is a ⅜-inch-radius quarter round, cut deep enough to leave a ¹⁄₁₆-inch step, or fillet. Rout this profile with a roundover bit in a table-mounted router.

Switch to a ¼-inch cutter, and rout a ⅜-inch-deep panel groove in the appropriate edges of each door-frame member. Use the router table fence to control the depth of the groove.

5 **Miter the sticking at the joints.** To enable the mortise-and-tenon joints to be assembled, the sticking must be trimmed away from the shoulders around the mortises and neatly mitered to present a good appearance.

On both the stiles and rails, lay out the areas that need to be trimmed away around the mortises. Cut the miters first, doing this on the table saw. Tilt the blade to 45 degrees and set the height to cut just through the profile. Make the miter cuts on both rails, the mullion, and the stiles. The waste around the mortises can be trimmed away with repeated table-saw cuts, with a jigsaw, or with the coping saw. Use a chisel to trim the cut surfaces and refine the fit of the joints.

6 **Make the door panels.** Assemble the door frame without glue, then measure the frame to confirm the panel dimensions. Cut the panels to size.

Lay out the arch at the top of each panel next. Cut the arch on the band saw or with a jigsaw, and smooth the edges with a fine rasp and sandpaper.

Rout the raised panel with a horizontal panel-raising bit in a table-mounted router. While you can use the router-table fence to guide the cut along three edges, you have to depend on the bit's pilot bearing to guide the cut on the curved section of each panel. Make several passes, increasing the cutting depth after each pass. The final pass should produce a $\frac{1}{16}$-inch step between the beveled edge and the raised field.

Using a sharp chisel, square the rounded corners that the bit leaves on either side of the arch.

7 **Mortise and fit the lock.** The doors in the original cabinet have no pulls. Instead, they are fitted with locks; you insert the key, unlock the door, then tug on the key to swing the door open. The locks used are called mortise locks because they are set into mortises. A source for appropriate locks is provided in the Materials List.

With the lock in hand, lay out and rout a mortise for it in the left door stile. Drill holes in the face of the stile for the keyhole, and shape it with files to fit the lock. Attach the lock after the door is sanded and assembled. Attach the escutcheon after the finish is applied.

8 **Assemble the door.** Sand the doors, removing all milling marks and blemishes. Prefinish the panels if you like so they have less chance of binding from misplaced glue. Glue the mullion between the rails of the bottom door, capturing the two panels as you pull the clamps tight. Glue and clamp the stiles to the rails. Make certain the door is flat and square.

9 **Peg the door joints.** Once the door is assembled, you can peg the tenons both for added strength and decoration. On the drill press, drill $\frac{1}{4}$-inch holes through each door joint, as shown in *Front View*. Note that the H-hinges interfere with one peg in each top rail. I drill the holes through the stiles, but you may stop them if you prefer. Whittle tapered pegs from $\frac{5}{16} \times \frac{5}{16} \times 1\frac{1}{4}$-inch blanks to fit each of the holes you have drilled. Do not worry if they are not perfect; irregularities add authenticity. Glue them in place, leaving them slightly proud of the face. When the glue is dry, sand them flush. Cut off the excess on the back side, and sand them flush as well.

10 **Fit the door to the cabinet.** Set the lower door in place in the cabinet opening. Aim for $\frac{1}{16}$-inch clearance on the sides and top and $\frac{3}{32}$-inch clearance on the bottom. Trim the doors with a hand plane or by making light passes on the jointer to get the fit. The H-hinges are surface-mounted, so just set them in place and mark for the screws. Remove the door, and drill pilot holes for the screws. Attach the door to check your fit, make any adjustments, and lay out the mortise for the lock strike. Cut the strike mortise with chisels, drilling some of the waste first. Remove the hinges until after the finish is applied.

Make the Upper Door

1 **Cut the upper door frame joinery.** The perimeter frame for the upper door is made in the same way as that of the lower door. However, there are some significant differences—the sticking profile, the substitution of a glazing rabbet for a panel groove, and the use of muntins.

Begin by laying out and cutting the mortise-and-tenon joints in the rails and stiles, as shown in *Upper Door Joinery Detail*.

When the joinery has been cut, miter the profile at the ends of the rails and stiles to fit together as you did for the lower door.

2 **Shape the top rail, and rout the edge profiles.** Lay out and cut the three arches in the top rail, as shown in the *Upper Door Joinery Detail*. Cut out these arches just as you cut out the arches in the lower doors.

Next, rout the double-filleted bead on the rails, stiles, and both face edges of each muntin, as shown in *Upper Door Joinery Detail*. Use a $\frac{1}{4}$-inch-radius beading bit in a table-mounted router. Adjust the setup so the cut produces $\frac{1}{16}$-inch fillets at each end of the quarter-round arc.

Quick tip

When fitting doors to a cabinet, coins make quick and handy shims. Nickels are about right for the space at the bottom of the doors, and dimes or pennies are good for the sides. When attaching hinges, drill only one hole in each half of the hinge, insert the screws, and check your position. If you need to adjust, you can correct the alignment with the other screws.

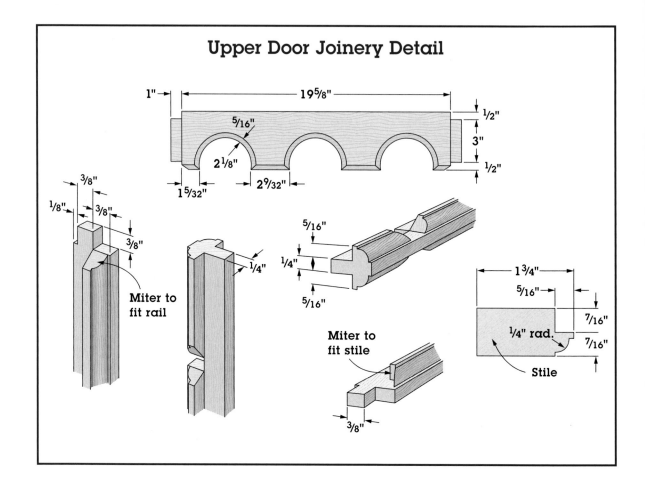

Upper Door Joinery Detail

3 **Cut the rabbets for the glass.** Cut a $\frac{5}{16}$-inch-wide × $\frac{7}{16}$-inch-deep rabbet for the glass in the back edge of both stiles, the bottom rail, and both edges of each muntin. Use a dado cutter in the table saw for this. For the top rail, rout the rabbet for the glass with a ball-bearing rabbeting bit in the router. To make fitting the glass easier, avoid a sharp inside corner on the glass by chiseling off the corner created by the rabbet at the base of each arch.

4 **Fit the upper door muntins to the rails and stiles.** The muntins on the upper glass door are tenoned to fit the rails and stiles in the same manner that the rails fit the stiles. Before cutting the joinery, dry assemble the upper door,

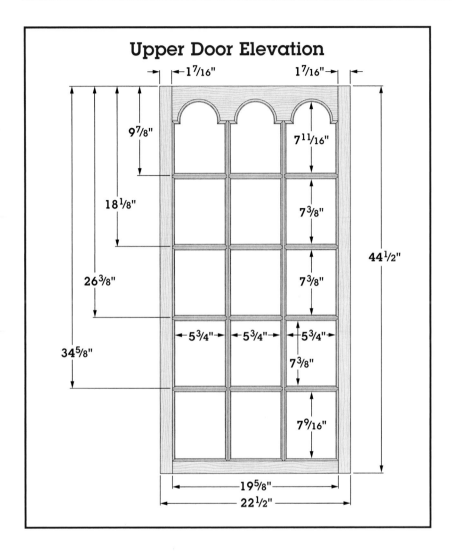

Upper Door Elevation

lay out the mortises, and measure the final length of the muntins. Make adjustments to the vertical and horizontal muntin length if necessary.

Cut tenons on the ends of the muntins, as shown in *Upper Door Joinery Detail.* Then drill out matching mortises in the rails and stiles, and square them up with a chisel.

In addition to the muntin-to-rail and muntin-to-stile joinery, the muntins also overlap one another. First fit the ends of the muntins to the rails and stiles, mitering the molded lip and removing the small ¼-inch section of waste between miter cuts.

Upper Door Joinery Detail shows the muntin lap joints, with the horizontal pieces running through and the vertical pieces "stopped." You may reverse the cuts to have the two vertical pieces run uninterrupted if you prefer. Carefully mark each vertical and horizontal muntin for the 45 degree miter cuts. If you clamp them together, you can mark them all at once. Hold the pieces against a stop for accuracy when mitering. Remove the waste between the miters with a $\frac{1}{4}$-inch dado blade on the table saw. Cut the $\frac{1}{4} \times \frac{7}{16}$-inch lap joint across the face of the vertical pieces and on the back of the horizontal pieces.

5 **Mortise and fit the lock.** Rout a mortise in the left stile of the upper door for the lock just as you did for the lower door.

6 **Assemble and fit the door.** Sand the door, removing all milling marks and blemishes.

Glue the two vertical muntins between the rails. Next, glue and clamp the horizontal muntins into the lap joints to form the grid for the glass. Finally, clamp the stiles to the rails and horizontal muntins. Make certain the door is flat and square.

Once the door is assembled, peg the tenons where the rails meet the stiles. Fit the upper door to its opening just as you did for the lower door. Then lay out and cut the mortise for the lock strike.

Finish the Cabinet

Sand all of the parts of the corner cabinet a final time, sanding progressively from 180 to 220 grit. My favorite finish is shellac, but I have also finished some of my cabinets with wiping varnish. At least three coats are necessary for the best results.

Install the glass after the finish has dried. I hold the individual glass panes in place with glazing compound, colored to match the wood.

Hall Table

by Robert A. Yoder

I've always enjoyed building tables, even when I was building them by the score in a production shop. It seems to me that building a table is like building a bridge on a small scale. You have to think about the mechanics—the span and stress. The legs need to be slight yet strong enough to support the weight of the table and anything that it is meant to hold. I think traditional tapered legs are elegant as they diminish in width as they stretch toward the floor. Cabinetmaker Bill Draper taught me to enhance their slimming appearance even more by jointing a chamfer on the inside corner of the legs after they have been tapered.

While I call this a hall table, it really can find a home in any room. My table currently resides in my eat-in kitchen, serving somewhat the function of a sideboard.

The construction is pretty simple: Pegged mortise-and-tenon joints fasten the aprons to the tapered legs, while the drawers are dovetailed in front and dadoed together in back.

Exploded View

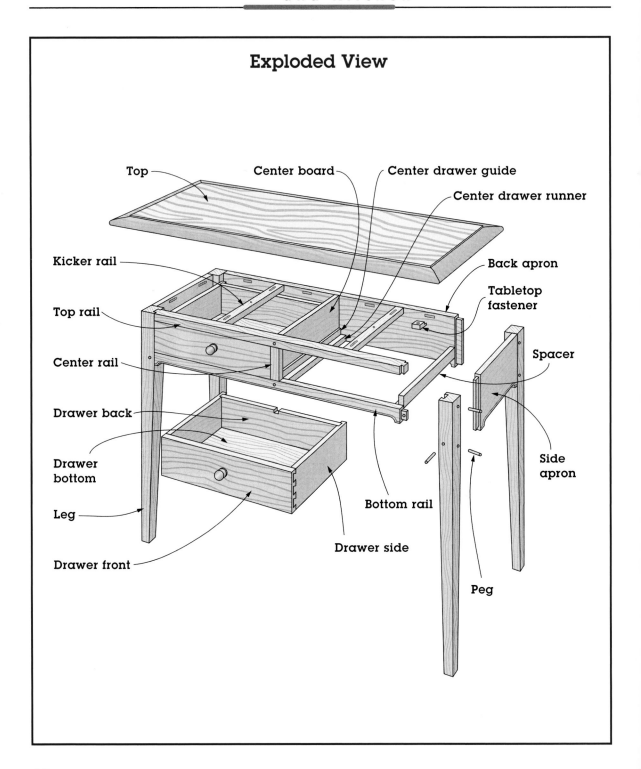

Top

Center board

Center drawer guide

Center drawer runner

Kicker rail

Back apron

Top rail

Tabletop fastener

Center rail

Spacer

Drawer back

Drawer bottom

Side apron

Leg

Bottom rail

Drawer front

Drawer side

Peg

Materials List

Part	Dimension	Part	Dimension
Table Base		**Drawers**	
Legs (4)	$2" \times 2" \times 31\frac{1}{4}"$	Fronts (2)	$1" \times 3\frac{5}{16}" \times 17\frac{3}{8}"$
Back apron	$\frac{3}{4}" \times 6\frac{7}{8}" \times 38\frac{1}{2}"$	Sides (4)	$\frac{1}{2}" \times 3\frac{5}{16}" \times 13"$
Side aprons (2)	$\frac{3}{4}" \times 6\frac{7}{8}" \times 13\frac{1}{2}"$	Backs (2)	$\frac{1}{2}" \times 2\frac{13}{16}" \times 16\frac{7}{8}"$
Bottom rail	$\frac{3}{4}" \times 2\frac{1}{2}" \times 38\frac{1}{2}"$	Bottoms (2)	$\frac{1}{4}" \times 12\frac{1}{4}" \times 16\frac{7}{8}"$
Top rail	$1" \times 1\frac{3}{8}" \times 36\frac{5}{8}"$	Stops (2)	$\frac{3}{16}" \times \frac{3}{8}" \times 1\frac{1}{2}"$
Center rail	$\frac{3}{4}" \times 1\frac{1}{4}" \times 5\frac{5}{8}"$		
Center drawer runners (2)	$\frac{3}{4}" \times 2\frac{3}{4}" \times 13\frac{3}{4}"$	**Hardware**	
Center board	$\frac{3}{4}" \times 4\frac{3}{8}" \times 13\frac{3}{4}"$	#8 × $1\frac{3}{4}"$ flathead wood screws (as needed)	
Center drawer guides (2)	$\frac{1}{4}" \times \frac{1}{2}" \times 13\frac{1}{4}"$	#8 × $1\frac{1}{4}"$ roundhead wood screws (as needed)	
Spacers (2)	$1\frac{1}{8}" \times 2" \times 11"$	#8 × $1"$ flathead wood screws (as needed)	
Side drawer runners (2)	$\frac{3}{4}" \times \frac{3}{4}" \times 13\frac{1}{4}"$	#6 × $\frac{3}{4}"$ roundhead wood screws (as needed)	
Pegs (16)	$\frac{1}{4}" \times \frac{1}{4}" \times 1\frac{1}{8}"$	4d nails (as needed)	
		2d box nails (as needed)	
Tabletop		$1\frac{1}{4}"$ dia. wooden drawer knobs (2)	
Top	$\frac{7}{8}" \times 18" \times 48"$		
Kicker rails (2)	$\frac{3}{4}" \times 1" \times 12\frac{5}{8}"$		
Tabletop fasteners (12)	$\frac{1}{2}" \times 1" \times 1\frac{1}{2}"$		

Make the Table Base

1 **Select the stock, and cut the pieces to size.** Cut the parts for the table base to the sizes specified in the Materials List. The legs, aprons, rails, and top should be made from walnut (like the original) or from another fine hardwood. The rest of the parts can be made from a less expensive species, such as birch or poplar.

2 **Mortise the legs.** Lay out the mortises on the legs, as shown in *Leg Joinery Detail*. Mount a $\frac{3}{8}$-inch mortising bit in a plunge router, and rout the mortises using the plunge router's edge guide to position and guide the cut. Alternatively, you can use the drill press to drill a series of $\frac{5}{16}$-inch holes between your layout lines and then clean out the rest of the waste with a chisel.

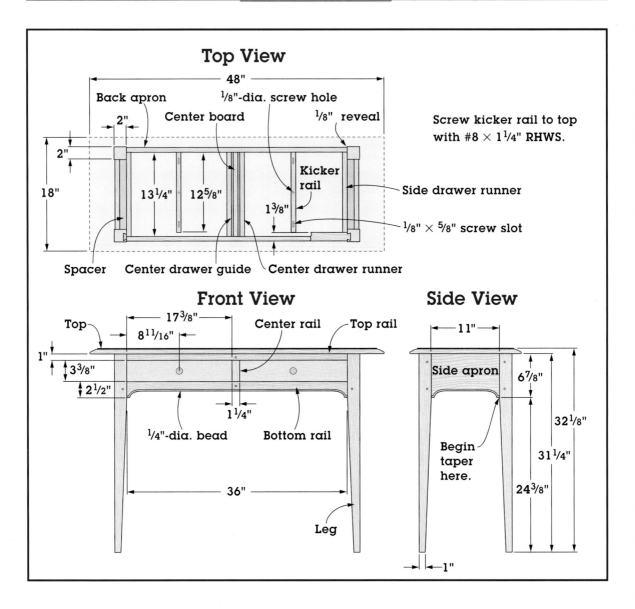

Top View

48"

Back apron

1/8"-dia. screw hole

1/8" reveal

2"

Center board

2"

2"

18"

13 1/4"

12 5/8"

Kicker rail

1 3/8"

Screw kicker rail to top with #8 × 1 1/4" RHWS.

Side drawer runner

1/8" × 5/8" screw slot

Spacer

Center drawer guide

Center drawer runner

Front View

Top

17 3/8"

8 11/16"

Center rail

Top rail

1"

3 3/8"

2 1/2"

1 1/4"

1/4"-dia. bead

Bottom rail

36"

Leg

Side View

11"

Side apron

6 7/8"

32 1/8"

Begin taper here.

31 1/4"

24 3/8"

1"

3 **Cut the apron and rail tenons.** Lay out the tenons on the ends of the aprons and the bottom rail, as shown in *Leg Joinery Detail*. Put a ¾-inch-wide dado blade in your table saw, and raise it ³⁄₁₆ inch above the surface of the table saw. Adjust the fence to cut the 1¼-inch tenon cheeks. Test the blade adjustment by cutting a tenon in a piece of scrap of the same thickness as the aprons and then fitting it in

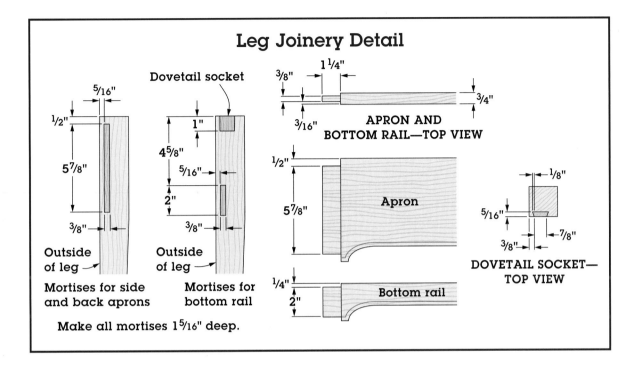

Leg Joinery Detail

Dovetail socket

5/16"

1/2"

5 7/8"

3/8"

Outside
of leg

**Mortises for side
and back aprons**

1"

4 5/8"

5/16"

2"

3/8"

Outside
of leg

**Mortises for
bottom rail**

Make all mortises 1 5/16" deep.

1 1/4"

3/8"

3/16"

3/4"

**APRON AND
BOTTOM RAIL—TOP VIEW**

1/2"

5 7/8"

Apron

1/4"

2"

Bottom rail

1/8"

5/16"

3/8"

7/8"

**DOVETAIL SOCKET—
TOP VIEW**

one of the leg mortises. Adjust the blade as necessary to get a snug-fitting tenon. When the settings are correct, guide the aprons and rail with a miter gauge as you make the cuts. Pull the stock away from the fence slightly, and take another pass to remove the stock that the dado blade missed.

Next, set the rail and aprons on edge, and cut the tenon shoulders, as specified in *Leg Joinery Detail*.

4 **Add the top rail.** The top rail is attached to the front legs via a dovetail joint. Lay out the dovetail socket on each leg, as shown in *Leg Joinery Detail*. Cut along the layout lines as far as possible with a dovetail saw, as shown in the photo on page 92. Chop out the waste with a chisel.

Place the top rail flat on your bench, bottom side up. Position each leg in turn in its desired location at the end of rail. To lay out the tails on the rail, trace the shape of the dovetail sockets with a sharp knife. Cut out the tails with a dovetail saw or on the band saw, and fit the rail to the legs.

Quick tip

When cutting two or more pieces to the same length on the table saw, screw a straight length of wood to your miter gauge to serve as an extension fence. Make the fence a couple of inches longer than the pieces you're cutting. Cut one end of each piece square, then clamp a stop block to the fence and cut the pieces to length with the square end butted against the stop.

By sawing on the diagonal, you'll be able to cut all the way along both layout lines. Once the lines are cut, you can chisel out the rest of the waste.

5 **Shape the aprons and bottom rail.** Lay out the curves along the bottom edge of the aprons and the bottom rail, as shown in *Apron and Bottom Rail Profile Detail*. Cut along the layout lines on the band saw, then scrape and sand the sawed edges smooth. Cut the bead along the curved edges with a scratch stock, as shown in the photo on the opposite page. Though there are commercial scratch stocks available (sometimes called "beading cutters"), you can easily make your own from a scrap of hardwood and a short piece of hacksaw blade, as shown in "Making a Scratch Stock" on page 94.

6 **Cut notches for the tabletop fasteners.** Each apron and the top rail needs ¼-inch-wide × ¼-inch-deep × 1¼-inch-long tabletop fastener notches cut near their top inside edge, as shown in *Tabletop Fastener Detail*. The notches should be spaced evenly along the aprons and top rail. Rout four notches in the back apron and top rail, and rout two notches in each side apron.

7 **Cut the center rail joinery.** The center rail is joined to the top and bottom rails with mortise-and-tenon joints, as shown in *Center Joinery Detail*. Mark the

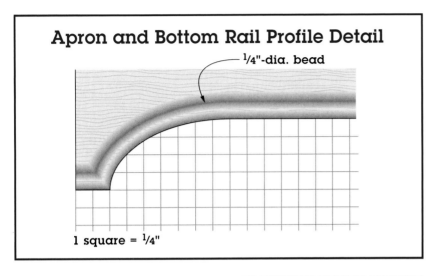

Apron and Bottom Rail Profile Detail

¼"-dia. bead

1 square = ¼"

To use a scratch stock, hold the stock in a vise and draw the tool along the edge. Experiment with different amounts of pressure until you discover what gives the best result.

center of the top and bottom rails and lay out the mortises as shown. Rout the mortises and cut the tenons as described earlier.

8 **Cut the center drawer runner joinery.** The center drawer runner attaches to the back apron and bottom rail with a short, or "stub," tenon, as shown in *Center Joinery Detail*. Rout the mortises, using the bottom edges of the pieces to guide the cuts. Using the same edge on each piece as a reference for the cuts makes it easier to locate the runner properly. Cut the stub tenons by rabbeting both faces of the runner with a dado blade on the table saw.

Making a Scratch Stock

I t's not often that you can make your own tools, especially for precision work. But over the centuries, woodworkers developed a long tradition of creating blades to cut their own, unique profiles in wood. Our forefathers weren't limited to a selection of router bits at the local building-supply store, and you shouldn't limit yourself either. Today, professional woodworkers who build reproductions almost always need to have special cutters made for the moldings and profiles they need to reproduce. The stock router and shaper cutters available in hardware stores or through catalogs just don't cut it.

Once you see how easily this scratch stock cuts, you may be inspired to design your own molding shapes. The knowledge of how to make and use a scratch stock gives you the opportunity to create some truly unique designs.

Scratch Stock Detail

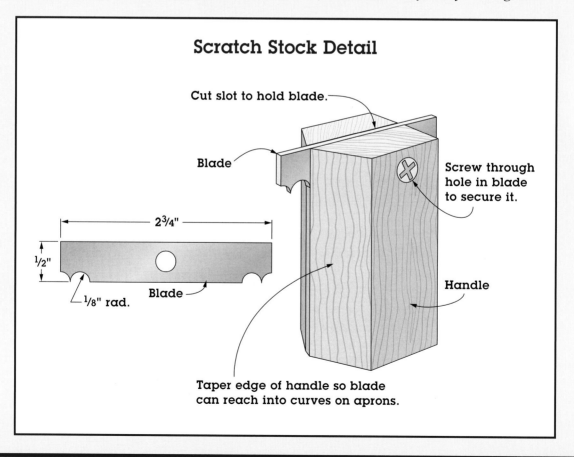

Cut slot to hold blade.

Blade

Screw through hole in blade to secure it.

2³/₄"

¹/₂"

¹/₈" rad.

Blade

Handle

Taper edge of handle so blade can reach into curves on aprons.

The simple beading scratch stock shown in *Scratch Stock Detail* isn't anything fancy, but it will cut a bead that no router bit can. A router bit is limited in how it can cut because the router's base needs a flat surface to sit on. It can't cut around an inside curve on the face of a board like that shown in the aprons of the hall table on page 93. The handle of this scratch stock was made from a piece of leg stock left over from the hall table. The cutter was shaped specifically for this project, but it could handle other shapes as well.

MAKE THE HANDLE

First, find a suitable piece of scrap wood. I made my scratch stock handle from a $2 \times 2 \times 4$-inch scrap of walnut. Yours can be sized according to the scrap you have available.

Next, draw a centerline across the end of the scrap, and then cut a slot along the line to hold the scratch stock blade. Cut the slot just deep enough to accommodate the width of your blade stock. I cut the slot on the band saw, but you could cut it with a backsaw or hacksaw. The width of the slot cut should closely match the thickness of the scratch stock blade stock.

When the blade slot has been cut, cut bevels in one side of the handle that meet the blade slot, as shown in *Scratch Stock Detail*. These bevels allow you to swing the blade around an inside corner like those in the apron of the hall table on page 93, while the square face of the handle allows you to cut accurately along the long, straight profile edge.

MAKE THE BLADE

Next, find a scrap of metal for the blade. I made my scratch stock blade from $\frac{1}{16}$-inch-thick stainless steel that I had lying around. Old hacksaw blades and band saw blades also make good cutters. Use a hacksaw to cut the metal to the right length and width. The scratch stock shown required a piece of metal $\frac{1}{2}$ inch wide $\times 2\frac{3}{4}$ inches long.

When the blade stock is ready, insert it into the slot in the handle and center it side to side. Then drill a screw hole through one side of the handle and just through the blade. Drive a #8 $\times 1\frac{1}{2}$-inch drywall screw through the hole to secure the blade in the handle.

Finally, clamp the scratch stock in a vise, and shape the blade with files. To make the $\frac{1}{4}$-inch bead cutter shown, simply lay out the $\frac{1}{4}$-inch-diameter half circles as shown, and cut away the metal with a round file.

CUT THE PROFILE

To use the scratch stock, simply draw it along the edge to be shaped. You basically scratch away the waste until the profile appears. Don't exert too much pressure on the scratch stock because the blade may slip and scratch where you don't intend. Instead, let the blade's sharp edge do its work in several light passes. This said, the scratch stock works much faster than you might imagine, and in no time the profile will be complete.

Where the profile curves, use the beveled portion of the scratch stock, and always work in the direction of the grain.

9 **Cut the center board joinery.** The center board is also attached with stub tenons. Mark vertical centerlines on both the center rail and the back apron. Use these lines to help lay out the mortises. Be careful as you set up to rout the pieces: Because the pieces lack a common reference surface, it is critical that the cuts be centered on each, or the center board won't align

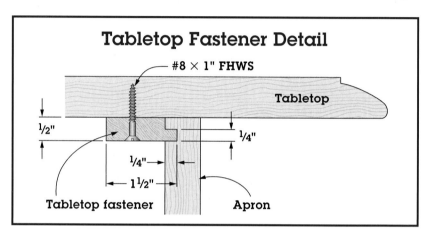

Tabletop Fastener Detail

#8 × 1" FHWS

Tabletop

1/2"

1/4"

1/4"

1 1/2"

Tabletop fastener

Apron

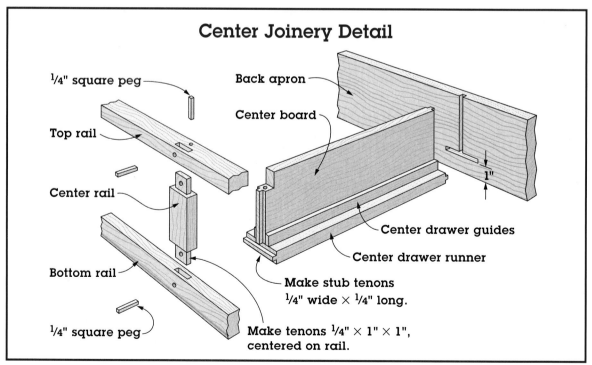

Center Joinery Detail

1/4" square peg

Top rail

Center rail

Bottom rail

1/4" square peg

Back apron

Center board

Center drawer guides

Center drawer runner

Make stub tenons
1/4" wide × 1/4" long.

Make tenons 1/4" × 1" × 1",
centered on rail.

1"

correctly. Rout the mortises and cut the tenons as usual. Notch the upper front corner of the center board to fit around the top rail, as shown in *Center Joinery Detail*. Fit the pieces together, and drill them for a ¼-inch pegs as shown.

10 **Taper the legs.** Make a tapering jig from a scrap of plywood, as shown in *Tapering the Legs*. Cradle each leg in the jig, and taper the two inside surfaces on the table saw.

To make the legs appear lighter yet, cut a ⅜-inch-wide chamfer along their inside corners on a jointer. Tilt the jointer fence to 45 degrees, and take two or three passes until the chamfer is roughly ⅜ inch wide. Alternatively, chamfer the inside corner of each leg with a chamfering bit in a table-mounted router.

11 **Sand and assemble the table base.** Sand all the visible surfaces of all the parts of the table base. It is far easier to sand everything before the pieces are assembled. Carefully clamp the base together without glue to make sure all the joints fit well. Disassemble the table, apply glue to the joints, and clamp the table together. Before the glue has a chance to dry, measure the piece diagonally from corner to corner to check that it's square. If the base is clamped properly, the diagonals will be equal.

12 **Attach the side drawer runners.** After the glue dries, cut the spacers to fit between the front and back legs, as shown in *Top View*. Screw them to the side aprons with #8 × 1¾-inch flathead wood screws, as shown in *Runner and Spacer Cross Section*. Glue the side drawer runners in place along the bottom edge of the spacers as shown. Also fit the center drawer guides along each side of the center board, and glue them in place.

Make the Tabletop

1 **Glue up the top.** Edge-glue narrow boards to make up a panel that is slightly (½ inch or so) wider and longer than the dimensions of the top specified in the Materials List. When the glue is dry, cut the panel to the required size.

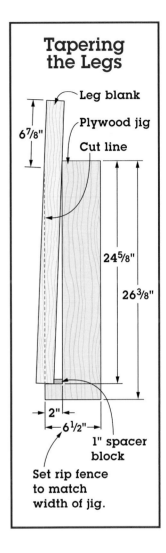

Tapering the Legs

Leg blank
Plywood jig
Cut line
6⅞"
24⅝"
26⅜"
2"
6½"
1" spacer block
Set rip fence to match width of jig.

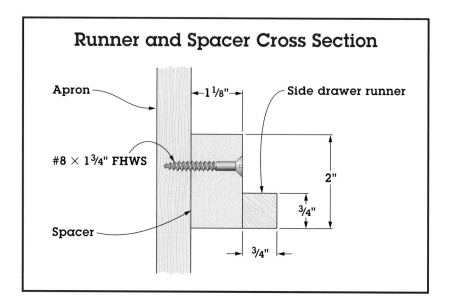

Runner and Spacer Cross Section

Apron

Side drawer runner

←1⅛"→

#8 × 1¾" FHWS

2"

¾"

Spacer

¾"

2 **Shape and sand the top.** Scrape and sand the top flat. Then rout a thumbnail profile on all four edges, as shown in *Front View* and *Side View.* The bit I used had a 1¼-inch wing with a slightly beveled end. A similar bit is available from Freud (catalog #99-027; call 800-472-7307 for names of dealers). After the thumbnail is cut, relieve the bottom edge of the tabletop slightly with a spokeshave and sandpaper.

3 **Make the tabletop fasteners.** Cut a couple pieces of stock for the tabletop fasteners that are the correct thickness and width, but about 12 inches long. Rabbet one end of each piece with a dado blade on the table saw to fit in the notches you cut in the side aprons, back apron, and top rail, as shown in *Tabletop Fastener Detail.* Then cut the rabbeted end off at the appropriate length to make an individual fastener. Repeat the process until you have 12 fasteners.

4 **Attach the tabletop.** Place the tabletop face down on top of your bench. You may want to pad the bench surface to avoid marring the top. Flip the table base over, and center it on the top. Slip the tabletop fasteners in the notches in the aprons and top rail. Predrill holes for #8 × 1-inch flathead wood screws through the holes in the tabletop fasteners. You may want to use a depth stop to avoid drilling through the tabletop. Screw the base to the top.

5 **Attach the kicker rails.** Cut the kicker rails to the size specified in the Materials List. Drill and counterbore a hole in the center of each rail, and rout a counterbored slot at either end, as shown in *Top View*. Screw the kicker rails to the top with #8 × 1¼-inch roundhead wood screws.

Make the Drawers

1 **Cut the parts to size.** Measure the drawer openings in your table, and modify the Materials List dimensions as necessary before cutting the drawer parts to size. The length of each drawer front should be about ¹⁄₁₆ inch less than the width of the drawer opening, and the width of all the drawer parts should be about ¹⁄₁₆ inch less than the height of the opening. Cut the front, back, and sides to the appropriate sizes, leaving the backs ½ inch or so long for now. Wait until the drawers are ready to assemble before cutting the bottoms.

2 **Cut the dovetail joints.** The sides are joined to the front with half-blind dovetails. Lay out the pins on the drawer fronts, as shown in *Drawer Joinery Detail*. Note that the distance from the shoulder line to the end of the board should be slightly *less* than the thickness of the sides. Cut along the layout lines with a dovetail saw, and chop out the waste with a chisel. Hold the fronts in position on top of the drawer sides, and trace around the pins to lay out the tail side of the joints. Again, saw along these layout lines and chop out the waste. Pare the joints to an exact fit if necessary. For more detailed information on cutting these joints, see "Cutting Dovetails" on page 164.

3 **Cut the dadoes for the back and bottom.** Set up a dado blade on the table saw that matches the thickness of the drawer backs. Cut a dado near the trailing end of each

Quick tip

When many woodworkers cut dovetail joints, they allow the ends of the pins and tails to protrude slightly beyond the adjoining surfaces. This works, but you have to make the pieces slightly longer than the finished size of the box you're after to allow these protruding ends to be cut away. A better strategy is to cut the boards to the exact length you want, then lay out the joint so the ends are just barely below the adjoining surfaces. Once the box is together, you can go back and sand or plane the surfaces flush with the ends. This will leave you with a box that is exactly the size you want.

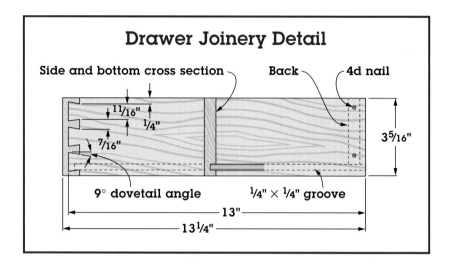

Drawer Joinery Detail

Side and bottom cross section

Back

4d nail

11/16"

1/4"

7/16"

3⁵/16"

9° dovetail angle

1/4" × 1/4" groove

13"

13¼"

drawer side to hold the back, as shown in *Drawer Joinery Detail*. Reset the dado to make a ¼-inch-wide groove. Cut a groove for the drawer bottom in the drawer fronts and sides.

4 **Sand and assemble the drawer boxes.** Sand the inside surfaces of the drawer fronts, sides, and backs. Assemble the drawer boxes without glue to make sure the joints fit well. Disassemble the boxes, paint glue on the joints, and put the pieces back together again. Drill small holes through the back dadoes and secure the back with 4d nails. Before the glue dries, measure from corner to corner diagonally to check that the drawer box is square. If necessary, squeeze the box across the longer diagonal to rack it into square. When you're sure the front, sides, and back are square, slide the drawer bottoms under the drawer back and into the grooves in the drawer sides and drawer front. Secure the drawer bottom to the bottom edge of the drawer back with two or three 2d box nails.

5 **Fit the drawers.** Once the glue dries, test the fit of the drawer box in its opening. Plane, scrape, or sand the drawer sides until the box slips in perfectly. You may also have to plane or sand the edges of the drawer box to reduce its height. Once the drawers run the way you want them to, sand the outsides smooth.

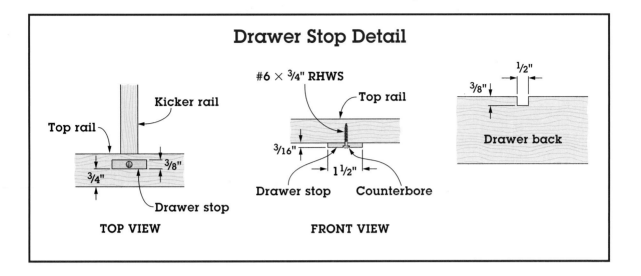

Drawer Stop Detail

6 **Attach the drawer stops.** Cut the stops to the size specified in the Materials List. Drill and counterbore them, then screw them to the top rail with #6 × ¾-inch round-head wood screws, as shown in *Drawer Stop Detail*. Notch the drawer backs to accommodate the stops as shown.

Finish the Table

1 **Install the pegs.** Cut the pegs to the dimensions specified in the Materials List. Carve each peg so it is square at one end and blends to round at the other. Drill ¼-inch-diameter holes through the legs and rails, as shown in *Front View* and *Side View*. Dab a little glue on the end of each peg, and drive it home. If you are using a particularly hard wood like maple, you may have to chisel the holes square for best results. Sand the ends of the pegs off flush.

2 **Attach the drawer knobs.** Find the center of each drawer front, and drill a ⅜-inch-diameter hole for the knob listed in the Materials List. I turned the knobs for the original table; if you have a lathe, you can, too, by following the pattern shown in *Knob Detail*.

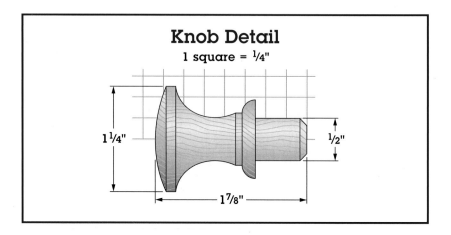

Knob Detail

1 square = ¼"

1¼"

½"

1⅞"

3 **Sand and apply the finish.** Do any touch-up sanding necessary, then apply your favorite finish. The table in the photo on page 281 was finished with four coats of Waterlox, a wiping varnish. This type of finish is fairly easy to apply—simply wipe it on with a rag, then wipe away the excess. Lightly sand or rub out with steel wool in between coats. After sanding the last coat, you can polish the finish with a little bit of pumice mixed with mineral oil to impart a warm, satiny glow. As a final touch, rub a little paraffin on the drawer sides and runners to lubricate the drawer action.

Living Room and Family Room

Three-Drawer Side Table

by Ben Erickson

With its frame-and-panel sides, scrolled base, and cock beading on the drawer fronts, this side table will dress up any room of the house. And its three spacious drawers offer beautiful storage for anything from coasters and magazines to linens and flatware.

Building this piece will hone your skills in solid wood construction. I built the entire side table from walnut. If you wish, you can use pricey walnut only for the visible exterior parts of the case. A secondary wood like poplar can be used as a less-expensive choice for the web frame sides and backs as well as the interior parts of the drawers.

The side and back frames are built with mortise-and-tenon joinery and house a floating solid wood panel that can expand and contract with the seasons. The simply constructed web frames serve as drawer dividers and front rails to hold the sides together. The hand-dovetailed drawers feature brass keyhole escutcheons and cock beading on the edges—very classy touches.

Exploded View

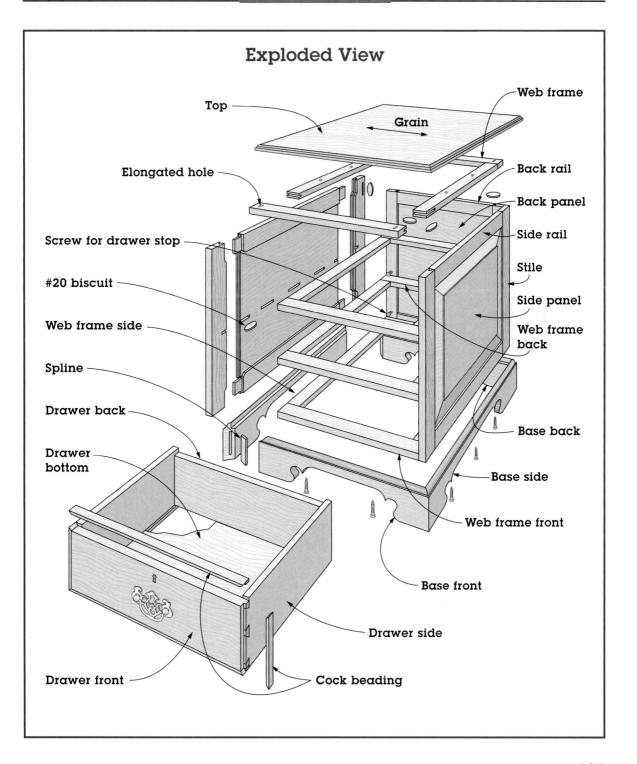

Top

Grain

Web frame

Elongated hole

Back rail

Back panel

Side rail

Screw for drawer stop

Stile

#20 biscuit

Side panel

Web frame side

Web frame back

Spline

Drawer back

Base back

Drawer bottom

Base side

Web frame front

Base front

Drawer side

Drawer front

Cock beading

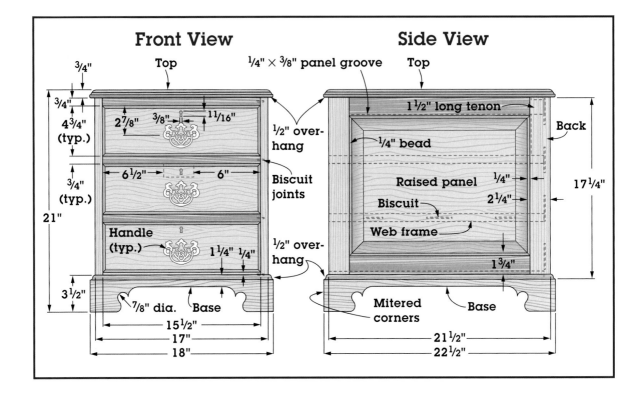

Front View

¾"

Top

¼" × ⅜" panel groove

¾"

¾"

4¾" (typ.)

2⅞"   ⅜"   11/16"

½" over-hang

6½"   6"

Biscuit joints

¾" (typ.)

21"

Handle (typ.)

½" over-hang

3½"

1¼" ¼"

⅞" dia.   Base

15½"

17"

18"

Side View

Top

1½" long tenon

Back

¼" bead

Raised panel   ¼"

17¼"

Biscuit   2¼"

Web frame

1¾"

Mitered corners   Base

21½"

22½"

Make the Top

1 **Choose the stock.** Unless you're able to find a very wide board for the top, you'll have to glue it up from several pieces. To maintain good color and grain match, cut all of the pieces from one board. Mating the same edges of the board will help you attain a good grain match.

2 **Glue and trim the top.** I use biscuit joints to help align the board during assembly. Glue the top up slightly oversized, then cut it on the table saw to the sizes given in the Materials List.

3 **Rout the edge profile.** I used a double Roman ogee bit (available from Jesada Tools, 310 Mears Boulevard, Oldsmar, FL 34677; [800] 531-5559; catalog #641-380), but you could use a different style of bit profile, if you like.

Quick tip

When routing a profile on all four edges of a board, cut the end-grain edges first. That way, any tear-out will be removed when routing the long-grain edges.

Materials List

Part	Dimension	Part	Dimension
Top		Drawer bottoms (3)	$1/4" \times 15" \times 19^7/8"$
Top	$3/4" \times 22^1/2" \times 18"$	Cock beading (6)	$3/16" \times 1/2" \times 4^3/4"$
		Cock beading (6)	$3/16" \times 1^1/8" \times 15^1/2"$
Case			
Stiles (6)	$3/4" \times 2^1/4" \times 17^1/4"$	**Hardware**	
Side rails (4)	$3/4" \times 2^1/4" \times 20"$	#8 × 1¾" drywall screws (10)	
Back rails (2)	$3/4" \times 2^1/4" \times 14"$	#8 × 1¼" drywall screws (8)	
Side panels (2)	$3/4" \times 13^1/2" \times 17^3/4"$	#8 × 1" drywall screws (6)	
Back panel	$3/4" \times 13^1/2" \times 11^3/4"$	#6 × ¾" flathead wood screws (12)	
Web frame fronts (4)	$3/4" \times 1^1/2" \times 15^1/2"$	#20 biscuits (as needed)	
Web frame backs (4)	$3/4" \times 1^1/2" \times 15^1/2"$	$11/16" \times 3/8"$ brass inset keyhole escutcheons (3).	
Web frame sides (8)	$3/4" \times 1^1/2" \times 17^3/4"$	Available from Woodcraft Supply, P.O. Box 1686, Parkersburg, WV 26102-1686; (800) 225-1153; part #02U01	
Base		$1^1/2" \times 3"$ brass drawer locks (3). Available from East Coast Refinisher's Warehouse, 13 Amy Elsey Drive, Charleston, SC 29407-1702; (800) 636-8555; part #S5G	
Front and back (2)	$1^1/4" \times 3^1/2" \times 18"$		
Sides (2)	$1^1/4" \times 3^1/2" \times 22^1/2"$		
Drawers		3" center-to-center brass pierced Chippendale handles (3). Available from Garret Wade, 161 Avenue of the Americas, New York, NY 10013; (800) 221-2942; fax (800) 566-9525; part #A28.04	
Drawer fronts (3)	$1" \times 4^3/8" \times 15^1/2"$		
Drawer backs (3)	$1/2" \times 3^3/4" \times 15^1/2"$		
Drawer sides (6)	$1/2" \times 4^3/4" \times 20^1/4"$		

Make the Case

To build the case, you'll make the side frames, the back frame, then the web frames. After that, you'll glue the frame-and-panel assemblies together with the web frames in between them.

1 **Prepare the stock.** Joint, plane, and cut the case pieces to the sizes given in the Materials List. Use flat, straight-grained wood for the rails and stiles. Make the stiles for the back frame-and-panel assembly slightly oversized in width. Also make the side pieces of the web frames slightly oversized in width. After assembling the panels and web frames, you'll trim the back panel and web frames to the same exact width before assembling the case.

I used clear walnut throughout, except for the side and back pieces of the web frames. Although you could use a common secondary wood like poplar for these, I prefer a harder wood like maple or ash to prevent wear over time from drawer operation.

2 **Mortise the stiles.** Begin by cutting the $\frac{1}{4} \times 1\frac{1}{4} \times 1\frac{3}{8}$-inch mortises in the stiles, as shown in *Frame-and-Panel Detail*. I cut mine with a hollow chisel mortiser, and if you have one, use it. You can also rout them with a plunge router, or drill a series of holes and chop them out.

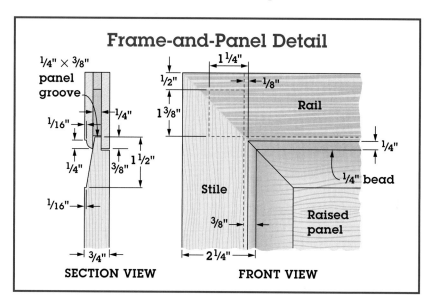

Frame-and-Panel Detail

$\frac{1}{4}" \times \frac{3}{8}"$ panel groove

$\frac{1}{16}"$ · $\frac{1}{4}"$

$\frac{1}{4}"$ · $\frac{3}{8}"$ · $1\frac{1}{2}"$

$\frac{1}{16}"$

$\frac{3}{4}"$

SECTION VIEW

$1\frac{1}{4}"$

$\frac{1}{2}"$ · $\frac{1}{8}"$

$1\frac{3}{8}"$

Rail

$\frac{1}{4}"$

$\frac{1}{4}"$ bead

Stile

$\frac{3}{8}"$

Raised panel

$2\frac{1}{4}"$

FRONT VIEW

3 **Cut the rail tenons.** Cut the rail tenons to fit the mortises. I cut the tenon cheeks on the table saw using a tenoning jig, then cut the shoulders on my radial arm saw. Alternatively, you could cut the tenons by feeding the workpiece flat across a dado cutter on the table saw.

4 **Rout the bead.** Rout a $\frac{1}{4}$-inch bead on the front inside edges of each rail and stile, as shown in *Frame-and-Panel Detail*. For a smooth bead, use a table-mounted router with a straight fence. Bury the bit in a recess in the fence so only the profile is exposed.

5 **Cut the panel groove.** Rout the ¼-inch-wide × ⅜-inch-deep panel groove, centered in the edge of the frame stock, as shown in *Frame-and-Panel Detail*. To do this, put a ¼-inch straight bit in a table-mounted router, and run the stock against a fence as you make the cut.

6 **Miter the bead on the rails and stiles.** In order to assemble the stiles and rails, the beads must be mitered where the stiles and rails meet, as shown in *Frame-and-Panel Detail*. Set the table saw blade at 45 degrees and raise it until it just touches the reveal above the bead. Miter the bead on the ends of the rail first. To cut the miter, guide the end of the rail's tenon along the table saw fence with a miter gauge set at 90 degrees, as shown in the photo below at left.

Once you've cut the miters in the rails, lay out and miter the bead at the ends of the stiles. Guide the miter cut on the ends of the stiles with both the miter gauge and the rip fence. Position the rip fence so that placing the end of the stile against it will align the miter with the blade, as shown in the photo below at right.

Quick tip

To ensure consistent width of narrow pieces when preparing stock, plane the stock, joint one edge, then feed the pieces through your planer jointed edge down.

Slide the tenon against the table saw fence as you miter the bead in the rail. The miter should meet the point where the bead's reveal and tenon shoulder intersect.

Slide the end of the stile against the table saw fence to position the miter in the stile's beaded edge. The miter should be positioned so that when the frame is assembled, the rail's outer edge is flush with the end of the stile. Make sure that the blade just kisses the reveal between the bead and face of the stile.

When the miters have been cut in the stiles, remove the waste between the miter and end of the stiles with several passes over the table saw blade. Then smooth the cut with a chisel, if necessary.

7 **Raise and rabbet the panels.** Cut the bevel on the front of the panels, as shown in *Frame-and-Panel Detail.* I raise my panels with a vertical panel-raising bit on the router table, as shown in "Routing Raised Panels" on page 14.

In *Frame-and-Panel Detail,* notice that the back of the panel is rabbeted to be flush to the inside of the frame. This is to ensure that the drawers slide smoothly against the sides of the case. You can rout or saw the rabbet.

8 **Assemble the case sides and back.** Test assemble the panels into their frames to make sure everything fits well. The panels can fit snugly between the grooves in the stiles, but they must be allowed to expand and contract seasonally between the grooves in the rails. If I'm building during the humid summer, I fit the panels snugly between the rail grooves. If it's the dry wintertime, I trim the panel about $1/16$ inch in height.

When everything fits well, glue up each frame-and-panel unit, making sure they're clamped up square and flat. Don't glue the panels into the grooves.

9 **Make the web frames.** I joined the web frames with biscuits, but mortise-and-tenon joinery or dowels would work as well. If you use #20 biscuits (which I recommend for their width), you'll have to trim off the extra length after assembling the frame. The trimmed area won't show on the completed piece.

Glue up the web frames square, and let them dry. Then set your table saw for a $15^1/2$-inch cut, and rip the web frames and the frame-and-panel back to their final widths.

10 **Cut the biscuit joints.** I used biscuit joints to join the case sides to the back and to the web frames. There's no need to join the case back to the web frames.

It is very important that the placement of the two middle web frames results in drawer openings that are the same size. To accomplish this, first cut the slots centered on the edges of the web frames, as shown in *Side View*. Then, lay out the side panel biscuit slots on a piece of scrap the same length as the side stiles.

Next, make a spacer, as shown in *Cutting the Center Biscuit Slots*. To determine the length of the spacer, measure the distance from the edge of the frame to the center of the intended slot. Then subtract the distance between the bottom of your biscuit joiner and the center of its cutter. Make the spacer slightly overlong; then make test cuts in your scrap, adjusting the length of the spacer until the drawer openings will be equal.

11 **Assemble the case.** Test assemble the entire case to check the joints and alignment and to do a clamping rehearsal. You can pull the centers of the case sides down to

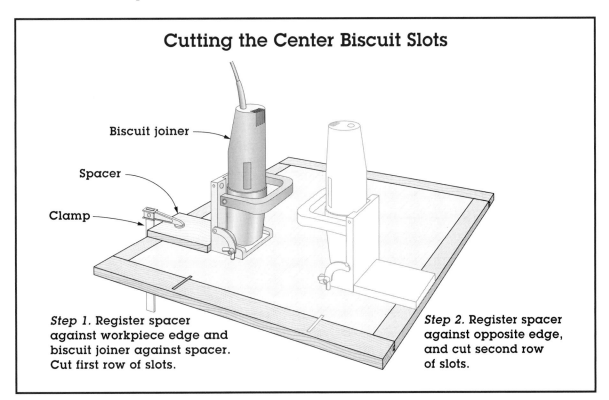

Cutting the Center Biscuit Slots

Biscuit joiner

Spacer

Clamp

Step 1. Register spacer against workpiece edge and biscuit joiner against spacer. Cut first row of slots.

Step 2. Register spacer against opposite edge, and cut second row of slots.

Quick tip

To distribute clamping pressure across wide case sides, use lengths of thick, stiff hardwood as cauls under your clamps. To increase clamping pressure at the center of a caul, first joint a slight bow in one of its faces, then place that face against the case side when clamping.

the inner web frames using long, slightly curved cauls. This case is a lot to assemble at one time, so be sure that you have everything you need right at hand, including a helper.

When you're ready to glue up, lay one case side down on the bench, and spread glue into its biscuit slots. Then apply a thick coat of glue to the mating slots and edge of each web frame. Insert the biscuits, and stand the web frames in place, carefully aligning their front edges with the front edges of the case sides. Next, attach the back in the same manner. Then apply glue to the opposite slots and edges, insert the biscuits, and attach the remaining case side. Lightly clamp up the assembly so you can adjust the spacing of the web frames as necessary. Then snug up the clamps, making sure the entire case is square.

Make the Base

1 **Mill the material.** Joint and plane the base pieces to the thickness and width given in the Materials List, but leave the pieces a bit long for right now.

2 **Cut the profile and rabbet.** Rout the ogee profile on the top of the base stock using a ¼-inch-radius Roman ogee bit set up in a table-mounted router (bit available from Jesada Tools; catalog #640-350).

Next, put a ¾-inch-diameter straight bit in a table-mounted router, and rout the ½ × ¾-inch rabbet in the base parts, as shown in *Base Detail*.

3 **Miter the ends and cut the scrollwork.** Cut miters on the ends of the base pieces, fitting them tightly against the case. Then reinforce each corner with a biscuit or a hidden spline, as shown in *Exploded View*.

Next, cut out the pattern on each piece. Begin by drilling out the holes, as shown in *Base Detail*. Then cut the rest of the profile on a band saw. Once cut, the straight sections of the base pattern can be smoothed with a block plane and sanding blocks.

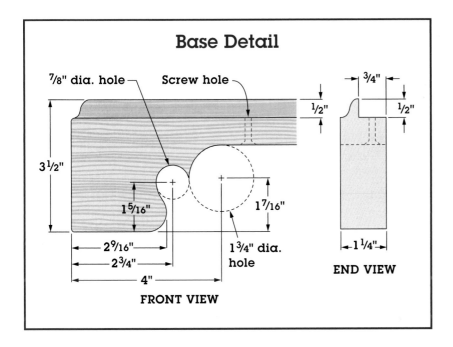

Base Detail

⁷⁄₈" dia. hole   Screw hole   ¾"

3½"   ½"   ½"

1⁵⁄₁₆"   1⁷⁄₁₆"

2⁹⁄₁₆"   1¾" dia.
2¾"   hole

1¼"

4"

END VIEW

FRONT VIEW

Clean up the curved edges with sandpaper and files or a drum sander, if you have one.

4 **Assemble the base.** Glue together the base, and clamp it up using band clamps. To prevent clamping pressure from bowing the thin sections inward, fit scrap sticks between the base sides during clamping.

Make the Drawers

The drawers are constructed traditionally, with half-blind dovetails at the front and through dovetails at the back. I used maple for the drawer sides and back because of its durability. The drawer bottoms are hardwood plywood.

Because the drawers are solid wood, you have to allow for seasonal wood movement when fitting them for their openings. In the dry season, I allow about a ¹⁄₁₆-inch gap above and below each drawer front. When it's humid, I allow about ¹⁄₃₂ inch.

1 **Cut the parts to size.** Cut out the drawer fronts to the sizes given in the Materials List, adjusting the width as necessary to allow for wood movement. Notice that each drawer back stops ¼ inch below the tops of the sides. This allows air displacement behind the drawer and prevents the back from scraping against the web frame above it.

2 **Make the joints.** Cut the dovetails using a fine-toothed saw and chisels. If you cut the pins first, remember to allow for the thickness of the top and bottom cock beading when laying out the tails, as shown in *Drawer Side View*. For more on dovetailing, see "Cutting Dovetails" on page 164.

Next, cut the bottom groove in the drawer sides and fronts on the table saw. Raise the blade to ¼ inch above the table, set the fence ½ inch from the blade, and cut a groove in the parts. Then, move the fence out ⅛ inch more, and take a second pass to widen the groove to ¼ inch (assuming that you have a standard blade that cuts a ⅛-inch-wide kerf).

When the joints have been cut, assemble the drawers, sliding the bottom into place and securing it to the back with #6 × ¾-inch flathead wood screws.

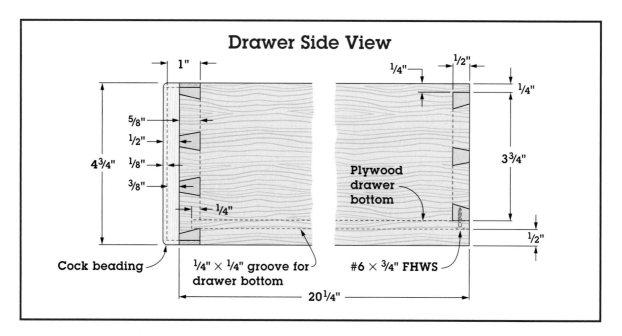

Drawer Side View

1"   ¼"   ½"   ¼"

5/8"   ½"   1/8"   3/8"

4¾"   3¾"

Plywood drawer bottom

¼"   ½"

Cock beading   ¼" × ¼" groove for drawer bottom   #6 × ¾" FHWS

20¼"

Fit the drawers into their openings, sanding or planing as necessary. Then, cut the $3/16 \times 3/8$-inch rabbet in the side of the drawer, as shown in *Drawer Cock Beading,* using a straight bit in a table-mounted router.

3 **Make and install the cock beading.** Sand the drawer fronts. Then make the cock beading stock—sanding, planing, or routing to create a bullnose on one edge. Fit and attach it to the drawers, as shown in *Drawer Cock Beading*. I use epoxy or polyurethane glue on the end grain.

4 **Install the escutcheons and locks.** For each escutcheon, drill a hole to accept its circular head, where shown in *Front View*. Use a spur point bit to prevent tear-out, and drill only to a depth the thickness of the escutcheon.

Next, lay the escutcheon in place, and scribe its outline onto the workpiece. (If the escutcheon is tapered; the smaller side should be down.) Alternatively, to transfer the outline, you can lay carbon paper under the lower section of the escutcheon and press it down with a bolt chucked in a stopped drill press, as shown in the top photo on page 116.

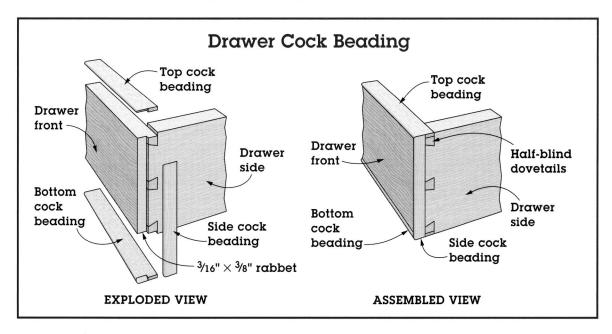

Drawer Cock Beading

Top cock beading

Drawer front

Bottom cock beading

Drawer side

Side cock beading

$3/16" \times 3/8"$ rabbet

EXPLODED VIEW

Top cock beading

Drawer front

Half-blind dovetails

Bottom cock beading

Drawer side

Side cock beading

ASSEMBLED VIEW

To mark the position of the escutcheon, first chuck a bolt in the drill press. Then, put the escutcheon in place on the door or drawer front with carbon paper underneath it. Press the escutcheon down gently with the bolt to create a mark.

Scribe around the lock's flange with a marking knife, and then chisel a recess for it. The flange should be flush with the surface of the wood edge.

Carefully chisel out the waste to the same depth as the hole you drilled. Test fit the escutcheon in its hole without pressing it all the way in. When you've gotten a good fit, mix a little walnut sanding dust with epoxy and line the hole with the mix, which will fill any slight imperfections. Then clamp the escutcheon flush into its hole, using waxed paper between the clamp and the escutcheon. Sand the escutcheon flush after the epoxy dries.

5 **Cut the lock mortises.** Place the lock in the mortise, aligning the pin with the hole, and scribe the outline of the lock's top flange onto the edge of the door or top edge of the drawer front. Cut the recess to the depth of the flange, as shown in the bottom photo at left.

Using a coping saw, cut out the remainder of the keyhole waste, being careful not to score the escutcheon. Hold the lock in place and check the key operation. Adjust the lock position, if necessary.

I like to mortise the lock's back flange flush with the wood surface, which looks much nicer than leaving it proud. If you do this, you'll have to widen the mortise for the edge flange. When you're done, install all of the locks temporarily with steel screws.

6 **Cut the lock bolt mortises.** To locate the position of a lock bolt mortise, close the drawer with the lock bolt raised, touching the bolt to the web frame rail. Then, transfer the bolt's position across the edge of the rail. Measure the distance from the face of the bolt to the face of the drawer front (not to the edge of the cock beading), and transfer this measurement onto the web frame to lay out the mortise. When laying out the mortise, allow an extra $1/16$ inch over the thickness and width of the lock bolt so that the bolt will slide easily into the mortise.

Next, drill a series of holes within the layout lines, and clean out the waste with a knife or chisel. Last, position the catch plate, if any, over the mortise. Scribe around the catch plate, then cut out a recess for mounting it flush.

7 **Drill holes for the pulls, and install the stops.** Drill the screw holes for the pulls, centering them in the middle of the drawer fronts, as shown in *Front View.* Install stops to keep the drawer fronts flush to the case front. For adjustable drawer stops, I simply install screws into the case back at the rear of the drawer sides, as shown in *Exploded View.*

Finish the Side Table

1 **Finish the wood.** Remove the locks and pulls, then sand the wood to 220 grit. Clean off any dust, and apply your favorite finish. I used tung oil varnish, topping it with paste wax. Finish the underside of the top to minimize warping. And be sure to wax the drawer sides and runners so they'll slide easily.

2 **Attach the top and base.** I attached the top with eight #8 × 1¼-inch drywall screws through the upper web frame, as shown in *Exploded View.* Attach the front and rear section of the top through slotted screw holes to allow it to expand and contract seasonally. Be sure to maintain a ½-inch overhang all the way around. Then place the base on the case, and attach it with #8 × 1¾-inch drywall screws through the base into the case.

3 **Do the final assembly.** Reinstall the locks with brass screws, and attach the pulls. Fill the drawers with all the things you haven't been able to find a place for until now.

Sewing Desk

by Robert J. Treanor

It's a good bet that if you make this piece of furniture, you won't make it for a sewing station. Not that it doesn't function well in the role the Shaker craftsmen originally intended it for. It's just that this desk is pretty handy for any of a number of uses you might want to put it to; and let's face it, people don't sew as they once did. At first glance you might wonder that it is called a desk at all, but beneath the work top is a pullout surface that allows you to slide up a chair and get to work.

This particular desk is a design based upon examples made at the Alfred, Maine, Shaker community in the last quarter of the nineteenth century. They might have used the piece as a worktable and may also have employed it in one of several capacities besides sewing.

The desk combines both hardwoods and softwoods, primarily maple and pine, with drawer fronts made of butternut. There are few limitations on the choice of wood here, particularly if

you intend to paint the case as I have. You can also easily make the panels out of ½-inch hardwood plywood. I left the drawers unpainted and added contrast with walnut knobs.

You can consider this sewing desk a sister to the "Shaker Counter" on page 296. The technique for building these pieces is similar, and both projects share construction advice.

Exploded View

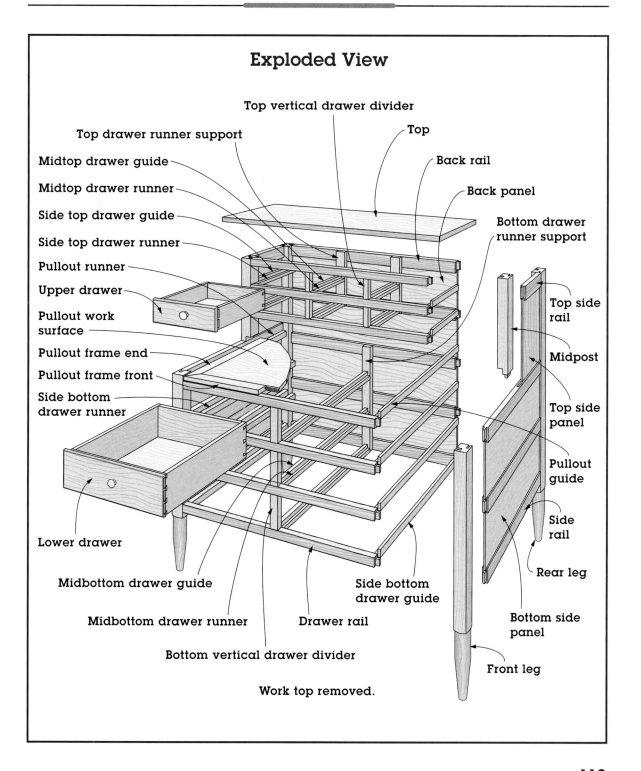

Top vertical drawer divider

Top

Top drawer runner support

Back rail

Midtop drawer guide

Back panel

Midtop drawer runner

Bottom drawer runner support

Side top drawer guide

Side top drawer runner

Pullout runner

Upper drawer

Top side rail

Pullout work surface

Midpost

Pullout frame end

Pullout frame front

Top side panel

Side bottom drawer runner

Pullout guide

Side rail

Lower drawer

Rear leg

Midbottom drawer guide

Side bottom drawer guide

Midbottom drawer runner

Drawer rail

Bottom side panel

Bottom vertical drawer divider

Front leg

Work top removed.

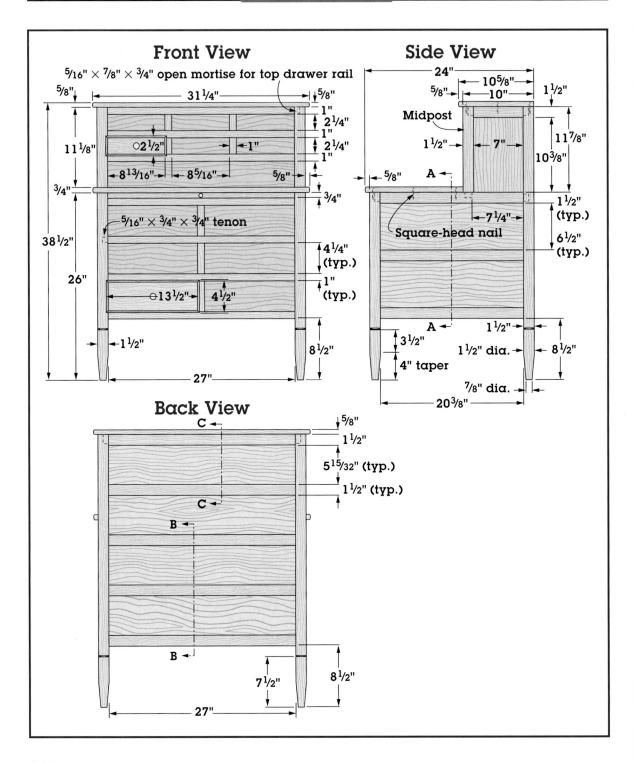

Front View

$^5/_{16}$" × $^7/_8$" × $^3/_4$" open mortise for top drawer rail

$^5/_8$"
31$^1/_4$"
$^5/_8$"
1"
2$^1/_4$"
1"
2$^1/_4$"
1"
11$^1/_8$"
$2^1/_2$"
1"
8$^{13}/_{16}$"
8$^5/_{16}$"
$^5/_8$"
$^3/_4$"
$^3/_4$"
$^5/_{16}$" × $^3/_4$" × $^3/_4$" tenon
38$^1/_2$"
4$^1/_4$"
(typ.)
1"
(typ.)
26"
13$^1/_2$"
4$^1/_2$"
1$^1/_2$"
8$^1/_2$"
27"

Side View

24"
10$^5/_8$"
$^5/_8$"
10"
1$^1/_2$"
Midpost
11$^7/_8$"
1$^1/_2$"
7"
10$^3/_8$"
$^5/_8$"
A
1$^1/_2$"
(typ.)
7$^1/_4$"
Square-head nail
6$^1/_2$"
(typ.)
A
1$^1/_2$"
3$^1/_2$"
1$^1/_2$" dia.
8$^1/_2$"
4" taper
$^7/_8$" dia.
20$^3/_8$"

Back View

C
$^5/_8$"
1$^1/_2$"
5$^{15}/_{32}$" (typ.)
1$^1/_2$" (typ.)
C
B
B
7$^1/_2$"
8$^1/_2$"
27"

Materials List

Part	Dimension	Part	Dimension
Case		Work top	$\frac{3}{4}$" × $23\frac{1}{4}$" × $31\frac{1}{4}$"
Front legs (2)	$1\frac{1}{2}$" × $1\frac{1}{2}$" × 26"	Top	$\frac{5}{8}$" × $10\frac{5}{8}$" × $31\frac{1}{4}$"
Rear legs (2)	$1\frac{1}{2}$" × $1\frac{1}{2}$" × $37\frac{7}{8}$"	Pullout work surface	$\frac{3}{4}$" × $18\frac{7}{8}$" × $24\frac{3}{4}$"
Midposts (2)	$1\frac{1}{2}$" × $1\frac{1}{2}$" × $12\frac{5}{8}$"	Pullout frame ends (2)	$\frac{3}{4}$" × $1\frac{1}{2}$" × 20"
Top side rails (2)	$\frac{3}{4}$" × $1\frac{1}{2}$" × $8\frac{1}{2}$"	Pullout frame front	$\frac{3}{4}$" × $1\frac{1}{2}$" × 27"
Side rails (6)	$\frac{3}{4}$" × $1\frac{1}{2}$" × $21\frac{7}{8}$"	Pullout guides (2)	$\frac{3}{4}$" × $\frac{3}{4}$" × 20"
Back rails (5)	$\frac{3}{4}$" × $1\frac{1}{2}$" × $28\frac{1}{2}$"	Pullout runners (2)	$\frac{3}{4}$" × $1\frac{1}{2}$" × 20"
Drawer rails (7)	$\frac{3}{4}$" × 1" × $28\frac{1}{2}$"	**Drawers**	
Bottom vertical drawer dividers (3)	$\frac{3}{4}$" × 1" × $5\frac{1}{4}$"	Lower drawer fronts (6)	$\frac{13}{16}$" × $4\frac{1}{2}$" × $13\frac{1}{2}$"
Top vertical drawer dividers (4)	$\frac{3}{4}$" × 1" × $3\frac{1}{4}$"	Lower drawer sides (12)	$\frac{1}{2}$" × $4\frac{1}{4}$" × 16"
Side top drawer guides (4)	$\frac{1}{2}$" × $1\frac{1}{2}$" × 8"	Lower drawer backs (6)	$\frac{1}{2}$" × $3\frac{1}{2}$" × 13"
Side top drawer runners (4)	$\frac{3}{4}$" × 1" × $8\frac{1}{2}$"	Lower drawer bottoms (6)	$\frac{7}{16}$" × $15\frac{3}{4}$" × $12\frac{1}{2}$"
Midtop drawer guides (4)	$\frac{3}{4}$" × 1" × 8"	Upper drawer fronts (6)	$\frac{13}{16}$" × $2\frac{1}{2}$" × $18\frac{13}{16}$"
Midtop drawer runners (4)	$\frac{3}{4}$" × $2\frac{1}{2}$" × $8\frac{1}{4}$"	Upper drawer sides (12)	$\frac{1}{2}$" × $2\frac{1}{4}$" × 8"
Side bottom drawer guides (6)	$\frac{1}{2}$" × $1\frac{1}{2}$" × $21\frac{3}{8}$"	Upper drawer backs (6)	$\frac{1}{2}$" × $1\frac{1}{2}$" × $8\frac{5}{16}$"
Side bottom drawer runners (6)	$\frac{3}{4}$" × 1" × 16"	Upper drawer bottoms (6)	$\frac{7}{16}$" × $7\frac{3}{4}$" × $7\frac{13}{16}$"
Midbottom drawer guides (3)	$\frac{3}{4}$" × 1" × 16"	Large knobs (6)	$1\frac{1}{4}$" dia. × $1\frac{13}{16}$"
Midbottom drawer runners (3)	$\frac{3}{4}$" × $2\frac{1}{2}$" × $21\frac{5}{8}$"	Small knobs (6)	$\frac{7}{8}$" dia. × $1\frac{21}{32}$"
Bottom side panels (4)	$\frac{1}{2}$" × 7" × $20\frac{7}{8}$"		
Top side panels (2)	$\frac{1}{2}$" × $7\frac{1}{2}$" × $10\frac{7}{8}$"	**Hardware**	
Back panel	$\frac{1}{2}$" × $5\frac{15}{16}$" × $27\frac{1}{2}$"	#10 × $1\frac{3}{4}$" flathead wood screws (as needed)	
Top drawer runner supports (2)	$\frac{3}{4}$" × $2\frac{1}{2}$" × $8\frac{15}{32}$"	#8 × $1\frac{1}{4}$" flathead wood screws (as needed)	
Bottom drawer runner support	$\frac{3}{4}$" × $2\frac{1}{2}$" × $15\frac{7}{16}$"	#6 × 1" flathead wood screws (as needed)	
		#10 × 1" cut nails (as needed)	
		$\frac{3}{4}$" porcelain knob. Available from Rockler Woodworking and Hardware, 4365 Willow Drive, Medina, MN 55340; (800) 279-4441; part #35808	

Construct the Case

Both parts of the case—the bottom section, containing six drawers, the pullout work surface, and the work top, and the smaller top section with six smaller drawers—should be made at the same time. The glue-up is done in a couple of stages.

Quick tip

As milled project parts sit in your shop, make sure that they are evenly exposed to the air. Don't leave a panel lying overnight on a bench where air can get to only one side. Either stack pieces so no air flow reaches either face of your parts, or put thin sticks crosswise between them so air reaches both faces equally. This simple precaution can save you the headaches that can result from excessive cupping.

1 Cut the sewing desk case parts to size. Mill wood for the case pieces to the sizes given in the Materials List. For now, leave 1 inch of extra length on each leg for a "horn," which will help with turning. Glue together narrower boards to get the required widths for the wider parts.

2 Mortise the legs and posts for the rails and drawer guides. Each of the legs and posts has numerous mortises cut into it for the horizontal drawer rails, the side and back panel rails, and the drawer guides. *Leg Joinery Detail* shows a typical layout of these mortises. However, the mortises at the top of the legs and posts are open mortises, as shown in *Leg and Post Top Mortise Detail—Top View*. This avoids the problem of breakable short grain just above a stopped mortise and makes for an easier glue-up. Carefully lay out all the joints according to the measurements shown in *Front View, Side View,* and *Back View*.

A square chisel-mortising machine is an excellent method for cutting mortises. Unlike routed mortises, you don't have to round the tenons or square the mortises for the joint to fit. Rout the mortises with a plunge router and fence attachment if you don't have the mortiser, making a number of shallow passes to reach the final depth. Secure the legs in a simple carriage like that shown in *Setup for Making Mortises* on page 300, or clamp several legs together on your bench to create a stable bearing surface for your router. Rail mortises are $5/16$ inch thick × $3/4$ inch deep, and drawer guide mortises are $1/4$ inch thick × $1/2$ inch deep. Don't forget to take into account the horn on the top of the legs when laying out the joints.

3 Cut mortises in the top of the side rails for the midpost tenons. The two short midposts that frame the small drawers in the top are tenoned into the top of the long side rails with $5/16$-inch-thick tenons, as shown in *Post-and-Rail Joinery Detail. Side View* shows the position of these mortises on the rails. Make these mortises just as you have made the previous mortises. If you rout the mortises, clamp several rails together to make a stable surface for your router base.

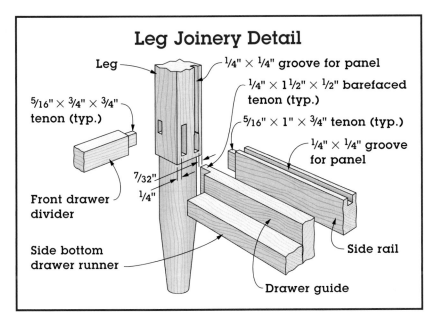

Leg Joinery Detail

Leg

1/4" × 1/4" groove for panel

1/4" × 1 1/2" × 1/2" barefaced
tenon (typ.)

5/16" × 3/4" × 3/4"
tenon (typ.)

5/16" × 1" × 3/4" tenon (typ.)

1/4" × 1/4" groove
for panel

7/32"

1/4"

Front drawer
divider

Side bottom
drawer runner

Side rail

Drawer guide

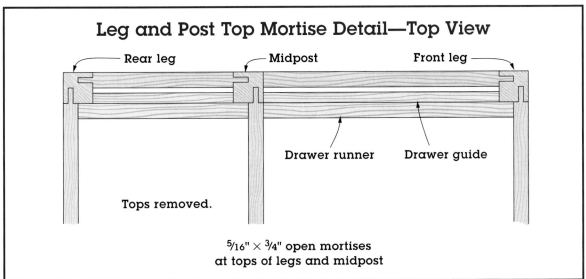

Leg and Post Top Mortise Detail—Top View

Rear leg

Midpost

Front leg

Drawer runner

Drawer guide

Tops removed.

5/16" × 3/4" open mortises
at tops of legs and midpost

4 **Make the panel grooves in the rails, posts, and legs.** The 1/4 × 1/4-inch grooves for the panels are centered in the rails and leg rail mortises. The fastest way to make them is with a table saw and 1/4-inch dado blade. Slide the side and back rails on edge against the rip fence to cut the panel

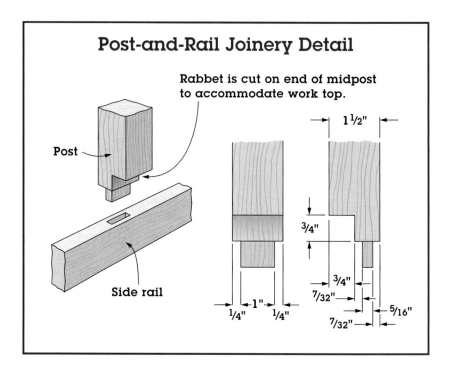

Post-and-Rail Joinery Detail

Rabbet is cut on end of midpost
to accommodate work top.

Post

Side rail

1 1/2"

3/4"

3/4"

7/32"

5/16"

7/32"

1"

1/4"   1/4"

grooves. Do the same for the posts. Remember that on each of the topmost side rails, the groove for the upper case side panel runs between the midpost and rear leg.

On the legs, the panel groove must be stopped at the bottom-most mortise. Push the leg against the rip fence and lift the leg off the blade at the end of the cut. Attach a stop to this fence to position the start of the cut. You will have to reset the rip fence position for half the cuts on the legs, or else drop the leg carefully onto the dado blade and run the groove out the top. Finish any small portion of the groove left to cut with your router, a 1/4-inch straight bit, and a fence attachment. If you choose, you can make the leg grooves entirely with the plunge router secured in a router table with a fence to ride the pieces against.

5 **Turn the feet on the bottoms of the legs.** On a lathe, turn the taper on the bottom of each leg, as shown in *Side View*. Sand the leg while it is still spinning on the lathe. If you don't have a lathe, you could also taper the legs square on a band saw and clean up the sawed surfaces with a hand plane.

The horn on the top of each leg allows you to chuck the leg blanks in the lathe spindle without disfiguring the leg. Cut off the horn on the table saw to bring the legs to final length.

6 **Mortise the drawer rails for drawer dividers and runners.** Vertical dividers separate each drawer from the others. The dividers join the horizontal drawer rails with ¼-inch-thick × ½-inch-long tenons, as shown in *Drawer Rail and Guide Joinery Detail*. You must mortise the top three drawer rails in the stepped-back part of the sewing desk for two vertical drawer dividers, and mortise the four rails in the bottom section of the desk for one divider. Cut these mortises with a mortising machine or a plunge router and router fence as you did for the legs.

Behind the drawer dividers, the drawers ride on runners that join into the inside of the drawer rails with ¼ × ¼-inch stub tenons, as shown in *Drawer Rail and Guide Joinery Detail*. Cut the mortises for these stub tenons on the inside of the drawer

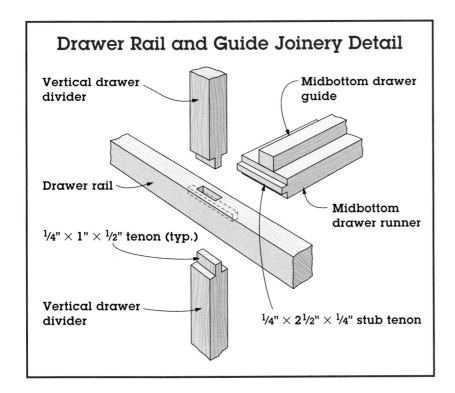

Drawer Rail and Guide Joinery Detail

Vertical drawer divider

Midbottom drawer guide

Drawer rail

Midbottom drawer runner

¼" × 1" × ½" tenon (typ.)

Vertical drawer divider

¼" × 2½" × ¼" stub tenon

rails just as you have done the other mortises. If you clamp several rails together, you create a suitable bearing surface for your router base. Always ride the router fence against the rail you are mortising.

When you finish them, you have completed all the mortises. Now, unless you used a square chisel mortising machine or plan on rounding over the edges of the tenons, you must go back and square the ends of each mortise with a chisel.

7 **Cut tenons on the rails, dividers, guides, runners, and posts to fit the mortises.** Now that you have cut all the mortises in the case, you must make the tenons to fit them. You can make tenons by whatever technique you are most familiar with. I cut the tenons on this project with a dado blade on the table saw. It is a quick and effective method that works best if you have milled the tenon pieces to accurate thickness. Since you register off both surfaces, any variations will cause differences in tenon thickness.

Lay the piece to be tenoned flat on the table saw. Screw a wooden face piece to your miter gauge, and clamp a stop block to it to determine the length of the tenon. Crosscut the tenon shoulder, then slide the piece away from the stop block while you remove the remainder of the waste on that face of the tenon. Flip the piece over and repeat the procedure. Adjust the height of the blade to adjust the thickness or width of the tenon. For the panel rail tenons, the drawer rail tenons, and the post tenons, you must stand the pieces on edge, and adjust the height of the blade to cut all four shoulders and cheeks of the tenons.

The outside drawer guides attach to the legs with barefaced tenons, or tenons with only one shoulder, as shown in *Leg Joinery Detail*. Remember to offset the tenons you make on the bottoms of the two posts, as shown in *Post-and-Rail Joinery Detail*. Remember also that the tenons that fit the open mortises on the legs and posts are wider than the other rail tenons. Make the tenons on the posts, the drawer rails and dividers, the panel rails, and the drawer guides and runners to fit the mortises you have already made.

Quick tip

It is always a good idea to make the mortise an extra $\frac{1}{32}$ to $\frac{1}{16}$ inch deeper than the length of the tenon, or conversely, make the tenon shorter than the depth of the mortise by this amount. This guards against those desperate situations when you discover in the middle of a heated glue-up that the tenon won't seat, regardless of the clamping pressure you exert. Before you begin gluing together your project, check each tenon length and mortise depth for accuracy.

8 **Rabbet the bottoms of the posts.** A ¾ × ¾-inch rabbet on the bottoms of the midposts, as shown in *Post-and-Rail Joinery Detail,* allows the work top to fit under the posts. Cut the rabbet with a dado blade on the table saw just as you have cut the tenons. Lay the post flat on the table saw with a stop block clamped to the miter gauge to determine the height of the rabbet. Cut the shoulder of the rabbet, and slide the post away from the stop block to cut the rest of the rabbet.

9 **Bevel the panels.** I beveled the back, or inside, edges of the panels to fit the panel grooves, creating a flat panel on the exposed surfaces. Bevel the edges with a combination blade on your table saw. Tilt the blade away from the rip fence about 15 degrees, then stand the panels on edge as you slide them against the fence to cut the bevel, as shown in *Cross Section A-A—Side Panels, Rails, and Drawers.* To add stability to the operation, clamp a scrap of plywood to the fence to increase the fence height, as shown in the photo below. You may want to cut the bevels slightly large, then take a couple passes with a hand plane to clean up the saw marks.

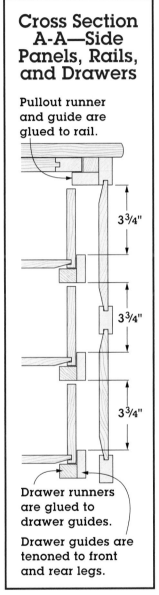

Cross Section A-A—Side Panels, Rails, and Drawers

Pullout runner and guide are glued to rail.

3¾"

3¾"

3¾"

Drawer runners are glued to drawer guides.

Drawer guides are tenoned to front and rear legs.

Increasing the height of the fence with a scrap of plywood decreases the likelihood of the panel flipping over the fence as you cut the bevel.

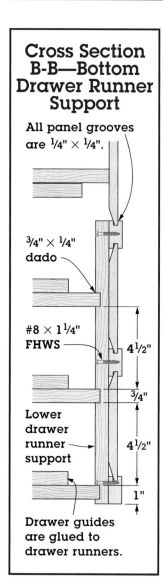

Cross Section B-B—Bottom Drawer Runner Support

All panel grooves are $1/4" \times 1/4"$.

$3/4" \times 1/4"$ dado

#8 × $1 1/4"$ FHWS

Lower drawer runner support

$4 1/2"$

$3/4"$

$4 1/2"$

$1"$

Drawer guides are glued to drawer runners.

10 **Make the drawer runner supports.** The midtop drawer runners and midbottom drawer runners tenon into the drawer rails at the front of the case and are glued into dadoes cut in the runner supports at the back of the case, as shown in *Cross Section B-B—Bottom Drawer Runner Support* and *Cross Section C-C—Top Drawer Runner Support*. When the case is assembled, the runner supports are glued and screwed to the panel rails.

Cut the $1/4$-inch-deep dadoes in the single runner support for the bottom drawers and the two runner supports for the top drawers with a $3/4$-inch dado blade in your table saw. Lay the support flat on the table, and crosscut the dadoes with the miter gauge at 90 degrees. Drill and countersink clearance holes for #8 × $1 1/4$-inch screws, as shown in the cross-section illustrations.

Assemble the Sewing Desk

1 **Sand and test assemble the case.** After all the joints have been made, sand each of the pieces to the desired smoothness. You should remove milling marks and any blemishes in the surfaces. Be careful when sanding any of the areas where pieces join. Putting the parts together without glue helps you to see where any problems in the fit may occur and allows you to correct them without rushing around in a glue-up panic later.

Fit the post tenons into the rail mortises, then clamp the side rails and panels between the front and back legs. Fit the side drawer guides into their corresponding leg and post mortises as you tighten the clamps. Clamp the drawer dividers between the drawer rails, and set the midtop drawer runners and midbottom drawer runners in place between the drawer rails and drawer supports. Clamp the drawer rails, back rails, and panels between the two side panel assemblies to form the case. Keep the drawer guides and center runners in place as you draw in the clamps, clamping the drawer support pieces to the back rails. Make certain all the joints seat tightly.

2 Drill holes to attach the drawer supports to the back panel rails. The midtop drawer runners and midbottom drawer runners are dadoed into the drawer supports, which are screwed and glued to the panel rails. Measure carefully to make certain the drawer supports are correctly positioned, then drill through the countersunk clearance holes already drilled in the supports for pilot holes in the rails. The position of the drawer support is shown in *Cross Section B-B* and *Cross Section C-C*. If you don't have room to drill with the case together, mark the screw positions on the back rails, and drill the pilot holes after you disassemble the case.

3 Fit the work top to the case. If you have not already done so, mill, edge-glue, and cut the wood to the sizes given in the Materials List for the work top, the pullout pieces, and the top of the sewing desk. Mill the wood for the pullout work surface and the work top $\frac{1}{64}$ inch less than the $\frac{3}{4}$-inch thickness shown.

The sides of the work top must be notched out to fit between the midposts and back legs, as shown in *Work Top—Top View*. First, set the work top on the case, and draw a line where its back edge meets the notches in the midposts. Double-check the length of the notch in the work top by measuring from the front edge of the midpost to the back of the case. Lay out the notch on the work top, and cut away the waste on the band saw or with a jigsaw. Clean up the cut with a file, if necessary.

Next, gently slide the work top under the notches in the midpost until the back edge of the work top hits the two back legs. Lay out notches in the back edge of the work top to fit around the back legs, and cut out the notches on the band saw or with a dovetail saw.

The edges of the top and work top have a slight radius on the sides and fronts, as shown in *Front View* and *Side View.* You can round the edges by hand with a sharp hand plane or block plane, and sand them smooth.

Sand the work top and top, and set them in place on the case. The work top and top are both nailed to the case. Predrill

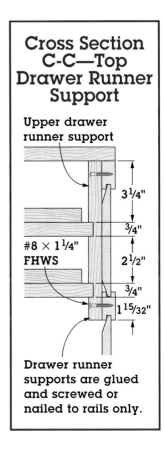

Cross Section C-C—Top Drawer Runner Support

Upper drawer runner support

$3\frac{1}{4}$"

$\frac{3}{4}$"

#8 × 1$\frac{1}{4}$" FHWS

$2\frac{1}{2}$"

$\frac{3}{4}$"

1 $\frac{15}{32}$"

Drawer runner supports are glued and screwed or nailed to rails only.

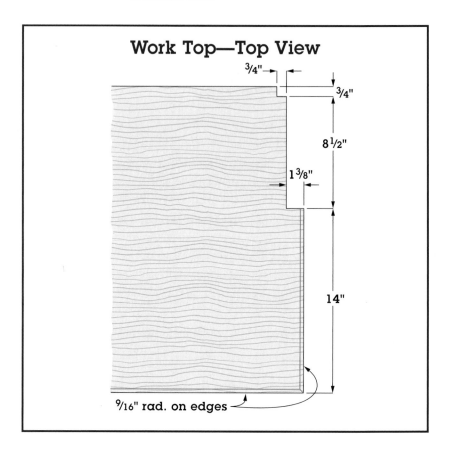

Work Top—Top View

3/4"

3/4"

8 1/2"

1 3/8"

14"

9/16" rad. on edges

nail holes in the work top and top and into the legs and posts. Make certain your case is square and that all the joints close completely.

4 **Glue together the runners and guides for the drawers and pullout.** Glue the drawer runners on the sides of the case to the guides, which are mortised into the legs and posts. Hold each runner in place against the guide, and mark to indicate the position to glue the runner. The bottom edge of each runner should line up closely with the bottom edge of the guide. The front edge of each runner butts against the inside surface of the drawer rails. You can glue the runners to the guides now if you have spring clamps or other small clamps that work in this small space. Otherwise, glue the runners to the guides after you disassemble the case.

The center midtop drawer runners and midbottom drawer runners are tenoned into the drawer rails and dadoed into the drawer supports. The drawer guides are glued to these runners. Glue and clamp the guides in position on the runners if you have clamps that work in this space, making certain you keep the measurements between drawer guides equal. If you don't have small clamps, mark the positions of the guides, and glue them after you disassemble the case.

Cross Section A-A shows the position of the pullout runner and guide glued to the inside of the side panel rails. Remove the work top, then glue and clamp these pieces in position.

5 **Glue the case together.** Completely disassemble the test assembly. Glue together the drawer guides and runners to your layout lines if you could not clamp them in place when the case was test assembled.

Have an assistant or two to help you as you begin gluing the case, and work quickly. First glue the side assembly mortise-and-tenon joints, including the legs, midpost, side rails, and side drawer guides. Slide the side panels between their rails, but do not glue them. They must be able to expand and contract freely in their grooves. Clamp the legs and posts securely to the panel rails. Make certain these side assemblies are square by carefully measuring across the diagonals. The piece is square if the diagonal measurements are equal. Stop at this point and clean up any excess glue with a damp rag. Allow the side assemblies to dry.

6 **Complete the case assembly.** Glue and clamp the drawer dividers to the drawer rails for both the upper and lower parts of the case.

With one of the side assemblies lying flat on your bench or on sawhorses, glue and stand the drawer rails and back panel rails upright in their mortises. For the back section, slide the panels into the panel rail grooves. Glue the midtop drawer runners and midbottom drawer runners to the drawer rails, then glue and slip the runner support pieces in place. Quickly glue the second side assembly in place, standing the case up-

Quick tip

When taking apart a test clamping run, a rubber mallet or a shot-filled dead blow mallet is very handy. Tap with only enough force to separate the joints, and whenever possible, place a block of scrap wood against your project pieces to tap against. Never hit your project with a metal-faced hammer.

right on its four legs. Pull all the joints snug with clamps. Glue and screw the three runner support pieces to the panel rails, not to the panels. Make certain the case is square and that the legs sit level so the case is not twisted. Clean up the excess glue.

Slide the work top in place under the post rabbets, nailing it through the predrilled holes to the legs and the case frame, as shown in *Side View*. Nail the top to the posts and back legs.

7 **Make the pullout work surface.** Make sure the pullout pieces slide in the case opening. With a dado blade on the table saw, cut a $\frac{1}{4}$-inch-thick × $\frac{3}{8}$-inch-long tongue along both ends and the front edge of the pullout. Ride the pullout board along the rip fence to make one shoulder and cheek of this tongue, then flip the board over to cut the other.

Adjust the dado to cut a matching $\frac{1}{4}$-inch-wide × $\frac{3}{8}$-inch-deep groove centered on the inside edges of the pullout frame pieces. Guide the pullout frame pieces along the rip fence as you cut the grooves.

Next, lay out and cut 45-degree miters on both ends of the pullout frame front piece, but miter only the front ends of the two pullout frame end pieces to complete the frame. Crosscut the back ends of the pullout frame end pieces at 90 degrees flush with the back edge of the pullout.

When the pullout frame pieces have been mitered and fit, drill three $\frac{3}{8}$-inch-deep counterbore and through clearance holes along each pullout frame end piece for #10 × $1\frac{3}{4}$-inch wood screws, as shown in *Pullout Detail*.

Sand the pullout and pullout frame pieces, and glue and clamp the pullout frame front to the pullout. Then, glue and clamp only the first 3 inches of each pullout frame end to the pullout, and screw them in place. This allows the pullout some seasonal movement.

After you remove the clamps, plug the screw holes, and sand the plugs flush. Screw a porcelain knob to the pullout frame front.

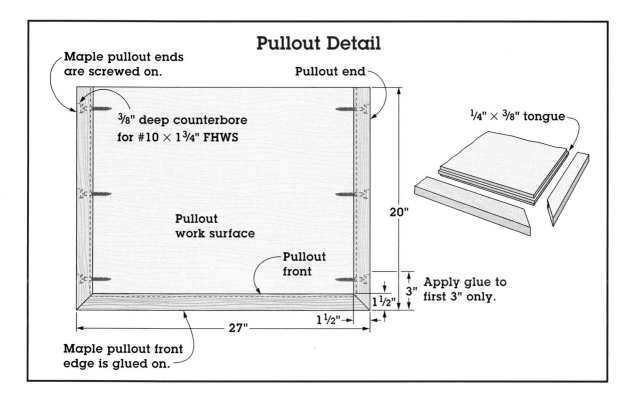

Pullout Detail

Maple pullout ends are screwed on.

Pullout end

$^3/_8$" deep counterbore for #10 × 1$^3/_4$" FHWS

$^1/_4$" × $^3/_8$" tongue

Pullout work surface

20"

Pullout front

3"

Apply glue to first 3" only.

1$^1/_2$"

Maple pullout front edge is glued on.

27"

1$^1/_2$"

Construct the Drawers

The dovetails on these drawers are strong and attractive, but they are time-consuming and more demanding to make than other joinery. You may decide to cut the dovetails with a router and a jig, or you may choose to make other drawer joinery. Plan this ahead so you can take into account any possible changes in dimensions. You can also replace solid wood drawer bottoms with $^1/_2$- or $^3/_8$-inch hardwood plywood, if you prefer.

1 **Cut the parts for the drawers.** Mill the parts for the drawers, but keep the drawer faces and backs $^1/_8$ to $^1/_4$ inch longer and wider and the sides $^1/_8$ inch wider than the dimensions given. Edge-glue wood for the drawer bottoms as needed, but do not cut them to final dimensions yet.

2 **Fit the drawer parts to the drawer openings.** Organize all the drawer parts first, putting all pieces for each drawer together and marking each piece for "top" and "inside" (or "front"). Then fit each part to the individual drawer openings. The processes of constructing and gluing together the case may have caused small variations in the dimensions of the drawer openings.

The drawer backs should have a total of $1/16$-inch clearance side to side inside the drawer frame. After the rabbets are cut in the ends of the drawer fronts (to create the lip), they should also have the $1/16$-inch clearance. The clearance above the drawer face depends upon its width. Wider drawer faces need greater clearance because the faces will expand more from season to season. If you are building the drawers in the summer, the clearance does not need to be quite as much as in the drier winter. In the sewing desk a maximum of $1/8$ inch is sufficient clearance above the larger drawers, and a maximum of $1/16$ inch is sufficient above the smaller drawers. Cut the sides $1/4$ inch narrower than the corresponding fronts.

Recess the beading bit in a router table fence, and guide the drawer fronts along the fence to rout the profile. To avoid tear-out, rout the ends of the drawer fronts first, and then rout the top and bottom edges.

3 **Rout the molded edge on the drawer faces.** This decorative edge is quickly made with a $1/4$-inch-radius beading bit in a table-mounted router. Bury the bit in a fence clamped to the table (even if the bit comes with a ball bearing). You can roughly band saw an opening in the fence board large enough for the bit to sit within. Slide the drawer fronts face down against the fence to rout the $1/4$-inch roundover with a $1/16$-inch fillet, or step, on the front of the drawer face, as shown in the photo at left. The fillet creates a distinct separation between the drawer front and edge.

4 **Rabbet the drawer faces for a lip, and cut the bottom grooves.** Each drawer face has a $1/4 \times 1/2$-inch lip on both ends and along the top (not on the bottom edge), as shown in *Drawer Joinery Detail*. Cut the lip with a rabbeting bit in your router table as you did the edge detail in the previous step. This time slide the drawer fronts against the fence face up.

The drawer bottoms fit into $\frac{1}{4} \times \frac{1}{4}$-inch grooves cut in the inside of the drawer faces and sides, as shown in *Drawer Joinery Detail*. Make the bottom grooves with a $\frac{1}{4}$-inch dado blade in the table saw, sliding the drawer pieces against the rip fence.

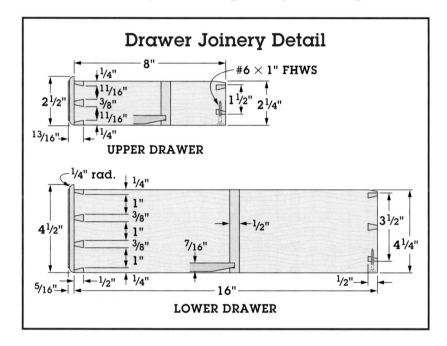

Drawer Joinery Detail

UPPER DRAWER

LOWER DRAWER

5 **Cut the dovetails joining the sides to the fronts and backs.** I cut these traditional dovetails by hand, making half-blind dovetails in the front and through dovetails on the back. I will explain the procedure for making the joints, but for a more detailed explanation, see "Cutting Dovetails" on page 164. Perform the same operation for all drawers before going on to the next operation. For example, lay out the tails on all the drawers at one time before you begin sawing.

Start by scribing a line around each end of the drawer sides with a marking gauge to mark the length of the tails (or the thickness of the pins). With a sharp pencil and your sliding T-bevel set at 12 degrees, lay out the tails on the drawer sides, as shown in *Drawer Joinery Detail*. With a square, carry the lines across the end grain on both ends of the drawer sides. Saw and chisel out the small pockets of waste between all the tails. Try to split the layout line to the waste side as you saw. Next, for each drawer, scribe the outline of the tails onto the end grain of the drawer face and back pieces. Clamp the pieces securely as you mark with a sharp, thin scribing or layout knife.

With your marking gauge, scribe a line across the inside of the drawer faces and around the ends of the drawer backs indicating the length of the pins (or the thickness of the tails). With a square, carry your pin layout lines down to this pin line. On the drawer backs you can saw out the pins and chisel the waste between them, but on the front half-blind dovetails, you must basically chisel all of it. When you have chiseled out all the waste, lightly tap the pins into the tails to check the fit of your joints. With your sharpest chisel, clean up any rough areas, and the dovetails are ready to assemble.

6 **Drill the drawer faces for the knobs.** On the drill press, drill $\frac{3}{8}$-inch-diameter holes through the small drawer faces and $\frac{1}{2}$-inch-diameter holes through the larger drawer faces for the turned knobs. Center the holes in each of the drawer faces.

7 **Glue the drawers together.** Scrape and sand the drawer parts to remove the milling marks, but avoid sanding the inside surfaces of the joints themselves. Glue one drawer at a time. I think the best way to glue dovetails is to get all of the joints tapped just barely together, perhaps for the first $\frac{1}{16}$ inch or so. With a small brush, apply the glue quickly to all the mating surfaces, which are easier to determine with all the joints partly together. One or two clamps across the face and back are all you need to pull the dovetails closed. If you place the clamp cauls right over the pins, place wax paper under the cauls so they don't stick to the drawer. Make certain the drawer is square and flat. Glue all the drawers together in the same way.

8 **Fit the drawer bottoms to each drawer.** First, cut the drawer bottoms to their final dimensions by custom fitting each drawer. Then, bevel the edges of the $\frac{7}{16}$-inch-thick bottoms to fit the $\frac{1}{4} \times \frac{1}{4}$-inch groove in the drawer faces and

Quick tip

When fitting a drawer, it helps to be able to test the drawer in the actual opening before the glue in the drawer joints is completely set. Even a square drawer won't look square in a crooked opening and may need to be adjusted to fit correctly. Ten to fifteen minutes after gluing up your drawer, unclamp it and fit it into the drawer opening. If it sits crooked, adjust the drawer by angling the clamps slightly to draw the drawer into the proper shape.

sides. Do this just as you did the panels in the case, standing the bottoms on edge on the table saw. Cut the bevels with a combination blade tilted away from the fence.

The drawer bottom must be allowed to move with seasonal dimensional changes, so the drawer bottoms are each held in place with two #6 × 1-inch flathead wood screws turned through the bottom and into the drawer back. Drill two clearance holes for each screw side by side. Then countersink each hole, overlapping the countersinks. Chisel away the waste between the two holes to make a screw slot.

Give each drawer bottom a final sanding, and slide the bottoms into place. Glue them only along the front edge, and drive the screws.

9 **Turn and attach the drawer knobs.** On a lathe, turn the drawer knobs, as shown in *Drawer Knob Detail*. Turn several knobs from one longer blank, as shown in the photo on page 138. Sand the knobs on the lathe, and cut them apart after you have removed the turned blank from the lathe. Chuck the stem gently in the drill press to sand down the rounded end where you cut it apart from its neighbor. Make the wedges as shown from scrap wood by cutting them out on the band saw. You need them in two widths.

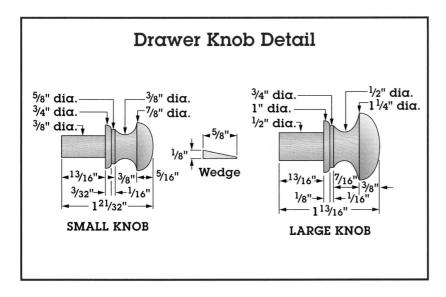

Drawer Knob Detail

SMALL KNOB

5/8" dia.
3/4" dia.
3/8" dia.
3/8" dia.
7/8" dia.
13/16"
3/32"
3/8"
1/16"
5/16"
1 21/32"

1/8"
5/8"
Wedge

LARGE KNOB

3/4" dia.
1" dia.
1/2" dia.
1/2" dia.
1 1/4" dia.
13/16"
1/8"
7/16"
1/16"
3/8"
1 13/16"

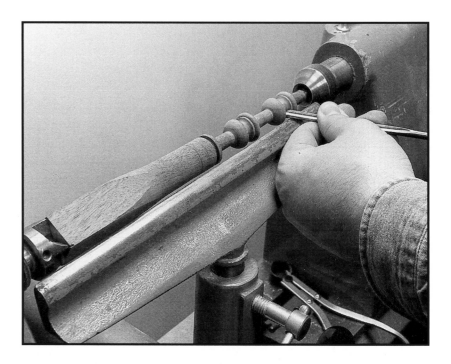

Turn several knobs from one piece of wood, and cut them apart after you remove them from the lathe.

Split the stem of each knob down the middle with a fine backsaw. Glue the knobs into the drilled holes in the drawer faces, turning the stems so the split is vertical. Glue and tap in the wedge, and do any final sanding on the drawers.

Finish the Desk

Finish is often a matter of personal choice and can be somewhat dictated by the woods you have used. I like to use shellac for the drawers because it won't bleed on clothes. Although it isn't the most durable finish, it works well where there is little chance something will spill on it. I used a tung oil wiping varnish on the drawer fronts to bring out the color of the butternut and walnut knobs. I painted the rest of the case, as the Shakers who inspired this adaptation quite likely would have done, which is why I built it from maple and pine.

TV House
by Glenn Bostock

Who says a TV cabinet has to look like a piece of furniture? Not the owner who came up with the concept for the entertainment center disguised as a dollhouse as a gift for his wife. He took the idea to a decorative artist, Angela Herder, who worked out the basic design, approximate size, and eventual painting scheme of the cabinet. She in turn called me for the construction of the gift. After consulting with her about what details were to be included and changes that needed to be made, Phil McGinnis and I constructed the piece.

It has plenty of room for a television set, a VCR, and a cable control box as well as a drawer for storing video games and equipment.

The roof is hinged, giving complete access to the attic—the perfect place for storing the remote control, videos, and current television listings.

Construction is pretty basic. The entire cabinet is built of birch veneer core plywood, assembled with

tongue-and-groove joinery. The doors are medium-density fiberboard. They are hinged to the case using flipper door hardware that allows them to disappear into the case for unobstructed TV viewing.

Exploded View

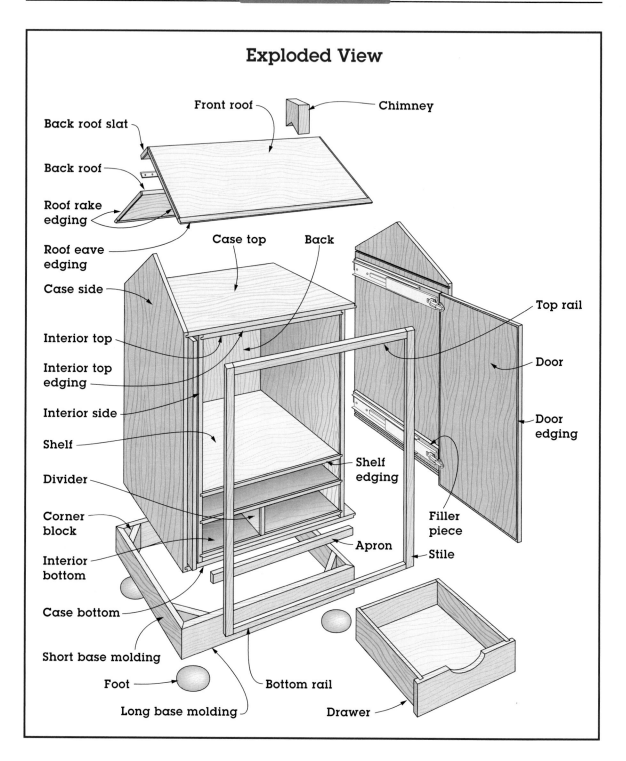

Back roof slat

Front roof

Chimney

Back roof

Roof rake edging

Case top

Back

Roof eave edging

Case side

Top rail

Interior top

Door

Interior top edging

Interior side

Shelf

Shelf edging

Door edging

Divider

Corner block

Filler piece

Interior bottom

Apron

Stile

Case bottom

Short base molding

Foot

Bottom rail

Long base molding

Drawer

Materials List

Part	Dimension
Case	
Case sides (2)	$\frac{3}{4}" \times 26\frac{1}{4}" \times 54\frac{1}{4}"$
Case top/bottom (2)	$\frac{3}{4}" \times 25\frac{1}{2}" \times 37\frac{3}{4}"$
Back	$\frac{3}{4}" \times 38" \times 44\frac{1}{4}"$
Filler pieces (as needed)	$\frac{3}{4}" \times 2" \times 25\frac{1}{2}"$
Top rail	$\frac{3}{4}" \times 2" \times 35\frac{1}{2}"$
Bottom rail	$\frac{3}{4}" \times \frac{3}{4}" \times 35\frac{1}{2}"$
Stiles (2)	$\frac{3}{4}" \times 1\frac{1}{2}" \times 44\frac{13}{16}"$
Front roof	$\frac{3}{4}" \times 18\frac{1}{2}" \times 40"$
Back roof	$\frac{3}{4}" \times 15\frac{1}{8}" \times 40"$
Back roof slat	$\frac{3}{4}" \times 3\frac{1}{4}" \times 40"$
Roof eave edging (2)	$\frac{3}{4}" \times 1\frac{1}{4}" \times 40\frac{1}{2}"$
Roof rake edging (4)	$\frac{1}{4}" \times \frac{3}{4}" \times 18\frac{1}{2}"$
Chimney	$3" \times 3" \times 3"$
Doors	
Doors (2)	$\frac{3}{4}" \times 17\frac{1}{4}" \times 41\frac{1}{2}"$
Door edging (6)	$\frac{1}{4}" \times \frac{3}{4}" \times 42"$
Interior	
Interior sides (2)	$\frac{3}{4}" \times 25\frac{1}{4}" \times 42\frac{3}{4}"$
Interior top/shelves (3)	$\frac{3}{4}" \times 25\frac{1}{4}" \times 30\frac{3}{4}"$
Interior bottom	$\frac{3}{4}" \times 24\frac{3}{4}" \times 30\frac{3}{4}"$
Divider	$\frac{3}{4}" \times 6" \times 25\frac{1}{4}"$
Apron	$\frac{3}{4}" \times 1\frac{1}{2}" \times 30"$
Interior side edging (2)	$\frac{1}{4}" \times \frac{3}{4}" \times 44"$
Interior top/shelf edging (3)	$\frac{1}{4}" \times \frac{3}{4}" \times 30"$
Drawer front	$\frac{3}{4}" \times 6" \times 17\frac{1}{4}"$
Drawer back	$\frac{1}{2}" \times 5\frac{3}{8}" \times 15\frac{1}{4}"$
Drawer sides (2)	$\frac{1}{2}" \times 6" \times 25"$
Drawer bottom	$\frac{1}{4}" \times 24\frac{3}{4}" \times 15\frac{3}{4}"$
Base	
Long base moldings (2)	$\frac{3}{4}" \times 3" \times 40"$
Short base moldings (2)	$\frac{3}{4}" \times 3" \times 28\frac{1}{2}"$
Corner blocks (4)	$1\frac{1}{4}" \times 2\frac{1}{4}" \times 6\frac{3}{4}"$

Hardware

#8 × $1\frac{5}{8}"$ drywall screws (as needed)

#8 × $1\frac{1}{4}"$ drywall screws (as needed)

4d finish nails (as needed)

42" piano hinge with screws

Flipper door hardware (2 sets). Available from most mail-order hardware suppliers or from Accuride, 12311 Shoemaker Avenue, Sante Fe Springs, CA 90670; (562) 903-0208; part #123-22

Bun feet (4). Available from Adams Wood Products, 974 Forest Drive, Morristown, TN 37814; (423) 587-2942; part #A0550

Lid stays (2). Available from Woodworker's Supply, Inc., 1108 North Glenn Road, Casper, WY 82601; (800) 645-9292; part #812-804

24" full-extension drawer slides

Make the Case

1 **Cut the case joinery.** The top and bottom are joined to the sides with tongue-and-groove joints. Cut the case sides, top, and bottom to the sizes given in the Materials List. Set up a $\frac{1}{4}$-inch-wide dado cutter on your table saw, and set the depth of cut to one-half the stock thickness. Set the rip fence to position the cuts, as shown in *Front View,* and cut the two grooves across each of the sides.

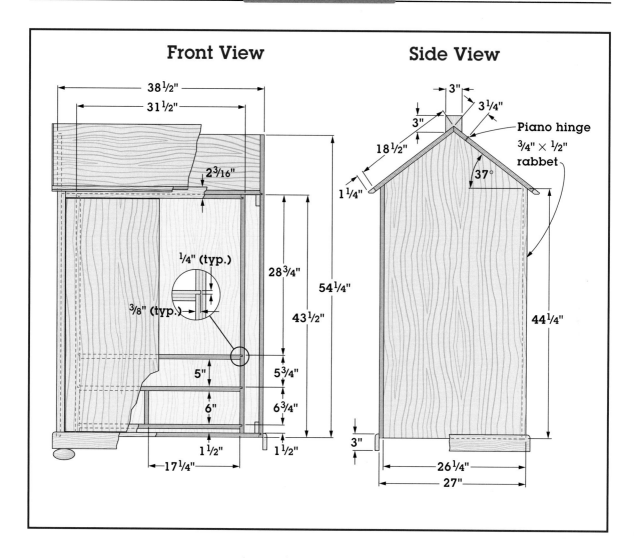

Readjust the width of the dado cutter to about ¾ inch and lower the blade just a tad (about 1/32 inch). Set the fence so it is ¼ inch from the blade. Hold a piece of scrap on edge against the fence, and feed it past the blade, cutting a tongue. Check the resulting tongue against the grooves in the sides, and adjust the table saw fence as necessary. Then make a second cut and check again. When you have the fence set to make a snug-fitting tongue, cut tongues on the ends of the top and bottom, as shown in the photo on the opposite page.

2 **Cut the sides and back to shape.** While you have
the dado cutter set up, cut ¾-inch-wide × ½-inch-deep
rabbets for the back along the back edges of the sides. Then install a saw blade and make the angled gable cuts on the sides, as
shown in *Side View*. Note that the front gable cut starts ⁹⁄₁₆ inch
higher than the back gable cut because of the face frame. Saw
the back to the size given in the Materials List.

3 **Assemble the case.** Place one side on your bench,
grooved side up. Apply glue to the grooves, and fit the
top and bottom in place with their back edges flush with the
edge of the rabbet. Apply glue to the grooves in the second
side, and flip it onto the upright tongues quickly so the glue
doesn't run.

Screw the case together with #8 × 1⅝-inch drywall screws
along the bottom edges to clamp the joints tight. These screws
will be covered by the base moldings so you don't have to worry
about covering them. Also, fasten the top with more screws
through the joints. Drill pilot and countersink holes for them,
and plug the holes to hide the screw heads. Before the glue dries,
glue and screw the back in place. Rack the case, if necessary, to
make the top and bottom flush with the edges of the back.

4 **Cut and install the filler pieces.** Cut the filler pieces
to the sizes given in the Materials List. These create
mounting surfaces for the flipper door slides flush with the
inner edges of the face frame. Glue and screw the filler strips
to the sides of the case. The strips should be installed right
against the top and bottom of the case.

5 **Make the face frame.** Make the face frame from a
hardwood such as poplar. Cut the rails and stiles to
the sizes given in the Materials List. Join the top rail to the
stile with mortise-and-tenon joints, as shown in *Face-Frame
Detail*. Cut the mortises with a ⅜-inch straight bit in a plunge
router guided by its edge guide. Cut the tenons flat on the
table saw with a dado blade. The bottom rail is simply a spacer
that will be nailed to the case later. After cutting the joints, but

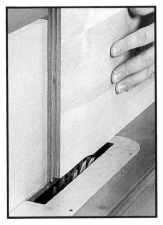

Cut the tongues on the
ends of the top and
bottom by running
them on end past a
dado cutter. Attach a
piece of plywood to
your fence with car-
riage bolts for added
support.

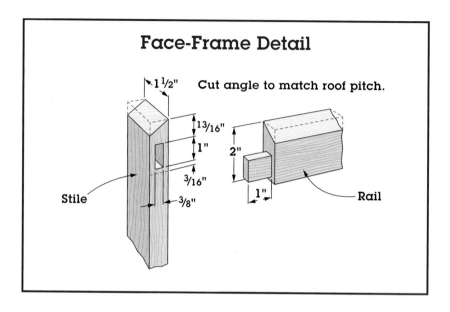

Face-Frame Detail

before gluing them together, trim the ends of the stiles and the top edge of the top rail to match the slope of the roof. Then glue the top rail to the two stiles. Put the bottom rail in place to keep the clamp from squeezing the frame out of shape. Set the frame aside until after you've installed the interior.

6 **Make the roof pieces.** The Materials List shows the roof as three separate parts, but it's easier to start making it as two parts. You'll cut the back roof slat from the back roof later—the kerf will make room for the piano hinge. Cut two pieces of plywood to the size given for the roof. Also cut the roof eave and rake edging from poplar. Glue the rake edging to the ends of the roof pieces. When the glue dries, trim the ends flush, then glue the eave edging along one edge of each piece. Sand all the edging flush with the surface of the plywood.

7 **Assemble the roof.** Tilt the blade on your table saw 37 degrees from vertical, and bevel the edges of the roof pieces where they meet at the roof ridge, as shown in *Side View*. Make this cut with the stock flat on the saw table. Move the fence up to about ¼ inch from the blade on the left side of the blade (unless you have a left-tilt saw), and bevel the eave edges of the roof pieces with the stock on edge against the fence. This leaves a child-safe ¼-inch-wide "blunt" on the eaves of the house.

Cut the back roof slat free from the back roof on the table saw. The wood lost to the saw kerf will create space for a hinge. Now glue the back roof slat to the front roof along the roof-ridge miter cuts. When the glue dries, attach the assembly to the back roof with a piano hinge.

Cut a piece of hardwood for the chimney to the shape shown in *Side View*. Glue and screw the chimney to the roof. Don't install the roof until you've completed the rest of the project.

Make the Doors

1 **Cut and edge the doors.** Cut the doors and edging to size, and glue the edging to the side edges of the doors. When the glue is dry, trim the ends of the edging flush with the ends of the doors, and glue the edging to the ends. Again, trim it flush after the glue dries.

2 **Install the door hardware.** The flipper door hardware comes with instructions that you should read and follow carefully. Keep in mind, however, that after building and installing the interior, you will add the face frame. So when the door hardware instructions tell you to position the slides inset from the front by ⅛ inch plus the thickness of the doors, you will need to install them ⅛ inch from the front edge of the case as it exists now—not from the edge of the face frame. Here is an overview of the procedure: Position the slides against the top and bottom of the case, and screw them in place. Pull the slides forward, and install a follower between them. This keeps the slides in vertical alignment, preventing the door from sagging. Bore the hinge holes in the backs of the doors, and screw the hinges in place, but wait to hang the doors until after the face frame is in place.

Make the Interior

1 **Assemble the interior.** Cut the interior sides, top, bottom, shelves, and divider to the sizes given in the Materials List. Cut tongue-and-groove joints as you did with the case. The spacing is shown in *Front View*. Double-check to make sure the interior will be 4 inches narrower than the inside of the case, measuring from filler piece to filler piece. You must have 2 inches of clearance on each side for the flipper doors. Screw the divider to the second shelf, then glue all the pieces together, and screw the divider to the bottom as well.

2 **Attach the apron and the edging.** Cut the apron to fit snugly between the interior sides, and glue it to the front edge of the interior bottom flush with the upper surface. Cut the edging to size, and glue the interior side edging to the front edges of the interior sides. Cut the edging for the interior top and shelves so it fits snugly between the side edging pieces, and glue it in place. Sand all the edging flush with the plywood surfaces.

3 **Install the interior.** Slide the interior into the case, and center it from side to side. Check that there are 2 inches of clearance on either side for the doors. Drive four #8 × 1⅝" drywall screws through the back into the interior sides and two up through the case bottom into the interior bottom apron to anchor the unit in place.

4 **Make the drawer.** The drawer is joined with simple rabbets and grooves, as shown in *Drawer Detail*. If you prefer a more robust drawer like I made for my client, see "Cutting Dovetails" on page 164. For a simpler drawer, cut the parts to the sizes given in the Materials List, then set up a ¼-inch dado cutter on the table saw, and cut the grooves for the bottom in the front and sides.

Reset the dado cutter to ½ inch, and cut the rabbets in the ends of the front.

Lay out the curved cut on the front, as shown in *Drawer Detail*. This cutout will serve as a drawer pull. Make the cut with a band saw, and sand away the saw marks. Spread glue on the mating surfaces of the drawer joints, and nail the pieces together with 4d finish nails. When the glue is dry, plane or sand the drawer for a nice, easy fit in the drawer opening.

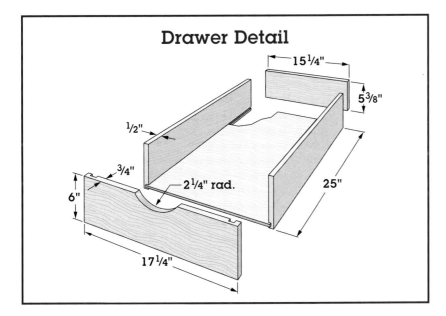

Drawer Detail

15¼"

5⅜"

½"

¾"

2¼" rad.

25"

6"

17¼"

Complete the Assembly

1 **Attach the face frame.** Turn the case face up on the floor. Glue and nail the bottom rail to the front edge of the case bottom. Apply glue to the front edges of the case sides and top, and position the face frame on top. Align the top of the frame with the angles on the sides, making sure the edges of the stiles are flush with the outside of the case. Nail the frame to the case with 4d finish nails. The frame can also be held in place with biscuits if you choose to do so.

2 **Hang the doors.** Fasten the hinges to the clips on the slides, and adjust the doors as necessary with the adjustment mechanisms built into the hinges.

Painting Scheme

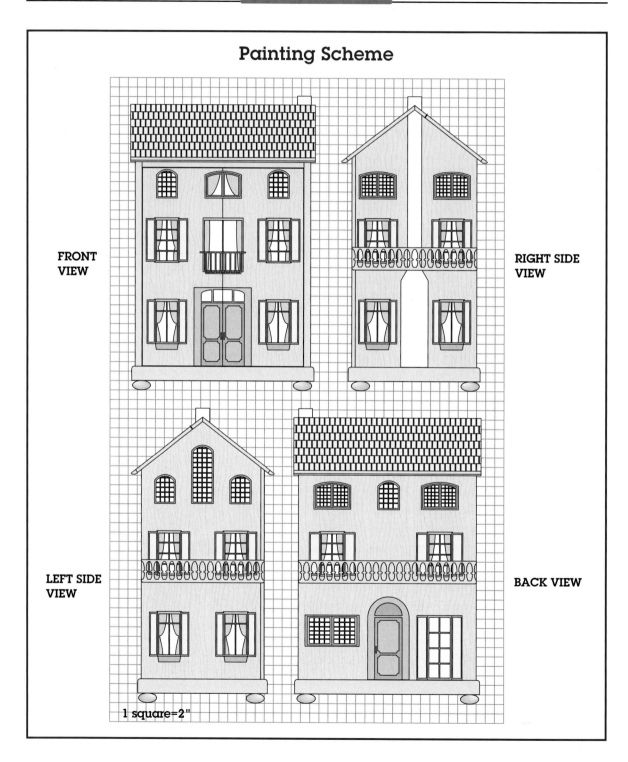

FRONT
VIEW

RIGHT SIDE
VIEW

LEFT SIDE
VIEW

BACK VIEW

1 square=2"

3 **Make the base.** Cut the long and short base moldings to the sizes given in the Materials List. Roundover one corner of each piece with a $\frac{1}{2}$-inch-radius roundover bit in a table-mounted router. Miter the corners of the molding so they fit around the case. Cut the corner blocks to fit, as shown in *Base Detail*. Glue the moldings to the case and to each other at the miter joints, holding them in position with a band clamp. While the glue dries, screw the corner blocks in place, flush with the bottom of the molding with #8 × $1\frac{1}{4}$-inch drywall screws. Screw the bun feet to the bottom edge of the corner blocks with #8 × $1\frac{5}{8}$-inch drywall screws.

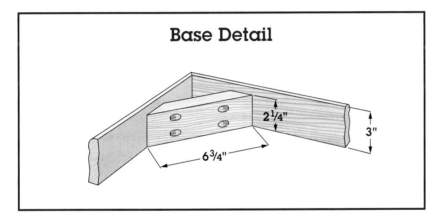

Base Detail

2$\frac{1}{4}$"

3"

6$\frac{3}{4}$"

4 **Install the drawer.** Hang the drawer on 24-inch full-extension drawer slides. Follow the manufacturer's instructions for attaching the slides to the drawer case and drawer sides.

5 **Finish the case.** Place the roof assembly on the case, and glue and screw the back roof to the sides with #8 × $1\frac{5}{8}$-inch drywall screws. Install the lid stays to finish the job.

Paint the cabinet with artists' acrylic paints, according to *Painting Scheme*. The interior of the case can be painted, too, or you can give it a coat or two of shellac.

Hanging Display Cabinet

by Voicu Marian

I originally made this cabinet to display my collection of Chinese soapstone chops, with their ink pads hidden away in the drawers below. Unfortunately, my collection never got big enough to use up all the space that the cabinet provides. Eventually, the chops got pushed aside by other small treasures.

I made this display cabinet out of black walnut with a curly maple back. The ¾-inch-thick back fits into a ½-inch rabbet in the back edge of the case. This pushes the cabinet away from the wall and makes it look as if it were floating. The leaded glass was made by my friend and stained-glass artist Jackie Zuffall.

If you aren't lucky enough to have a friend like Jackie, check with your local glass supplier for names of people in your area who do this kind of work, or simply use plain or leaded glass.

My approach to woodworking is conceptual. I tend to work from sketches that address the aesthetic nature of the piece, not from measured drawings. So, my first-time cabinets are really prototypes, and I usually make changes to them the second time around. In this case, I decided that the cabinet would look better with the drawer dividers reduced from the ¾ inch shown in the photo above to ½ inch. The dimensions in the Materials List and the drawings reflect this change.

Exploded View

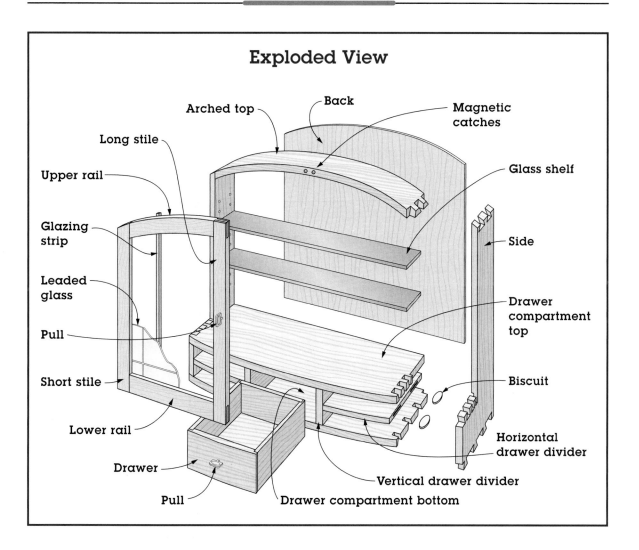

Arched top

Back

Magnetic catches

Long stile

Glass shelf

Upper rail

Glazing strip

Leaded glass

Side

Drawer compartment top

Pull

Biscuit

Short stile

Lower rail

Horizontal drawer divider

Drawer

Pull

Vertical drawer divider

Drawer compartment bottom

Make the Case

The case consists of two L-shaped sides, an arched top, a drawer compartment, a back, and two adjustable glass shelves. All the case pieces (with the exception of the back and the shelves) are cut from walnut.

1 **Choose the wood, and cut the parts.** Plane, joint, rip, and cut the sides, arched top, and drawer compartment top and bottom to the sizes given in the Materials

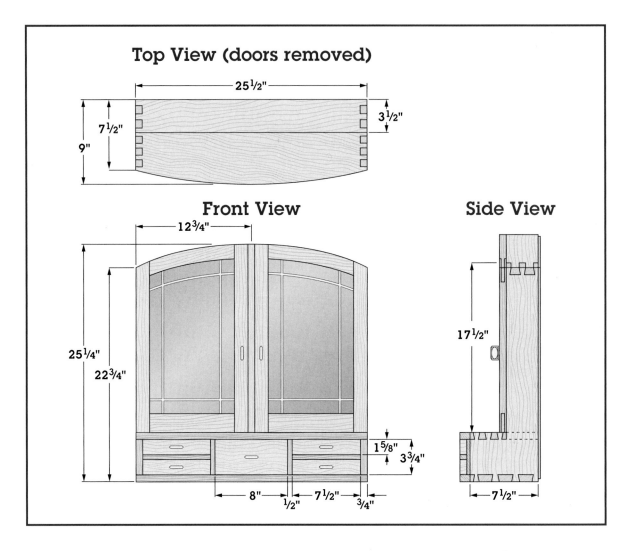

Top View (doors removed)

25 1/2"

7 1/2"

3 1/2"

9"

Front View

Side View

12 3/4"

25 1/4"

22 3/4"

17 1/2"

1 5/8"

3 3/4"

8"

1/2"

7 1/2"

3/4"

7 1/2"

List. Although for the arched top I used a 3 × 3 1/2-inch piece of solid walnut I'd been hoarding for years, you'll likely need to glue this up from thinner pieces. (*Note:* Don't cut the arched profile at this time.)

Also, the drawer compartment top is 1/2 inch narrower than the drawer compartment bottom so the back of the case can extend all the way to the drawer compartment bottom.

Don't cut the curved profile along the front edges of the drawer compartment pieces at this time—this is done after the case is assembled.

Materials List

Part	Dimension	Part	Dimension
Case		**Doors**	
Sides (2)	$\frac{3}{4}" \times 7\frac{1}{2}" \times 22\frac{3}{4}"$	Short stiles (2)	$\frac{3}{4}" \times 1\frac{1}{2}" \times 18"$
Arched top	$3" \times 3\frac{1}{2}" \times 25\frac{1}{2}"$	Long stiles (2)	$\frac{3}{4}" \times 1\frac{1}{2}" \times 20"$
Drawer compartment top	$\frac{3}{4}" \times 8\frac{1}{2}" \times 25\frac{1}{2}"$	Lower rails (2)	$\frac{3}{4}" \times 2" \times 12\frac{3}{4}"$
Drawer compartment		Upper rails (2)	$\frac{3}{4}" \times 3\frac{1}{2}"$ (rough) $\times 12\frac{3}{4}"$
bottom	$\frac{3}{4}" \times 9" \times 25\frac{1}{2}"$	Pulls (7)	$\frac{1}{4}" \times \frac{7}{8}" \times 1\frac{1}{2}"$
Back	$\frac{3}{4}" \times 25" \times 24\frac{3}{4}"$	Glazing strips (8)	$\frac{1}{4}" \times \frac{1}{4}" \times$
Vertical drawer dividers (2)	$\frac{1}{2}" \times 3\frac{3}{4}" \times 8\frac{1}{2}"$		as long as needed
Horizontal		Door lip	$\frac{1}{4}" \times 1\frac{1}{8}" \times 20"$
drawer dividers (2)	$\frac{1}{2}" \times 7\frac{1}{2}" \times 8\frac{1}{2}"$		
Large Drawer		**Hardware**	
Front (2)	$\frac{3}{4}" \times 3\frac{5}{8}" \times 8"$	#6 × 1¼" flathead wood screws	
Sides (2)	$\frac{3}{8}" \times 3\frac{5}{8}" \times 8\frac{1}{4}"$	¾" wire brads (as needed)	
Backs (2)	$\frac{3}{8}" \times 3\frac{5}{8}" \times 7\frac{5}{8}"$	#20 biscuits (as needed)	
Bottoms	$\frac{1}{8}" \times 7\frac{1}{2}" \times 8"$	Leaded glass panels (2)	
		No-mortise door hinges (4). Available from Paxton	
Small Drawers		Hardware, Ltd., 7818 Bradshaw Road, Upper	
Fronts (4)	$\frac{3}{4}" \times 1\frac{1}{2}" \times 7\frac{5}{8}"$	Falls, MD 21156; (410) 592-8505; part #4168	
Short drawer sides (4)	$\frac{3}{8}" \times 1\frac{1}{2}" \times 7\frac{1}{16}"$	¼" dia. shelf support pins (8). Available from Wood-	
Long drawer sides (4)	$\frac{3}{8}" \times 1\frac{1}{2}" \times 8\frac{3}{16}"$	worker's Supply, 1108 North Glenn Road, Casper,	
Backs (4)	$\frac{3}{8}" \times 1\frac{1}{2}" \times 8\frac{1}{8}"$	WY 82601; (800) 645-9292; part #867-365	
Bottoms (4)	$\frac{1}{8}" \times 7\frac{1}{8}" \times 8"$	¼" × 3⅛" × 23⅞" glass shelves (2)	
		Magnetic door catches (2)	

2 **Cut a dado for the drawer compartment top.** Lay out and cut a stopped ¾-inch-wide × ⅜-inch-deep dado across the inside face of each side piece for the drawer compartment top, as shown in *Inside View of Side*. The dado stops before the first dovetail, which is used later to join the drawer compartment top to the sides, as shown in the photo on page 154.

3 **Drill holes for shelf supports.** The adjustable shelves rest on pins that fit into holes drilled into the case sides. The easiest way to get the holes drilled in the right places is to make up a simple drilling jig from a strip of ½-inch-thick × 3-inch-wide plywood. Lay out a series of ¼-inch

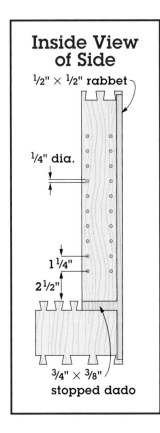

Inside View of Side

½" × ½" rabbet

¼" dia.

1 ¼"

2 ½"

¾" × ⅜"
stopped dado

holes on the jig to the dimensions shown in *Inside View of Side*, and then bore the holes on the drill press. Mark one end of the jig to indicate the bottom. A similar jig is illustrated on page 348.

To use the jig, clamp it to the inside of the side with its edge aligned with the front edge of the side and its bottom aligned with the dado for the drawer compartment top. Drill the ½-inch-deep pin holes with a handheld electric drill. Use a drill stop or a masking tape flag on the drill to set the drilling depth.

4 **Notch the drawer compartment top.** Unlike the drawer compartment bottom, which is dovetailed along its full width into the sides, the drawer compartment top is only partially dovetailed. The rear portion is notched to slip into the dado you cut earlier in the sides, as shown in *Drawer Compartment Top—Top View*. Cut the notch on the band saw, and clean up the cut with a sanding block.

5 **Cut the dovetails.** Lay out and cut dovetails on the sides of the case for the drawer compartment top and bottom, matching pins on the ends of the drawer compartment top and bottom, as shown in *Dovetail Layout*.

Also, lay out and cut the dovetails that will join the arched top piece to the sides of the case. Cut small tails on the ends of

A T-shaped edge guide guarantees a straight dado. A stop clamped to one end ensures that the cut stops where it should.

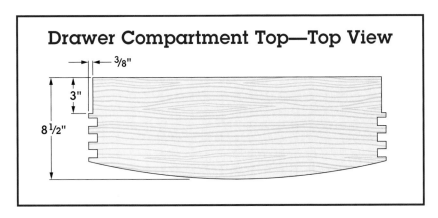

Drawer Compartment Top—Top View

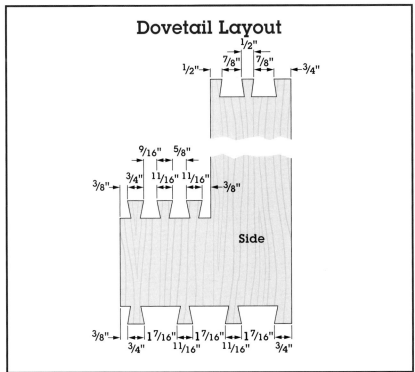

Dovetail Layout

the sides and pins on the ends of the arched top piece. Note that the arched top is not arched yet—it's just a big hunk of wood. So, you need to cut a half-blind tail in it, as shown in *Side-to-Top Joinery Detail*. These dovetails aren't really traditional—the dovetails are usually wider than the pins—in fact, just the opposite is true here. It is also unusual to cut "half"

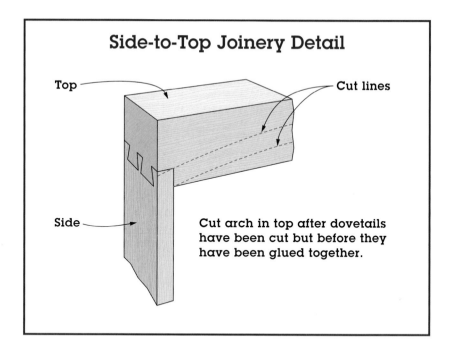

Side-to-Top Joinery Detail

Top

Cut lines

Side

Cut arch in top after dovetails
have been cut but before they
have been glued together.

dovetails like those where the sides join the top. A dovetail jig won't help you here. See "Cutting Dovetails" on page 164 for information on cutting dovetails by hand.

When they have been cut, test assemble the case to check how the dovetails fit together and make any adjustments needed.

Cut the Arched Profile

1 **Lay out the curve.** With the case assembled and lying on its back, lay out the curved profile of the arched top along the outside edge, as shown in *Front View*. (Be sure to extend your pencil lines across the front edge of each side.)

2 **Cut the outside profile.** With an oversized auxiliary table attached to the table of a band saw and the case lying on its back, band saw the curved profile along the top of the case, cutting through the ends of the case sides as well, as shown in *Side-to-Top Joinery Detail*. When done, sand the arched profile until smooth and symmetrical.

Quick tip

A pipe clamp and a flexible straightedge are all it takes to lay out a graceful curve. Simply clamp the straightedge between the jaws and adjust the clamp for the desired curve.

3 **Cut a matching inside profile.** With a marking gauge or a set of dividers set to a width of $\frac{3}{4}$ inch, follow the top profile to lay out the inside edge, as shown in the photo at right. Then remove the arched top from the case, and band saw the inside edge to shape. Sand the curve smooth.

4 **Rout a rabbet for the back.** The arched top, sides, and drawer compartment bottom all need to be rabbeted to accept the cabinet's back. To cut the rabbet, temporarily assemble these parts and clamp their dovetail joints together securely.

Next, put a $\frac{1}{2}$-inch piloted rabbet bit in your router, and adjust it to cut a $\frac{1}{2} \times \frac{1}{2}$-inch rabbet. Using the bit's bearing as a guide, rout a rabbet around the inside back edge of the case.

When the rabbet has been cut, square the corners of the rabbet at the bottom of the case with a sharp chisel. The corners of the rabbet where the arched top meets the case sides should be chiseled to match the arch of the top. Since the back is $\frac{3}{4}$ inch thick, it will stand $\frac{1}{4}$ inch proud of the back of the case. This brings the cabinet $\frac{1}{4}$ inch out from the wall and creates a "floating" effect.

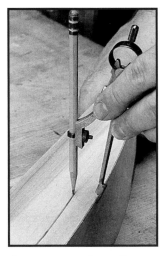

An easy way to scribe a matching curve is to use a set of dividers open to the appropriate width—in this case, $\frac{3}{4}$ inch.

Make the Dividers, and Fit the Back

1 **Choose the wood, and cut the parts.** Although you could cut the dividers to the sizes given in the Materials List, it's safer to cut them to fit. To do this, first test assemble the case. Then measure inside the drawer compartment, and cut the $\frac{1}{2}$-inch-thick vertical and horizontal drawer dividers to size.

2 **Cut slots for the biscuits.** Disassemble the case, and then lay out and cut slots for biscuits to join the dividers to the drawer compartment.

If you don't have a biscuit jointer, drill $\frac{1}{4}$-inch-diameter $\times$ $\frac{1}{2}$-inch-deep holes for dowels where the dividers, sides, and drawer compartment top and bottom join.

3 **Assemble the case.** To start, glue the vertical drawer dividers in between the drawer compartment top and bottom pieces. Then glue the horizontal dividers, compartment top and bottom, and the arched top in between the sides of the case. Clamp and square up the cabinet.

4 **Cut and fit the back.** Using $\frac{3}{4}$-inch-thick stock (I used curly maple to lighten up the cabinet interior), glue up enough pieces to slightly surpass the width of the back given in the Materials List. When dry, cut the back to fit between the rabbets in the back of the case, allowing for a $\frac{1}{8}$-inch gap top and bottom and $\frac{1}{4}$ inch on each side for seasonal wood movement. Carefully lay out the arch where the back meets the arched top, and cut it to shape on the band saw or with a jigsaw. Once the back fits within the rabbets correctly, lightly chamfer the edge that's exposed on the back of the case to soften the corners.

5 **Install the back.** Use #6 × $1\frac{1}{4}$-inch flathead wood screws to attach the back. Drill pilot holes centered on the top and bottom edges of the back to fix it in place. Then cut elongated holes for the other screws to allow the back to move. To hang the cabinet, I routed a pair of keyhole slots in the back on 16-inch centers to match the studs in the wall.

Cut the Curved Front

1 **Lay out the curved profile.** After the case is assembled and the glue has dried, you can lay out the curved profile on the drawer compartments. Here again, I used a flexible straightedge to lay out this line.

2 **Cut the profile.** Cut the curved profile in the face of the drawer compartment on a band saw with the cabinet sitting upright on the saw table. On standard band saws, the top of the cabinet will clear the top wheel and blade guard without any problem. Sand all of the edges smooth.

Make the Large Drawer

All of the drawer fronts are cut from ¾-inch-thick walnut that is a shade lighter than the other walnut used. The sides and backs are ⅜-inch maple, and the bottoms are cut from ⅛-inch plywood. I cut dovetails in the original drawers, and you can do this, too. Be aware, however, that these are very tricky angled dovetails that almost deserve a book in themselves to describe.

As an alternative, I suggest that you cut simple rabbet joints, as shown in *Drawer Detail*. These joints work just fine since the drawers are relatively small and aren't designed to carry a lot of weight. For added strength, I glued the plywood bottoms in place (no wood movement worries here).

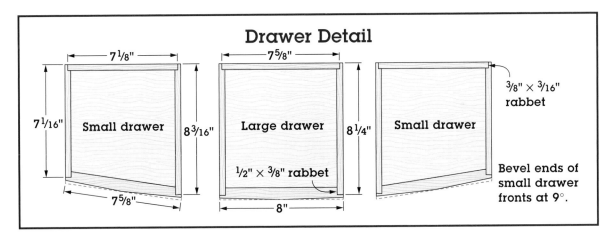

Drawer Detail

7⅛" — Small drawer — 7¹/₁₆", 8³/₁₆", 7⅝"

7⅝" — Large drawer — 8¼", 8", ½" × ⅜" rabbet

Small drawer — ⅜" × ³/₁₆" rabbet

Bevel ends of small drawer fronts at 9°.

① Choose the wood, and cut the parts. Plane, joint, rip, and cut the large drawer parts to size.

② Cut the rabbets. Cut ½-inch-wide × ⅜-inch-deep rabbets on the ends of the drawer front and ⅜-inch-wide × ³/₁₆-inch-deep rabbets at the back of the drawer sides.

③ Cut grooves for the bottom. Cut a ³/₁₆-inch-deep groove for the ⅛-inch plywood drawer bottom on the inside face of each drawer part. Position the groove ¼ inch up from the bottom edge of the drawer sides, back, and front.

4 **Assemble the drawer.** Test assemble the drawer sides, front, and back; and measure for the drawer bottom. Trim the bottom stock to fit in the bottom grooves. When satisfied with the fit, glue up the drawer with the bottom in place.

Make the Small Drawers

The four small drawers are constructed in much the same manner as the large drawer. The main difference is the front of each drawer is angled so that a curve can be cut to match the profile of the drawer compartments, as shown in *Drawer Detail*.

1 **Choose the wood, and cut the parts.** Plane, joint, rip, and cut the small drawer parts to the sizes given in the Materials List. Note that the ends of the drawer fronts are beveled at a 9-degree angle to provide sufficient material when band sawing the front to shape.

2 **Cut the rabbets.** Cut $\frac{1}{2}$-inch-wide $\times$ $\frac{3}{8}$-inch-deep angled rabbets in the ends of the drawer fronts, and square the rabbets in the drawer sides with a dado blade. To cut the angled rabbets, angle the dado blade to match the beveled ends of the drawer fronts, as shown in the photo at left.

3 **Cut grooves for the drawer bottoms.** Cut $\frac{1}{8}$-inch-wide $\times$ $\frac{3}{16}$-inch-deep grooves for the drawer bottoms on the inside face of each drawer part as you did for the large drawer.

4 **Assemble the drawers.** Test assemble the drawer sides, fronts, and backs; and measure for the drawer bottoms. Trim the bottom stock to fit in the bottom grooves. When satisfied with the fit, glue up each drawer with its bottom in place.

Angle your dado blade to match the beveled ends of the drawer fronts to cut matching rabbets.

5 **Cut a matching profile.** Slide the small drawers in their openings, and trace the curved front of the drawer compartment onto each drawer front. Curve the drawer front of each drawer with a stationary belt sander or band saw the face, and then sand all of them smooth.

6 **Add the pulls.** Drill a hole in the center of each drawer front for a pull. I made my own pulls from maple to resemble the tuning pegs of a violin. I cut them to shape on the band saw and then finished them with a whittling knife and a small gouge, as shown in *Pull Detail*.

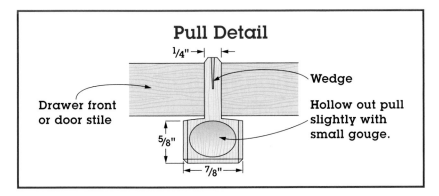

Pull Detail

1/4"

Wedge

Drawer front
or door stile

Hollow out pull
slightly with
small gouge.

5/8"

7/8"

Make the Doors

The stiles and rails for the doors are made from 3/4-inch-thick walnut. A through mortise-and-tenon slip joint is used to hold the stiles and rails together. The leaded glass fits in a rabbet in the inside edge of each door. The glass is held in place with a simple wood glazing strip nailed in place with wire brads.

1 **Choose the wood, and cut the parts.** Plane, joint, rip, and cut the door parts to the sizes given in the Materials List.

2 **Cut the slip joints.** Cut a through mortise on the end of each stile and tenons on the ends of each rail, as shown in *Door Joinery Detail*. I cut the mortises with a tenoning jig and a standard carbide-tipped blade on my table saw, flipping the piece between cuts to ensure a centered mortise. I also used the tenoning jig to cut the tenons, but you could cut them flat on the table saw with a dado blade, taking multiple passes to remove the waste.

When the upper rails have been tenoned, cut away a portion of the tenons that join the long stiles, as shown in *Door Joinery Detail*.

3 **Cut the outside profile.** Test assemble the door frames, and temporarily clamp them to the face of the case. Now trace the arched profile onto the back side of each door. Remove and disassemble the doors. Then band saw the outside edge of the upper rails to shape. Sand each edge smooth.

4 **Cut the matching inside curve.** Then transfer the profile to the inside edge of each upper rail with a marking gauge or dividers set to a width of $1\frac{1}{2}$ inches. Band saw the inside edge, and sand the curve smooth.

5 **Cut the rabbets for the glass.** Using a $\frac{1}{2}$-inch-rabbet bit, cut a $\frac{1}{2} \times \frac{1}{2}$-inch rabbet along the back inside edge of each frame piece to accept the leaded glass.

6 **Add the door lip.** Cut a door lip to the size given in the Materials List, and round-over the outside edges. Position the door lip so that it is centered between the stiles of each door when closed, as shown in *Front View*, and glue it to the right-hand door.

7 **Add the pulls.** Drill a hole in each door for a pull, and attach the pulls to the doors.

8 **Cut the glazing strips to fit.** To hold the glass in place, miter the glazing strips to length. Don't install the glass and strips at this time, as it's a lot easier to apply the finish first.

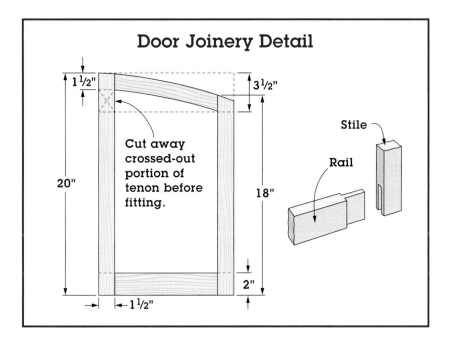

Door Joinery Detail

1½"

3½"

Stile

Rail

Cut away
crossed-out
portion of
tenon before
fitting.

20"

18"

2"

1½"

Finish the Cabinet

1 **Apply a finish.** I applied three coats of polyurethane
to the case, shelves, drawers, doors, and glazing strips,
sanding lightly between coats with 320-grit sandpaper.

2 **Install the glass.** After the finish dries, set the glass
in the doors, and secure the glass in place by fastening
the glazing strips with wire brads.

3 **Mount the doors.** Mount the doors to the case using
two no-mortise hinges for each door.

4 **Add the shelves.** Finally, install shelf pins, and add
the adjustable shelves.

Cutting Dovetails

If you have a commercial dovetailing router jig, you can cut scads of dovetails quickly if you follow the directions that come with the jig. However, not all dovetails (like those in the "Hanging Display Cabinet" on page 150) can be cut with a jig and router, and I think cutting dovetails by hand is much more enjoyable anyway.

Whether I'm cutting through dovetails or half-blind dovetails, I always start by cutting the tails, and then I cut the pins to fit them. Some woodworkers swear that you have to start with the pins, but I really don't think it makes any difference.

Through dovetails, like through mortises, pass all of the way through the stock they are joined with. They are commonly used for the corner joints of boxes and blanket chests, and for joining cabinet sides to cabinet tops and bottoms. They are also traditionally used to join drawer sides to drawer backs.

Half-blind dovetails do not pass all of the way through the stock they are joining. This type of joint is traditionally used in joining drawer sides to drawer fronts. In this case, the dovetails are visible only when the drawer is pulled open.

THROUGH DOVETAILS

1 Lay out the length of the tails. When cutting through dovetails, the length of the tails is equal to or *slightly* longer than the thickness of the stock the dovetails will join. Set a marking gauge to this length, and use it to scribe around all four sides of the tail stock and the pin stock.

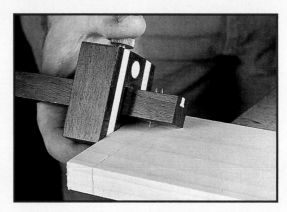

2 Lay out the tails. With a sharp pencil and a bevel gauge set somewhere between 9 and 14 degrees off perpendicular (I generally use 12 degrees), lay out the tails on the tail stock. Traditionally, there are wider dovetails in the midsection of the stock and smaller dovetails toward the edges. I usually space the tails by eye because some slight irregularity in spacing gives the tails a hand-cut look.

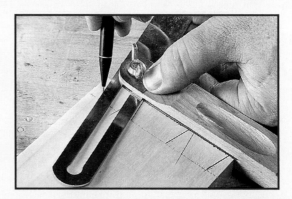

3 **Cut away the waste between the dovetails.** Cut away most of the waste between the tails on the band saw or with a coping saw. Then carefully chisel to the layout lines.

5 **Extend the pin layout lines.** Draw lines that extend from the ends of the pin layout lines down to the scribe line left by the marking gauge with a square and pencil.

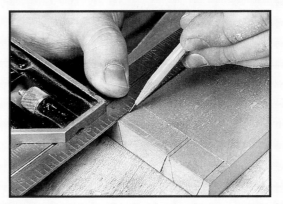

4 **Lay out the pins.** Using the dovetails you just cut and chiseled as a template, lay out the pins on the end of the pin stock. Use a sharp pencil or a sharp craft knife with a #11 blade to trace the tails, as shown in the photo below.

6 **Cut the pins.** With a fine-tooth backsaw or a dovetail saw, cut along the pin layout lines down to the scribe line left by the marking gauge. Always cut about $\frac{1}{64}$ inch to the waste side of the layout lines, and just as a reminder, clearly "ex" out the waste between the pins.

7 **Remove the waste between the pins.** Carefully tap a chisel along the marking gauge line to define the waste between the pins. This cuts through the grain of the wood, allowing you to pop off slivers of the waste wood when you drive the chisel into the end grain of the stock.

8 **Fit the pins into the tails.** When the waste has been removed from between the tails, test fit the pins into the tails. Pare away the edges of the pins until a snug fit is achieved.

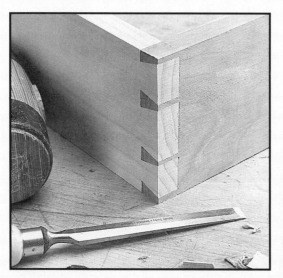

HALF-BLIND DOVETAILS

The only difference between through dovetails and half-blind dovetails is that the tails extend only partway into the thickness of the pin stock (not *through* it). This joint is usually used where thin drawer sides meet a thicker drawer front.

1 **Lay out the length of the tails.** This is exactly like Step 1 under "Through Dovetails," except that this time use the marking gauge to mark the end grain and inside surface of the pin stock. Then, lay out the cut for the tails just as you did in Steps 2 and 3 on pages 164–165.

2 **Lay out the dovetail sockets in the pin stock.** Use the dovetails as a template to lay out the dovetail sockets on the end of the pin stock.

3 **Extend the dovetail socket layout lines.** Draw lines that extend from the bottom of the dovetail socket layout lines down to the scribe line left by the marking gauge with a square and pencil. Notice that the dovetail socket layout lines on the end of the pin stock extend only to the marking gauge scribe line.

5 **Trim the dovetail sockets to accept the tails.** Carefully pare the edges of the dovetail sockets until the dovetails fit in them snugly. Note that the half-blind dovetails are visible only from the side of the assembly.

4 **Cut along the dovetail socket layout lines.** Using a backsaw or dovetail saw, cut to the waste side of the dovetail socket layout lines. As shown in the photo at top right, cut across the edge of the stock down to both scribe lines. Then, chisel away the waste within the dovetail sockets just as you did between the pins in Step 7 on the opposite page.

Entertainment Center

by Tony O'Malley

While the TV is the centerpiece in most entertainment centers, it's the ever-growing array of accessories and related equipment that leads many people to consider buying or making a large entertainment center.

Designing one is challenging because it's hard to come up with a design that's not overbearing. When I was asked to make one for a friend, we decided right away that it should be painted to match the doors and trim of the room it would be in. The result is an entertainment center that blends into the room instead of overwhelming it.

This project is designed as three separate cabinets. The center cabinet houses the TV and VCR, while the side cabinets hold the stereo equipment and accessories. The stereo speakers go in the top compartments of the side cabinets, which have speaker-cloth–covered frames in the doors. You could choose to build just the center cabinet if that's all you need for your equipment. In any case, you should carefully check the dimensions of your equipment to make sure it will fit, and make the necessary changes in the dimensions of the cabinets.

These cabinets are simply constructed—birch plywood with solid wood edges joined with biscuits. The doors are cope-and-stick construction. The large pocket doors slide back into the cabinet to provide full view of the TV. The sides of the side cabinets have an applied molding, which provides the look of frame-and-panel construction but is easier to make. The cases are trimmed with store-bought crown and base moldings.

Exploded View

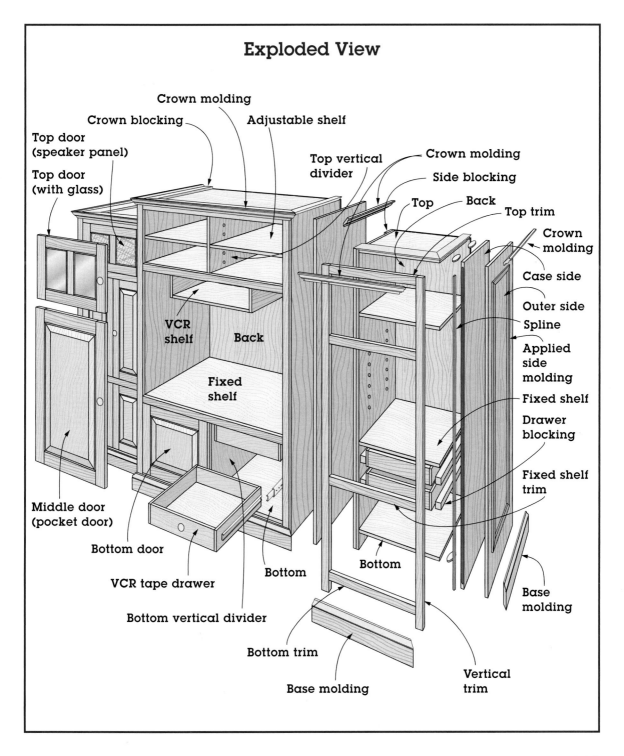

Crown molding

Crown blocking

Adjustable shelf

Top door (speaker panel)

Top door (with glass)

Top vertical divider

Crown molding

Side blocking

Top

Back

Top trim

Crown molding

Case side

Outer side

Spline

Applied side molding

Fixed shelf

Drawer blocking

Fixed shelf trim

VCR shelf

Back

Fixed shelf

Middle door (pocket door)

Bottom door

VCR tape drawer

Bottom vertical divider

Bottom

Bottom

Base molding

Bottom trim

Base molding

Vertical trim

Front View

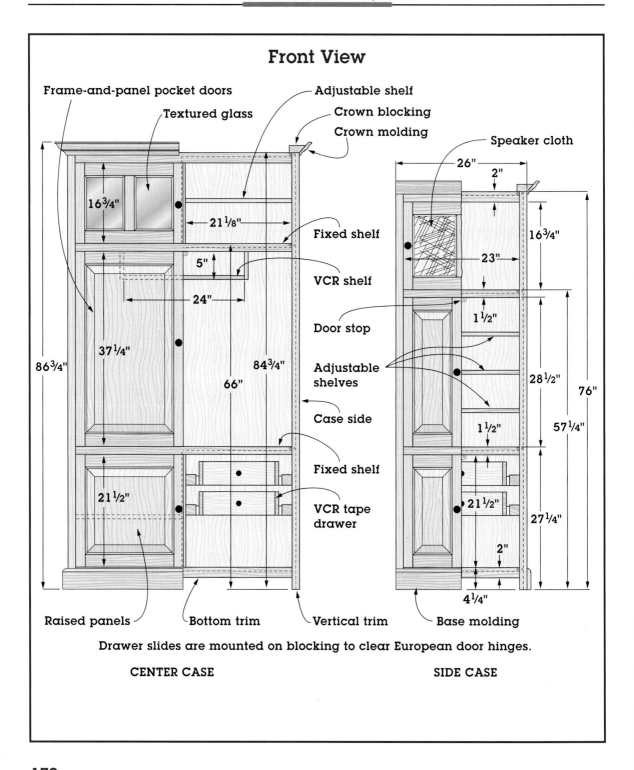

Frame-and-panel pocket doors

Textured glass

Adjustable shelf

Crown blocking

Crown molding

Speaker cloth

$16^3/4"$

$21^1/8"$

Fixed shelf

$5"$

VCR shelf

$24"$

Door stop

$37^1/4"$

$84^3/4"$

Adjustable shelves

$86^3/4"$

$66"$

Case side

$21^1/2"$

Fixed shelf

VCR tape drawer

$26"$

$2"$

$16^3/4"$

$23"$

$1^1/2"$

$28^1/2"$

$76"$

$1^1/2"$

$57^1/4"$

$21^1/2"$

$27^1/4"$

$2"$

$4^1/4"$

Raised panels

Bottom trim

Vertical trim

Base molding

Drawer slides are mounted on blocking to clear European door hinges.

CENTER CASE

SIDE CASE

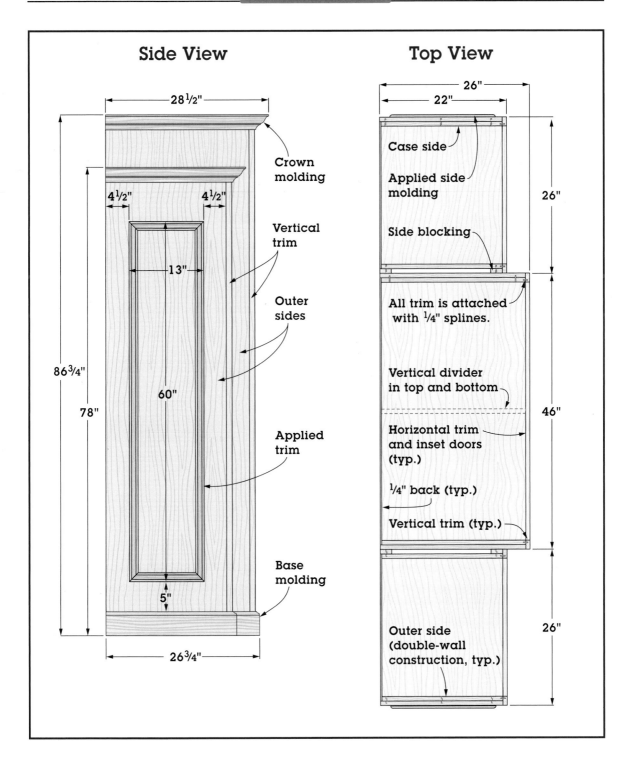

Side View

28¹/₂"

Crown
molding

4¹/₂"   4¹/₂"

Vertical
trim

13"

Outer
sides

86³/₄"

60"

78"

Applied
trim

Base
molding

5"

26³/₄"

Top View

26"

22"

Case side

Applied side
molding

26"

Side blocking

All trim is attached
with ¹/₄" splines.

Vertical divider
in top and bottom

46"

Horizontal trim
and inset doors
(typ.)

¹/₄" back (typ.)

Vertical trim (typ.)

Outer side
(double-wall
construction, typ.)

26"

Materials List

Part	Dimension
Center Case, Plywood Parts	
Case sides (2)	$\frac{3}{4}$" × 25" × $84\frac{3}{4}$"
Outer sides (2)	$\frac{3}{4}$" × $25\frac{1}{4}$" × $84\frac{3}{4}$"
Top, bottom (2)	$\frac{3}{4}$" × 25" × 43"
Back	$\frac{1}{4}$" × $44\frac{1}{2}$" × $81\frac{1}{4}$"
Fixed shelves (2)	$\frac{3}{4}$" × 25" × 43"
Adjustable shelves (3)	$\frac{3}{4}$" × $21\frac{1}{8}$" × $24\frac{7}{8}$"
Top vertical divider	$\frac{3}{4}$" × 18" × 25"
Bottom vertical divider	$\frac{3}{4}$" × $22\frac{1}{4}$" × 25"
VCR shelf	$\frac{3}{4}$" × 20" × 24"
VCR shelf supports (2)	$\frac{3}{4}$" × 5" × 25"
Drawer sides (4)	$\frac{3}{4}$" × $4\frac{1}{2}$" × 18"
Drawer fronts, backs (4)	$\frac{3}{4}$" × $4\frac{1}{2}$" × $16\frac{5}{8}$"
Drawer bottoms (2)	$\frac{1}{4}$" × 17" × $17\frac{1}{8}$"
Side Cases, Plywood Parts	
Case sides (4)	$\frac{3}{4}$" × 21" × 76"
Outer sides (2)	$\frac{3}{4}$" × $21\frac{1}{4}$" × 76"
Top, bottom (4)	$\frac{3}{4}$" × 21" × 23"
Back	$\frac{1}{4}$" × $24\frac{1}{2}$" × $72\frac{1}{2}$"
Fixed shelves (4)	$\frac{3}{4}$" × 21" × 23"
Adjustable shelves (6)	$\frac{3}{4}$" × $20\frac{7}{8}$" × $22\frac{15}{16}$"
Drawer sides (4)	$\frac{3}{4}$" × $4\frac{1}{2}$" × 18"
Drawer bottoms (2)	$\frac{1}{4}$" × 17" × 17"
Side blocking (4)	$\frac{3}{4}$" × 3" × 76"
Center Case, Solid Wood Parts	
Vertical trim (2)	$\frac{3}{4}$" × $1\frac{1}{2}$" × $84\frac{3}{4}$"
Fixed shelf trim (4)	$\frac{3}{4}$" × $1\frac{1}{2}$" × 43"
Bottom and top trim (2)	$\frac{3}{4}$" × 2" × 43"
Splines (vertical) (2)	$\frac{1}{4}$" × $\frac{3}{4}$" × $84\frac{3}{4}$"
Splines (horizontal) (4)	$\frac{1}{4}$" × $\frac{3}{4}$" × 43"
Top door stiles (4)	$\frac{3}{4}$" × $2\frac{1}{4}$" × $16\frac{3}{4}$"
Top door rails (4)	$\frac{3}{4}$" × $2\frac{3}{4}$" × $17\frac{5}{8}$"
Top door muntins (2)	$\frac{3}{4}$" × $2\frac{1}{4}$" × 12"
Middle door stiles (4)	$\frac{3}{4}$" × $2\frac{1}{4}$" × $37\frac{1}{4}$"
Middle door rails (4)	$\frac{3}{4}$" × $2\frac{3}{4}$" × $17\frac{5}{8}$"
Middle door panels (2)	$\frac{5}{8}$" × $17\frac{5}{8}$" × $32\frac{3}{8}$"
Bottom door stiles (4)	$\frac{3}{4}$" × $2\frac{1}{4}$" × $21\frac{1}{2}$"

Part	Dimension
Bottom door rails (4)	$\frac{3}{4}$" × $2\frac{3}{4}$" × $17\frac{5}{8}$"
Bottom door panels (2)	$\frac{5}{8}$" × $17\frac{5}{8}$" × $16\frac{5}{8}$"
Door stop	$\frac{1}{4}$" × $1\frac{1}{2}$" × $1\frac{1}{2}$"
Top door glazing strips (vertical) (8)	$\frac{1}{4}$" × $\frac{3}{8}$" × 12"
Top door glazing strips (horizontal) (8)	$\frac{1}{4}$" × $\frac{3}{8}$" × $8\frac{1}{8}$"
Drawer blocking (2)	2" × 2" × 8"
Side Cases, Solid Wood Parts	
Vertical trim (2)	$\frac{3}{4}$" × $1\frac{1}{2}$" × 76"
Bottom and top trim (2)	$\frac{3}{4}$" × 2" × 23"
Fixed shelf trim (2)	$\frac{3}{4}$" × $1\frac{1}{2}$" × 23"
Splines (vertical) (2)	$\frac{1}{4}$" × $\frac{3}{4}$" × 76"
Splines (horizontal) (4)	$\frac{1}{4}$" × $\frac{3}{4}$" × 23"
Top door stiles (4)	$\frac{3}{4}$" × $2\frac{1}{4}$" × $16\frac{3}{4}$"
Top door rails (4)	$\frac{3}{4}$" × $2\frac{3}{4}$" × $19\frac{1}{4}$"
Top door muntins (2)	$\frac{3}{4}$" × $1\frac{1}{2}$" × 12"
Middle door stiles (8)	$\frac{3}{4}$" × $2\frac{1}{4}$" × $28\frac{1}{2}$"
Middle door rails (8)	$\frac{3}{4}$" × $2\frac{3}{4}$" × $7\frac{3}{4}$"
Middle door panels (4)	$\frac{5}{8}$" × $7\frac{5}{8}$" × $23\frac{5}{8}$"
Bottom door stiles (8)	$\frac{3}{4}$" × $2\frac{1}{4}$" × $21\frac{1}{2}$"
Bottom door rails (8)	$\frac{3}{4}$" × $2\frac{3}{4}$" × $7\frac{5}{8}$"
Bottom door panels (4)	$\frac{5}{8}$" × $7\frac{5}{8}$" × $16\frac{5}{8}$"
Speaker panel frame parts (vertical) (8)	$\frac{3}{8}$" × $\frac{3}{4}$" × 12"
Speaker panel frame parts (horizontal) (8)	$\frac{3}{8}$" × $\frac{3}{4}$" × $8\frac{7}{8}$"
Speaker panel turnbuckles (16)	$\frac{1}{4}$" × $\frac{3}{4}$" × $1\frac{1}{2}$"
Door stops (6)	$\frac{1}{4}$" × $1\frac{1}{2}$" × $1\frac{1}{2}$"
Drawer blocking (4)	2" × 2" × 18"
Stock Moldings	
Base molding	20 linear feet
Crown blocking	2" × 4" × 20 linear feet
Crown molding	20 linear feet
Applied side molding	26 linear feet

Materials List—Continued

Hardware

#8 × 2¼" drywall screws (as needed)
#8 × 1⅝" drywall screws (as needed)
#8 × 1¼" drywall screws (as needed)
#8 × 1" drywall screws (as needed)
#6 × ¾" flathead wood screws (as needed)
4d finish nails (as needed)
1" brads (as needed)
#20 biscuits (as needed)
Iron-on veneer edge banding (50 ft.)
Speaker cloth

Self-closing "inset" European hinges (14 pairs)
20" pocket door slides (2 pairs)
Rubber door bumpers (12)
Amerock colonial knobs, hammered finish (16).
  Available from hardware stores and from Woodworker's Hardware, P.O. Box 784, St. Cloud, MN
  56302; (800) 383-0130; #A03403
18" full-extension drawer slides (4 pairs)
1" dia. wooden knobs (4)
Glass, ⅛" thick, cut to fit (4)
Shelf support pins (36)

Make the Cases

1 **Cut the plywood case parts to size.** Lay out and cut all of the plywood case parts to the sizes given in the Materials List. Carefully label the individual parts as you cut them so you can keep them organized.

2 **Cut and attach the edge trim.** As shown in *Front View*, the case sides, tops, bottoms, and fixed shelves are trimmed with strips of solid poplar. The strips are not as-sembled as a face frame; they're just glued to the individual case parts with splines, as shown in *Top View, Center Case Cross Section,* and *Side Case Cross Section.*

Cut spline slots in the edges of the plywood parts with a router and slot-cutting bit, and then cut matching slots in the back face of the trim on the table saw. Plane solid wood strips to fit in the slots, then cut them to width, allowing some room in the slots for excess glue. Masonite and plywood also make good splines, as long as the thickness matches the slot. Once the trim pieces are attached, sand them flush with the inside faces of the panels.

Apply veneer edge-banding tape to the two vertical di-viders in the center cabinet, as shown in the top photo on page 174.

Quick tip

Depending on the size of your table saw, it is sometimes difficult to cut large pieces of ply-wood. One approach is to rough out the case parts with a handheld circular saw and straightedge. Then you can make the final cuts on the table saw, trimming the case parts to their final sizes. For the cabinet sides, you may need to make all the cuts with a circular saw and straightedge.

Several case parts, as well as the drawers, are trimmed with iron-on veneer edge-banding tape. Use a hot iron to adhere the tape, then trim it flush to the sides of the part with a sharp chisel.

3 **Lay out and cut the biscuit joints.** Biscuit joinery, once you get the hang of it, simplifies case construction. I've found that compared to cases joined with dado and rabbet joints, biscuit-joined cases take less time and are more likely to go together square without any fuss.

First cut the biscuit slots in the edges of all the horizontal parts and vertical dividers, as shown in the photo at bottom left. Next, lay out the locations of the top, bottom, and fixed shelves on the cabinet sides and the position of the vertical dividers, as shown in *Front View, Center Case Cross Section,* and *Side Case Cross Section.* Draw lines representing both edges of the parts. Use a "story stick" to mark the locations of the individual slots. (A story stick is a strip of wood on which you lay out dimensions, which can be used to transfer the layout marks accurately onto several pieces.) Clamp a straightedge along the top line to position the biscuit joiner, and cut the slots.

The top of the cabinet presents a unique situation because you can't use the same flat fence to guide the biscuit joiner. Instead, use an L-shaped fence, as shown in the photo on the opposite page.

4 **Assemble the cases.** Clamping up large cases like these can be awkward. Since these cabinets have double walls, you can use screws instead of clamps, as they won't show once you apply the outer sides. Predrill for #8 × 1⅝" drywall screws between the biscuits from inside the sides, then countersink the holes on the outside face of the sides. Position one side with the inside surface facing up on a set of high sawhorses. Then glue and screw one joint at a time, checking for square as you go. In the center case, the vertical dividers need to be glued between the fixed shelves and top and bottom at this point. These can also be screwed in place. Once all the horizontal parts are attached to one side, apply glue to all the other joints, position the second side, then screw each joint together.

Lay the parts face down on a bench, and cut the slots with the base of the joiner held tightly on the bench.

5 **Drill the shelf-support holes.** The adjustable shelves rest on support pins that fit into holes in the cabinet sides, as shown in *Center Case Cross Section* and *Side Case*

Center Case Cross Section

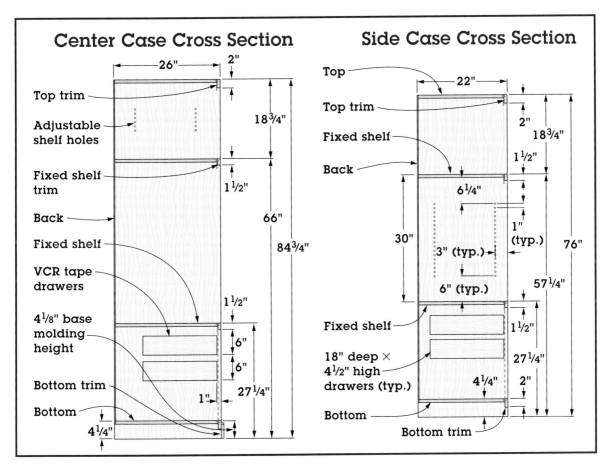

- Top trim
- Adjustable shelf holes
- Fixed shelf trim
- Back
- Fixed shelf
- VCR tape drawers
- 4$^{1}/_{8}$" base molding height
- Bottom trim
- Bottom

26" — 2"

18$^{3}/_{4}$"

1$^{1}/_{2}$"

66"

84$^{3}/_{4}$"

1$^{1}/_{2}$"

6"

6"

1"

27$^{1}/_{4}$"

4$^{1}/_{4}$"

Side Case Cross Section

- Top
- Top trim
- Fixed shelf
- Back
- Fixed shelf
- 18" deep × 4$^{1}/_{2}$" high drawers (typ.)
- Bottom
- Bottom trim

22"

2"

18$^{3}/_{4}$"

1$^{1}/_{2}$"

6$^{1}/_{4}$"

1" (typ.)

30"

3" (typ.)

6" (typ.)

76"

57$^{1}/_{4}$"

1$^{1}/_{2}$"

27$^{1}/_{4}$"

4$^{1}/_{4}$"

2"

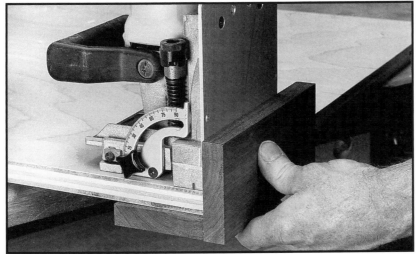

You can also use the base of the joiner as the reference surface on the outside corner joints. This is easy with an L-shaped fence clamped or held tightly against the edge of the side.

175

Whenever possible, use the base of the biscuit joiner, not the fence, as the reference surface for cutting all the slots. The fence can move or be knocked out of adjustment, but the distance between the base and the cutter is always the same.

Cross Section. To drill accurate holes, make a template from a $\frac{1}{4} \times 6 \times 15$-inch scrap of plywood. Drill a row of $\frac{1}{4}$-inch-diameter holes centered on its width, starting 6 inches from the bottom of the scrap and spaced 1 inch apart. Next, mark the 6-inch section of the template clearly as the bottom, and clamp it in the center case resting on the top fixed shelf with its edge flush with the front edge of the case. Drill a set of $\frac{1}{2}$-inch-deep holes in the case side using the template as a guide. Position the template against the back edge of the side to drill the back set of holes, and then repeat the procedure on the other side.

Use the same template to drill the shelf holes in the side cases, as shown in *Side Case Cross Section.* In order to drill more holes than the template's length allows, slide it up along the case side, and position it accurately by pushing a $\frac{1}{4}$-inch dowel through the template into one of the holes that was already drilled. Then, clamp it in place and continue drilling.

6 **Cut and edge-band the shelves.** Cut the adjustable shelves to fit in their cases, and apply veneer edge-banding tape to the front edges, as shown in the top photo on page 174.

7 **Assemble and attach the VCR shelf.** The VCR shelf is a simple U-shaped assembly held together with biscuit joints and held to the fixed shelf with biscuits and screws. Apply veneer edge-banding tape to the front edges of each part. Next, cut the biscuit slots, and assemble the parts with glue and clamps. Position the assembled VCR shelf under the upper fixed shelf in the center case, and mark its location. Cut biscuit slots in both parts, then predrill holes for #8 $\times$ $1\frac{5}{8}$-inch drywall screws between the biscuit slots. Glue and screw the VCR shelf in place.

8 **Screw and glue on the finished sides.** The outer sides of the cabinets form double walls. These panels can be just glued and clamped in place with a few #8 $\times$ $1\frac{1}{4}$-inch drywall screws added from inside the cases, if needed. After adding the outer walls, screw blocking to the inside walls of the side cabinets. Then, once the cases have been finished, you will be ready to screw the side cabinets to the center one, again from inside the cabinets, using #8 × 2¼-inch drywall screws, as shown in *Top View* and *Front View.*

9 **Screw the backs to the cases.** The backs fully overlap the case sides, tops, and bottoms (but not the outer sides or spacers), as shown in *Top View.* Draw center lines indicating the position of each fixed shelf (and vertical dividers for the center case) onto the back of the backs. Predrill holes and screw on the backs using #8 × 1-inch drywall screws.

Make the Doors

All the doors are joined using cope-and-stick joints cut with a cope-and-stick router-bit set. Cope-and-stick joinery is illustrated in *Typical Cope-and-Stick Door Construction.* The bottom and middle doors are frame-and-panel construction, the center cabinet top doors have textured glass, and the side cabinet top doors get speaker-cloth–wrapped panels.

Note that some cope-and-stick cutter sets are designed to make both kinds of doors (grooved and rabbeted), but some are designed to cut the panel groove only. With the latter type, you can improvise to make both types of doors by routing away the lip on the back edge of the door, thereby turning a groove into a rabbet.

1 **Rout the sticking cut.** Rout the sticking cut, or edge profile, on the inside edge of all the rails and stiles and on both edges of the muntins. Use a featherboard to hold the frame parts tightly to the table, as shown in the photo at right.

Note that the upper doors all get rabbets instead of panel grooves. The rabbet holds either glass or the speaker panel, as shown in *Door Detail,* instead of a solid raised panel.

Rout the sticking cut profile on the edge of all the parts and on both edges of the muntins. The featherboard ensures a consistent profile.

Quick tip

When using a cope-and-stick router bit set, it's a good idea to go through the entire process of setting up and making each cut on extra pieces of stock. That way you'll be familiar with the process and will get good results when cutting the real door stock.

Typical Cope-and-Stick Door Construction

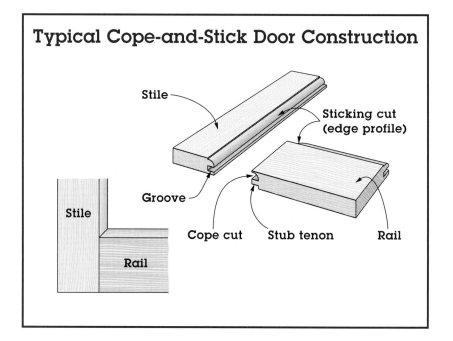

Stile

Sticking cut (edge profile)

Groove

Cope cut   Stub tenon   Rail

Stile

Rail

2 **Rout the cope cut.** Reset the cutters to make the cope cut. Start by coping the edge of a wide board—a backer board—that will cradle the profiled edge of each rail as it's fed past the cutter, as shown in the top photo on page 180. The backer board prevents the profiled edge from tearing out and also acts like a miter gauge by keeping the workpiece square to the fence. Reset the cope cutter for the rabbeted upper door parts, and cope all their ends.

3 **Raise the panels.** I used a horizontal panel-raising bit to raise the panels, as shown in the bottom photo on page 180. Attach a high auxiliary fence to the router table fence to support the panel stock, and remove the waste in light passes. See "Routing Raised Panels" on page 14.

4 **Sand and finish the panel bevels.** It's much easier to sand and finish the panel bevels before they're surrounded by the frame. Finish the profile to ensure that when the wooden panels shrink the newly exposed wood will not stand out as unfinished.

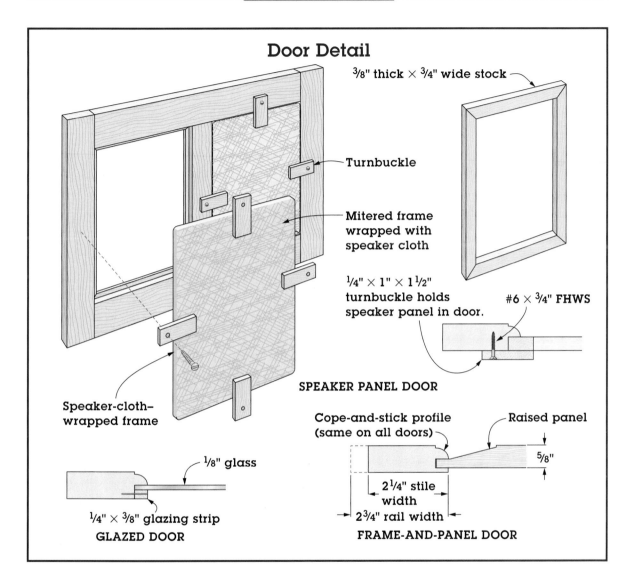

Door Detail

3/8" thick × 3/4" wide stock

Turnbuckle

Mitered frame
wrapped with
speaker cloth

1/4" × 1" × 1 1/2"
turnbuckle holds
speaker panel in door.

#6 × 3/4" FHWS

SPEAKER PANEL DOOR

Speaker-cloth–
wrapped frame

1/8" glass

1/4" × 3/8" glazing strip

GLAZED DOOR

Cope-and-stick profile
(same on all doors)

Raised panel

5/8"

2 1/4" stile
width

2 3/4" rail width

FRAME-AND-PANEL DOOR

5 **Assemble the doors.** Clamp the doors together on a flat surface, and sight across them with winding sticks to make sure they are flat.

6 **Make the speaker panels.** Mill strips of solid wood for the speaker panel frames, and miter them to the lengths given in the Materials List, checking the sizes against the actual openings in the door. The speaker frames should be

Make a backer board with a coped edge to cradle and support the rail stock as you guide the end of it past the router bit to cut the cope. The cope cut in the backer board interlocks with the sticking cut in the edge of the rail (see *inset*).

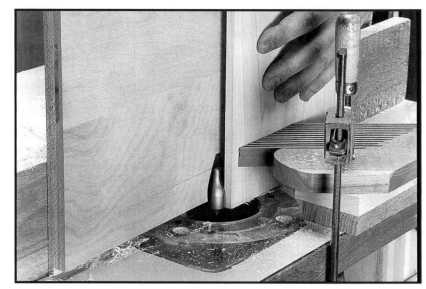

With a panel-raising bit in the router table, raise the panels in a series of light cuts, routing the ends of each panel first, then the long grain.

about $\frac{1}{8}$ inch smaller than the openings. Glue the frames together, and reinforce each corner with a brad, as shown in the photo at left on the opposite page. Then spray the frame with flat black spray paint so the wood won't show through the thin speaker cloth. After the paint is dry, wrap the frame with the speaker cloth, and staple it in place, as shown in the photo at right on the opposite page.

Secure the speaker panel frames with small brads.

Pull the speaker cloth tightly around the frame, and staple it into the back of the frame.

Hang the Doors

The door parts are dimensioned so the assembled doors match their openings exactly. I fit each door individually, aiming for a heavy $\frac{1}{16}$-inch gap all around the doors. I used European hinges because they can be finely adjusted to equalize the gaps around each door.

1 **Trim the doors to fit their openings.** Check the fit of the doors in their openings, and then trim them to fit. To do this, first take a jointing cut from each stile to get the finished door width. (You could also joint one edge, then rip the other edge.) Then crosscut the bottom and top edges of the doors on the table saw, taking just a slight cut. You may need to fine-tune the fit with a block plane after hanging the doors.

2 **Drill the hinge mortises.** Drill the hinge mortises in the doors with a 32-mm Forstner or multispur bit in a drill press. Always read and follow the specifications of the hinge you're using because hinges from different manufac-

Quick tip

European hinges have three advantages over butt hinges: The hinges are quick and easy to mount; they are adjustable in three directions, which makes it easier to get consistent gaps all around the doors; and most manufacturers make a clip-on style—the doors snap on and off in an instant once the two parts of the hinge are mounted.

turers may vary slightly. Cut a 4-inch-wide strip of scrap wood to the same length as one of the doors, and hinge it as a test piece for getting the hinge mortise just right. Then drill all the hinge mortises, as shown in the photo below, with a fence attached to your drill press table. When the fence is set up correctly, draw offset marks on it to indicate the ends of the stiles.

3 Screw on the hinges, and mount the doors. Screw the hinges to the doors, and connect the hinge plates to the hinges. Position each door in its opening, using $\frac{1}{16}$-inch shims underneath to compensate for the gap. Then reach inside the cabinet and screw the hinge plates to the cabinet side. Adjust the hinges so that there's consistent spacing around the doors.

4 Hang the pocket doors. A pocket door slide combines a drawer slide with a hinge (typically a European hinge). The door swings on the hinge, which is mounted to the slide. Mounting this hardware as a unit is little different from mounting each of these pieces of hardware separately. Specifications vary, so follow the instructions that come with the slides carefully. I used BLUM brand pocket door slides.

5 Screw on the door stops. The bottom and top doors on the center cabinet close against the vertical dividers. All the other doors need a stop to prevent them from closing beyond 90 degrees. (Stops are necessary with "self-closing" hinges; if you prefer, you can use "free-swinging" hinges and install magnetic or mechanical catches to stop the doors and hold them closed.)

Cut the stops from $\frac{1}{4}$-inch-thick stock, and round the corners. Add rubber door bumpers. Then predrill and countersink two holes for #6 × $\frac{3}{4}$-inch flathead wood screws in each stop. The stops attach to the back face of the fixed shelf edges, as shown in *Door Stop Detail* and *Front View*. Mount the stops for the top doors at the inside corners. Mount the other stops for paired doors centered in the openings so they stop both doors in each pair.

Drill the hinge mortises on the drill press, aligning the end of each door with the offset marks on the fence.

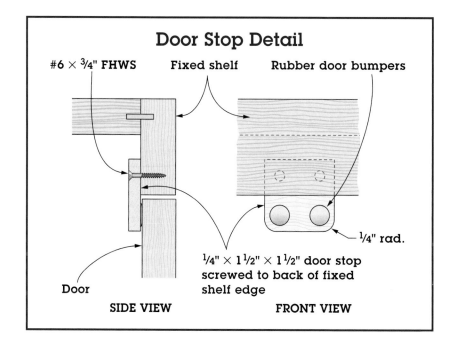

Door Stop Detail

#6 × ¾" FHWS   Fixed shelf   Rubber door bumpers

¼" rad.

¼" × 1½" × 1½" door stop
screwed to back of fixed
shelf edge

Door

SIDE VIEW   FRONT VIEW

6 **Drill bolt holes and attach the knobs.** Lay out knob
bolt holes centered along the length of the door stiles,
as shown in *Front View.* Choose a bit that is slightly larger in
diameter than the knob's bolt, and drill the holes. When the
holes have been drilled, screw the knobs in place.

Make and Hang the Drawers

I made the drawers from plywood, since there was plenty
left over from the cases. I trimmed the plywood with the same
veneer edge-banding tape I used on the adjustable shelves. Because the drawers are concealed behind the doors, I didn't
apply a false front to conceal the drawer slides, but you could
add one if you want. You could also make more or fewer
drawers, depending on your needs.

Note that the drawer slides need to be mounted on blocking
so the drawers don't interfere with the door hinges, as shown
in *Front View.* Screw the blocking to the cabinet before veri-
fying the exact dimensions of the drawer parts. Alternately,

you could forget the blocking and hang the drawers only in the middle area of the cabinet where they would not interfere with the hinges.

1 **Cut out the drawer parts.** Cut the drawer parts to the sizes given in the Materials List.

2 **Cut the drawer joinery and apply the edge-banding.** Cut $\frac{1}{4} \times \frac{1}{4}$-inch grooves in the fronts, backs, and sides for the drawer bottoms. You can cut this groove on the table saw with two passes over the regular blade or with a $\frac{1}{4}$-inch-thick dado blade.

Next, apply a strip of veneer edge-banding tape to the top edges of the four parts and to the front edges of the sides. Then cut biscuit slots, as shown in *Drawer Construction*.

3 **Assemble the drawers.** Apply glue to the biscuits, slots, and grooves, and clamp the drawers together. Make sure they are flat and square.

4 **Screw the blocking to the cabinet sides.** Locate the drawers, as shown in *Front View.* Screw the drawer blocking to the cabinet side where necessary—the bottom of the blocking should be aligned with the bottom of the drawers, and the front of the blocking should be 1 inch back from the front edge of the case. Make sure the blocking is square to the front edge of the case. Note that the blocking is needed only on the hinge side of the door openings—two sides on the side cases, and one side on the center case.

5 **Attach the drawer slides, and mount the drawers.** Mount the drawer slides according to the instructions provided with the hardware. Use the bottom edge of the drawer and the bottom edge of the blocking as the reference points for mounting the slides.

6 **Drill holes and attach the drawer knobs.** Lay out knob screw holes centered on the drawer fronts. Choose a bit that is slightly larger in diameter than the knob's

Drawer Construction

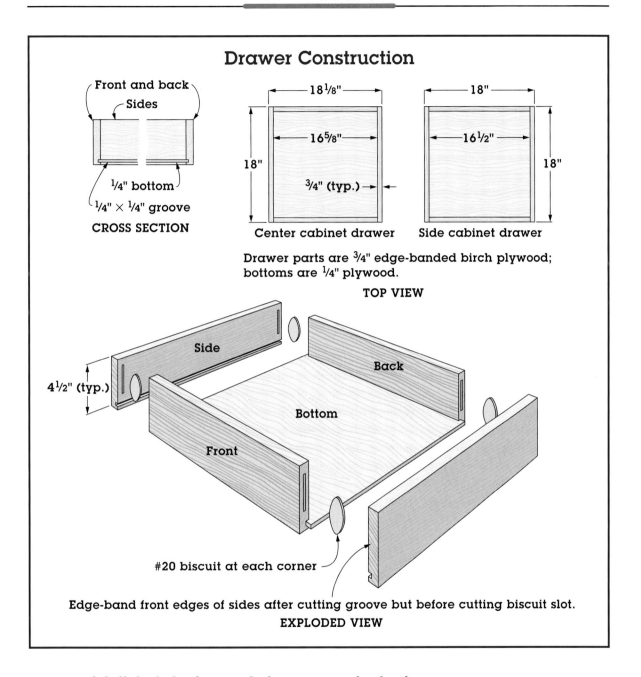

Front and back
Sides

1/4" bottom
1/4" × 1/4" groove

CROSS SECTION

18 1/8"
16 5/8"
18"
3/4" (typ.)

Center cabinet drawer

18"
16 1/2"
18"

Side cabinet drawer

Drawer parts are 3/4" edge-banded birch plywood; bottoms are 1/4" plywood.

TOP VIEW

Side
Back
Bottom
4 1/2" (typ.)
Front

#20 biscuit at each corner

Edge-band front edges of sides after cutting groove but before cutting biscuit slot.

EXPLODED VIEW

screw, and drill the holes for 1-inch-diameter wooden knobs. These are pretty standard and should be available in your local hardware store. When the holes have been drilled, screw the knobs in place.

Cut and Apply the Molding

Because this project was to be painted, I purchased all the molding in clear pine at my local building-supply store. Of course, you can make your own, if you prefer, but I think buying it is a good shortcut. In any case, the profiles don't have to be identical to the ones in the drawings.

1 **Miter and attach the base molding.** Hold the front center base molding stock against the cabinet, mark the back side of the miter cut, then cut the miters. Secure the molding with 4d nails and glue, where shown in *Base Detail*. Work from the center around to each side, cutting and nailing the molding one piece at a time.

2 **Cut and attach the crown molding.** Start by ripping the required lengths of 2 × 4 blocking at the appropriate bevel for the crown molding you're using, as shown in *Crown Molding Detail*. It's typically—but not always—45 degrees. Miter the edges of the blocking on the table saw. Secure the blocking along the top edges of the cases with glue and #8 × 2¼-inch drywall screws, as shown in *Exploded View*.

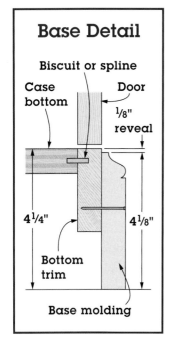

Base Detail

Biscuit or spline

Case bottom

Door

1/8" reveal

4¼"

4⅛"

Bottom trim

Base molding

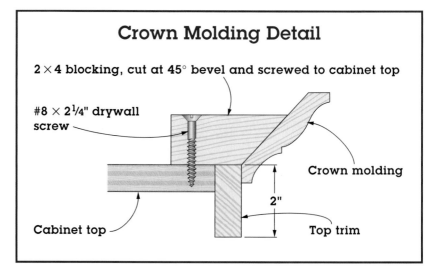

Crown Molding Detail

2 × 4 blocking, cut at 45° bevel and screwed to cabinet top

#8 × 2¼" drywall screw

Crown molding

Cabinet top

2"

Top trim

When the blocking is in place, miter the crown molding to fit around the case and blocking. Then, secure the molding with glue and 4d finish nails.

3 **Cut and apply the side panel molding.** This molding breaks up the large flat plane of the cabinet sides and gives the look of a framed panel without nearly as much work.

Locate and mark the corners of the molding frame on the cabinet sides, as shown in *Side Molding Detail*. Miter the moldings and position all four pieces with the cabinet lying on its side. Secure the molding to the cabinet with 4d finish nails and glue.

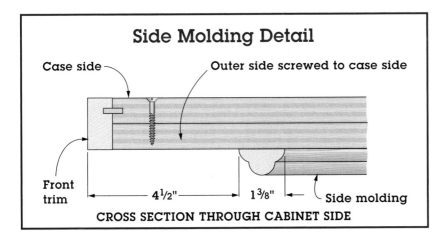

Side Molding Detail

Case side

Outer side screwed to case side

Front trim

4¹/₂" 1³/₈" Side molding

CROSS SECTION THROUGH CABINET SIDE

Finish the Cabinet

I painted the cabinet in a spray booth using a spray gun. This gives a very smooth result. I started with a coat of KILZ brand primer, added a shellac-based sealer, and then applied two coats of latex paint.

Use a clear finish such as shellac, wax, or a water-based finish on the drawers.

When the cabinet has been finished, have glass cut to fit the glass doors, and install it with glazing strips cut to the dimensions given in the Materials List. Secure the glazing strips with 1-inch brads.

Library, Den, and Office

Slant-Front Desk

by Kenneth S. Burton Jr.

As I was growing up, my mother's slant-front desk played a key role in keeping our family going. Its ample writing surface set the stage for paying bills, writing Christmas cards, and re-viewing book reports, while the drawers below held the family archives—baby books, diplomas, and numerous other treasures. The pigeonholes held all sorts of useful stuff like tape, stamps, and pencils, which, much to my mother's dismay, we all sort of viewed as community property. With so many fond memories of that piece of furniture, when I was given the chance to build such a desk, I leaped at the chance.

While this desk has the look of a piece of eighteenth-century furniture, it is not a reproduction. Rather it is an original interpretation that makes use of many of the design elements from that era. The dimensions evolved from a detailed study of several historic pieces, combined with a knowledge of what sorts of tasks would be done while seated at the writing surface. The pigeon-hole unit in particular was designed around the trappings of modern life—checkbook ledgers, business paper, and other office necessities.

Construction is fairly straightforward but involves some pretty heavy-duty woodworking. Handcut dovetails are what keep the case as well as all the drawers together, and the writing flap must be precisely made and fit to cover the opening. In all it is a challenging project, but the result is a piece of real, honest-to-goodness furniture that will last through generations of holiday greetings.

Exploded View

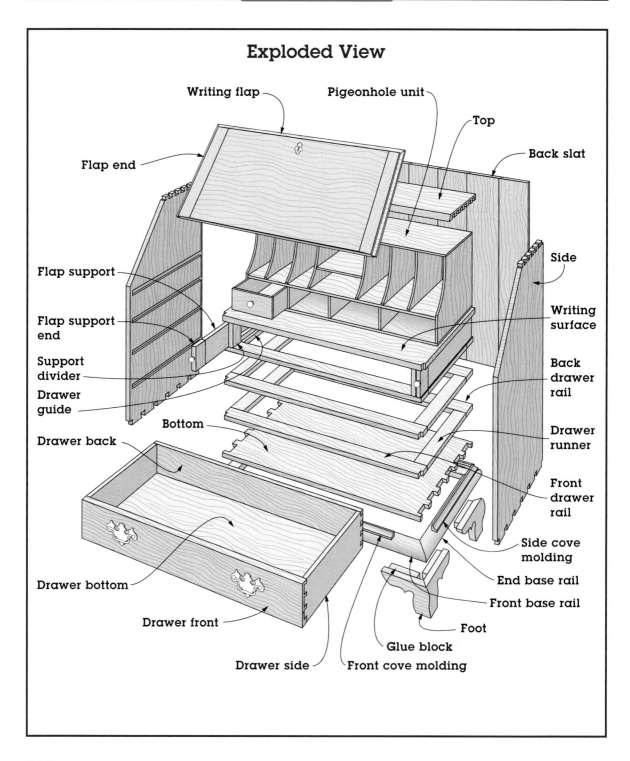

Writing flap

Pigeonhole unit

Top

Back slat

Flap end

Flap support

Flap support end

Support divider

Drawer guide

Side

Writing surface

Back drawer rail

Drawer runner

Front drawer rail

Bottom

Drawer back

Drawer bottom

Drawer front

Drawer side

Front cove molding

Glue block

Foot

Front base rail

End base rail

Side cove molding

Materials List

Part	Dimension	Part	Dimension
Case		**Pigeonhole Unit**	
Sides (2)	$^{13}/_{16}$" × $18^1/_8$" × $37^3/_{16}$"	Ends (2)	$^3/_8$" × $10^7/_8$" × 13"
Top	$^{13}/_{16}$" × $10^1/_{16}$" × 36"	Top	$^3/_8$" × $8^7/_8$" × $34^3/_8$"
Bottom	$^{13}/_{16}$" × $18^1/_8$" × 36"	Bottom	$^3/_8$" × $10^7/_8$" × $34^3/_8$"
Writing surface	1" × $17^5/_8$" × $35^1/_8$"	Long shelf	$^3/_8$" × $10^3/_8$" × $33^7/_8$"
Front/back drawer rails (6)	$^3/_4$" × 2" × $35^1/_8$"	Drawer dividers (3)	$^3/_8$" × $10^5/_8$" × $3^1/_8$"
Drawer runners (6)	$^3/_4$" × 2" × $13^5/_8$"	Dividers (6)	$^1/_4$" × $10^1/_8$" × $9^3/_8$"
Tenon stock	$^3/_8$" × $1^1/_4$" × 26"	Short shelf	$^3/_8$" × $8^5/_8$" × 10"
Support dividers (2)	$^5/_8$" × 2" × $4^3/_8$"	Back	$^1/_4$" × $12^5/_8$" × 34"
Drawer guides (2)	$^5/_8$" × $^3/_4$" × $13^5/_8$"	Top drawer front	$^5/_8$" × $2^1/_2$" × $9^3/_4$"
Back slats (8)	$^1/_2$" × $4^7/_8$" × $36^5/_8$"	Top drawer sides (2)	$^3/_8$" × $2^1/_2$" × $8^1/_4$"
Writing flap	$^7/_8$" × $15^9/_{16}$" × $31^5/_8$"	Top drawer back	$^3/_8$" × 2" × $9^3/_4$"
Flap ends (2)	$^7/_8$" × $2^1/_4$" × $15^9/_{16}$"	Top drawer bottom	$^1/_4$" × $8^1/_4$" × $9^3/_8$"
End base rails (2)	$^7/_8$" × $2^1/_2$" × $21^1/_8$"	Outside drawer fronts (2)	$^5/_8$" × $2^7/_8$" × 8"
Front/back base rails (2)	$^7/_8$" × $2^1/_2$" × 39"	Outside drawer backs (2)	$^3/_8$" × $2^7/_8$" × 8"
Base rail tenon stock	$^3/_8$" × $1^1/_4$" × 12"	Inside drawer fronts (2)	$^5/_8$" × $2^7/_8$" × $8^1/_4$"
Feet (8)	$1^1/_4$" × $5^1/_8$" × $9^1/_8$"	Inside drawer backs (2)	$^3/_8$" × $2^7/_8$" × $8^1/_4$"
Glue blocks (8)	$^3/_4$" × $^3/_4$" × 3"	Drawer sides (8)	$^3/_8$" × $2^7/_8$" × 10"
Foot tenon stock	$^1/_2$" × $3^1/_2$" × 12"	Outside drawer bottoms (2)	$^1/_4$" × 10" × $7^5/_8$"
Cove molding stock	$^3/_4$" × $^{13}/_{16}$" × 11'	Inside drawer bottoms (2)	$^1/_4$" × 10" × $7^7/_8$"
Top drawer front	$^7/_8$" × $3^7/_8$" × $31^7/_8$"	Drawer stops (5)	$^1/_8$" × $^1/_2$" × 2"
Top drawer sides (2)	$^1/_2$" × $3^7/_8$" × 17"		
Top drawer back	$^1/_2$" × $3^1/_4$" × $31^7/_8$"	**Hardware**	
Top drawer bottom	$^3/_8$" × $16^3/_4$" × $31^3/_8$"	#12 × $1^1/_2$" roundhead wood screws with washers (4)	
Second drawer front	$^7/_8$" × $4^3/_{16}$" × $34^3/_8$"	#8 × $1^5/_8$" drywall screws (as needed)	
Second drawer sides (2)	$^1/_2$" × $4^3/_{16}$" × 17"	#8 × $1^1/_4$" flathead wood screws (as needed)	
Second drawer back	$^1/_2$" × $3^9/_{16}$" × $34^3/_8$"	#6 × 1" flathead wood screws (2)	
Third drawer front	$^7/_8$" × $4^7/_8$" × $34^3/_8$"	3d cut finish nails (as needed)	
Third drawer sides (2)	$^1/_2$" × $4^7/_8$" × 17"	2d finish nails, 1" brads (as needed)	
Third drawer back	$^1/_2$" × $4^1/_4$" × $34^3/_8$"	Brass flap hinges with screws (2). Available from Woodcraft Supply Corp., 210 Wood County Industrial Park, P.O. Box 1686, Parkersburg, WV 26102-1686; (800) 225-1153; part #16Q62	
Fourth drawer front	$^7/_8$" × $6^3/_8$" × $34^3/_8$"		
Fourth drawer sides (2)	$^1/_2$" × $6^3/_8$" × 17"	3" Chippendale drawer pulls (8). Available from Ball and Ball, 463 W. Lincoln Highway, Exton, PA 19341; (610) 363-7330; part #C2-010	
Fourth drawer back	$^1/_2$" × $5^3/_4$" × $34^3/_8$"		
Drawer bottoms (3)	$^3/_8$" × $16^3/_4$" × $33^7/_8$"	$^1/_2$" dia. knobs (7). Available from Ball and Ball; part #G17-135	
Drawer stops (8)	$^1/_8$" × $^3/_4$" × 2"		
Flap support ends (2)	$^5/_8$" × 3" × $3^7/_8$"	Desk lock and escutcheon. Available from Ball and Ball; parts #TAB-001 and #L98	
Flap supports (2)	$^5/_8$" × $3^7/_8$" × 14"		
Support stops (2)	$^1/_4$" dia. × $1^1/_8$"		

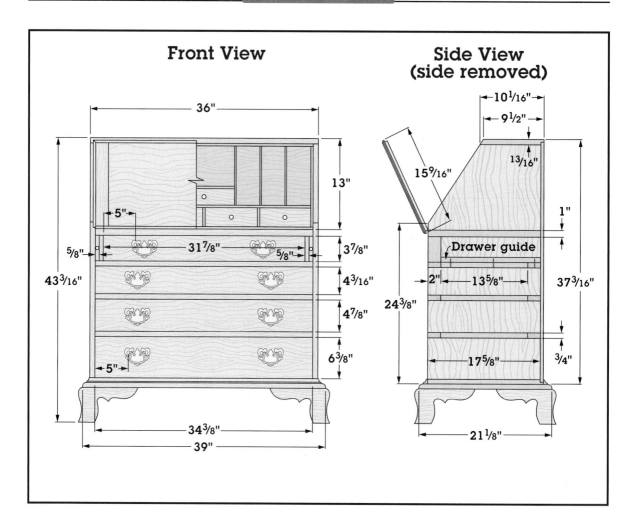

Front View

36"

13"

5"

5/8" 31⁷/₈" 5/8" 3⁷/₈"

43³/₁₆" 4³/₁₆"

4⁷/₈"

6³/₈"

5"

34³/₈"

39"

**Side View
(side removed)**

10¹/₁₆"

9¹/₂"

13/16"

15⁹/₁₆"

1"

Drawer guide

2" 13⁵/₈" 37³/₁₆"

24³/₈"

17⁵/₈" 3/4"

21¹/₈"

Make the Case

The visible parts of the desk's case were made from solid cherry; the drawer frames, drawer parts, and back were made from soft maple. The main pieces of the case (top, sides, bottom) are dovetailed together. Then the writing surface and drawer frames are dadoed into the sides.

1 **Cut the case joinery.** Surface and glue up panels wide enough for the case sides, top, and bottom. Cut the pieces to the sizes given in the Materials List. Then lay out the diagonal cut on each of the sides, as shown in *Side View*. Make the cuts on the band saw, staying ⅛ inch or so away from the line to allow for trimming later. Lay out the pins for the dovetail joints on the ends of the top and bottom, as shown in *Case Dovetail Detail*.

Cut along the layout lines with a dovetail saw, and chop out the waste with a sharp chisel. Hold the top and bottom in place on the sides, and trace around the pins to lay out the tails on the sides. Cut out the tails and fit the joints together. For more information on cutting dovetails, see "Cutting Dovetails" on page 164.

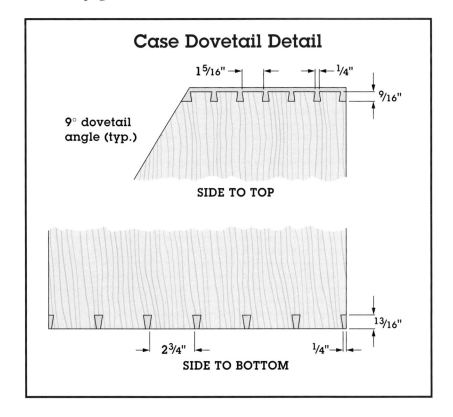

Case Dovetail Detail

1⁵/₁₆"   ¼"   ⁹/₁₆"

9° dovetail
angle (typ.)

SIDE TO TOP

13/16"

2¾"   ¼"

SIDE TO BOTTOM

2 **Dado the case sides.** Lay out the dadoes for the writing surface and the drawer frames on the sides, as shown in *Front View*. Mount a 1-inch straight bit in a hand-held router, and rout the dadoes for the writing surface, guiding the router along a shop-made T-square, as shown in

Two pieces of scrap wood screwed together perpendicular to one another make a useful router guide. After you use the jig the first time, you'll have routed dadoes in the crosspiece that will help you align the jig on the work.

the photo at left. Switch to a ¾-inch straight bit, and rout the dadoes for the drawer frames. Note that all the dadoes should be ⅜ inch deep and should stop ¼ inch from the front edge.

3 **Make the writing surface.** Assemble the desk case so you can get an accurate dado-to-dado measurement to determine the length of the writing surface. Plane the stock for the surface until it fits snugly in the appropriate dadoes, then edge-glue the pieces to make up a wide enough panel. When the glue dries, cut the panel to the size given in the Materials List, adjusting the length if necessary.

4 **Make the drawer frames.** Plane the stock for the drawer runners and rails until they fit snugly in the dadoes. Cut the pieces to the sizes listed in the Materials List; the length of the front and back rails should match that of the writing surface. Assemble the frames with loose tenon joints, as shown in *Drawer Frame Detail*. With loose tenon joints, both of the adjoining pieces are mortised and a separate tenon piece is cut to fit in between. The tenons can be made from a secondary wood, if desired, because they won't be seen.

First, lay out and rout the mortises with a ⅜-inch-diameter straight bit in a plunge router. Rout the mortises in several passes, lowering the bit a little each time. To support the stock while you cut the mortises, consider making the simple jig shown in *Mortising Jig*. Clamping the jig and the stock in a bench vise (see the photo on page 201) supports the stock while providing a wide surface for the router.

Next, relieve the edges of the tenon stock (its dimensions are given in the Materials List) with a spokeshave or sandpaper so that it will fit into the rounded ends of the mortises. Cut individual tenons to equal the combined depth of the mortises minus about ¹⁄₁₆ inch.

Once the joints are cut, glue the frames together. Measure across the diagonals to make sure each frame is square. (The diagonal measurements should be equal.)

After the glue dries, notch the front corners of the frames as well as the front corners of the writing surface to fit in the

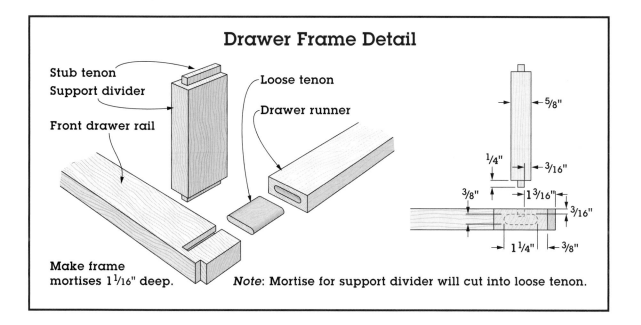

Drawer Frame Detail

Stub tenon

Support divider

Front drawer rail

Loose tenon

Drawer runner

5/8"

1/4"

3/16"

3/8"

1 3/16"

3/16"

1 1/4"

3/8"

**Make frame
mortises 1 1/16" deep.**

Note: **Mortise for support divider will cut into loose tenon.**

stopped dadoes. Hold the pieces on edge against the miter gauge of the table saw. (You might want to attach a 6-inch-wide × 36-inch-long auxiliary fence to the gauge for added support.) Set the saw blade height at 1/4 inch, and make several passes to complete the notches.

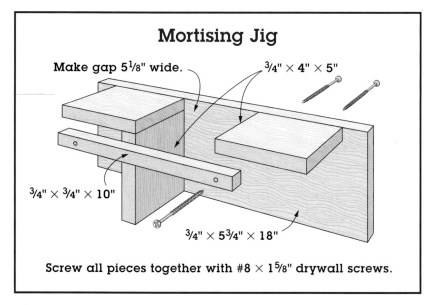

Mortising Jig

Make gap 5 1/8" wide.

3/4" × 4" × 5"

3/4" × 3/4" × 10"

3/4" × 5 3/4" × 18"

Screw all pieces together with #8 × 1 5/8" drywall screws.

Rather than trying to find a router bit that makes the exact width of rabbet you're after, use a fairly large diameter (1 inch or so) straight bit instead. Chuck the bit in a table-mounted router, and set up a fence with a cutout that allows you to bury part of the bit behind the guiding surface. To cut your rabbet, position the fence to expose only the amount of bit you need.

5 **Cut the support divider joinery.** The support dividers must be mortised into the underside of the writing surface and the top of the uppermost drawer frame. Lay out the $\frac{1}{4}$-inch-wide × $1\frac{1}{2}$-inch-long × $\frac{1}{4}$-inch-deep mortises, as shown in *Drawer Frame Detail*. Cut the mortises with a $\frac{1}{4}$-inch straight bit in a plunge router. Guide the router with its edge guide.

Cut the dividers to the size given in the Materials List. Cut two rabbets on each end to create the stub tenons that fit into the mortises you just routed. Trim the stub tenons away from the edge of the dividers to complete the tenons.

6 **Attach the drawer guides.** Clamp the support dividers in their mortises in the drawer frame. Their front edges should be flush with the front edge of the frame. Screw the drawer guides to the frame directly behind the supports with #8 × $1\frac{1}{4}$-inch flathead wood screws, as shown in *Side View*. Check to make sure the distance between the guides remains consistent from front to back.

7 **Rabbet the case for the back.** While you have the case together, rout a $\frac{1}{2}$-inch-deep rabbet around the back edges for the case back. Cut the rabbet in several light passes with a $\frac{3}{8}$-inch rabbeting bit in a handheld router, as shown in the photo on the opposite page. The router will leave the corners of the rabbet round where the parts meet. Cut these square with a sharp chisel.

8 **Assemble the case.** Gluing up a case this large and complex is tricky and can be stressful. You may want to enlist some dependable help or at least wait until you're fresh and well rested before tackling the job. Take the case apart, and sand all the inside surfaces that will be visible after the desk is finished. Apply glue to the dovetails on one side, and place it on your assembly table (or on the floor) with the dadoes facing up. Put an old towel or a scrap of carpet under the side to avoid marring its surface. Apply glue to the pins on the top and bottom, and start them into their mating sockets.

Apply glue to the dadoes that will hold the writing surface and to the front 3 inches of the drawer frame dadoes. (You don't want to glue the frames all the way across, or you'll prevent the side from expanding and contracting with changes in humidity.) Slide the writing surface and the frames into their respective dadoes. Also apply glue to the tenons on the support dividers, and slip them in place while you can still spread apart the writing surface and the first drawer frame.

Once all the pieces are in place, apply glue to the joints on the second side and the pins on the top and bottom. Flip the second side over and put it in place, driving the joints home with a mallet if necessary. This last step should be done as quickly as possible to avoid glue drips. Once the case is together, turn it upright and clamp the joints tight. Measure the diagonals to check that the case is square. If necessary, you can adjust the positions of the clamps to square the case.

9 **Make and attach the back.** The back is made traditionally of individual, shiplapped boards secured with nails. Cut the pieces to the sizes given in the Materials List, leaving one of the pieces about 1 inch wide for now. Rabbet both sides of six of the pieces, as shown in *Shiplap Detail—Top View.*

On the remaining two pieces (one of which should be the wide one), rabbet only one side, as shown. These two pieces go at each side of the back. Sand the pieces, breaking any sharp corners along the rabbets. Start attaching the back pieces by nailing one of the single-rabbeted pieces (not the wide one) along one side of the case. Use three 3d cut finish nails per slat: one into the rabbet in the top, one into the rabbet in the bottom, and one into the back edge of the writing surface. Place the nails near the nonrabbeted edge as shown, predrilling the holes to avoid splitting. Nail the next piece in place alongside the first, leaving a slight gap (a thin $1/16$ inch) between the pieces to allow for expansion. Again, use three nails to hold the piece, as shown. Continue in this manner until you are ready to install the last piece (the wide one). Trim the piece to fit the opening, and nail it in place, as shown, using six nails.

Because the rabbet for the case back must stop before it reaches the ends of the pieces, it is easier to rout it with a piloted rabbeting bit when the case is assembled. This way the case itself serves as a stop for the bit. Clamp a straight piece of wood along the outside of the case to give the router a surface on which to ride.

Shiplap Detail—Top View

Install this piece last, trimming
to fill remaining space.

Note: Leave a little space (¹/₁₆") between
slats as you install them to allow back
to move with changes in humidity.

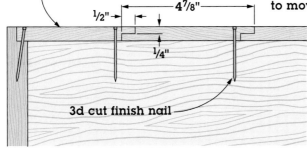
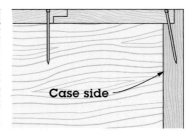

½" ← → 4⁷/₈" ←

¼"

3d cut finish nail

Case side

All slats except last one are attached with 3 nails driven close to overlapping edge.
Last slat is nailed in place with 6 nails, 3 along each edge.

10 **Glue up the writing flap.** Edge-glue a number of
narrow pieces to make up a panel wide enough for the
writing flap. If possible, choose quartersawn material, as it
tends to stay flatter. However, if all you have is flatsawn, you
shouldn't have a problem if you just cut the pieces down so
they are less than 4 inches wide. While you are cutting up this
material, also surface two pieces for the flap ends. Once the
glue dries, cut the panel to the size given in the Materials List,
and sand it smooth.

11 **Cut the writing flap joinery.** The flap ends are attached to the writing flap with tongue-and-groove
joints. Set up a ¼-inch-wide dado blade, and cut the grooves
in the flap ends, as shown in *Writing Flap Cross Section*. The
tongues on the ends of the flap are also cut on the table saw,
but the process is a little more complex.

Screw a 10-inch-wide piece of plywood to the saw fence to
make it taller. Set up a ½-inch-wide (approximately) dado
blade on the saw, and lower it completely below the table surface. Move the fence over so that when you raise the blade it
will cut into the plywood piece, leaving one side of the blade
exposed. Lock the fence in position, turn on the saw, and raise

the blade up into the plywood about ¾ inch. Turn off the saw, and reposition the fence to expose ¼ inch of the dado blade. Set the depth of cut to ½ inch. Stand the writing flap on end, and guide it past the blade with its outside face against the tall fence. Repeat the process with the second end. Also make the same cut on a piece of scrap wood so you'll have a piece on which to test the next setup. Mark on the scrap which face you ran against the fence.

To cut the second side of the tongues, move the fence over until it is a little more than ½ inch away from the blade. Make a cut on the test piece. Again, the marked face should be against the fence. The resulting tongue should be slightly too big for the grooves in the flap ends. Bump the fence over a little, and make another test cut. Keep moving the fence until the tongue fits snugly in the groove. Make the cuts on the ends of the flap. Note that by using the same face of the flap as a reference for both cuts, you can be sure the tongue will be a consistent thickness. If you try to make the cuts from both sides, any variation in the flap's thickness will be transferred to the tongue.

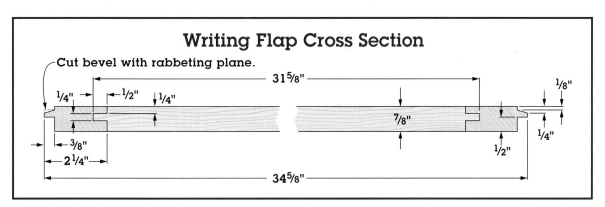

Writing Flap Cross Section

Cut bevel with rabbeting plane.

12 **Assemble the writing flap.** The flap ends are glued to the flap itself. But to prevent problems with expansion and contraction, apply glue only to the center 3 inches of the tongue-and-groove joints. This will leave the flap free to move across its width with changes in humidity. Clamp the joints tight and allow the glue to dry. After removing the clamps, sand the flap and the ends flush.

When mounting brass hardware, attach it initially with steel screws rather than brass ones. The steel screws will cut the threads and stand up to repeated insertion and removal far better than brass screws will. Switch to brass screws when you screw the hardware in place for the final time.

13 **Shape the flap.** Cut a rabbet around three sides of the inside surface of the writing flap with a rabbeting bit in a table-mounted router. The exact dimensions are shown in *Writing Flap Cross Section*. Leave uncut the edge that will be hinged to the writing surface. Also cut a decorative profile around all four edges on the outside surface of the flap as shown. To create the profile shown, I first cut a $\frac{1}{8}$-inch-deep rabbet on three top edges of the writing flap and then cut the bevel with a sharp rabbeting plane. While you're shaping the flap, also bevel the front edge of the case top with a block plane to match the angle of the sides.

14 **Attach the writing flap.** Locate the flap hinges on the writing flap, 5 inches in from each side. Hold each hinge in place with its leaves open and its barrel centered over the unrabbeted edge of the flap. Trace around the leaves with a marking knife to lay out the hinge mortises. Chuck a $\frac{3}{8}$-inch straight bit in your router, and set the depth of cut to match the thickness of the hinge's leaf. Rout away the bulk of the waste from the mortises, then square them up with a sharp chisel. Screw the hinges in place.

Next, prop the flap in its open position against the edge of the writing surface on a pair of sawhorses. Open the hinges, and check to make sure the barrel is centered on the seam between the flap and the writing surface. Trace around the leaves with a marking knife to lay out their mortises on the writing surface. Set the flap aside, and rout and chisel the mortises as you did before. Screw the hinges in place and check the action of the flap. You may have to plane the angle on the desk sides slightly to get a perfect fit.

Make the Base

1 **Prepare the stock.** Cut the base rails and the feet to the thickness and width given in the Materials List. Leave the pieces 1 inch or so on the long side for now to allow for mitering and shaping.

2 **Cut the frame joinery.** Miter the ends of the base rails by angling the miter gauge on the table saw, cutting the pieces to the right length in the process. Join the corners with loose tenon joints as you did for the drawer frames. The only difference is that you'll have to modify your mortising jig slightly to hold the pieces at the correct angle, as shown in the photo below left. The dimensions for the joints are shown in *Base Frame Detail*. Rout the mortises in the faces of the miters, and cut the tenon stock to fit. Cut the tenons to the appropriate length, and glue the frame together. To get the joints to draw up tight, clamp them in both directions, as shown in the photo below right.

When mortising mitered stock, the mortises must be cut perpendicular to the faces of the miters.

Clamp the mitered base frame together as shown, and measure diagonally across the corners to make sure the base is square.

3 **Rout the screw slots for attaching the base.** When you screw the base to the case, you'll have do so in a way that will allow the case to expand and contract with changes in humidity. The easiest way to do this is to run the screws through elongated holes, or slots. Chuck a ¼-inch straight bit in a table-mounted router, and rout these slots in several shallow passes. The placement of the slots is shown in *Base Frame Detail*.

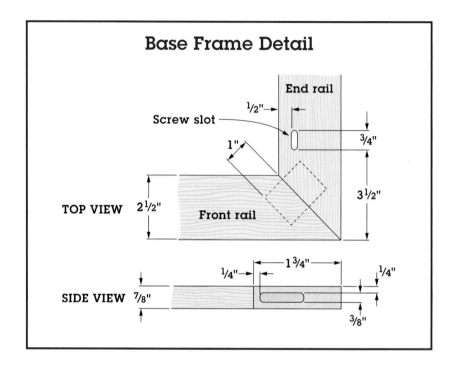

Base Frame Detail

End rail

Screw slot

$1/2"$

$3/4"$

$1"$

TOP VIEW $2^{1}/_{2}"$ Front rail $3^{1}/_{2}"$

SIDE VIEW $^{7}/_{8}"$ $^{1}/_{4}"$ $1^{3}/_{4}"$ $^{1}/_{4}"$

$^{3}/_{8}"$

④ Miter the feet. The feet are mitered and tenoned together, as shown in *Foot Detail*. Tilt the blade on the table saw to 45 degrees, and miter the ends of the foot blanks, cutting them to length in the process. The mortises in the feet run across the width of the miter faces rather than along the length. To cut these mortises, clamp the feet with the miter facing up in a bench vise. Then clamp a straightedge to the bench to guide the router, as shown in the photo on the opposite page. Rout the mortises, then cut the tenon stock to fit.

⑤ Shape the feet. From ¼-inch plywood, make a template that matches the foot silhouette shown in *Foot Detail*. Trace the silhouette onto the blanks, and cut the pieces to shape on the band saw. Sand and file the pieces to smooth away the saw marks and true the curves.

⑥ Assemble the feet. The best way to guarantee that a miter joint will go together tightly is to apply clamping pressure directly perpendicular to the mating surfaces. In order

Foot Detail

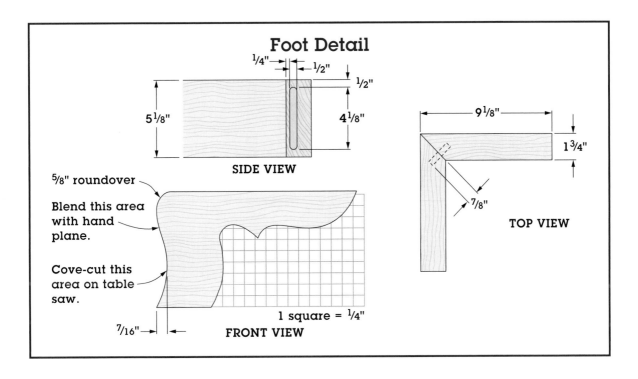

1/4" 1/2"

1/2"

5 1/8"

4 1/8"

SIDE VIEW

9 1/8"

1 3/4"

7/8"

TOP VIEW

5/8" roundover

Blend this area with hand plane.

Cove-cut this area on table saw.

1 square = 1/4"

7/16"

FRONT VIEW

Routing the mortises in the feet calls for a mortising setup that provides a straightedge along which to run the router. Clamp the feet with the miter facing up in a bench vise. Then clamp a straightedge to the work bench to guide the router.

Angled glue blocks
allow pressure to be ap-
plied directly across a
miter joint.

to be able to apply pressure this way to the feet, you'll have to glue some angled clamping blocks to the foot blanks, as shown in the photo at left. Once the clamp blocks are secure, spread glue in the mortises, on the tenons, and on the miter faces. Clamp the pieces together. When the glue dries, you can split the blocks off with a chisel and a mallet.

7 **Cove the feet.** After the feet are glued up, you can cut them to their final shape, as shown in *Foot Detail*. Round-over the top edges with a ⅝-inch roundover bit in a table-mounted router. While you have the router set up, also round-over the top outside edge of the bottom frame.

Next, cove the faces by feeding the foot across the table saw at an angle, as described in "Cove Cutting on the Table Saw" on page 24. Scrape and sand the sawed surfaces.

8 **Attach the feet.** Glue the feet to the underside of the base frame. The outside edges of the feet should be offset from the edges of the frame by ¾ inch, as shown in *Base Cross Section*. After the glue dries, add glue blocks to the underside of the frame as shown to strengthen the joints.

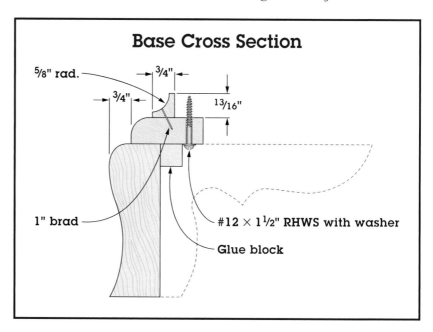

Base Cross Section

⅝" rad.

¾"

¾"

13/16"

1" brad

#12 × 1½" RHWS with washer

Glue block

9 **Attach the base.** Place the case on its back on a set of sawhorses. Have a helper hold the base in position while you drill ⅛-inch pilot holes for the screws through the slots. Screw the base to the case with #12 × 1½-inch round-head wood screws and washers.

10 **Make the cove molding.** As a finishing touch to the base, attach a small cove molding to serve as a transition between the base frame and the case. Rather than cutting the molding to the exact size specified before shaping it, start with a piece of wood of the appropriate length that has been planed to the correct thickness but that is about 6 inches wide. Rout the cove profile on both edges of the board with a table-mounted router, then rip the moldings to the proper width on the table saw. Repeat the procedure to make the other pair of moldings. Cutting moldings in this manner is much safer than trying to rout thin strips of wood, where your fingers might get uncomfortably close to the spinning bit.

11 **Attach the molding.** Cut the moldings to wrap around the case, mitering the corners as you go. Nail the pieces in place with 1-inch brads, as shown in *Base Cross Section*.

Make the Drawers

1 **Prepare the stock.** Measure the case, and double-check the sizes of the drawer openings compared to the sizes given in the Materials List for the drawer parts. The width of the parts should be just a little (a thin ¹⁄₁₆ inch) less than the height of the drawer openings, and the length of the front and back should be slightly (about ¹⁄₃₂ inch) less than the width of the opening. Make any necessary adjustments to the Materials List dimensions, and cut the pieces to size. If you opt to use solid-wood drawer bottoms as specified, edge glue narrower pieces together to make up panels wide enough.

2 **Cut the corner joinery.** Lay out the pins for the dovetail joints, as shown in *Drawer Detail*. When you scribe the shoulder line, set your marking gauge $1/64$ inch *less* than the thickness of the sides. When you assemble the drawers, the sides will be slightly proud of the pin ends. Once you have planed them flush, the drawer should be a perfect side-to-side fit in its opening.

Cut along the layout lines with a dovetail saw, and remove the waste with a sharp chisel. Transfer the layout to the drawer sides by holding the front and back in position and tracing around the pins with a sharp knife. Saw out the tails, chop away the waste, and pare the joints until they fit. For more on cutting dovetails, see "Cutting Dovetails" on page 164.

3 **Add the drawer bottoms.** On your router table, rout a $1/4$-inch groove for the drawer bottoms in the drawer fronts and the drawer sides, as shown in *Drawer Detail*. (The drawer backs are cut down so the bottoms can be slipped in from the rear after the drawer is assembled.) Rabbet the ends and front edge of the drawer bottoms to fit in the grooves.

4 **Assemble the drawers.** Starting with the top drawer, spread glue on the sides of the pins and tails, and push the joints together. Put a dab of glue in the groove in the drawer front, and slide the bottom into place. Clamp the drawer from side to side to completely seat the dovetails. (Another advantage of leaving the sides slightly proud of the pin ends is that you can clamp the joints up without having to make special clamping blocks that fit over the pin ends.) Check to make sure the diagonals are equal, meaning the drawer is square. Glue up all the other drawers one by one.

5 **Fit the drawers.** When the glue dries, remove the clamps and plane the drawer sides flush with the ends of the front and back. Check the fit of the drawer in its opening. It should slide right in; but if it doesn't, plane the sides some more to remove any high spots. Keep fussing with it until the drawer slides in perfectly.

Drawer Detail

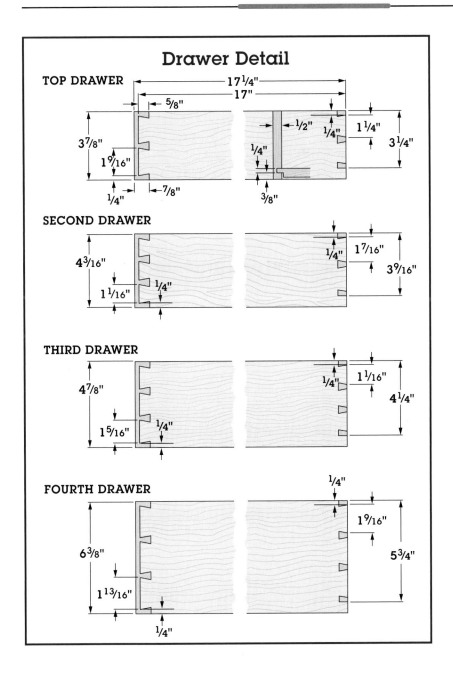

6 **Add the drawer stops.** The drawer stops get glued to the front rails of the drawer frames. Measure the thickness of the drawer fronts and set this distance off along the rails. Cut the drawer stops to the size given in the Materials

List, and glue them in place slightly in front of the line you just drew on the rails. It is easier to remove a little of the stop later than it is to add it if the stop is set too far in. When the glue dries, try the drawers to see if they stop where you want them to. If necessary, trim the stops with a rabbeting plane.

7 **Make the flap supports.** Cut the flap supports and the flap support ends to the sizes given in the Materials List. Join the pieces with loose tenon joints as you did with the drawer frames. The joinery layout is shown in *Support Detail*.

Check the fit of the supports in their slots, and trim the supports if necessary. To keep the supports from being pulled out too far, you'll have to add stops to them once they're in position. Pull the supports out so they extend 14 inches from the front edge of the writing surface. Remove the top drawer from the case, and set it aside. Reach inside the drawer opening, and mark the supports along the back edge of the support dividers. Pull the supports out and drill a ¼-inch hole through each support. The holes should be centered from top to bottom and tangent to the line you just drew. Put the supports back in their slots, and slip a snug-fitting length of ¼-inch dowel through each of the holes. The dowels will bump against the back of the support divider, preventing the support from being pulled out too far. The dowels are removable, however, so you can get the supports out if you need to.

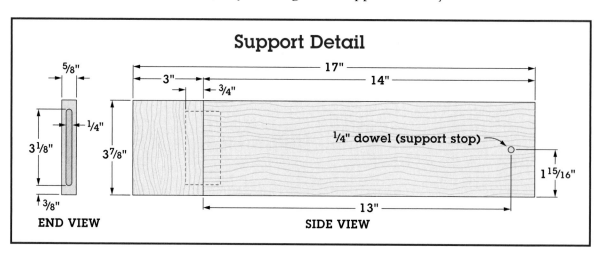

Support Detail

END VIEW

SIDE VIEW

¼" dowel (support stop)

Make the Pigeonhole Unit

1 **Prepare the stock.** The pigeonhole unit is a separate assembly that fits inside the main case. To make getting it into the case easier, make it $\frac{1}{16}$ inch smaller than the opening in both height and width. Start by measuring the opening in the top of the desk. Compare the measurements to those given in the Materials List, and note any necessary changes. Cut all the parts except for the drawers to size. Edge-glue narrower boards to make up the wide pieces.

2 **Cut the corner joinery.** The corners of the pigeonhole unit are dovetailed together. Lay out the curves on the ends, as shown in *Pigeonhole Unit—Cross Section,* but don't make the cuts until after you've cut all the joinery. Lay out the dovetail pins on the ends of the top and bottom, as shown in *Pigeonhole Joinery Detail.* Saw along the lines and chop out the waste as you did with the main case joints. Lay out the tails by tracing around the pins. Saw and chop away the waste as usual. Pare the joints to a perfect fit.

3 **Cut the dadoes.** The rest of the pigeonhole unit is assembled with $\frac{3}{16}$-inch-deep stopped dado joints. Cut the dadoes with the appropriate-size straight bit in a handheld router. Guide the router with a shop-made T-square similar to the one you used to rout the dadoes in the case sides. The spacing of the pieces is shown in *Pigeonhole Unit—Front View.* Rout the $\frac{3}{8}$-inch dadoes for the long shelf in the ends, stopping the cuts $\frac{1}{4}$ inch from the ends' front edges. Then rout more $\frac{3}{8}$-inch dadoes for the drawer dividers in the underside of the long shelf and top side of the bottom. Stop the dadoes $\frac{1}{4}$ inch from the front edge of the pieces. Switch bits and rout $\frac{1}{4}$-inch dadoes for the dividers in the top side of the long shelf and the underside of the top, again stopping $\frac{1}{4}$ inch from the front edge. Square the ends of these dadoes with a sharp chisel. Finally, lay out the curves on two of the dividers, as shown in *Pigeonhole Unit—Cross Section.* Rout $\frac{3}{8}$-inch dadoes across the dividers to hold the short shelf. Stop them $\frac{1}{4}$ inch from the layout lines.

Pigeonhole Unit—Cross Section

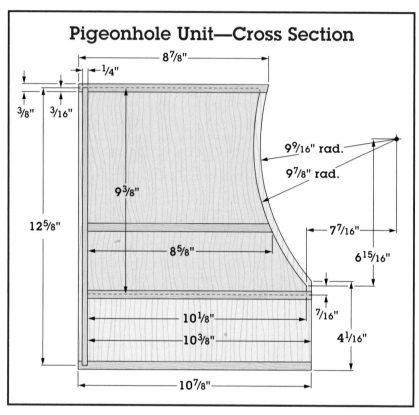

Pigeonhole Joinery Detail

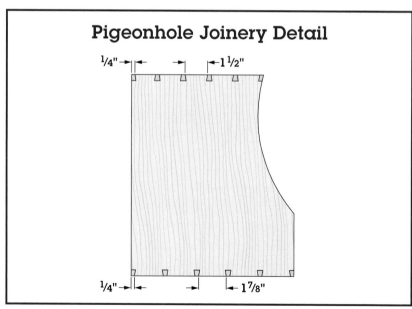

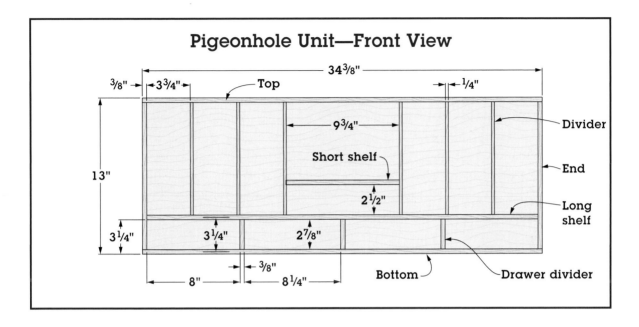

Pigeonhole Unit—Front View

4 **Cut the grooves for the back.** Cut ¼-inch-wide grooves for the back in the top, bottom, and ends, as shown in *Pigeonhole Unit—Cross Section*. Don't worry about stopping the grooves before they run out the ends of the pieces—they won't be seen once the pigeonhole unit is installed.

5 **Cut the pieces to their final shapes.** On the band saw, cut the curves on the ends and the partitions, and sand away the saw marks. Notch the front edges of the long shelf, the short shelf, and the drawer partitions to fit in the stopped dadoes. To make the cuts, hold the pieces on edge against the miter gauge on the table saw. Set the blade height at slightly more than ¼ inch. Make a couple of passes over the blade to complete the notches, as shown in the photo on page 212.

6 **Assemble the pigeonhole unit.** Spread glue on all the mating surfaces. Join the top and bottom to one of the ends. Then add the long shelf, drawer partitions, regular partitions, and short shelf. Slide the back into place, followed by the second end. Clamp the joints, and check the diagonals to make sure the unit is square. Set it aside to allow the glue to

To keep the notches a consistent length, position a stop block against the rip fence and butt the workpieces up against it for the first cut. The distance from the block to the outside of the blade should equal the length of the notch.

dry. After the glue dries, trim the front edge of the top to match the curve of the ends and the front edge of the short shelf to match the curve of the partitions.

7 **Make the drawers.** Check the actual dimensions of the drawer openings in the pigeonhole unit against the dimensions given for the drawer parts in the Materials List. Make any necessary adjustments, then cut the parts to size. Dovetail the corners together as you did with the larger drawers. Cut the grooves for the bottoms, and assemble the drawers. When the glue dries, plane and sand the drawers to a perfect fit.

Glue the drawer stops in place so they catch the bottom edge of each drawer front and stop the drawer flush with the shelf above.

Finish the Desk

1 **Apply the finish.** Pull the drawers out of their openings, remove the writing flap, and do any last-minute sanding that is necessary. Then dust off all the pieces and apply your chosen finish. The desk in the photo on page 189 was finished with four coats of Waterlox, a transparent wiping varnish. Everything was rubbed with steel wool in between coats, and the final coat was rubbed out with a mixture of pumice and mineral oil. The finish has a satiny glow to it; and while the cherry started out on the light side, it has begun to take on that warm, dark look associated with cherry.

2 **Attach the hardware.** Attach the drawer pulls and knobs, as shown in *Front View.* Also mortise the desk lock into the writing flap and the strike plate into the underside of the top.

Finally, nail the escutcheon in place. You may also want to take a few minutes to polish and buff the flap hinges before reinstalling the flap.

3 **Install the pigeonhole unit.** Put a layer or two of kraft paper on the writing surface to protect it. Then slide the pigeonhole unit into place. Drive one #6 × 1-inch flathead wood screw through each end of the unit from inside the outer drawer hole into the desk sides to hold the unit in place. Rub a little paraffin on the bottoms of the drawers to help them slide well, and put them into their holes to finish the job.

Shaker-Style Storage and Workstation

by Andy Rae

When a customer asked for storage in a small guest room in her house, I had just the answer: "Fill one wall with built-in cabinetry," I advised. On the face of it, the idea sounded suspiciously space-consuming, not space-saving. But wall-to-wall and floor-to-ceiling built-ins fit more utility into less space than freestanding furniture does. That leaves more open living space in the room.

The upper cases of these built-in cabinets offer plenty of shelf space for books. Deep, smooth-action drawers in the lower cases provide plenty of storage. The work surface built into the center of two units is handy for tasks ranging from writing and studying to craftwork.

The simple construction uses hardwood plywood and dimensioned #2 pine from the lumberyard or building-supply store. The casework is joined with dadoes, rabbets, grooves, and splines. And the hard-working drawers pull out on modern, full-extension metal slides, providing easy access to the entire contents.

Exploded View

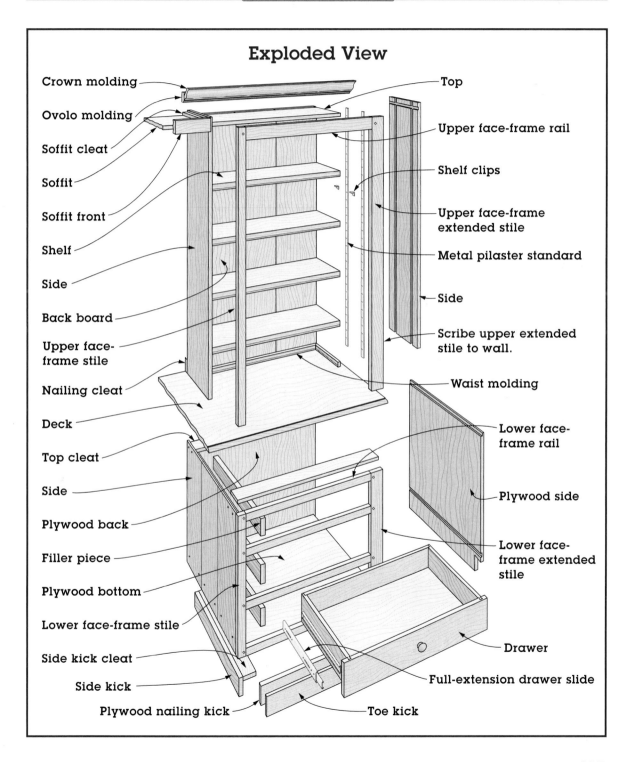

Crown molding

Ovolo molding

Soffit cleat

Soffit

Soffit front

Shelf

Side

Back board

Upper face-frame stile

Nailing cleat

Deck

Top cleat

Side

Plywood back

Filler piece

Plywood bottom

Lower face-frame stile

Side kick cleat

Side kick

Plywood nailing kick

Top

Upper face-frame rail

Shelf clips

Upper face-frame extended stile

Metal pilaster standard

Side

Scribe upper extended stile to wall.

Waist molding

Lower face-frame rail

Plywood side

Lower face-frame extended stile

Drawer

Full-extension drawer slide

Toe kick

Customize the Cabinets

The photo on page 214 shows two storage units, one on each side of an existing window and a desk-height work surface. A soffit, a cornice, and the work surface join the three elements visually and structurally. This arrangement works well for walls about 8 feet high and 10 feet wide. You need to adjust the dimensions to fit your specific room, of course. You can also adapt the design to other needs. Some of the options available to you include the following:

• Build the cabinets essentially as shown, adjusting only the width between the cabinets so the overall cabinetry fills the wall. The work surface can be as narrow as 30 inches or as wide as 4 feet. If your wall has no window, you can panel it to match the backs of the upper cases.

• Combine two or more storage units with no work surface. These storage units can be as narrow as 2 feet wide or as wide as 3 feet and still look good and function well. If you build this way, all of the lower case sides can be plywood since none of them will be fully visible. Join the units with face-frame stiles that cover the edges of the adjoining sides.

• Fill a wider wall by flanking a work surface with two or more storage units on one or both sides.

The dimensions shown in the drawings are for the room in my customer's house. Increase or decrease the widths and heights of the cabinets to suit your own room, but I suggest you keep the height of the work surface, or deck, as it is. At $31\frac{1}{2}$ inches high, it's a comfortable writing height when sitting on a standard chair. To tailor the overall height of the cabinetry, find where the floor-to-ceiling distance is the smallest, then make the height of the stacked cabinets 1 inch less than this distance. With the work surface kept at $31\frac{1}{2}$ inches high, the height adjustment will have to come in the upper cases.

Fitting cabinetry to a room for a truly seamless look often frightens woodworkers who haven't done it before. It shouldn't. By making the cabinets 1 or 2 inches less than the total width of the room and by fastening wider face-frame

Materials List

Part	Dimension
Lower Cases	
Sides (2)	$\frac{3}{4}$" × $23\frac{1}{4}$" × $25\frac{3}{4}$"
Plywood sides (2)	$\frac{3}{4}$" × $22\frac{3}{4}$" × $30\frac{3}{4}$"
Plywood backs (2)	$\frac{1}{4}$" × $32\frac{3}{4}$" × $25\frac{3}{4}$"
Plywood bottoms (2)	$\frac{3}{4}$" × $22\frac{1}{2}$" × 32"
Top cleats (4)	$\frac{3}{4}$" × 4" × 32"
Nailing cleats (4)	$\frac{1}{2}$" × $2\frac{1}{2}$" × $33\frac{1}{8}$"
Plywood nailing kicks (2)	$\frac{3}{4}$" × $5\frac{3}{4}$" × 29"
Toe kicks (2)	$\frac{1}{4}$" × $5\frac{3}{4}$" × $29\frac{3}{4}$"
Side kicks (2)	$\frac{3}{4}$" × $5\frac{3}{4}$" × $19\frac{3}{4}$"
Side kick cleats (2)	$\frac{3}{4}$" × $5\frac{3}{4}$" × $19\frac{3}{4}$"
Upper Cases	
Back boards (6)	$\frac{3}{4}$" × $10\frac{1}{2}$" × 60"
Sides (4)	$\frac{3}{4}$" × $11\frac{1}{4}$" × 60"
Tops (2)	$\frac{3}{4}$" × $10\frac{1}{2}$" × 32"
Shelves (6)	$\frac{3}{4}$" × $10\frac{3}{8}$" × $31\frac{1}{8}$"
Nailing cleats (4)	$\frac{3}{4}$" × $2\frac{3}{4}$" × $17\frac{5}{8}$"
Splines (4)	$\frac{1}{8}$" × $\frac{3}{4}$" × 60"
Face Frames	
Lower face-frame stiles (2)	$\frac{3}{4}$" × $1\frac{1}{2}$" × $25\frac{3}{4}$"
Lower face-frame extended stiles (2)	$\frac{3}{4}$" × $1\frac{1}{2}$" × $25\frac{3}{4}$"
Lower face-frame rails (8)	$\frac{3}{4}$" × $1\frac{1}{2}$" × $33\frac{1}{8}$"
Upper face-frame stiles (2)	$\frac{3}{4}$" × $1\frac{1}{2}$" × 60"
Upper face-frame extended stiles (2)	$\frac{3}{4}$" × 3" × 60"
Upper face-frame rails (2)	$\frac{3}{4}$" × 3" × $33\frac{1}{8}$"
Peg stock	$\frac{1}{4}$" × $\frac{1}{4}$" × as long as needed
Drawers	
Lower drawer fronts (4)	$\frac{3}{4}$" × $7\frac{1}{4}$" × $30\frac{3}{8}$"
Lower drawer sides (8)	$\frac{1}{2}$" × $7\frac{1}{4}$" × $22\frac{1}{2}$"

Part	Dimension
Lower drawer backs (4)	$\frac{1}{2}$" × $6\frac{3}{4}$" × $28\frac{7}{8}$"
Upper drawer fronts (2)	$\frac{3}{4}$" × $4\frac{7}{8}$" × $30\frac{3}{8}$"
Upper drawer sides (4)	$\frac{1}{2}$" × $4\frac{7}{8}$" × $22\frac{1}{2}$"
Upper drawer backs (2)	$\frac{1}{2}$" × $4\frac{3}{8}$" × $28\frac{7}{8}$"
Plywood bottoms (6)	$\frac{1}{4}$" × $22\frac{1}{4}$" × $28\frac{7}{8}$"
Filler pieces (6)	$\frac{3}{4}$" × 3" × 22"
Trim	
Deck	$\frac{3}{4}$" × $25\frac{1}{2}$" × 10' 2"
Crown molding	$\frac{3}{4}$" × $2\frac{1}{2}$" × 10' 2"
Ovolo molding	$\frac{3}{4}$" × 2" × 10' 2"
Waist moldings (2)	$\frac{3}{4}$" × $1\frac{1}{2}$" × $31\frac{1}{4}$"
Waist moldings (4)	$\frac{3}{4}$" × $1\frac{1}{2}$" × 14"
Soffit	$1\frac{1}{8}$" × $11\frac{1}{4}$" × 56"
Soffit front	$\frac{3}{4}$" × 3" × as long as needed
Soffit cleats (2)	1" × 1" × $11\frac{1}{4}$"

Hardware

#8 × 3" drywall screws (as needed)

#8 × 2" drywall screws (as needed)

#8 × $1\frac{1}{2}$" drywall screws (as needed)

#8 × $1\frac{1}{4}$" drywall screws (as needed)

6d box nails (as needed)

6d cut nails (as needed)

4d finish nails (as needed)

57" pilaster standards (8)

Shaker-style knobs (6). Available from Woodcraft Supply Corp., 210 Wood County Industrial Park, P. O. Box 1686, Parkersburg, WV 26102–1686; (800) 225-1153; part #125434

22" full-extension drawer slides (6 pairs)

Shelf clips (32)

Front View

Side View Cross Section

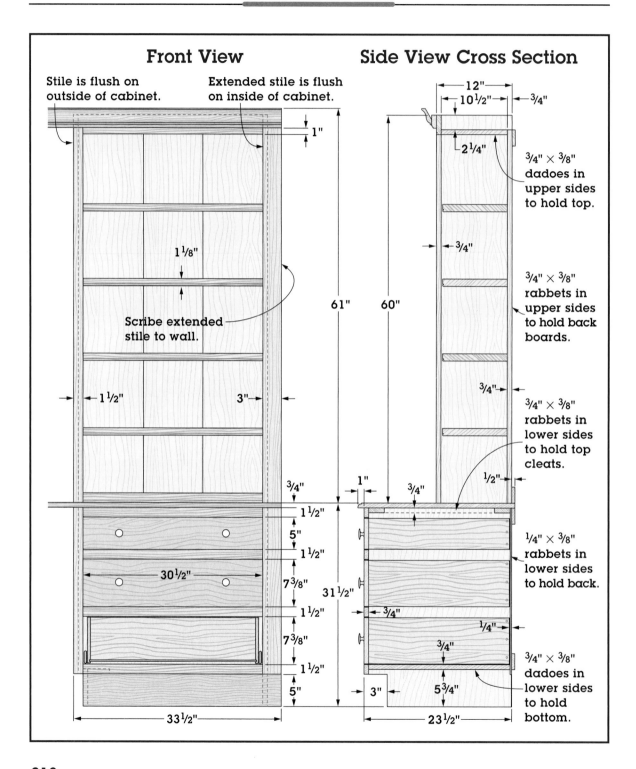

Stile is flush on outside of cabinet.

Extended stile is flush on inside of cabinet.

1"

Scribe extended stile to wall.

1 1/8"

61"

1 1/2"

3"

3/4"

1 1/2"

5"

1 1/2"

30 1/2"

7 3/8"

1 1/2"

7 3/8"

1 1/2"

5"

33 1/2"

12"

10 1/2"

3/4"

2 1/4"

3/4"

3/4"

60"

1"

3/4"

3/4"

1/2"

31 1/2"

1"

3/4"

3/4"

1/4"

3/4"

3"

5 3/4"

23 1/2"

3/4" × 3/8" dadoes in upper sides to hold top.

3/4" × 3/8" rabbets in upper sides to hold back boards.

3/4" × 3/8" rabbets in lower sides to hold top cleats.

1/4" × 3/8" rabbets in lower sides to hold back.

3/4" × 3/8" dadoes in lower sides to hold bottom.

stiles to the fronts of the cases after the cases are in place, the cabinets go in easily and fit perfectly. The same approach fits the cabinetry to the house wherever the two meet and allows you to install straight and square cabinets even in a room with crooked or irregular walls.

Make the Lower and Upper Cases

1 **Prepare the sides and backs.** To make the lower case sides facing the kneehole, you need to glue up several pine boards to create a panel. Cut the boards about 1 inch longer than the dimension given in the Materials List, so they can be trimmed after gluing. Use a ¼-inch-diameter beading bit in a table-mounted router to bead an edge of each board to be joined. While you have the router set up, bead an edge of each upper case back board as well. Remember to bead only one edge of each board, as shown in *Upper Case Back Joinery.* Glue up the boards for the side panels.

2 **Cut the pine and plywood parts.** After the glue has dried in the side panels, cut all the pine and plywood parts for the lower and upper cabinets to the sizes given in the Materials List. Don't forget to modify the dimensions of the Materials List provided here to suit your particular installation. Cut out the kick-space notches in the lower front corners of the lower case plywood sides, as shown in *Front View* and *Side View Cross Section.*

3 **Dado, groove, and rabbet the parts.** All the case sides are assembled to their adjoining parts with simple rabbets and dadoes, as shown in *Exploded View* and *Side View Cross Section,* and the back boards are grooved to accept ⅛-inch-thick splines. Shallow grooves in the upper case sides hold metal pilaster standards for the adjustable shelves. Cut the dadoes, grooves, and rabbets with a table-mounted router and straight bits of appropriate diameters,

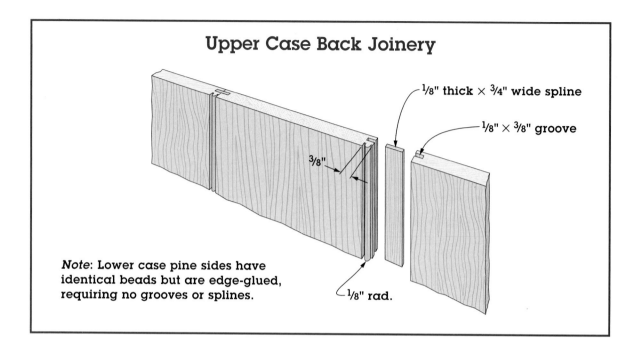

Upper Case Back Joinery

⅛" thick × ¾" wide spline

⅛" × ⅜" groove

⅜"

Note: Lower case pine sides have identical beads but are edge-glued, requiring no grooves or splines.

⅛" rad.

or use a dado blade on the table saw. I used a standard kerf saw blade to cut the spline grooves in the back boards, as shown in *Upper Case Back Joinery*.

4 **Prepare the shelf stock.** The material I used for the shelves is 1⅛-inch-thick pine, which is referred to as 5/4 (five-quarter) stock. The extra thickness provides strength so the shelves won't sag under a heavy load of books. Rout the ¼-inch-diameter bead on the lower front edges of the shelves.

5 **Assemble the cases.** Finish sand all of the case parts. Install the pilaster standards in the grooves in the upper case sides. Assemble the sides to the tops and bottoms with glue and nails or screws—6d square-cut nails where fasteners will show and #8 × 2-inch drywall screws where they won't show. Then install the backs to square up the cases. Spread glue in the rabbets, and install the backs with 6d box nails, checking that each cabinet is square as you go. Don't glue the splines into the grooves in the upper case back boards; just tap them into place. Attach the top cleats to the lower cases

with glue and #8 × 1½-inch drywall screws, and attach the
nailing cleats to the backs of the cases with #8 × 2-inch drywall
screws. The nailing cleats will stiffen the upper cases, which
don't have bottoms to keep them rigid and square.

Next, attach the side kicks to the side kick cleats with #8 ×
2-inch drywall screws, and then attach them to the lower cases
with more #8 × 2-inch drywall screws. Position the assembly,
as shown in *Front View.* Then, attach the plywood nailing
kicks in front of the side kicks and to the inside edge of the
plywood sides with #8 × 2-inch drywall screws. The toe kick
will be nailed in place after the cabinets have been installed.

Make the Face Frames

1 **Size the frame parts, and cut the beads.** Cut the
frame stiles and rails to the sizes given in the Materials List.

When the rails and stiles have been cut to size, rout a
¼-inch-diameter bead on all the face-frame stock. Remember
to bead both sides of the center rails on the lower case frames,
as shown in *Face-Frame Joinery.*

2 **Cut the mortise-and-tenon joinery.** The beaded
frames are held together with pegged mortise-and-
tenon joinery, and the beads are mitered where the joints come
together, as shown in *Face-Frame Joinery.* I cut the miters on
the table saw with the blade tilted to 45 degrees and pushed
the stock past the blade with the miter gauge. I cut away the
beads between the miters with a chisel.

Once the miters are cut, mortise the stiles with a $5/16$-inch-
diameter spiral upcut bit in the router or with a hollow-chisel
mortiser. Then cut tenons to fit the mortises. You can rip them
with a tenoning jig on the table saw or waste away the cheeks
with a dado cutter. If you routed the mortises, either chisel the
ends square to fit the square tenons, or round-over the tenon
edges with a rasp. Test assemble the frames to check that the
miters are tight and that the frames are the correct width.

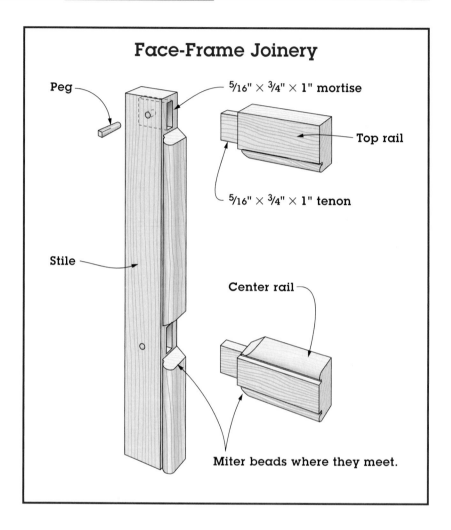

Face-Frame Joinery

Peg

$5/16" \times 3/4" \times 1"$ mortise

Top rail

$5/16" \times 3/4" \times 1"$ tenon

Stile

Center rail

Miter beads where they meet.

3 **Assemble and attach the frames.** Glue and clamp the face frames together, and then check to see if they are square by measuring diagonally from corner to corner. The frames are square when the measurements are equal.

Next, make peg stock by ripping $1/4 \times 1/4$-inch sticks from some scraps of pine. Then, cut individual $1\frac{1}{2}$-inch pegs (approximately) from the peg stock. When the pegs have been cut, whittle one end of each peg into a bullet shape.

When the pegs are ready, drill $1/4$-inch-diameter holes through the frames where the rail tenons and stile mortises converge. Before you start hammering pegs, decide how you want the pegs to appear once they are driven in place. I like to drive the pegs so that once they are flush with the surface of the frame, they form little diamonds set at 45 degrees to the frame. Some woodworkers prefer to set the pegs square to the frame to form little squares. Once you have decided on an orientation for the pegs, drive them—bullet shape down—into their holes.

When the glue is dry, unclamp the frames, and cut the pegs flush to the back of the frames with a dovetail saw. Then glue and nail the frames to the cases, using 6d cut nails every 10 inches or so.

Make the Drawers

1 **Cut the drawer parts.** Measure the drawer openings in the face frames before cutting the drawer parts to the sizes given in the Materials List, as slight variations in each case can affect the fit of the drawers. Cut the drawer fronts ⅛ inch less than the width of the case openings.

2 **Rout the dovetails.** Sliding dovetails secure the drawer sides to the fronts for unbeatable strength. Note that the correct location of these joints is determined by the thickness of the drawer slides—in my case, ½ inch. Cut the dovetails and the dovetail sockets on the router table with a ½-inch dovetail bit, as shown in the photos on page 224. I like to rout the sockets in the drawer fronts first, then I cut a test dovetail on a piece of scrap wood to get the correct fit to the sockets. Once the scrap dovetail fits into the sockets with light taps from a hammer, I rout all the dovetails in the sides.

3 **Groove, rabbet, and drill the parts.** Use a straight router bit or a table-saw dado cutter to cut the groove for the drawer bottom in the drawer fronts and drawer sides and the rabbet in the drawer sides for the drawer backs, as shown in *Drawer Construction*. Then drill the holes in the drawer fronts for the knobs.

4 **Assemble the drawers.** Spread glue into the dove-tail sockets, and tap the drawer sides into the drawer fronts. Then spread glue in the grooves and along the rabbets, and install the backs and bottoms. Secure the backs and bottoms with 6d box nails. Spread glue on the knob tenons, and install them into the drawer fronts with light taps from a mallet.

5 **Install the drawers in the cases.** Screw the metal drawer slides to the drawer sides. Before screwing the drawer slides to the case sides, you'll need to screw ¾-inch-thick filler pieces to the pine sides to bring the slides even with the edge of the face frame. Screw the filler pieces to the pine sides with #8 × 1¼-inch drywall screws, and attach the drawer slides to the filler pieces and plywood case side, as shown in *Drawer Construction*. Test fit the drawers in the cases. If they bind, reduce the thickness of the fillers. If the drawers rattle or feel loose, shim between the fillers and the slides with cardboard.

Rout the dovetail socket ⅜ inch deep, guiding the drawer front with a miter gauge.

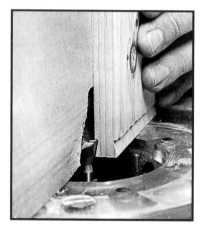

Leave the bit at ⅜ inch high, move the fence over to bury most of the bit, then rout both sides of the dovetail on scrap wood the same thickness as the drawer sides.

Test the fit in a socket. If the dovetail is loose, bury more of the bit. If it won't go in, expose more of the bit. When the dovetail on scrap wood fits snugly but assembles without trouble, rout the dovetails on the drawer sides.

Drawer Construction

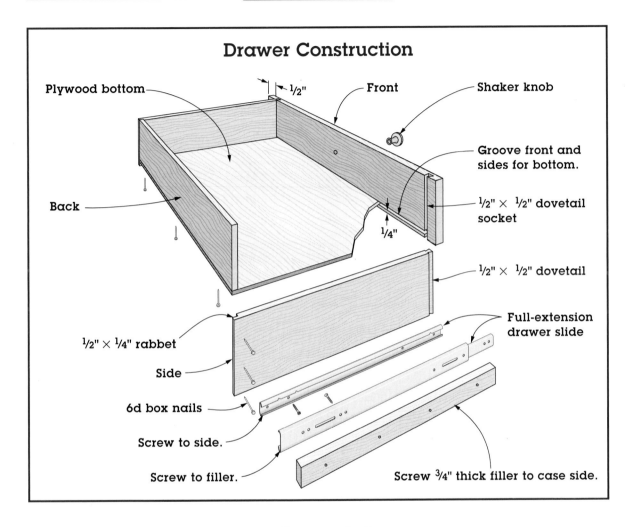

Plywood bottom

1/2"

Front

Shaker knob

Back

Groove front and sides for bottom.

1/2" × 1/2" dovetail socket

1/4"

1/2" × 1/2" dovetail

1/2" × 1/4" rabbet

Side

Full-extension drawer slide

6d box nails

Screw to side.

Screw to filler.

Screw 3/4" thick filler to case side.

Make the Trim and Moldings

1 **Make the moldings.** You can buy most of the moldings for this project at a lumberyard or building-supply store; just choose a style that's similar to the one shown in *Cornice and Soffit Construction*. I made the moldings shown in the drawing using a combination of straight and beveled cuts on the table saw and an assortment of readily available router bits with different profiles. A few passes with a block plane and some sanding using coarse paper wrapped around shaped wooden blocks completed the profiles.

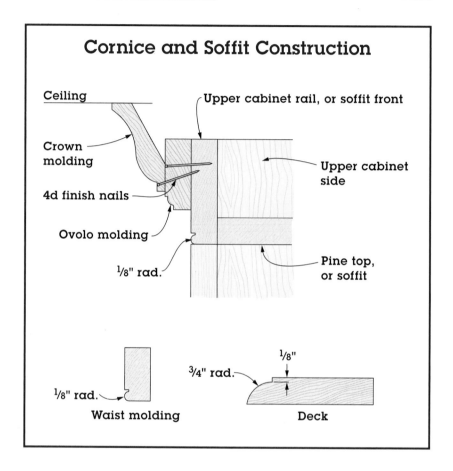

Cornice and Soffit Construction

Ceiling

Upper cabinet rail, or soffit front

Crown molding

4d finish nails

Ovolo molding

Upper cabinet side

⅛" rad.

Pine top, or soffit

⅛" rad.

Waist molding

¾" rad.

⅛"

Deck

You need to make or buy the crown and ovolo moldings that run the full width of the installed cabinets and the beaded waist moldings that locate the upper cases on the work surface.

2 **Glue up the deck.** Glue together three pine boards that are a couple of inches longer than the total width of the room. Use a handheld router equipped with an edge guide to rout the thumbnail profile on the front edge of the deck.

3 **Make the soffit.** The final detail is to make a soffit board for above the window. The soffit visually ties together the cabinets for a seamless appearance. Like the deck, cut it a few inches long so you can trim it to an exact fit when you install it.

Finish and Install
the Casework

1 **Finish the parts.** I like the look of worn, decades-old cabinetry. To achieve the look, I use a "secret" finish commonly called "scrub pine" because it looks as if the wood has been painted, then stripped or scrubbed of paint, leaving a worn look. Even though they aren't attached yet, you should also apply finish to the molding, trim, and toe kicks.

For a scrub pine finish, start with a light wood stain with a honey-colored tone. Once you've stained all the parts, give all the woodwork a clear coat of lacquer or wiping varnish to seal the surface. When the clear finish is dry, sand all the parts lightly with 220-grit sandpaper.

Now brush or wipe on a single coat of latex paint in a light color such as baby blue or light green. Immediately wipe off the paint with clean rags. You'll find it's best to work on small sections at a time. The paint will remain in all the nooks and crannies, while broad, flat surfaces such as drawer fronts and sides will gain a pleasing tone that "ages" the wood. Finish up by sealing the dried paint coat with two or more clear coats of lacquer or wiping varnish.

2 **Install the casework.** Even though you have a lot of cabinetry to install, the job is manageable because it's broken down into small sections. Begin by leveling and installing the lower cases, making sure to scribe the extended stiles and the extended pine sides to the walls for a tight fit. (See "Scribing to Fit" on page 228.) Nails or #8 × 3-inch drywall screws driven from inside the cabinets through the nailing cleats and into studs in the wall will hold everything securely.

Next, install the deck. For accuracy, make a cardboard or paper template for each end of the deck to determine the exact contours of the walls. Then transfer the contours of the templates onto the deck, and cut the ends of the deck with a jigsaw. Aim for a tight fit only where the joint will

Scribing to Fit

Few walls are as flat as they look. For a neat cabinet installation, you almost always have to either scribe the cabinet edge to fit the irregularities of the wall or tack on molding to cover gaps. Since tacked-on moldings tend to look tacky, scribing is usually the better choice.

Most how-to advice on scribing assumes great irregularities in the surface you must fit. Such surfaces require the compass approach, as shown in the photo top right. In the real world, though, most surfaces that you need to fit are only mildly irregular—a wall that looks flat but isn't quite. Scribing to a mildly irregular wall allows you to take a simple approach, using only an ordinary pencil, as shown in the photo bottom right.

To fit a countertop or other work surface between two walls, scribe pattern pieces to the walls at both ends, then trace them onto the countertop. Make sure the overall length is correct before trimming the countertop to the traced lines.

When a cabinet or countertop has been scribed to fit a wall, trim to the scribe line with a jigsaw or circular saw. The jigsaw's ease of maneuvering makes it a good choice for very irregular cuts, while the circular saw is more appropriate for straighter cuts. In general, a circular saw will produce a more finished cut.

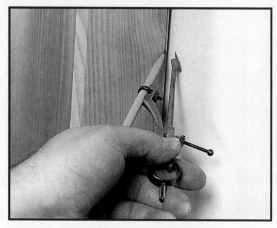

To trace the shape of a wall onto a scribing stile, set a compass to bridge the largest gap, then keep the point of the compass in touch with the wall while the pencil draws the shape on the stile. After trimming the stile to the line, the cabinet will move over the distance that you set the compass to.

Quite often, the wall surface is only mildly wavy. If the largest gap is ⅛ inch or less, simply hold an ordinary pencil flat against the wall while tracing the shape onto the stile. After trimming the stile to the line, the cabinet will move over half the diameter of the pencil, typically ⅛ inch.

not be hidden by other woodwork. Secure the deck by driving #8 × 1¼-inch drywall screws up through the lower case's top cleats.

When the deck has been installed, attach the toe kicks to the front of the nailing kicks with 4d finish nails.

Level and scribe the upper cases to the walls, then secure them as you did the lower cases. Install the beaded waist molding inside the upper cases to conceal any gaps.

When the cabinets have been secured to the wall and the deck is in place, install the moldings and trim. Use a hand or power miter saw to cut the moldings to the correct length, then attach them with glue and 4d finish nails, as shown in *Cornice and Soffit Construction*.

Finally, install the adjustable shelves with shelf clips, and load them with books.

Home Office Cabinetry

by Glenn Bostock

As the world of business becomes more and more electronically based, there is less need to get in a car each morning and drive to a big city office. Instead of slurping their morning cup of coffee on the interstate while dodging other bleary-eyed workers doing the same, many more people are finding it possible to walk in their stocking feet with coffee in hand to their very own home office.

Like other jobs my associate Phil McGinnis and I put together, this office was a custom job that was tailored to the individual needs of our customer. Linda Daly, A.S.I.D. (American Society of Interior Designers), developed this office concept for her client, who needed lots of storage space, bookshelves, ample work area for a computer and typewriter, and room to spread out when a job called for it. And all of this had to fit in an 8 × 9½-foot space.

Don't slavishly follow the layout of this office, since it was designed specifically for the room where it resides. I'll

give you an overview of the design and details on building the individual components, which you can combine and resize to fit your space.

I made these cabinets from plywood—cherry-faced plywood where the outside or inside of the cabinet is in

view and standard birch plywood for the drawer bases and anywhere that the plywood would be hidden. The drawer boxes are made from Baltic birch, which has even veneer for an attractive edge. The doors and drawer faces are made from cherry frames with cherry or glass panels.

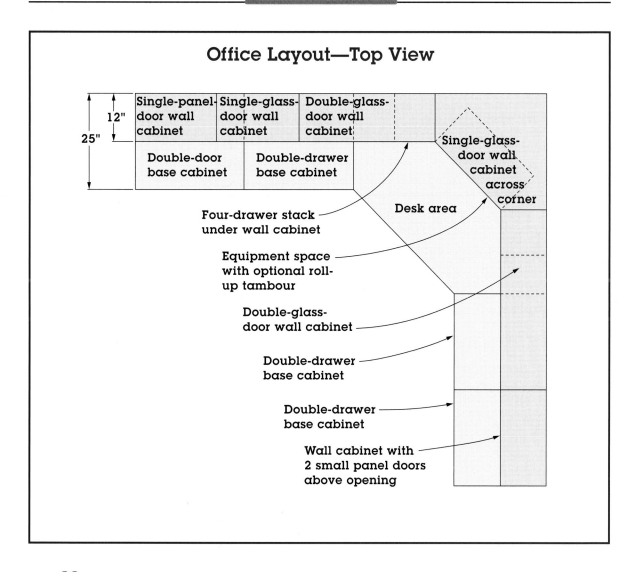

Office Layout—Top View

Single-panel-door wall cabinet

Single-glass-door wall cabinet

Double-glass-door wall cabinet

Single-glass-door wall cabinet across corner

Double-door base cabinet

Double-drawer base cabinet

12"

25"

Four-drawer stack under wall cabinet

Desk area

Equipment space with optional roll-up tambour

Double-glass-door wall cabinet

Double-drawer base cabinet

Double-drawer base cabinet

Wall cabinet with 2 small panel doors above opening

Office Design

As shown in *Office Layout—Top View*, Linda Daly designed this office around a corner desk, or workstation. Working from a corner puts most everything within reach of the user. Three of the base cabinets have drawers installed—two per cabinet—to hold file folders. The remaining base cabinet has two doors and an adjustable shelf to hold boxes and supplies such as typing or printer paper.

Materials List

Part	Dimension
Base Cabinet Case	
Sides (2)	$3/4" \times 23" \times 24^1/2"$
Top/bottom (2)	$3/4" \times 23" \times 27^1/4"$
Back	$1/4" \times 27^1/4" \times 24^1/2"$
Filler strip	$3/4" \times 2" \times 26^1/2"$
Adjustable shelf	$3/4" \times 23" \times 26^3/8"$
Plinth stock (as needed)	$3/4" \times 4" \times$ as long as needed
Plinth corner blocks (as needed)	$1" \times 1" \times 4"$
Base Cabinet Doors (2)	
Stiles (4)	$3/4" \times 2^1/4" \times 24^1/2"$
Top rails (2)	$3/4" \times 2^1/4" \times 10^1/4"$
Bottom rails (2)	$3/4" \times 2^3/4" \times 10^1/4"$
Dowels (16)	$3/8"$ dia. $\times 3"$
Panels (2)	$3/4" \times 10^1/4" \times 20^1/2"$
Base Cabinet Drawers (2)	
Drawer face stiles (4)	$3/4" \times 2^1/4" \times 12^1/4"$
Drawer face rails (4)	$3/4" \times 2^1/4" \times 24^1/4"$
Drawer face panels (2)	$3/4" \times 7^3/4" \times 24^1/4"$
Drawer box sides (4)	$1/2" \times 10" \times 21"$
Drawer box front/back (4)	$1/2" \times 10" \times 25"$
Drawer box dividers (2)	$1/2" \times 9^1/4" \times 24^1/2"$
Drawer box bottoms (2)	$1/4" \times 20^1/2" \times 25"$
Countertop	
Work surface	$3/4" \times 24^1/4" \times$ as long as needed
Solid wood edging stock	$3/4" \times 1^5/8" \times$ as long as needed
Attaching strip stock	$3/4" \times 4" \times$ as long as needed
Wall Cabinet Case	
Sides (2)	$3/4" \times 11^1/4" \times 46^1/2"$
Top/bottom (2)	$3/4" \times 11" \times 41^1/4"$
Back	$1/4" \times 41^1/4" \times 46^1/2"$
Filler strips (3)	$3/4" \times 2" \times 40^1/2"$
Adjustable shelves (3)	$3/4" \times 11" \times 40^3/8"$
Molding spacer stock	$3/4" \times 3" \times$ as long as needed
Crown molding	$1^1/4" \times 3" \times$ as long as needed
Wall Cabinet Doors (2)	
Stiles (4)	$3/4" \times 2^1/4" \times 43^1/2"$
Top rails (2)	$3/4" \times 2^1/4" \times 17^1/4"$
Bottom rails (2)	$3/4" \times 2^3/4" \times 17^1/4"$
Glazing strip stock	$5/16" \times 3/8" \times$ as long as needed
Dowels (16)	$3/8"$ dia. $\times 3"$

Hardware

#8 $\times$ 3" drywall screws (as needed)
#8 $\times$ 1$^1/2$" drywall screws (as needed)
#8 $\times$ 1$^1/4$" drywall screws (as needed)
#8 $\times$ 1" drywall screws (as needed)
#6 $\times$ $3/4$" flathead wood screws (as needed)
4d finish nails
$3/4$" brads
Iron-on edge-banding tape (as needed)
European-style full-overlay cup hinges with winged base plate (8). Available from Outwater Hardware Corp., 11 West End Road, Totowa, NJ 07512; (201) 890-0940; parts #1006 and #63204
20" full-extension drawer slides (2 pairs). Available from C. H. Briggs Hardware Company, P. O. Box 15188, Reading, PA 19612; (800) 355-1000; Accuride part #4032
1$^1/4$" dia. door knobs (4). Available from Woodworker's Supply, 1108 North Glenn Road, Casper, Wyoming, 82601; (800) 645-9292; part #874-358
3" center drawer pulls (4). Available from Woodworker's Supply; part #859-525
Glass, $1/8$" thick, cut to fit
$1/4$" dia. shelf support pins (bag of 20). Available from Woodworker's Supply; part #867-365

Most of the wall cabinets have glass doors for displaying books. The shelves are adjustable here, too, so that books of different heights can be accommodated. The bottom of each wall cabinet is flush with the top edge of the bottom door rails so that the books placed there are completely visible and none of the book titles are obscured by the door rail.

Two of the wall cabinets have paneled doors: One of these has a single panel door that is the same height as the glass doors, and the other has two small panel doors over an opening that fits a small television.

The corner work area has a single, glass-door wall cabinet bridging the corner above a computer monitor cabinet with a roll-up tambour. I bought the roll-up tambour from C. H. Briggs Hardware Company (P.O. Box 15188, Reading, PA 19612; 800-355-1000), which has a selection of sizes and styles. If you have one of today's larger monitors, the size of this cabinet would need to be increased. I think the combination of the tambour cabinet and small drawer cabinets flanking it give a traditional, desklike feel to the office corner.

The work surface, or countertop, for this office is made from cherry plywood with an applied solid cherry edge. If you plan on heavy, abrasive use of the work surface, a plastic laminate surface will last longer, but you could still apply a solid wood edge.

When designing your office, first consider how you will be using it and what equipment it needs to house. Also try to think ahead to your future needs as well as up-and-coming technology that you may want to accommodate.

Some standards should be observed in your office design. The most crucial of these relates to the height and depth of the countertop and the depth of the cabinets themselves. As shown in *Height Layout,* the work surface should be 30 inches high. This would be too low for a kitchen counter, but it is just right for a sit-down countertop. The 18 inches between the countertop and the bottom of the wall cabinets gives you enough space to shuffle paper and equipment around without feeling cramped. The height of the ceiling in your office room will determine the actual height your wall cabinets can be— from 18 inches above the work countertop to the ceiling.

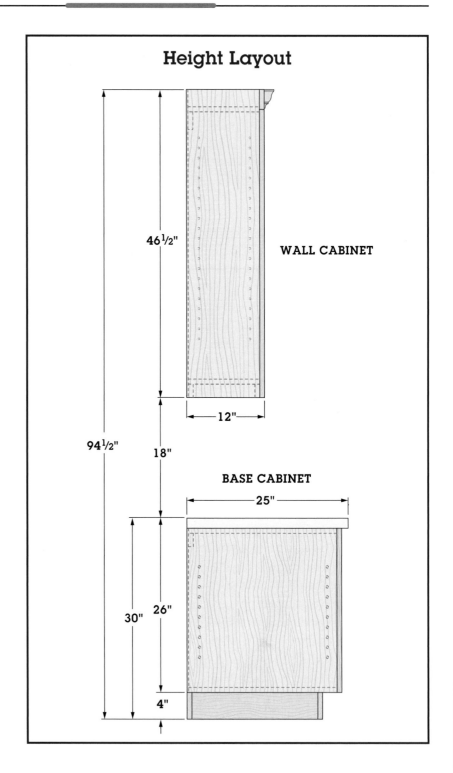

Height Layout

46¹/₂"

WALL CABINET

12"

94¹/₂"

18"

BASE CABINET

25"

26"

30"

4"

Building Base Cabinets

My basic base cabinets are simple plywood boxes that sit on top of a plywood plinth. The case construction is the same for cabinets with doors or those with drawers, so I'll show you how to build one case and install doors or drawers on it. The exposed plywood case edges are covered with cherry veneer edge-banding tape, and the doors and drawer faces overlay the front edges of the case. The dimensions shown in the drawings, given in the Materials List, and referred to in the text come directly from the cabinets shown below, but your cabinets may vary. The pullout work surface shown is not described in the text, but it simply slides into a cutout in the solid wood edging and attaching strip.

Base Cabinet—Exploded View

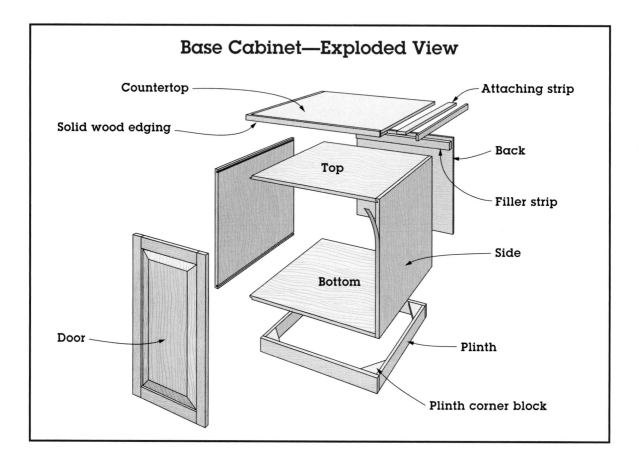

Countertop

Solid wood edging

Attaching strip

Back

Filler strip

Top

Side

Door

Bottom

Plinth

Plinth corner block

Make the Case

1 **Prepare the case parts.** Cut the case sides, top, back, bottom, and filler strips to the sizes given in the Materials List. Use cherry-faced plywood for any exposed surfaces.

2 **Cut the grooves in the sides.** As shown in *Base Cabinet—Front View* and *Base Cabinet Joinery Detail*, the base cabinet top and bottom are joined to the base cabinet sides with tongue-and-groove joints. To cut the grooves in the cabinet side, set up a ¼-inch-wide dado blade in the table saw. (You will need just the outside blades and no chippers.) Raise the blade ⅜ inch above the table, and position the table saw fence ½ inch from the blade.

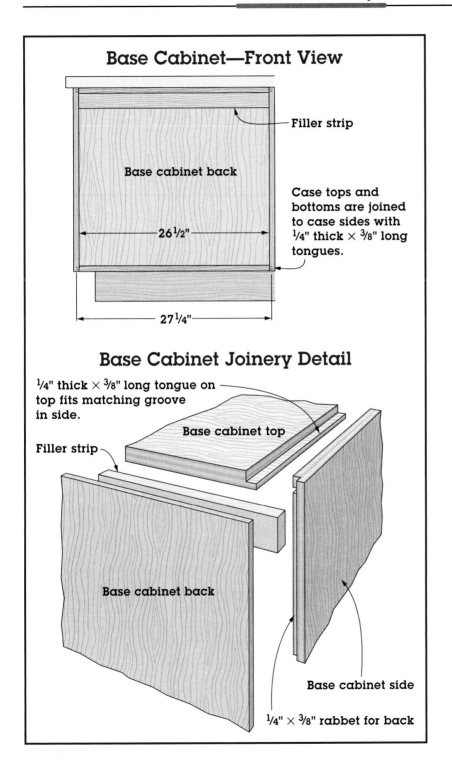

Base Cabinet—Front View

Filler strip

Base cabinet back

26½"

27¼"

Case tops and bottoms are joined to case sides with ¼" thick × ⅜" long tongues.

Base Cabinet Joinery Detail

¼" thick × ⅜" long tongue on top fits matching groove in side.

Base cabinet top

Filler strip

Base cabinet back

Base cabinet side

¼" × ⅜" rabbet for back

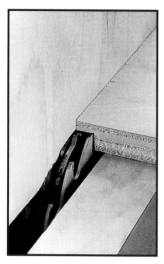

Guide the base cabinet top against the wooden auxiliary fence to cut the tongue. The wooden auxiliary fence allows the blade to cut all the way to the edge of the stock.

Quick tip

In my shop we often wait to install the cabinet back until after the cabinet has a finish applied. This allows the finisher easy access to the interior of the cabinet. Depending on your finishing method, you may want to consider this option as well.

Next, guide the top and bottom edges of the sides against the fence to cut $\frac{1}{4}$-inch-wide × $\frac{3}{8}$-inch-deep grooves, as shown in *Base Cabinet Joinery Detail*.

3 **Cut the tongues in the top and bottom.** To cut the tongues on each end of the base cabinet top and bottom, first put a $\frac{1}{2}$-inch-wide dado blade in the table saw and attach an auxiliary wooden fence to the table saw fence.

Next, raise the spinning dado blade into the auxiliary fence so that only $\frac{3}{8}$ inch of the blade's width is exposed beyond the fence. At the same time raise the blade $\frac{1}{2}$ inch above the table surface. The setup should create a $\frac{3}{8}$-inch-wide × $\frac{1}{2}$-inch deep rabbet, which leaves a $\frac{1}{4}$-inch-thick × $\frac{3}{8}$-inch-long tongue, as shown in *Base Cabinet Joinery Detail*. Test the cut in a piece of plywood scrap, and check the tongue's fit in the groove that you cut in the base cabinet side in the previous step.

When the saw is adjusted so that the tongue fits snugly in the groove, cut the tongue on the ends of the base cabinet top and bottom, as shown in the photo at left.

4 **Rabbet the sides to accept the back.** The base cabinet back fits in rabbets cut in the base cabinet sides, as shown in *Base Cabinet Joinery Detail*. Adjust the dado blade setup from cutting the last step to cut a $\frac{1}{4}$-inch-wide × $\frac{3}{8}$-inch-deep rabbet in the back edge of the base cabinet sides. Guide the base cabinet sides against the fence as you make the cut.

5 **Assemble the base cabinet case.** First, lay one base cabinet side flat on a low worktable, and spread a bead of glue in each groove. Next, insert the base cabinet top and bottom into their grooves in the base cabinet sides. The front edges of the top and bottom should be flush with the front edges of the sides. Use bar clamps to secure the assembly across the top and bottom.

With the bar clamps in place, lay the assembly on its face, and drop the case back into its rabbets in the base cabinet sides. Then, attach it with glue and #6 × $\frac{3}{4}$-inch flathead wood screws.

Next, set the case upright, and glue and screw the filler strip in place, as shown in *Base Cabinet—Front View* and *Base Cabinet—Side View*. Drive the #8 × 1½-inch drywall screws through the base cabinet top into the filler strip.

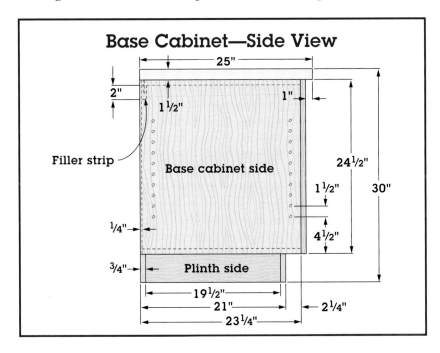

Base Cabinet—Side View

25"

2"

1½"

1"

Filler strip

Base cabinet side

24½"

1½"

30"

¼"

4½"

¾"

Plinth side

19½"

21"

2¼"

23¼"

6 **Apply the edge-banding tape.** When the case has been assembled and the glue has dried, apply iron-on veneer edge-banding tape to the exposed edges of the plywood at the front of the case. This type of edge banding has glue on its back that is activated with heat from an iron. Special edge-banding irons are made for this application, but a regular clothing iron will work as well.

Start by applying the edge banding to the front edge of the sides. With the case on its back, lay the edge banding in place, and press down on it with the hot iron until it begins to adhere. Then, slide the iron over the edge banding along the length of the side.

When both sides have edge banding applied, carefully trim off the excess with a razor. Then apply edge banding to the front edge of the top and bottom. This edge banding must fit between

and butt up against the edge banding you just applied to the case sides. Carefully trim it to fit with the razor as you apply it. Finally, trim the edges flush with the edges of the plywood. Also edge-band the front edge of the adjustable shelf, if applicable.

7 **Drill holes for the adjustable shelf.** Base cabinets with doors also have an adjustable shelf, which rests on ¼-inch brass shelf supports. Drill the ¼-inch-diameter × ½-inch deep holes for the shelf supports, as shown in *Base Cabinet—Side View.*

Make the Base Cabinet Doors and Drawer Faces

1 **Cut the door and drawer-face parts to size.** Since the construction for the doors and drawer faces is the same, you should prepare the parts at the same time. Cut all of the stiles, rails, and panels for the base cabinet doors and drawers to the sizes given in the Materials List and shown in *Base Cabinet Door and Drawer Options.* You may need to edge-glue stock to get the necessary width for the panels. All of these parts should be cut from solid cherry.

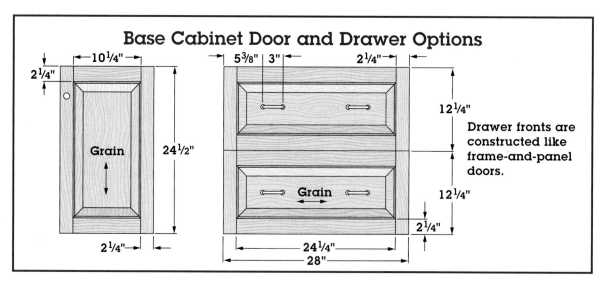

Base Cabinet Door and Drawer Options

Drawer fronts are constructed like frame-and-panel doors.

2 Drill dowel holes in the rails and stiles. Even though these doors use cope-and-stick construction, I like to reinforce the connection between the rails and stiles with dowels, as shown in *Door Joinery Detail*. To do this, the dowel holes must be cut in the ends of the rails and edges of the stiles before the parts are shaped. Drill the ⅜-inch-diameter dowel holes with a commercial doweling jig if you have one, or make your own from a ¾-inch-thick scrap of maple and some scraps of ¼-inch plywood, as shown in *Shop-Made Doweling Jig* and the photo on the left on page 242. Space the holes as shown in *Door Joinery Detail*, and drill them 1¾ inches deep.

3 Rout the sticking cut, or profile, in the rails and stiles. Once the dowel holes have been drilled in the rails and stiles, set up a cope-and-stick door bit set in a router table to cut the sticking cut along the edges of the door frame parts. The bit set I used cuts the profile shown in *Door Joinery Detail*—a ¼-inch-radius quarter round and a ¼-inch-wide × ⅜-inch-deep panel groove. When reconfigured, it cuts a matching cope in the ends of the rails. Each cope-and-stick

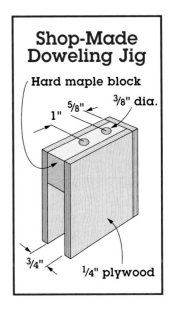

Shop-Made Doweling Jig

Hard maple block

5/8"   3/8" dia.

1"

3/4"   1/4" plywood

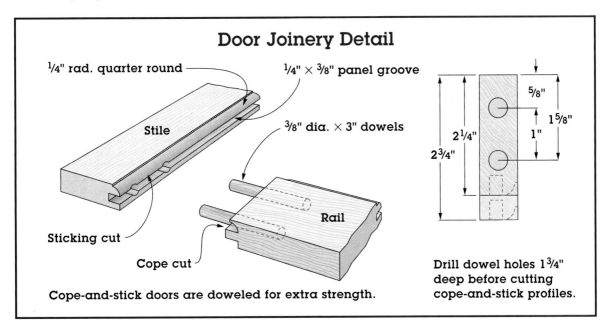

Door Joinery Detail

¼" rad. quarter round

¼" × ⅜" panel groove

Stile

⅜" dia. × 3" dowels

Sticking cut

Rail

Cope cut

Cope-and-stick doors are doweled for extra strength.

5/8"

1⅝"

2¼"

1"

2¾"

Drill dowel holes 1¾" deep before cutting cope-and-stick profiles.

Quick tip

To regulate the depth of the dowel holes quickly and easily, stick a flag of masking tape to the shank of your drill bit, which acts as a visual stop. To locate the flag, add the desired hole depth to the depth of the doweling jig, and then measure up the shank of the bit that far.

door bit set is slightly different, so you may need to adjust the dimensions and your setup accordingly. Make sure you read the directions that come with your bit set.

Set up the bit in a table-mounted router, and cut the sticking cut on the inside edge of each stile and rail, as shown in the photo below right. Bury most of the bit in a cutout in the router table fence, and guide the stock along the fence as you cut.

4 **Cut the cope in the ends of the rails.** Reconfigure the cope-and-stick door bit set to cut the counterprofile, or cope, in the ends of the rails, as shown in *Door Joinery Detail*. Test the cut in scrap, and make adjustments to the bit height and fence position until the cope interlocks perfectly with the profile you cut in Step 3 above.

Next, cut the cope in the edge of a 7 × 7-inch piece of scrap to use as a backer board when cutting the counterprofile in the ends of the rails. The counterprofile in the backer board can interlock with the profiled edge of the rail to provide support as you rout.

Finally, cut the counterprofile in the ends of each rail using the backer board for support, as shown in the photo on the opposite page.

Trap the end of the door stile in the doweling jig. If you wish, you can clamp the sides of the jig tight to the stile or rail with a C-clamp. Drill through the holes in the jig to drill the dowel holes in the edge of the stile.

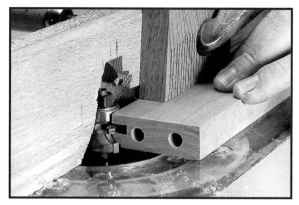

Guide the stock against a fence clamped to the router table as you rout the profile in the edge of the rails and stiles. The cope-and-stick door bit cuts the ¼-inch-radius bead and the ¼-inch-wide × ⅜-inch-deep panel groove at the same time.

5 **Raise the panels.** To raise the panels, I use a wing-shaped panel cutter in a shaper, but you can cut the same profile on the router table with either a horizontal or vertical panel-raising bit. As you set up the bit you choose in the router table, make some test cuts to make sure the panel will fit snugly in the panel groove in the rails and stiles. For details, see "Routing Raised Panels" on page 14.

6 **Assemble the doors and drawer faces.** Start by finish sanding the panels because they are difficult to sand well after assembly. Then trim about $\frac{1}{16}$ inch off the long edge of each panel so that they will be able to expand and contract across the grain in their frames as humidity changes with the seasons.

Next, assemble the doors and drawer faces one at a time by first gluing the dowels into the ends of the rails, gluing and inserting the rails into one of the stiles, inserting the panel into the panel grooves, and then gluing the other stile in place. When each frame and panel has been assembled, clamp it together with bar clamps and check to make sure the assembly is square.

Use a square backer board to guide the end of the rails past the cutter when making the cope cut. The edge of the backer board is counter-profiled to fit into the profiled edge of the rail.

Build the Drawer Boxes

1 **Cut the parts to size.** All of the drawer box parts except for the drawer bottom are made from $\frac{1}{2}$-inch Baltic birch plywood and are joined at the corners with tongue-and-groove joints, as shown in *Drawer Box Construction*. Cut all of the drawer box parts to the sizes given in the Materials List.

2 **Cut the tongue-and-groove joints.** Set up and cut the tongue-and-groove joinery on the table saw with a dado blade. You've already gone through this type of operation when cutting the joinery for the case. All you need to do is make the necessary adjustments for cutting these tongues and grooves, as shown in *Drawer Box Construction*.

Drawer Box Construction

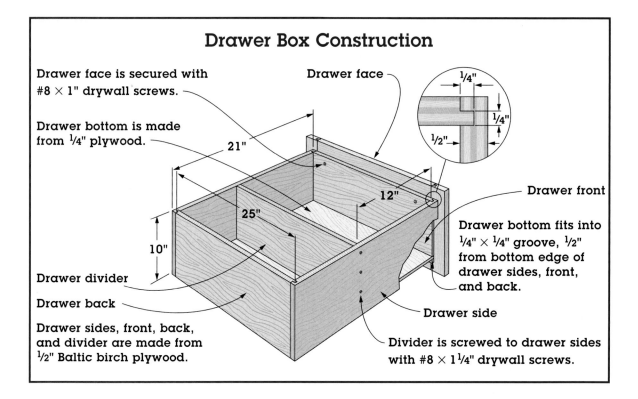

Drawer face is secured with #8 × 1" drywall screws.

Drawer face

Drawer bottom is made from ¼" plywood.

21"

25"

12"

10"

Drawer divider

Drawer back

Drawer sides, front, back, and divider are made from ½" Baltic birch plywood.

¼"

¼"

½"

Drawer front

Drawer bottom fits into ¼" × ¼" groove, ½" from bottom edge of drawer sides, front, and back.

Drawer side

Divider is screwed to drawer sides with #8 × 1¼" drywall screws.

3 **Cut the grooves for the drawer bottom.** Since you already have the dado blade set up in the table saw, use it to cut the grooves for the drawer bottom in the drawer sides, front, and back, as shown in *Drawer Box Construction*.

4 **Assemble the drawer box.** Glue the drawer sides, front, back, and bottom together. Clamp the assembly from side to side with bar clamps, and make sure the drawer is square.

When the glue is dry, position the drawer divider, as shown in *Drawer Box Construction*, and screw it in place with #8 × 1¼-inch drywall screws.

5 **Attach the drawer face.** Center the frame-and-panel drawer face against the drawer front, and secure it with #8 × 1-inch drywall screws, as shown in *Drawer Box Construction*.

Quick tip

When screwing the drawer face to the drawer front, be careful to position the screws so they will not come through the thin bevel of the panel. Driving a screw through a drawer-face panel can ruin your day.

Install the Doors
and Drawers

1 **Install the doors.** The doors are mounted on European-style, full-overlay cup hinges. One-half of these hinges fits into a stopped hole in the door stile, and then the hinge is screwed in place. The hole has to be drilled with a Forstner bit in a drill press. Even if you have to go out and buy a special Forstner bit, I think these hinges are worth it because they are very adjustable and allow me to achieve the full-overlay look that I like on the doors. Follow the manufacturer's instructions included with the hinges for precise installation.

2 **Install the drawers.** The drawers are mounted on heavy-duty full-extension slides, which mount directly to the sides of the case. These slides are strong enough to support heavy files and allow the drawer to extend out of the cabinet completely for easy access. Follow the manufacturer's instructions for installing the slides.

Position the slides in the case so that the drawer faces have about $\frac{1}{8}$-inch space between them.

Make the Plinth

1 **Cut the parts to size.** The plinth is simply a plywood frame that boosts the cabinet off the floor and helps to level it at the same time. Cut the plinth stock to the sizes given in the Materials List. The lengths you cut are based on the dimensions given in *Base Cabinet—Side View* and your own custom design.

2 **Assemble the plinth.** On a flat work surface, set up your plinth frame and put a plinth corner block at each corner. Next, predrill and drive #8 × 1$\frac{1}{2}$-inch drywall screws through the plinth corner blocks and into the plinth frame.

Finish and Install the Base Cabinet

1 **Sand the base cabinet, and apply the finish.** Finish sand the base cabinet and plinth progressively to 180 or 220 grit. The cabinets pictured here have a mahogany stain sealed with varnish.

When the varnish is dry, install the door knobs and drawer pulls, as shown in *Base Cabinet Door and Drawer Options*.

2 **Attach the base cabinet.** When the plinth frame is finished, put it in position in your office space, and set the base cabinet on top of it. Generally adjacent base cabinets are screwed together, and then the connected cabinets are leveled on top of the plinth. To level the cabinets, drive small shims between the bottom of the cabinets and the plinth.

When the cabinet (or cabinets) is level, screw through the bottom of the base cabinet into the plinth frame with #8 × 1½-inch drywall screws. Then, predrill and screw through the filler strip at the back of the cabinet and into the wall studs to secure the structure to the wall with #8 × 3-inch drywall screws.

Make and Install the Countertop

1 **Cut and assemble the countertop.** The countertop has to be customized to your space, but there are some basic construction steps that you can follow. As shown in *Countertop—Bottom View,* the cherry plywood work surface has a solid wood edging attached to its front and exposed side edges. Start by cutting the plywood work surface to the width given in the Materials List. Also, cut the solid wood edging stock and attaching strip stock to the thickness and width given in the Materials List. Then, glue the solid wood edging to the work surface with miters cut at the corners, as shown in *Countertop—Bottom View.* The edging is ⅛ inch wider than necessary so that it will extend slightly above the work surface when gluing and can be trimmed back later. Clamp the solid wood edging to the work surface with bar clamps.

When the glue is dry, trim the edge of the solid wood edge flush to the top of the work surface with a trim router and flush-trimming bit.

Next, secure the attaching strip to the bottom of the work surface with glue and #8 × 1¼-inch drywall screws, as shown in *Countertop—Bottom View.* Miter the attaching strips at the corner as shown, and also place an attaching strip across the bottom of the work surface wherever two cabinets meet. When the attaching strips are in place, trim the solid wood edging flush to them with a trim router and flush-trimming bit.

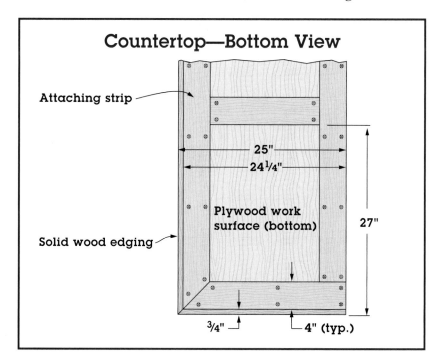

Countertop—Bottom View

Attaching strip

25"

24¼"

Plywood work surface (bottom)

27"

Solid wood edging

¾"

4" (typ.)

2 **Attach the countertop.** Set the completed countertop on top of the leveled base cabinet (or cabinets) and push it firmly against the wall. Check to make sure that the overhang is correct, and then drive #8 × 1½-inch drywall screws up through the top of the cabinet and into the attaching strips.

Building the Wall Cabinets

The wall cabinets, like the base cabinets, are simple plywood boxes. The joinery is very similar to that of the base cabinets, but the dimensions and positioning of the elements are somewhat different. One major difference is the glass doors included on the wall cabinets, and I'll tell you how to make them.

Again, you need to customize these cabinets to fit your space. The dimensions in the Materials List and text refer to the specific cabinets in the photos.

Wall Cabinet—Exploded View

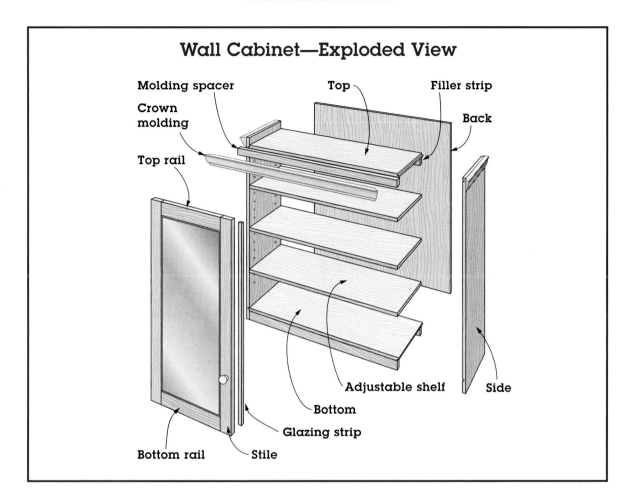

Molding spacer

Crown molding

Top rail

Top

Filler strip

Back

Bottom rail

Stile

Glazing strip

Bottom

Adjustable shelf

Side

Make the Case

1 **Cut the parts to size.** I've included drawings for a narrow wall cabinet and a wide wall cabinet, as shown in *Narrow Wall Cabinet—Front View* and *Wide Wall Cabinet—Front View*, but since the construction is the same for both, I will only discuss the wide wall cabinet. Cut the wall cabinet case parts to size.

2 **Cut the case joinery.** The wall cabinet case top and bottom are joined to the case sides with tongue-and-groove joinery like that used for the base cabinets.

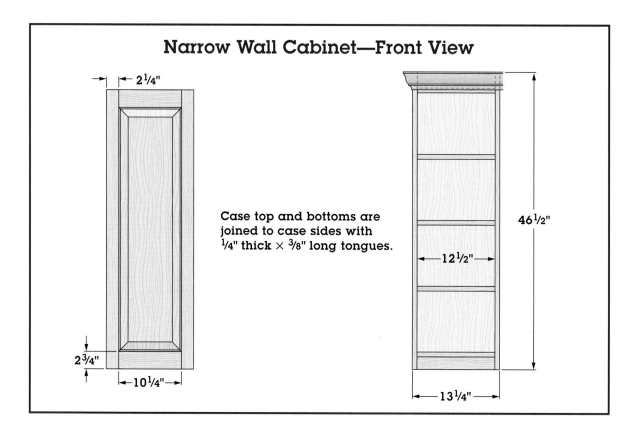

Narrow Wall Cabinet—Front View

2¼"

Case top and bottoms are
joined to case sides with
¼" thick × ³⁄₈" long tongues.

46½"

12½"

2³⁄₄"

10¼"

13¼"

Lay out the grooves in the case side, as shown in *Wide Wall Cabinet—Front View.* Then, cut the grooves in the case sides with a dado blade just as you cut the grooves in the base cabinet case sides, readjusting the table saw fence as necessary to position the grooves.

When the grooves have been cut, set up and cut the tongues in the ends of the case top and bottom. Do this exactly as you did for the base cabinet case top and bottom. First, make the tongue in some scrap plywood to test its fit in the groove.

Next, cut the ¼-inch-wide × ³⁄₈-inch-deep rabbet for the case back in the case sides, as shown in *Wall Cabinet—Side View* and *Base Cabinet Joinery Detail.*

3 **Assemble the wall cabinet case.** First, lay one of the wall cabinet sides flat on a low work table, and spread a bead of glue in each groove. Next, insert the wall cab-

Wide Wall Cabinet—Front View

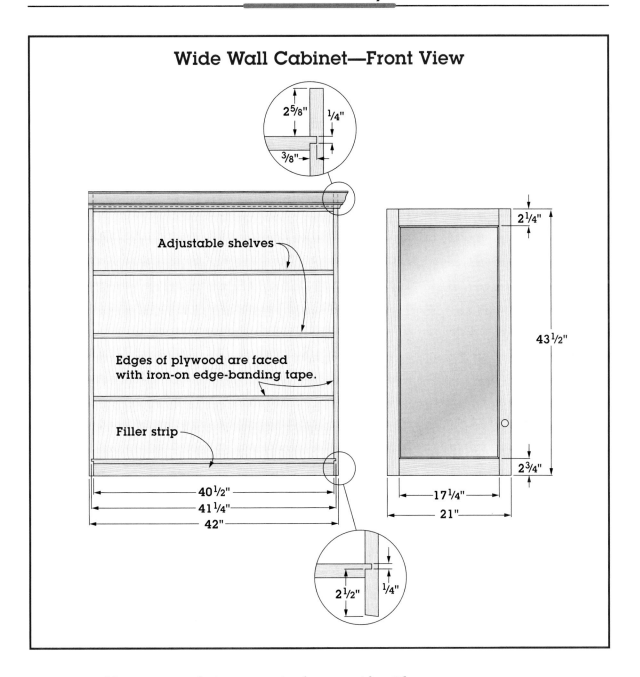

2⁵/₈" 1/4"

³/₈"

Adjustable shelves

Edges of plywood are faced
with iron-on edge-banding tape.

Filler strip

40¹/₂"

41¹/₄"

42"

2¹/₄"

43¹/₂"

2³/₄"

17¹/₄"

21"

2¹/₂" 1/4"

inet top and bottom into their grooves in the case sides. The
front edges of the top and bottom should be flush with the
front edges of the sides. Use bar clamps to secure the assembly
across the top and bottom.

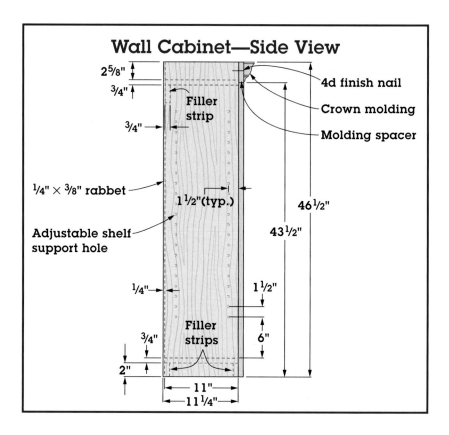

Wall Cabinet—Side View

$2^5/8$"

$3/4$"

Filler strip

$3/4$"

4d finish nail

Crown molding

Molding spacer

$1/4$" × $3/8$" rabbet

$1^1/2$"(typ.)

$46^1/2$"

$43^1/2$"

Adjustable shelf support hole

$1/4$"

$1^1/2$"

$3/4$"

Filler strips

6"

2"

11"

$11^1/4$"

With the bar clamps in place, lay the assembly on its face, and drop the case back into its rabbets in the base cabinet sides. Then, attach it with glue and #6 × ¾-inch flathead wood screws.

4 **Apply the edge-banding tape.** When the case has been assembled and the glue has dried, apply iron-on veneer edge-banding tape to the exposed edges of the plywood at the front of the case just as you did to the base cabinets. Also, apply edge banding to the front edge of each adjustable shelf.

5 **Add the filler strips.** Set the case upright, and glue the filler strips in place, as shown in *Wide Wall Cabinet—Front View* and *Wall Cabinet—Side View*. The filler strips that fit against the case back can be secured with #8 × 1½-inch screws, but the filler strip at the front of the case should be glued and clamped in place only.

6 **Drill holes for adjustable shelves.** The wall cabinet has three adjustable shelves, which rest on $\frac{1}{4}$-inch brass shelf supports. Drill the $\frac{1}{4}$-inch-diameter × $\frac{1}{2}$-inch-deep holes for the shelf supports, as shown in *Wall Cabinet—Side View.*

Make the Glass Doors

The glass door rails and stiles are joined with dowels and cope-and-stick joints just like panel doors that were discussed earlier. Of course, instead of a panel, glass is installed in the door after the rails and stiles are joined. In order to allow the glass to fall in place, the bottom edge of the groove needs to be cut away.

1 **Size the parts.** Cut the door parts to the sizes given in the Materials List. You can cut the glazing strip stock now, or wait until you install the glass.

2 **Drill dowel holes in the rails and stiles.** Drill the dowel holes exactly as you did for the panel doors, using either a commercial doweling jig or your own shop-made jig. (See *Shop-Made Doweling Jig* on page 241.)

3 **Rout the profile in the rails and stiles.** Once the dowel holes have been drilled in the rails and stiles, set up a cope-and-stick door bit set in a router table to cut the profile along the edges of the frame parts just as you did for the panel doors.

4 **Cut the cope in the ends of the rails.** When the rail and stile edges have been shaped, cope the ends of the rails by following the procedure you used for the panel doors.

5 **Assemble the glass doors.** Assemble the doors one at a time by first gluing the dowels into the ends of the rails, gluing and inserting the rails into one of the stiles, and then gluing the other stile in place. When each door frame has been assembled, clamp it together with bar clamps, and check to make sure the assembly is square.

Rabbet all around the inside edge of the door to remove the bottom edge of the panel groove. The bit's pilot bearing should ride against the bead as shown.

6 **Prepare the door for glass.** When the glue is dry, put a ³⁄₈-inch, piloted rabbeting bit in a table-mounted router. With one of the doors face up on the router table, adjust the height of the bit so that the pilot will run against the innermost portion of the bead, as shown in *Glass Door Detail.* Then, push the frame clockwise around the rabbet bit to remove the bottom edge of the panel groove, as shown in the photo at left.

When the bottom edge of the panel groove has been rabbeted away, square the corners of the rabbet with a chisel.

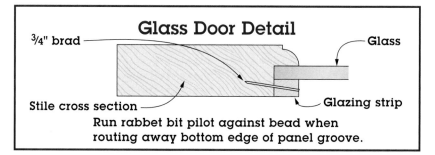

Glass Door Detail

³⁄₄" brad

Glass

Stile cross section

Glazing strip

Run rabbet bit pilot against bead when routing away bottom edge of panel groove.

7 **Install the glass.** Measure the rabbeted openings for the glass, and purchase ¹⁄₈-inch-thick glass to fit the door frames. Miter the glazing strip stock to fit around the rabbet. When the glazing strips have been mitered to fit, drill clearance holes for ³⁄₄-inch brads through the edge—one brad hole spaced every 4 inches or so. Start the brads in their holes, put the glazing strips in place behind the glass, and gently tap the brads into the door frame, as shown.

8 **Hang the doors.** Install the doors using European-style hinges like those used for the base cabinet doors.

Finish and Install the Wall Cabinet

1 **Prepare the cabinet for installation.** Sand the wall cabinet and doors progressively to 180 or 220 grit. Then, finish the cabinet to match the base cabinet.

When the finish is dry, install the door knobs.

If you are installing two or more adjacent wall cabinets, screw the cabinets together in manageable groups before attaching them to the wall. Make sure the edges of the cabinets align as you screw them together.

2 **Prepare the wall.** To aid in installing your cabinet, draw a level line along the wall to indicate the bottom edge of the wall cabinet. The line should be at least 18 inches above the countertop, as shown in *Height Layout*. Then, screw a temporary ledge below the level line—make sure you screw into the wall studs. This ledge will help you support the cabinet as you screw it to the wall.

3 **Hang the wall cabinet.** Hanging wall cabinets is a two-person job. Start by lifting the cabinet onto the ledge and positioning it on the wall.

Next, secure the cabinet to the wall by predrilling and driving #8 × 3-inch drywall screws through the back filler strips and into the wall studs. Remove the temporary ledge after the cabinet is in place.

When the cabinet is screwed in place, check its front edge for plum with a level, and if necessary, make adjustments by loosening the screws in the bottom filler strip and driving shims up between the cabinet back and the wall. When the cabinet is plum, retighten the screws, and trim the shims flush with the bottom of the cabinet.

4 **Install the molding spacer and crown molding.** Tack the molding spacer stock along the top of the wall cabinet with 4d finish nails, as shown in *Wall Cabinet— Side View*. The edge of the spacer should be flush with the outside side of any end cabinet, as shown in *Narrow Wall Cabinet—Front View*.

I made my crown molding with my shaper, but you can purchase similar moldings at a building-supply store. Tack the crown molding in place with 4d finish nails, and miter it to fit around the corners.

255

Mission Bookcase

by Tony O'Malley

It was a set of Golden Book Encyclopedias in the bookcase of my childhood living room that got me hooked on books. As an adult, I've always found that a room without books is lacking an important life ingredient. So as a woodworker, bookcases are among my favorite projects.

This bookcase design is a variation on the work of Gustav Stickley, who pioneered the honest, sturdy designs that came to be known as the Craftsman style and later the Mission style during the early twentieth century. The chamfered through tenons on the sides are a Stickley trademark. Quarter-sawn white oak was the preferred wood in Craftsman furniture, and I was able to find some nice planks for the sides and top. I settled for plain-sawn white oak for the shelves, knowing they'd be covered with books. White oak plywood serves for the back. The light walnut stain helps complete the Craftsman look.

I simplified construction of the glass doors by

making the divider bars, or muntins, a separate assembly that fits into notches in the door frame. As a result, each door gets one large pane of glass, which is held in place by small glazing strips.

Exploded View

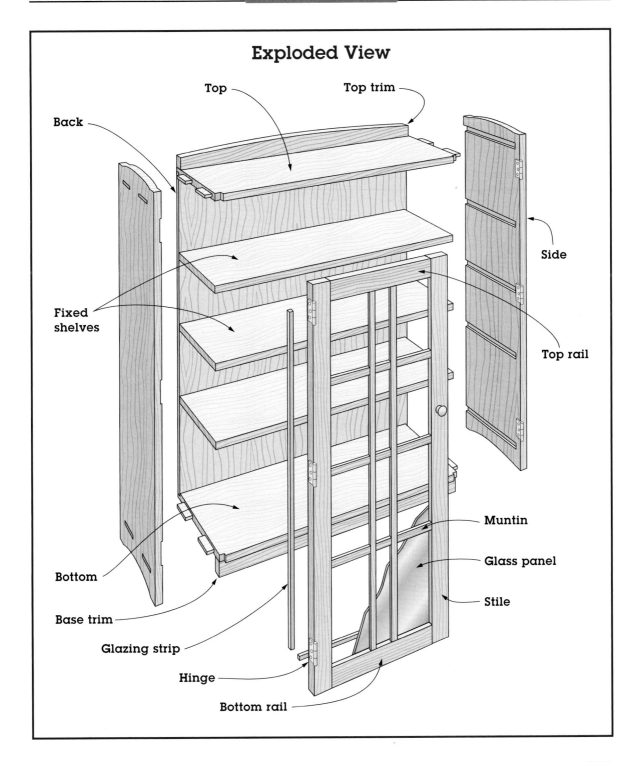

Top

Top trim

Back

Side

Fixed
shelves

Top rail

Muntin

Glass panel

Bottom

Stile

Base trim

Glazing strip

Hinge

Bottom rail

Top View

Stop rabbets in sides at intersection with top.

¼" plywood back fits in ¼" × ½" rabbet in sides, top, and bottom.

Attach top trim with glue and #8 × 1½" FHWS.

Attach back with #6 × ¾" drywall screws.

Front View

Side View

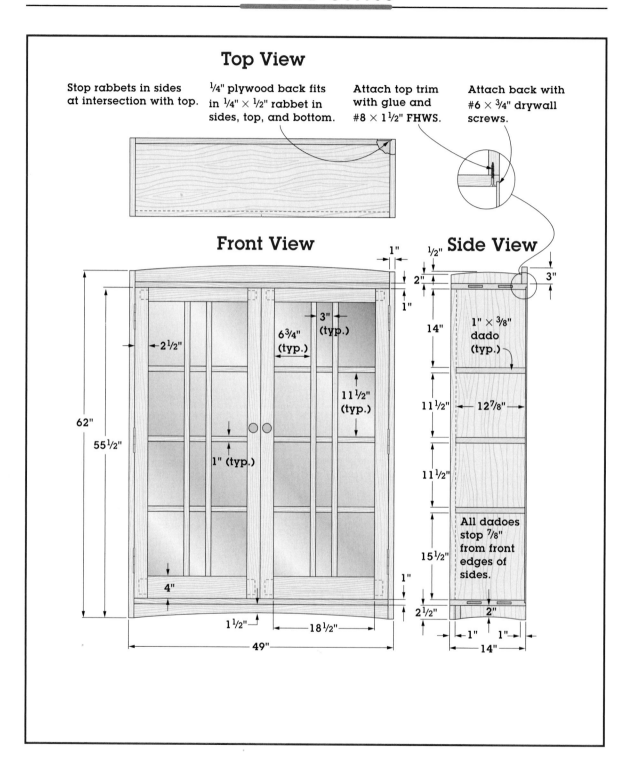

Materials List

Part	Dimension	Part	Dimension
Case		Horizontal muntins (6)	$\frac{3}{8}$" × 1" × $19\frac{1}{4}$"
Sides (2)	1" × 14" × 62"	Vertical glazing strips (4)	$\frac{1}{4}$" × $\frac{3}{8}$" × $49\frac{3}{4}$"
Top, bottom (2)	1" × 14" × $49\frac{1}{4}$"	Horizontal glazing strips (4)	$\frac{1}{4}$" × $\frac{3}{8}$" × $19\frac{1}{4}$"
Shelves (3)	1" × $12\frac{7}{8}$" × $47\frac{3}{4}$"		
Back	$\frac{1}{4}$" × 48" × $56\frac{1}{2}$"	**Hardware**	
Base trim	1" × 47" × $2\frac{1}{2}$"	#8 × $1\frac{1}{2}$" drywall screws (as needed)	
Top trim	1" × 47" × 3"	#6 × $\frac{3}{4}$" flathead wood screws (as needed)	
		$2\frac{1}{2}$" butt hinges (6)	
Doors		Glass, $\frac{1}{8}$" thick, cut to fit (2)	
Stiles (4)	$\frac{3}{4}$" × $2\frac{1}{2}$" × $55\frac{1}{2}$"	$\frac{1}{2}$" dia. felt bumpers (12)	
Top rails (2)	$\frac{3}{4}$" × $2\frac{1}{2}$" × $21\frac{1}{2}$"	$1\frac{1}{4}$" dia. oak door knobs (2)	
Bottom rails (2)	$\frac{3}{4}$" × 4" × $21\frac{1}{2}$"	Magnetic catches (2)	
Vertical muntins (4)	$\frac{3}{8}$" × 1" × $49\frac{3}{4}$"		

Make the Case

1 **Prepare the lumber.** The Materials List specifies a final thickness of 1 inch for most of the bookcase parts, excluding the doors. This is primarily an aesthetic issue for the sides, top, and bottom—if these parts were made thinner, they would not support the visual weight of the bookcase quite as well. In contrast, the shelves need to be 1 inch thick to support a load of books over their 47-inch span. However, if you cannot get the 5/4 stock necessary to get a 1-inch finished thickness, plane 4/4 stock so it's as thick as possible.

You'll probably be joining at least two boards on edge to get each case part. Make sure that each glued panel has $\frac{1}{2}$ inch or so of extra width, plus a couple inches of extra length for trimming.

2 **Cut the case parts to size.** Once glued up, joint one edge of each case part, then rip them all to width. I recommend using a crosscut sled on the table saw for crosscutting these parts to length. It is also good to use an outfeed support to hold the weight of the heavy oak boards.

Quick tip

In my shop, I often plane and cut the sides to size, and rout the dadoes. Then plane the top, bottom, and shelves to fit snugly in the dadoes. This is easier than routing dadoes to match the shelf thickness.

3 **Rout the stopped dadoes in the sides.** The top, bottom, and shelves fit into $\frac{3}{8}$-inch-deep stopped dadoes routed into the sides. The top and bottom are notched at their front edges, which are assembled flush with the sides. The shelves, set back behind the doors, fit fully in the dadoes. The net result is that all the dadoes are stopped an equal distance from the front edge—$\frac{7}{8}$ inch, as shown in *Side View*.

Clamp the sides together edge to edge, and lay out the dado locations across both sides. Use a T-square or straightedge to guide a plunge router. Use a $\frac{3}{4}$-inch straight bit ($\frac{1}{2}$ inch would also work), and rout each dado in two passes.

To do this, first set the straightedge to rout the near edge of each dado, then use a spacer between the straightedge and router to make the second pass, as shown in the photo below. With a $\frac{3}{4}$-inch bit and 1-inch-thick stock, for example, the spacer would be $\frac{1}{4}$ inch thick.

Instead of trying to find a bit that exactly matches the thickness of your shelf, it's better to make two passes with a smaller diameter bit. Instead of moving the fence, use a spacer to locate the second cut.

4 **Rout the through mortises.** Rout the mortises in the sides for the top and bottom with a plunge router, using the sides of the dadoes and a template guide on the router to determine the width of the mortises. The most practical combination of router bit-to-template guide is a $\frac{7}{8}$-inch outside diameter (O.D.) template guide and a $\frac{3}{8}$-inch-diameter straight bit, as shown in *Dado-Guided Mortising*.

Lay out the ends of the mortises right on the stock. To stop the router at the ends of the mortise cut, make a U-shaped template from a piece of $1/4$-inch plywood, as shown in the top photo on page 262. The distance between the two sides of the U should equal the width of the router base plus the width of the mortise minus the diameter of the router bit. Center the template using the mortise layout lines, and clamp it in place.

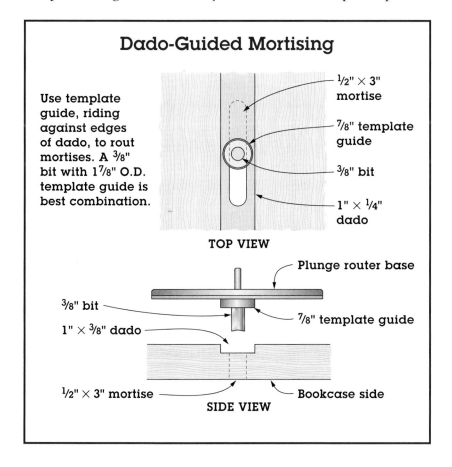

Dado-Guided Mortising

Use template guide, riding against edges of dado, to rout mortises. A $3/8"$ bit with $1^7/8"$ O.D. template guide is best combination.

$1/2" \times 3"$ mortise

$7/8"$ template guide

$3/8"$ bit

$1" \times 1/4"$ dado

TOP VIEW

Plunge router base

$3/8"$ bit

$1" \times 3/8"$ dado

$7/8"$ template guide

$1/2" \times 3"$ mortise

Bookcase side

SIDE VIEW

5 **Shape the top and bottom edges of the sides.** Lay out the soft curve at the top and bottom of each side, as shown in *Side View.* I simply bend a flexible rule to get the right curve and trace a pencil line against it. Cut the curves with a saber saw, and smooth them with a belt sander or sanding block.

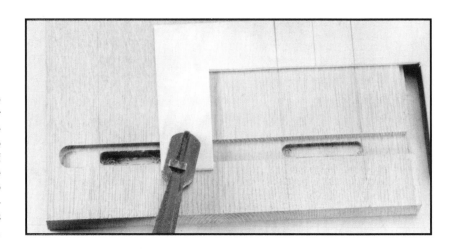

Center the mortise within the dado by using a template guide. To stop the router at the ends of the mortise cut, make a U-shaped template from a piece of ¼-inch-thick plywood, as shown here.

6 **Cut the tenons and notches on the top and bottom.** Start by cutting 1⅛-inch-wide × ¼-inch-deep rabbets along the ends of the top and bottom to form a ½-inch-thick continuous tenon, as shown in *Case Tenon Detail*. This can be done with a router and edge guide or on the table saw with a dado blade.

Next, lay out the ends of the smaller tenons on the continuous tenon. Use a small try square to strike the lines, which need to be square to the ends of the board.

When the tenons have been laid out, saw away the waste from around the tenons on the band saw. Don't try to cut the waste flush to the shoulders. Instead, set a fence on the band saw that will leave ½₂ inch or more of the waste, as shown in the photo at left. Trim the excess away with a flush-trimming router bit and a chisel.

Next, make the two ⅞-inch-deep cuts into the front edge of the top and bottom on the band saw. Clamp a fence on the band saw table, and position it to produce a ⅜-inch notch. This dimension is important and should correspond exactly to the depth of the dado. Work with a scrap piece of stock first to get the fence setting right. Once you have cut in ⅞ inch, back the blade out of the kerf. When the band saw kerf has been cut, tap a sharp chisel into the end grain to pop off the waste piece.

Finally, chamfer the ends of the tenons with a file, chisel, block plane, or sanding block, as shown in *Case Tenon Detail*.

To trim the waste between the tenons, set a fence on the band saw that will leave a little waste. What remains can be trimmed away with a chisel.

Case Tenon Detail

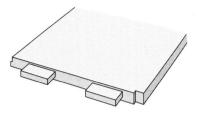

Step 1. Rout or saw $1\frac{1}{8}" \times \frac{1}{4}"$ rabbets on both sides of top and bottom.

Step 2. Lay out individual tenons.

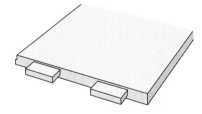

Step 3. Form tenons by bandsawing away most of excess stock. Then trim to final dimensions with chisel.

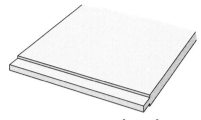

Step 4. Cut $\frac{3}{8}" \times \frac{7}{8}"$ notches at front corners.

Step 5. Shape $\frac{1}{8}"$ chamfer on ends of tenons.

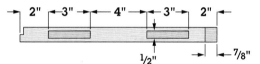

$\frac{1}{2}" \times 3" \times 1\frac{1}{8}"$ tenons centered in stock
TENON LAYOUT

⑦ Rout the back rabbet in the sides, top, and bottom. Make the rabbet for the back $\frac{1}{2}$ inch wide × $\frac{1}{4}$ inch deep. The easiest approach is to rout the rabbet with a bearing-guided router bit. Most rabbeting bits can be fitted with a smaller bearing guide to increase the cut from the standard $\frac{3}{8}$ inch to $\frac{1}{2}$ inch. You can also use a straight bit and an edge guide. Note that the rabbets in the sides must be stopped where they intersect the top.

8 **Cut and shape the base and top trims.** The arches in the base and top trims are identical, so you can cut both pieces from a single piece of 4⁹⁄₁₆-inch-wide stock and only have to cut the curve once. Lay out the curve on the stock with a thin flexible stick, and cut along the layout line on the band saw, as shown in the photo below. Then smooth the curves with a spokeshave and sanding blocks shaped to match the curves.

9 **Assemble the case.** Test assemble the case without glue to make sure all the parts fit together correctly. Then, assemble the top, bottom, and shelves to the sides with glue. Clamp the case from side to side along the shelves until all the parts are pulled together correctly.

Next, glue and clamp the base trim under the front edge of the bottom, set back 1 inch, as shown in *Side View*. Then, predrill and counterbore holes up through the underside of the base trim, and screw it to the bottom of the shelf, using #8 × 1½-inch drywall screws.

When the base trim is in place, glue and screw the top trim piece flush with the back edge of the case top, as shown in *Side View*.

Through all of this gluing, make sure that the case remains square. When the glue has had time to set up, screw on the back to help hold the case square, using #6 × ¾-inch flathead wood screws.

Cut one curve to get both curved parts. Lay out the curve on a piece that is 4⁹⁄₁₆ inch wide. Band saw on the line and you get both the base trim and the top trim pieces.

Make the Doors

1 **Cut the door parts to size.** Cut the rails and stiles to the sizes given in the Materials List. Wait until the frames are assembled and rabbeted before cutting the muntins.

2 **Cut the joinery.** Cut the rail tenons to the dimensions shown in *Door Detail*. I cut the tenons on the table saw with a dado blade, but you can cut them on the table saw with a tenoning jig if you have one.

Lay out the mortises on the stiles to accept the tenons, as shown in *Door Detail*. Rout the mortises with a plunge router

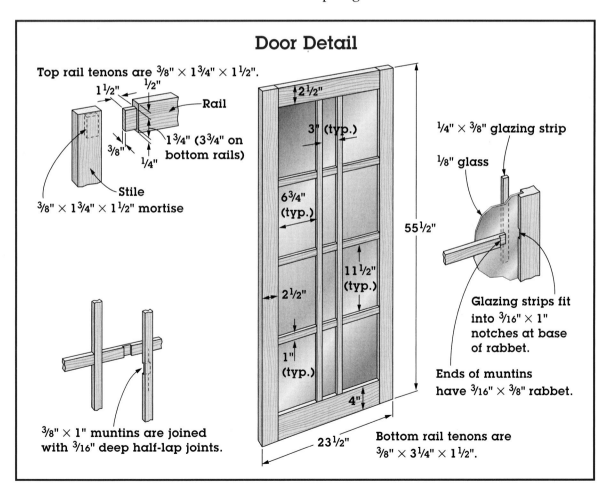

Door Detail

Top rail tenons are ³⁄₈" × 1³⁄₄" × 1¹⁄₂".

1¹⁄₂"   ¹⁄₂"

Rail

1³⁄₄" (3³⁄₄" on bottom rails)

³⁄₈"   ¹⁄₄"

Stile

³⁄₈" × 1³⁄₄" × 1¹⁄₂" mortise

³⁄₈" × 1" muntins are joined with ³⁄₁₆" deep half-lap joints.

2¹⁄₂"

3" (typ.)

6³⁄₄" (typ.)

2¹⁄₂"

11¹⁄₂" (typ.)

1" (typ.)

4"

23¹⁄₂"

55¹⁄₂"

¹⁄₄" × ³⁄₈" glazing strip

¹⁄₈" glass

Glazing strips fit into ³⁄₁₆" × 1" notches at base of rabbet.

Ends of muntins have ³⁄₁₆" × ³⁄₈" rabbet.

Bottom rail tenons are ³⁄₈" × 3¹⁄₄" × 1¹⁄₂".

and edge guide, or drill a series of holes within the layout lines and clean out the waste with a chisel.

3 **Assemble the doors.** Glue the door frames together on a flat surface, and measure across the diagonals to make sure the door is square. After the glue dries, rout a $\frac{3}{8} \times \frac{3}{8}$-inch rabbet for the glass and glazing strips around the inside edge of the door frames with a $\frac{3}{8}$-inch piloted rabbeting bit.

4 **Cut and assemble the muntins.** Cut the muntins to size, using the door frames as a guide. Lay out the muntin intersections using the case itself as a guide—the horizontal muntins should fall directly over the shelves. Then lay out and cut the half-lap joints where the muntins intersect, as shown in *Door Detail*. Use a dado blade, and guide the stock with the miter gauge. Glue the muntin assemblies together.

Next, lay out and cut the notches in the door frame rabbet for the muntins. I set up a router with a straight bit to give me a clean bottom and routed most of the notches freehand, as shown in the photo below left. Then I cleaned up the back and ends of the notches with a sharp chisel, as shown in the photo below right.

Use the muntin assembly to lay out the muntin notches in the rabbets of the doors, and then use a trim router and ¼-inch-diameter or smaller straight bit to cut the ³⁄₁₆-inch-deep notches.

When all of the notches have been routed, square the corners with a sharp chisel.

5 **Fit the doors, and cut the hinge mortises.** With the case lying flat on its back, test the fit of the doors in the opening. Trim the doors as necessary to fit. You can give the edges of the doors a light trim with a single pass over the jointer until they fit with about a $\frac{1}{16}$-inch gap all around. Push the door across the jointer with some scrap wood to avoid tearout.

The $2\frac{1}{2}$-inch butt hinges need to be mortised into the doors and case sides, as shown in *Front View*. To cut the hinge mortises, first put them in position on the edge of the door and scribe around them with a marking knife. Then, position each door in its opening with shims underneath. Transfer the hinge locations to the face frames.

After the hinge mortises have been laid out, use a small laminate trimmer with a straight bit to cut away most of the mortise to the depth of the hinge leaf. This method gives the mortise a flat consistent bottom. Finally, square the corners of each mortise with a chisel.

Finish the Bookcase

1 **Sand and finish the bookcase.** Sand the bookcase with progressively finer sanding grits to about 180 or 220 grit. You can make a 45-degree sanding block from a piece of scrap to sand the edges of the top and bottom tenons, as shown in the photo at right. When the piece was completely sanded, I brushed on three coats of satin polyurethane, sanding lightly between each coat with 400-grit wet-dry paper.

2 **Install the glass.** Glass panes this large are apt to rattle when the doors are closed. To prevent this, I placed a small circular felt pad behind each of the muntin intersections.

With the doors lying face down on a clean surface, install each large glass panel. Miter the glazing strips to fit, and install them with a thin bead of silicone caulk. Leave the doors lying horizontally until the caulk cures.

Cut a 45-degree bevel on the edge of a scrap piece to use as a sanding block for the chamfered ends of the through tenons. Glue a piece of sandpaper to the bevel, and sand away.

③ Hang the door, and install the hardware. When the caulk has cured, install the hinges and hang the doors. Since white oak is very hard, predrill for the screws supplied with the hinge.

Next, install the door knobs by drilling bolt or screw holes, positioning the knobs roughly where shown in *Front View*. You can buy oak knobs, or make your own as I did, as shown in *Knob Detail*.

Finally, install the magnetic catches under the top shelf, and load the bookcase with your favorite tomes.

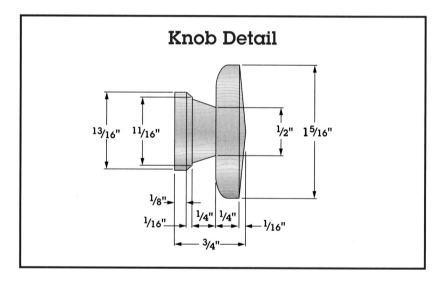

Knob Detail

Open-Shelf Bookcase

by Jim Probst

Simple, sturdy, and elegant—these are the three criteria I had in mind when I sat down to design an open-shelf bookcase. To keep things simple, yet elegant, I went with the clean lines of the Arts and Crafts movement. Stout, square legs, thin spindles, an overhanging top, and gracefully arched rails combine to create a visually interesting yet simple case.

Those clean lines allow this piece to be comfortable teaming up with almost any other decor, and the bookcase could be used in any room of the house. Although the bookcase was designed to hold a load of books, its shelves are also great places to display collectibles given its open design. The slatted sides allow light to penetrate the sides of the bookcase.

Since this case was designed to hold the considerable weight of books, I used mortise-and-tenon joinery throughout. The books rest on hefty 1-inch-thick shelves. And a series of shallow holes drilled inside the case accept shelf pins so

you can adjust the position of the shelves to fit different sizes of books.

This shelf was made from cherry, but white oak would also be a good choice. To build the open-shelf bookcase, I started by making two identical sides, then I joined these together with arched rails at the top and bottom of the case. Finally, I added a top and the shelves.

Exploded View

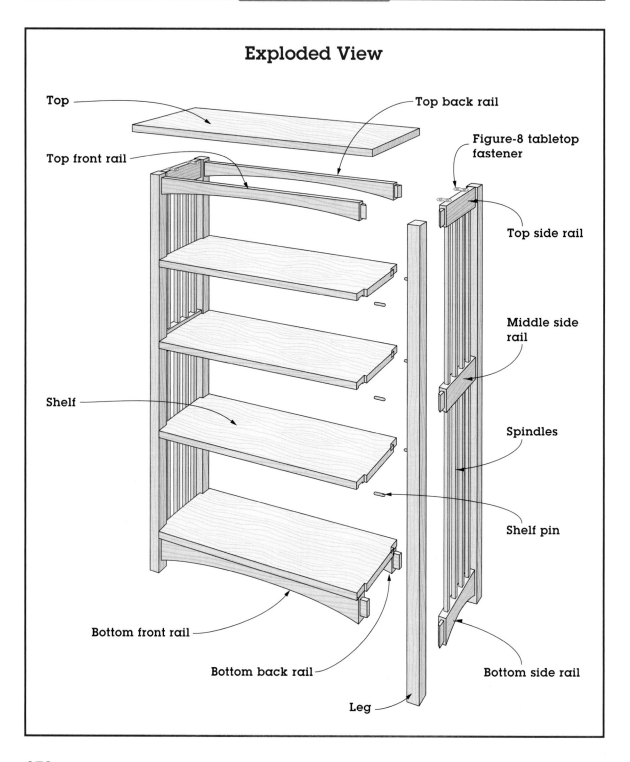

Top

Top back rail

Figure-8 tabletop fastener

Top front rail

Top side rail

Middle side rail

Spindles

Shelf

Shelf pin

Bottom front rail

Bottom back rail

Bottom side rail

Leg

Materials List

Part	Dimension	Part	Dimension
Sides		Top front and back rails (2)	1" × 2" × 30"
Legs (4)	$1\frac{1}{2}$" × $1\frac{1}{2}$" × 59"	Top	1" × 14" × 35"
Top side rails (2)	1" × $2\frac{1}{2}$" × 11"	Shelves (4)	$\frac{7}{8}$" × $11\frac{3}{4}$" × $28\frac{1}{2}$"
Middle side rails (2)	1" × 3" × 11"	Shelf pin stock	$\frac{1}{4}$" dia. × 24"
Bottom side rails (2)	1" × 4" × 11"	Cleats (4)	1" × 1" × $2\frac{1}{2}$"
Spindles (8)	$\frac{3}{4}$" × $\frac{3}{4}$" × $28\frac{1}{2}$"		
Spindles (8)	$\frac{3}{4}$" × $\frac{3}{4}$" × 21"	**Hardware**	
		#8 × $1\frac{1}{2}$" drywall screws (16)	
Front		Figure-8 tabletop fasteners with screws (4)	
Bottom front and back rails (2)	1" × 4" × 30"		

Make the Sides

1 **Cut the parts to size.** Joint, plane, rip, and cut the pieces for the legs, top side rails, middle side rails, bottom side rails, and spindles to the sizes given in the Materials List. Face-glue narrow boards to make up the $1\frac{1}{2}$-inch-thick legs, if necessary. (I prefer using 8/4 stock as it eliminates the glue line.)

2 **Lay out mortises in the legs.** Lay out five mortises in each leg (three for the side rails and two for the front and back rails), as shown in *Leg Mortise Layout*. (*Note:* Make sure to lay out the mortises as mirror images to ensure that you end up with two identical side assemblies.)

3 **Cut mortises in the legs.** Cut the mortises by taking a series of light cuts with a plunge router, and then square up the corners with a chisel. Clamp the legs on your workbench, and guide the cuts with the router's fence attachment, as shown in the photo at right. If you don't have a plunge router, you can remove the waste by drilling a series of holes, then square up the sides and corners of the mortises with a chisel.

Cut the mortises on the legs with a plunge router and a straight bit. Take a series of light cuts to reach the full depth.

Front View

Side View

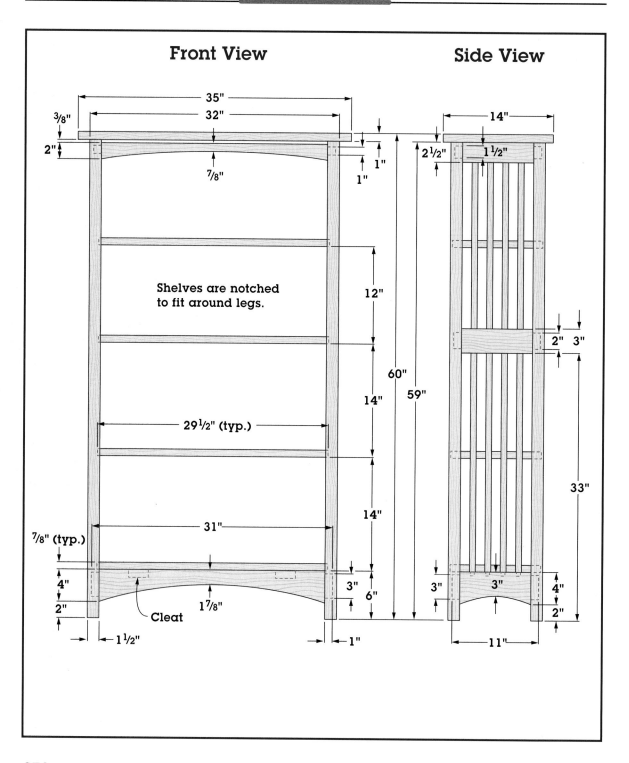

Shelves are notched
to fit around legs.

Cleat

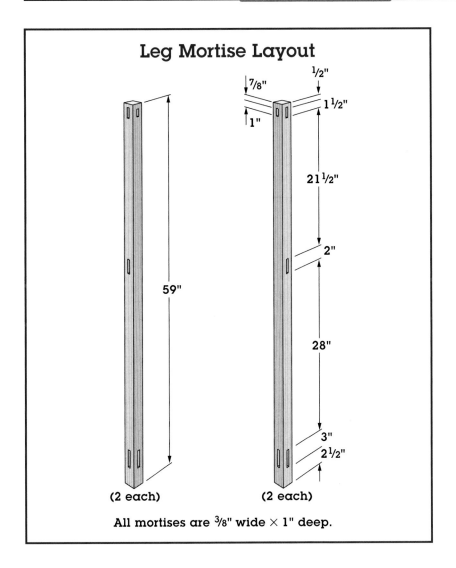

Leg Mortise Layout

1/2"

7/8"

1"

1 1/2"

21 1/2"

2"

59"

28"

3"

2 1/2"

(2 each)   (2 each)

All mortises are 3/8" wide × 1" deep.

4 **Cut tenons on the side rails.** Cut 1-inch-long tenons on the ends of each side rail to fit the mortises. To make quick work of this, I used the table saw with a stacked dado blade. Flip each piece between passes to remove an equal amount of material from each side.

Since the top and bottom side rails are adjacent to the front and back rails, the tenons on the top and bottom side rails and the front and back rails (made later) need to be mitered, as shown in *Mortise-and-Tenon Detail*.

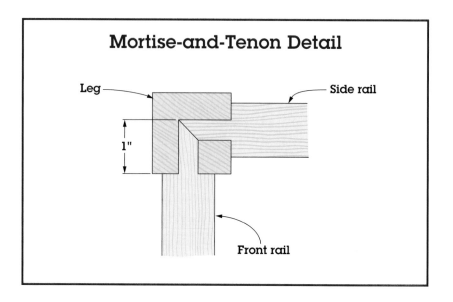

Mortise-and-Tenon Detail

Leg

Side rail

1"

Front rail

5 **Cut spindle mortises in the side rails.** When laying out the mortises for the spindles, keep in mind that the top side rails only have mortises on their bottom edges, and the bottom side rails are only mortised along their top edges—the middle rail is mortised along both edges. The layout of the mortises is shown in *Spindle Mortise Detail.* Once

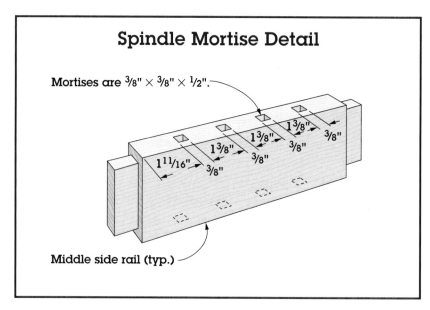

Spindle Mortise Detail

Mortises are $3/8" \times 3/8" \times 1/2"$.

$1^{3}/8"$ $1^{3}/8"$ $1^{3}/8"$ $3/8"$

$1^{11}/16"$ $3/8"$ $3/8"$ $3/8"$

Middle side rail (typ.)

the mortises are laid out, cut them by first drilling a series of $\frac{3}{8}$-inch-diameter holes, $\frac{1}{2}$ inch deep, and then squaring up the corners with a chisel.

6 **Cut tenons on the spindles.** Before cutting the tenons on the ends of the spindles, it's a good idea to test assemble the rails and legs, and check the dimensions one more time. Now cut a $\frac{3}{8}$-inch-thick × $\frac{3}{8}$-inch-wide × $\frac{1}{2}$-inch-long tenon on the ends of each spindle to fit the mortises in the rails. Here again, I used a stacked dado blade and a stop block attached to a miter gauge, flipping the spindle between each pass to ensure a centered tenon.

7 **Cut arcs on the bottom rails.** There's one last thing to do before gluing up the sides, and that's to cut a graceful arc on the bottom edge of each bottom side rail. To lay out the arc, simply bend and hold a flexible straightedge to the desired radius, as shown in the photo below. Then with a pencil, trace the curve onto the rail. After sawing the curve to shape, sand the edges smooth.

Quick tip

In order to ensure consistent tenons when using a dado blade to cut them, first make sure that matching parts are all the same thickness. If the stock thickness varies, so will the thickness of the tenons. Check the thickness of your rail and spindle stock for variations, or mill all of the stock at the same time to ensure consistent thickness.

Lay out the arc on the bottom rails using a flexible straightedge clamped between the jaws of a clamp. Adjust the clamp to achieve the desired radius.

8 **Assemble the sides.** Test assemble the sides without glue, and make any necessary adjustments. When you're satisfied with the fit, start by gluing the spindles in the side rails. Then apply glue to the leg mortises and rail tenons, and clamp the sides together.

Make the Front and Back Rails, Top, and Shelves

Once the sides are glued and clamped, you can turn your attention to the rails that connect the sides, the top, and the shelves.

1 **Cut the parts to size.** Joint, plane, rip, and cut the front and back top and bottom rails, the top, and the shelves to the sizes given in the Materials List. Edge-glue narrow boards to make up the wide pieces as necessary. *Note:* To create a deep shadow line between the top rail and the top, there's a $\frac{3}{8}$-inch gap between them. If you want to eliminate this, simply cut the top rails $\frac{3}{8}$ inch wider.

2 **Cut the tenons.** As you did with the side rails, cut tenons on the ends of each front and back rail.

3 **Cut arcs on the rails.** Lay out the arcs on the bottom edges of the front top and bottom rails and the back top and bottom rails. Here again, a flexible straightedge makes quick work of this. *Note:* The top rail is $\frac{7}{8}$ inch wide at the center of the arc. The bottom rail is $1\frac{7}{8}$ inches wide.

Assemble the Case

1 **Test fit the case.** Assemble the sides and front and back rails without glue to make sure the parts fit well. Make any necessary adjustments.

2 **Glue up the case.** Apply glue to the mortises and tenons, and clamp the case together. After you've applied clamps, measure on the diagonal to check that the case is square. Adjust the clamps as necessary.

3 **Add the top.** The top is secured to the case with metal figure-8 tabletop fasteners that sit in shallow mortises drilled into the top of each side rail, as shown in the photo below. Center the top on the case so there's an equal overhang on each side, and screw it in place with the screws provided with the fasteners.

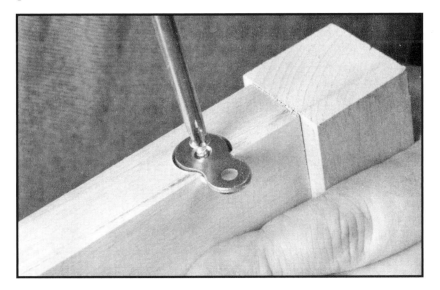

To attach the top, drill shallow mortises in the side rails to accept metal figure-8 tabletop fasteners.

4 **Add the shelves.** The corners of each shelf are notched to "wrap" around the inside corner of each leg. The bottom shelf sits on the bottom rails and is held in place in front and back by short cleats, as shown in *Front View*. These cleats are fastened into each front and back bottom rail and the underside of the bottom shelf with glue and #8 × 1½-inch drywall screws driven through slotted holes.

5 **Drill holes for shelf pins.** The shelves rest on shelf pins made from ¼-inch dowels that fit into holes drilled in the inside face of each leg. Lay out and drill holes to position the shelves, as shown in *Front View.* You can also drill a series of holes to adjust the shelves to fit different sizes of books. To make the dowels "invisible," I rout shallow open mortises in the bottom edge of the three adjustable shelves, as shown in *Shelf Pin Detail.* Rout the mortises with a ³⁄₈-inch-diameter straight bit, and guide the cut with the router's edge guide.

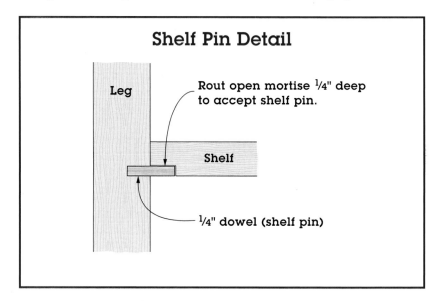

Shelf Pin Detail

Leg

Rout open mortise ¼" deep to accept shelf pin.

Shelf

¼" dowel (shelf pin)

Finish the Case

1 **Prepare the surface.** Sand all parts of the bookcase with progressively finer grits starting with 120 grit and ending with 220 grit. Remove all dust and sanding residue with a vacuum or tack cloth.

2 **Apply the finish.** I applied three coats of a wiping varnish, buffing lightly between coats with a fine-grade (gray) abrasive pad. Finally, I applied a coat of paste wax and buffed it out to a dull sheen.

3 **Install the shelves.** Install the shelf pins and the shelves.

Gallery of Fine Cabinetry

▲ The butternut drawer fronts add striking contrast to the painted maple case of furniture maker Robert J. Treanor's "Sewing Desk" (page 118). Simple lines and ample drawer space make the desk a practical addition to any room of the house.

▲ The Shakers used long counters like this for tasks such as measuring and cutting fabric, while the drawers provided extra storage for the ever-practical sect. The "Shaker Counter" (page 296) is also ideal for a bedroom because of its dresserlike drawers.

◀ If the sign of a true craftsman is attention to details, furniture maker Robert J. Treanor passes the test with carefully fitted joinery, even at the back of the counter.

▲ There is some Shaker influence in woodworker Rob Yoder's "Hall Table" (page 87), but the shaped edge of the top and the curves at the ends of the front rail and aprons result in a slightly more elegant design. Rob used a simple but effective scratch stock to cut the curving face beads on the front rail and aprons—a detail not easily created with a router.

◀ Cabinetmaker Voicu Marian used curves to set the style for his "Hanging Display Cabinet" (page 150). He cut all of the curves on a band saw so there was no complicated bending involved. Since the piece was originally designed to display Chinese soapstone stamps, or "chops," the Asian style is appropriate.

▲ Conservative walnut, maple inlay, and solid brass hardware distinguish cabinetmaker Ben Erickson's decidedly southern "Classic Huntboard" (page 26). A huntboard was originally used for serving a stand-up dinner to saddle-sore huntsmen. Today, a huntboard can still serve as a great staging area for special family dinners.

◀ Carefully inset escutcheons and inlay set off the huntboard's showy walnut grain.

The combination of walnut and bird's-eye maple creates this elegant little "Jewelry Box" (page 331). Cabinetmaker Ben Erickson joined his box with simple but strong splined miter joints and cut off the raised panel top to form a lid. Two small, velvet-lined, compartmental trays lift out to provide access to the treasures hidden inside.

The Shakers knew that built-in cabinets provide more efficient storage than free-standing cabinets. Furniture maker Andy Rae's "Shaker-Style Storage and Workstation" (page 214) proves this by utilizing the whole wall and even the space in front of the window.

◀ Cabinetmaker Ben Erickson's "Three-Drawer Side Table" (page 104) combines functionality with traditional elegance. Its height makes it perfect as a side table for a sofa or even as a bedside table. The side table is solidly constructed with frame-and-panel assemblies that rest on a traditional cut-out base. The locking, dovetailed drawers are set off with thin cock beading and provide ample storage for books, magazines, and reading glasses.

▶Every home needs a bit of whimsy, and the "TV House" (page 139) certainly provides some. The parents who commissioned designer Glenn Bostock to build a TV cabinet for their children requested "something light-hearted and fun." Glenn's design exceeded all of their expectations. The cabinet mimics a dollhouse (*far right*), but the facade opens with pocket doors (*right*) to reveal the TV hidden inside. The hinged roof of the TV house opens up to provide storage for the TV listing and remote control.

◀ Gustav Stickley started the Arts and Crafts movement in the United States, which included the Craftsman style of furniture that inspired woodworker Tony O'Malley's design for this "Mission Bookcase" (page 256). Made almost exclusively from oak, Craftsman furniture was made to last with thicker than usual hardwood and tough, often visible joinery. The chamfered through tenons in this piece are a Stickley trademark, as is the almost gaudy, quartersawn white oak.

◀ The swooping bottom rail of furniture maker Jim Probst's "Cherry Sideboard" (page 41) makes a potentially heavy piece seem ready to leap into the air. Parallel raised inlays in the drawer fronts also enhance the illusion of lightness (*inset*).

▼ Although a Pennsylvanian at heart, woodworker Ken Burton shows some Southwestern influence in his "Cherry Vanity" (page 371). The angular back-splash, panel doors, and door pulls bring to mind Native American art. The little protru-sions under the countertop, which Ken calls "lookouts," are certainly reminiscent of beams protruding from adobe houses.

▶Imagine Ben Franklin or Thomas Jefferson writing important documents at this "Slant-Front Desk" (page 189), a classic piece of American furniture. Woodworker Ken Burton designed an interpretation, rather than a reproduction, of this early but familiar form specifically to accommodate twentieth-century writing paper, checkbooks, calculators, and such. He made the slant-front desk from cherry, but walnut would also be an appropriate choice.

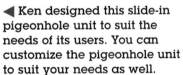

◀ Ken designed this slide-in pigeonhole unit to suit the needs of its users. You can customize the pigeonhole unit to suit your needs as well.

▶In the eighteenth century, German settlers in North America developed the "Step-Back Cupboard" (page 2), often called a Dutch cupboard. The word "Dutch" is simply a corruption of *Deutsche,* the German word for "German."

Cherry was a good traditional choice for the cupboard, since over time it darkens to a rich, reddish brown.

Woodworker Mitch Mandel designed his cupboard with modern tools and modern materials in mind—the back of the bottom case is cherry plywood, and Mitch joined a few of the parts with biscuits. The walnut handles that replace traditional turned knobs also give the piece an updated look.

◀ Simple, sturdy, and elegant—furniture maker Jim Probst kept these three criteria in mind as he designed his "Open-Shelf Bookcase" (page 269). The Arts and Crafts movement inspired the simplicity and elegance in the shelf's airy, clean lines. Yet the stout legs and arched rails give a sense of strength. The vertical spindles that form the sides of the shelf help to relieve the heaviness of the legs. All of these subtle elements work together to create a unified piece that would fit well within most contemporary and traditional homes.

◀ The design for this "Eastern Shore of Virginia Corner Cabinet" (page 61) by cabinetmaker Lonnie Bird dates from 1745 with its roots in Virginia's Eastern Shore region. The fluted columns, crown molding, waist molding, and baseboard in the original piece indicate that the cupboard was probably made by a house joiner (an interior carpenter). It was likely the high point of the joiner's craft—an elaborate freestanding cabinet that clearly shows the joiner's skill. The exceptional proportions and thoughtfully placed decorative moldings make it a fine example of cabinetry from the colonial Piedmont.

▲ Although the wide crown and waist moldings on the original corner cupboard were almost certainly cut with various molding planes, they can be built up from a series of smaller, routed profiles.

▲ Cabinetmaker Jim Michaud's "Platform Bed" (page 316) puts the wasted space under a bed to the best possible use. Painted bright blue, it looks great in a teen's room. Painted another color such as honey white and expanded to queen- or king-size, it works well in a master bedroom. For ease of moving, build beds larger than twins in two identical, back-to-back halves.

▶ A home office should be tailored to suit the occupant's needs. Woodworker Glenn Bostock's "Home Office Cabinetry" (page 230) can be customized to combine file drawers, bookshelves, storage, and work surfaces.

▲ The center cabinet in woodworker Tony O'Malley's stylish "Entertainment Center" (page168) holds a large TV and a VCR, while the side cabinets house a stereo system and speakers. Drawers store CDs and videos. When the TV is in use, pocket doors disappear into the sides of the cabinet. You can customize this design to meet your own unique electronic entertainment needs.

◀ Furniture maker Jim Probst designed this cherry "Sweater Cabinet" (page 340), which looks like a small wardrobe. Sweet-smelling cedar lining in the interior repels moths but not people. Two movable shelves allow the most efficient use of the space. Practical Shaker designs inspired Jim to create the simple lines of the cabinet, which would be at home in both country and contemporary decors.

293

▶ Walnut burl graces the drawer fronts of a traditional "Philadelphia Highboy" (page 352) reproduction by cabinetmaker Lonnie Bird—certainly one of the more challenging projects in this book. The top and bottom of the case are two separate, interlocking cabinets—just like the original. Although the exterior is walnut, the interior parts of the cases are poplar.

▼ To make the cabriole legs, Lonnie first rough cut them on a band saw. Then he shaped them with a drawknife, rasp, spokeshave, and file.

Bedroom and Bath

Shaker Counter

by Robert J. Treanor

Anyone who has worked with cloth knows the necessity of having a surface on which to lay out the pieces to be measured and cut. Practical people that they were, members of the Shaker community combined this work surface with drawers for storage and called the piece of shop furniture that resulted a counter. The design I show here is based on one made at the Watervliet Shaker community during the first half of the nineteenth century.

The materials in my counter are typical of what might have been used by Shaker craftsmen of old: maple for the case; pine for the drawer backs, sides, and bottoms; and poplar for the drawer runners and guides. The maple, including the figured maple for the drawer fronts, makes a durable and attractive surface for the counter.

Traditionally, the secondary woods used in places not readily visible, helped keep the cost down and were more easily worked than the primary wood, since they were softer. Today, clear white pine can cost as much as premium hardwood, so adapt the materials if you wish. The secondary wood in the drawers could be poplar; or make them all from plain maple, which is relatively inexpensive.

Exploded View

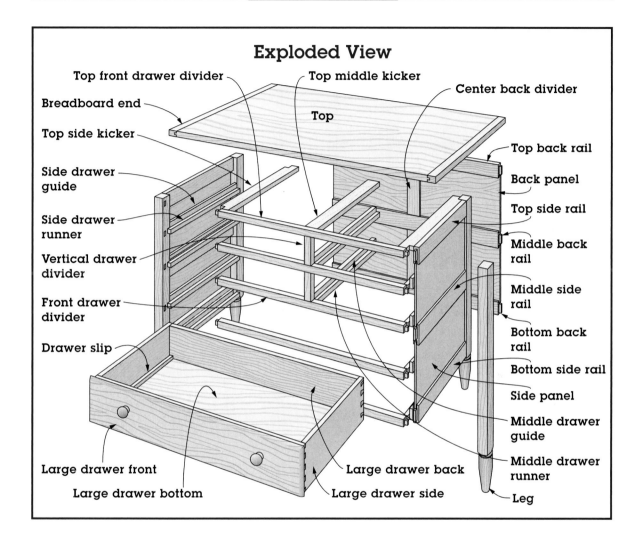

Top front drawer divider

Top middle kicker

Center back divider

Breadboard end

Top

Top side kicker

Top back rail

Back panel

Side drawer guide

Top side rail

Side drawer runner

Middle back rail

Vertical drawer divider

Middle side rail

Front drawer divider

Bottom back rail

Drawer slip

Bottom side rail

Side panel

Large drawer front

Middle drawer guide

Large drawer bottom

Large drawer back

Middle drawer runner

Large drawer side

Leg

Make the Case

1 **Select the stock and mill the parts to size.** Mill the wood for the case parts to the dimensions given the Materials List. For now, leave a 1-inch-long "horn" at the top of the leg blanks as an aid in turning. Since all the pieces of the counter are solid wood, you may have to edge-glue narrow boards to get pieces wide enough for some of the panels. If you wish, ½-inch hardwood plywood could also be used for the panels.

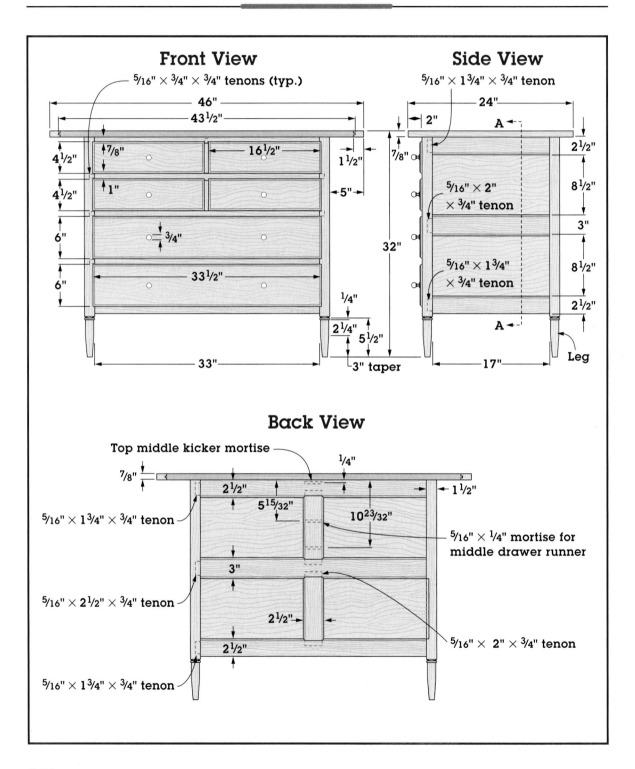

Front View

5/16" × 3/4" × 3/4" tenons (typ.)

46"
43½"
16½"
7/8"
4½"
1½"
1"
4½"
5"
3/4"
6"
33½"
6"
32"
1/4"
2¼"
5½"
33"
3" taper

Side View

5/16" × 1¾" × 3/4" tenon

24"
2"
A
7/8"
2½"
5/16" × 2"
× 3/4" tenon
8½"
3"
5/16" × 1¾"
× 3/4" tenon
8½"
2½"
A
17"
Leg

Back View

Top middle kicker mortise
1/4"
7/8"
2½"
1½"
5/16" × 1¾" × 3/4" tenon
5 15/32"
10 23/32"
5/16" × ¼" mortise for
middle drawer runner
5/16" × 2½" × 3/4" tenon
3"
2½"
5/16" × 2" × 3/4" tenon
2½"
5/16" × 1¾" × 3/4" tenon

Materials List

Part	Dimension	Part	Dimension
Case		Top side kickers (2)	$\frac{7}{8}$" × $2\frac{1}{2}$" ×$18\frac{3}{8}$"
Top	$\frac{7}{8}$" × 24" × $43\frac{1}{2}$"	Top middle kicker	$\frac{7}{8}$" × $2\frac{1}{2}$" × $18\frac{7}{8}$"
Breadboard ends (2)	$\frac{7}{8}$" × $1\frac{1}{2}$" × 24"		
Dowel stock	$\frac{1}{4}$ " dia. × 24"	**Drawers**	
Legs (4)	$1\frac{1}{2}$" × $1\frac{1}{2}$" × $31\frac{1}{8}$"	Small drawer fronts (4)	$\frac{13}{16}$" × $4\frac{1}{2}$" × $16\frac{1}{2}$"
Front drawer dividers (4)	$\frac{13}{16}$" × 1" × $34\frac{1}{2}$"	Small drawer sides (8)	$\frac{1}{2}$" × $4\frac{1}{4}$" × 16"
Top front drawer divider	$\frac{13}{16}$" × $\frac{7}{8}$" × $34\frac{1}{2}$"	Small drawer backs (4)	$\frac{1}{2}$" × $3\frac{3}{8}$" × 16"
Vertical drawer dividers (2)	$\frac{13}{16}$" × 1" × $5\frac{1}{4}$"	Small drawer bottoms (4)	$\frac{7}{16}$" × $15\frac{3}{4}$" × $14\frac{3}{4}$"
Top side rails (2)	$\frac{13}{16}$" × $2\frac{1}{2}$" × $18\frac{1}{2}$"	Large drawer fronts (2)	$\frac{13}{16}$" × 6" × $33\frac{1}{2}$"
Bottom side rails (2)	$\frac{13}{16}$" × $2\frac{1}{2}$" × $18\frac{1}{2}$"	Large drawer sides (4)	$\frac{1}{2}$" × $5\frac{3}{4}$" × 16"
Middle side rails (2)	$\frac{13}{16}$" × 3" × $18\frac{1}{2}$"	Large drawer backs (2)	$\frac{1}{2}$" × $4\frac{7}{8}$" × 33"
Top back rail	$\frac{13}{16}$" × $2\frac{1}{2}$" × $34\frac{1}{2}$"	Large drawer bottoms (2)	$\frac{7}{16}$" × $15\frac{3}{4}$" × $31\frac{1}{4}$"
Bottom back rail	$\frac{13}{16}$" × $2\frac{1}{2}$" × $34\frac{1}{2}$"	Drawer slips (12)	$\frac{3}{8}$" × $\frac{7}{8}$" × $15\frac{3}{4}$"
Middle back rail	$\frac{13}{16}$" × 3" × $34\frac{1}{2}$"	Knob stock	$\frac{3}{4}$" × $\frac{3}{4}$" × 20"
Center back dividers (2)	$\frac{13}{16}$" × $2\frac{1}{2}$" × $10\frac{1}{2}$"		
Side panels (4)	$\frac{1}{2}$" × 9" × $17\frac{1}{2}$"	**Hardware**	
Back panels (4)	$\frac{1}{2}$" × 9" × $15\frac{3}{4}$"	#10 × 2" flathead wood screws (as needed)	
Side drawer runners (8)	1" × 1" × $18\frac{3}{8}$"	#10 × $1\frac{1}{4}$" roundhead wood screws (as needed)	
Side drawer guides (8)	$\frac{1}{2}$" × 2" × 18"	#10 × 1" roundhead wood screws (as needed)	
Middle drawer runners (2)	1" × $2\frac{1}{2}$" × $18\frac{7}{8}$"	#8 × 1" flathead wood screws (as needed)	
Middle drawer guides (2)	1" × 1" × $18\frac{3}{8}$"	#10 flat washers (as needed)	

2 **Cut the mortises and panel grooves in the legs.**
Lay out these mortises and grooves carefully, as shown in *Leg Joinery Detail;* and don't let the extra length on the legs throw you off. Cut the $\frac{5}{16}$-inch-wide mortises for the front drawer dividers and side drawer guides with a hollow-chisel mortiser, if you have one, or you can clamp several of the legs to-gether on your bench to create a stable base for a plunge router. I have constructed a simple plywood box, as shown in *Setup for Making Mortises,* which I use to cut most of my mortises. Rout the mortises with several shallow passes, riding the router fence against the outside of the leg you are mortising or the outside of the mortising box. In the same manner, lay out and cut the $\frac{1}{4}$-inch-wide × $\frac{1}{2}$-inch-deep mortises for the side drawer guide tenons. Square the ends of all the routed mortises with a chisel.

The $\frac{1}{4} \times \frac{1}{4}$-inch panel grooves in the legs run between the top and bottom side rail mortises. Rout them in several passes in the same manner as the mortises.

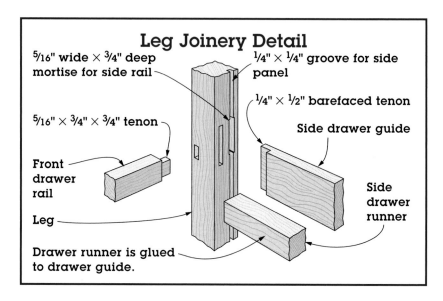

Leg Joinery Detail

$\frac{5}{16}$" wide $\times \frac{3}{4}$" deep mortise for side rail

$\frac{5}{16}$" $\times \frac{3}{4}$" $\times \frac{3}{4}$" tenon

Front drawer rail

Leg

Drawer runner is glued to drawer guide.

$\frac{1}{4}$" $\times \frac{1}{4}$" groove for side panel

$\frac{1}{4}$" $\times \frac{1}{2}$" barefaced tenon

Side drawer guide

Side drawer runner

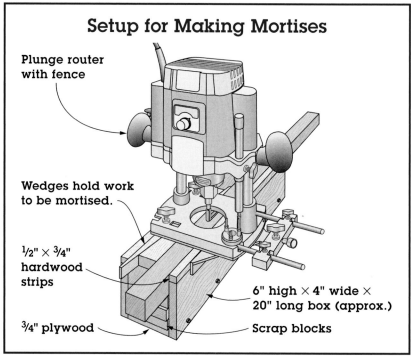

Setup for Making Mortises

Plunge router with fence

Wedges hold work to be mortised.

$\frac{1}{2}$" $\times \frac{3}{4}$" hardwood strips

$\frac{3}{4}$" plywood

6" high $\times$ 4" wide $\times$ 20" long box (approx.)

Scrap blocks

3 **Cut the mortises in the top and front drawer dividers and back rails.** In the counter, vertical dividers separate the four small drawers. The vertical dividers are attached to the top and front drawer dividers with $^5\!/_{16}$-inch-thick tenons, as shown in *Drawer Divider Joinery Detail*. Rout these mortises in the drawer dividers with a mortising machine or with a plunge router and router fence, as you did for the legs. If you do not use the mortising box, clamp the drawer rails together for a stable router-bearing surface, and ride the fence against the rail you are routing.

The middle drawer runners and top kickers for the small drawers join the drawer dividers in the front and the top rail and center divider in the back with $^5\!/_{16} \times ^1\!/_4$-inch stub tenons. Cut the mortises on the inside of the drawer dividers just as you have the other mortises. If you cut the corresponding mortises in the top back rail and center back divider now, you must lay them out carefully so they line up when you go

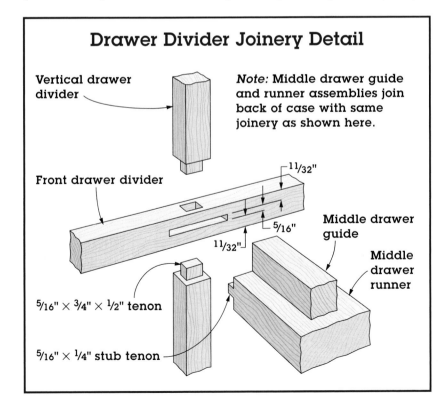

Drawer Divider Joinery Detail

Vertical drawer divider

Note: Middle drawer guide and runner assemblies join back of case with same joinery as shown here.

Front drawer divider

11/32"

5/16"

11/32"

Middle drawer guide

Middle drawer runner

$^5\!/_{16}" \times ^3\!/_4" \times ^1\!/_2"$ **tenon**

$^5\!/_{16}" \times ^1\!/_4"$ **stub tenon**

Turned Foot Detail

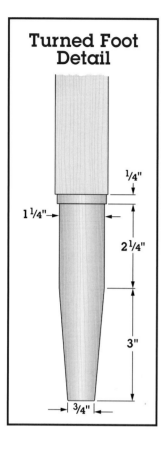

1¼"

¼"

2¼"

3"

3/4"

to assemble the case. You can cut these mortises at a later stage if you prefer. (See Step 9 on page 304.)

4 **Turn the bottom leg detail.** On a lathe, turn the ¼-inch collar and the taper on the bottom of each of the legs, as shown in *Turned Foot Detail*. Sand the leg turning while it is still on the lathe. The horn at the top of each leg allows you to attach it to the lathe spindle without worrying about disfiguring the leg, as shown in the photo below. After the legs have been turned and sanded, use a table saw to cut off the horns, bringing the legs to their final length.

5 **Rout the molded edge on the panel rails and dividers.** The side and back rails and center back dividers have a ¼-inch-radius roundover with a 1/16-inch step routed into the edges that border the panels. To cut this detail, secure your router in a router table, and fit it with a ¼-inch radius beading bit. Guide the rails and dividers against a fence clamped to the table as you rout. If your router bit has a ball-bearing guide, you could also secure the pieces to your bench, and then slide the router along each rail to cut the molded edges.

A 1-inch horn, or extension, on the leg allows you to cut off any chuck marks left by the lathe after the piece has been turned and sanded. Cut the leg to its final length as you cut away the waste.

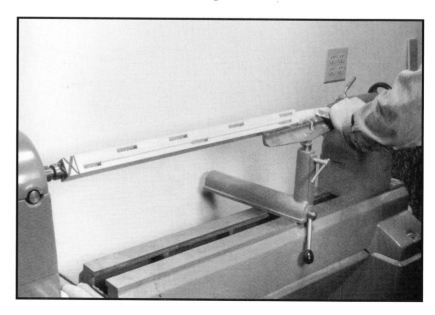

6 **Make mortises and grooves in the side and back rails and center back dividers.** On the paneled back of the counter, the two center dividers are tenoned into the rails with $5/16$-inch-thick × $3/4$-inch-long tenons. However, since you will eventually cut away the $1/4$-inch-wide molded edge where the divider and rail meet, the mortises you make must be 1 inch deep. Cut them with a hollow-chisel mortiser (or attachment to your drill press), if you have one. Otherwise, rout these mortises in the same manner as the others with your plunge router. Cut the $1/4$ × $1/4$-inch panel grooves in the side rails, back rails, and center back dividers with a dado head on your table saw. Slide the rails and dividers on edge against the rip fence as you cut the grooves.

7 **Cut the tenons in the side and back rails and center back dividers to match the mortises.** There are numerous ways to cut tenons, and you may have a technique you favor. I cut the tenons on this project with a dado blade on the table saw. It is a quick and effective method that works best if you have milled the tenon pieces to the accurate thickness. Since you register off both surfaces, any variation will cause a variations in the tenon's thickness. Lay the piece to be tenoned flat on the table saw. Screw a wooden face piece to your miter gauge that extends to the dado blade. Clamp a stop block to the rip fence, and adjust the fence to cut a tenon of the correct length.

Crosscut the shoulder; then slide the piece away from the stop block while you remove the remainder of the waste, as shown in the photo on page 304. Flip the piece over, and repeat the procedure. On the rail and divider tenons, you must stand the pieces on edge to cut all four shoulders and cheeks of the tenons. The side drawer guides have barefaced tenons, or tenons with only one shoulder, as shown in *Leg Joinery Detail*. Make the tenons on the top and front drawer dividers, vertical drawer dividers, side and back rails, center back dividers, and side and middle drawer guides and runners to fit the mortises you have already made.

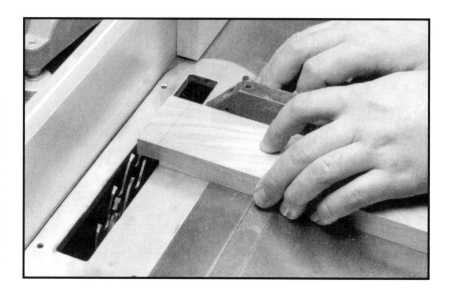

A stop block screwed to the rip fence ahead of the blade allows you to gauge the length of the tenon without scraping the stock along the fence as you cut. When the initial cut has been made, simply slide the stock back along the miter gauge and remove the waste at the end of the tenon.

8 Relieve the panels to fit the panel grooves. I beveled the back or inside edge of the panels to fit the panel grooves, thus creating a flat panel on the exposed surfaces. You can bevel these edges with a combination blade on your table saw. Tilt the blade away from the rip fence about 15 degrees; then stand the panels on edge as you slide them against the fence to cut the bevel, as shown in *Cross Section A-A—Top, Side Panels, and Rails*. You may want to cut the bevels slightly larger than necessary, and then take a couple of passes with a hand plane to clean up the saw marks.

9 Fit the center back dividers to the back rails. Because of the molded radius detail on the edges of the rails and dividers, the shoulders of the divider tenons won't seat against the edges of the rail mortises. To solve this problem, crosscut a 45-degree miter on the rails to the depth of the molded edge ($\frac{1}{4}$ inch) with your table saw. Crosscut the corresponding corners of the molded edge on the dividers, as shown in *Back Rail and Divider Joinery Detail*. Then remove the section of the rail molding where the divider meets it by crosscutting with the dado blade on the table saw. Cut only to the depth of the molded edge, and clean this cut up with a sharp chisel, if necessary.

If you haven't done so before, you need to cut the mortises in the center back divider for the small drawer runners and in the top back rail for the top middle kicker. You can feel more confident laying these out if you temporarily assemble the dividers and rails. Rout the $\frac{1}{4}$-inch-deep × $\frac{5}{16}$-inch-thick mortises with your plunge router where shown in *Back View*.

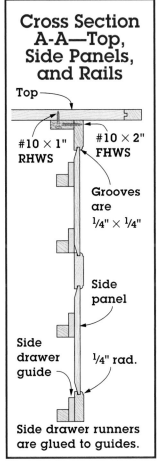

Cross Section A-A—Top, Side Panels, and Rails

Top

#10 × 1" RHWS

#10 × 2" FHWS

Grooves are $\frac{1}{4}$" × $\frac{1}{4}$"

Side panel

Side drawer guide

$\frac{1}{4}$" rad.

Side drawer runners are glued to guides.

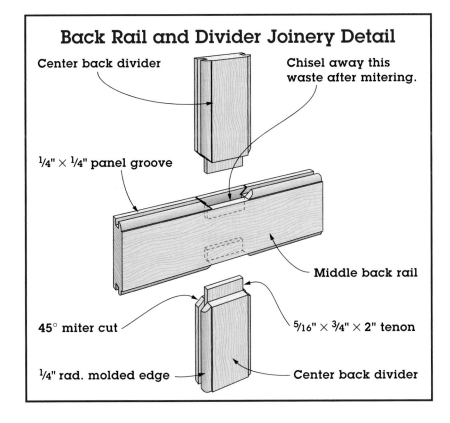

Back Rail and Divider Joinery Detail

Center back divider

Chisel away this waste after mitering.

$\frac{1}{4}$" × $\frac{1}{4}$" panel groove

Middle back rail

45° miter cut

$\frac{5}{16}$" × $\frac{3}{4}$" × 2" tenon

$\frac{1}{4}$" rad. molded edge

Center back divider

10 **Drill the top kickers for screws to attach the counter top.** In a runner-kicker drawer system, the runner and the kicker are usually the same piece of wood. It is a runner when the bottom of the drawer sides slide along it as the drawer is opened or closed. It is a kicker when the top of the drawer sides slide along it, preventing the drawer from sagging down from the weight of the contents. So except for the topmost and bottommost drawers, the kicker is simply the bottom surface of the runner that the drawer above is riding on.

The three kickers for the topmost drawers of this Shaker counter have holes drilled in them for screws that hold the top to the base. Clearance holes for the front and back screws must be enlarged to allow the top to move with seasonal moisture changes. Lay out the three holes in each kicker, as shown in *Top Kicker Detail*. Counterbore a shallow ¾-inch-diameter hole for the screw holes that must be slotted. To make the slots, drill two holes side by side on the drill press, and chisel away the waste between them. To prevent the screws in the middle kicker from interfering with the operation of the drawers, position them down the center of kicker, and they will not need to be counterbored. Attach the top with #10 × 1¼-inch roundhead wood screws and washers in the slotted holes and just the screws without washers in the center holes.

Counterbore 1-inch × ⅜-inch-diameter holes in the edges of the top side kickers for screws to hold them to the rails. Drill screw clearance holes in the center of the counterbores, as shown in *Top Kicker Detail*.

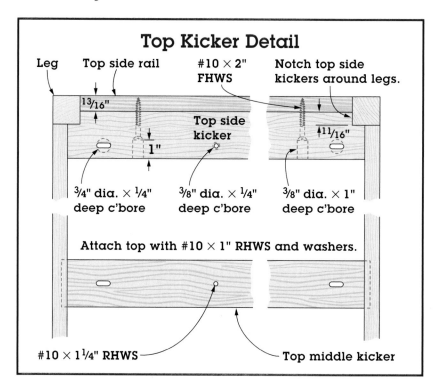

Top Kicker Detail

Leg   Top side rail   #10 × 2" FHWS   Notch top side kickers around legs.

13/16"

Top side kicker

1"

11/16"

¾" dia. × ¼" deep c'bore   ⅜" dia. × ¼" deep c'bore   ⅜" dia. × 1" deep c'bore

Attach top with #10 × 1" RHWS and washers.

#10 × 1¼" RHWS   Top middle kicker

Assemble the Case

1 **Sand and test assemble the case.** After all the joints have been made, sand each of the pieces to the desired smoothness. You should remove milling marks and any blemishes in the surfaces. Be careful when sanding any of the areas where parts join. Putting the pieces together without glue helps you see where any problems in the fit may occur and allows you to correct them without rushing around in a glue-up panic. Clamp the drawer rails between the two front legs, and the back rails and panels between the two back legs. Then clamp each of these assemblies together with the side rails and panels to form the case, fitting the drawer runners and guides in place as you draw in the clamps. Make certain all joints are tight.

While the case is together, notch the two top side kickers to fit around the legs, as shown in *Top Kicker Detail*. After you lay out the cuts, you can make them on the band saw. Attach these kickers once your glue-up is complete.

2 **Glue together the drawer runners and guides.** On the sides of the case, the drawer runners are glued to the drawer guides, which are mortised into the legs. Hold each runner in place against the guide, and mark to indicate the position to glue the runner. The front edge of each runner butts against the inside surface of the drawer rails.

The middle drawer runners for the small drawers are tenoned into the case, and the middle drawer guides are glued to them. Position and mark the runners for the middle guides. Disassemble the case; then glue and clamp the runners and guides to your marks.

3 **Glue together the front and back assemblies.** Start by gluing and clamping the vertical drawer dividers between the front drawer dividers to form the openings for the small drawers. Then glue and clamp the drawer dividers between the front legs. Make certain the pieces are square to each other by carefully measuring across diagonal corners and

Quick tip

One of the problems with drawer cases over the years, particularly when drawer runners are made of softer secondary woods, is that the drawer sides rub grooves in the drawer rails. You can guard against this now by attaching the runners a shade higher than the drawer rails. Then as the drawer opens and closes, it clears the drawer rail without rubbing.

Quick tip

When making a frame-and-panel construction, it is often helpful to finish the panels before you glue the frame together. This has two advantages. The first is that glue will not adhere to the panel if you get any on it, so the panel will float properly with seasonal moisture changes and not be accidentally bound by misplaced glue. The second is that, as the panel contracts with winter dryness or age, lines will not appear on the edges of the panel when unfinished wood is exposed.

adjusting until you get equal measurements. For the back assembly, glue and clamp the center back dividers to the back rails, capturing the panels as you pull the joints together. Try not to get glue on the panels or in the panel grooves, so the panels will float in the frames. Then glue and clamp the back legs to the back rails. Check as you did before to be sure the back assembly is square. Both panels should lie perfectly flat.

4 **Complete the case assembly.** You may want to wait until the glue has dried and the clamps are removed from the first two parts of the glue-up before continuing, but it isn't necessary. Glue the side rails and the drawer runner/guide pieces to the front assembly mortises, placing the side panels into position. Then glue and clamp the back assembly to the side rails and drawer runner/guide pieces. Check the case carefully to make certain that each side is square and the case is not twisted. The entire surface you sight across should be in the same plane. If one corner sits high, relieve the clamp pressure somewhat, place a 1-inch block under one leg and correct the twist by applying pressure down on the two lifted legs.

Make and Attach the Counter Top

1 **Edge-glue boards to make the top.** Mill the wood for the top and the breadboard ends, leaving the top boards about 1 inch longer than the final dimension listed in the Materials List. The top of this counter is solid maple and must be glued up from narrower boards. If you have a biscuit joiner, you can insert biscuits between the boards for better alignment and extra strength. Clamp the top together in two or three stages if you wish, gluing two boards at a time.

2 **Cut the top to size.** When glued together, the top should be slightly longer and wider than the final dimensions. The size and weight of the top make crosscutting it to length on the table saw awkward, but here is a method to make it easier. Measure the distance from the saw blade to the outside edge of the saw table. Clamp a straight 2 × 2 × 48-inch fence this distance plus ½ inch from the end of the top to be crosscut. The fence will extend about 12 inches on each side of the top. Make certain it is square to the sides of the counter top. Flip the top over so the fence is on the bottom, and set it with the fence running against the outside edge of the saw table. Turn on the saw, and slide the fence against the saw table, removing the last ½ inch of material from the top. Repeat the procedure to cut the second end to the final length.

When the top is cut to length, rip it against the fence on the table saw if necessary, and run each edge along the jointer to trim it to the final width.

3 **Cut the tongues and grooves for the breadboard ends.** Make the grooves in the breadboard pieces; then make the tongues to match the grooves. With a dado blade in the table saw, rip the $\frac{5}{16}$ × $\frac{3}{8}$-inch grooves in the breadboards by running the stock against the rip fence. Rout the tongues with a rabbeting bit equipped with a ball bearing, or clamp a straightedge fence across the ends of the top to ride the base of the router against as you rout the tongues with a straight bit. If you ride the router against a fence, set it up carefully when making the second cut so the shoulders align.

4 **Pin the breadboard to the counter top.** Clamp the breadboard ends in position on the top, with the top upside down on your bench. Drill ¼-inch stopped holes through the edge of the breadboard end and through the top tongue, but stop the bit ⅛ inch before it exits through the top. Drill three holes in each breadboard, one in the middle and one on each end, as shown in *Breadboard Detail*. Unclamp and remove the breadboard pieces; and with a small round file or coarse sandpaper wrapped around a length of $\frac{3}{16}$-inch dowel, elongate the two outer holes in the tongue on each end of the top.

Quick tip

When attaching a breadboard end to a top, you can create a better fit if the groove edge of the bread-board is slightly concave; that is, it bows slightly away from the top in the middle. Then as you clamp the breadboard tightly to the top, the ends hold more securely with no tendency to pull away. You can do this by hand planing about a $\frac{1}{32}$-inch curve along the length of the breadboard before you cut the groove.

Reclamp the breadboard end pieces to the top, this time gluing the middle 4 or 5 inches of tongue into the groove. When you have pulled the breadboard tight, tap ¼-inch hardwood dowels into the drilled holes to pin the ends. Glue the middle dowels, but glue only the last ¼ inch of the outside dowels. Cut off any excess dowel, and sand the ends flush with the breadboard when the glue has dried. The elongated holes in the tongue will allow the top to expand and contract as it needs. The small end grain circles from the dowels will be barely visible on the bottom side.

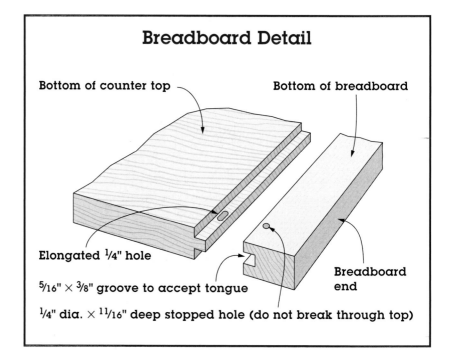

Breadboard Detail

Bottom of counter top

Bottom of breadboard

Elongated ¼" hole

5⁄16" × 3⁄8" groove to accept tongue

Breadboard end

¼" dia. × 11⁄16" deep stopped hole (do not break through top)

5 **Attach the counter top to the case.** Lay the counter top upside down on a pad on your bench, and set the case upside down on it. Position it and mark through the holes in the top kickers for screws. Remove the case, and use a handheld drill to bore pilot holes on your screw hole marks for #10 × 1¼-inch roundhead wood screws. Then replace the case on the top, and secure it with the screws (use flat washers in the slotted holes).

Make the Drawers

These drawers have traditional joinery that goes well with the overall nature of the Shaker counter, but they are time-consuming to make. You may decide to cut routed dovetails with a commercial dovetail jig, if you have one, or you can use some other drawer joinery, such as box joints. Plan this ahead of time so you can take into account any possible changes in dimensions.

1 **Mill the parts, and fit the drawer parts to the drawer openings.** Mill the drawer parts to the dimensions given in the Materials List, keeping in mind that the drawers have to be fitted to the openings in the case. So check your work to make certain your drawer openings are accurate. I made the bottoms from solid stock, which was glued up from narrower stock. It would be fine to make the bottoms from $\frac{1}{2}$-inch birch (or other appropriate hardwood) plywood.

Organize all the drawer parts first, putting all pieces for each drawer together and marking each piece for "top" and "inside" (or "front"). Then fit each part to the individual openings. The drawer faces should have a total of $\frac{1}{8}$ inch of clearance top to bottom and side to side. The drawer back should be $\frac{1}{2}$ inch less in length than the drawer fronts, and the sides should have the same $\frac{1}{8}$-inch top clearance as the faces. Let the drawer bottoms remain slightly oversize for now, and remember that the grain of the bottoms runs parallel to the drawer faces.

2 **Rout the molded edge on the drawer faces.** This decorative edge is quickly made with a $\frac{1}{4}$-inch-radius beading bit in a router table. Bury the bit in a fence clamped to the table (even if the bit comes with a ball bearing). Using a band saw or dado bit, you can roughly cut an opening in the fence board large enough for the bit to sit within. Slide the drawer fronts face down against the fence to rout the $\frac{1}{4}$-inch roundover with a $\frac{1}{16}$-inch fillet.

3 **Rabbet the drawer faces to create a lip, and cut the bottom groove.** Each drawer has a $\frac{1}{4} \times \frac{1}{2}$-inch lip on both ends and the top, which overlaps the drawer opening. Cut the lip with a rabbeting bit in your router table as you did the edge detail in the previous step. This time, slide the drawer faces against the fence face up. Do not cut a rabbet on the bottom edge.

The drawer bottom fits into a $\frac{1}{4} \times \frac{1}{4}$-inch groove cut in the inside of the drawer face, as shown in *Drawer Detail*. Make this groove with a dado blade on your table saw, sliding the drawer faces against the rip fence. The dovetails will hide the hole where the groove exits the end grain.

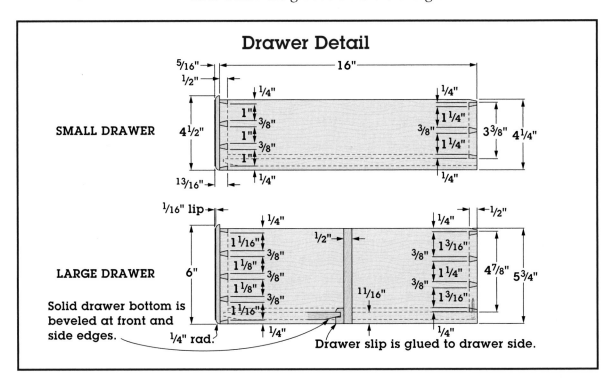

Drawer Detail

SMALL DRAWER

LARGE DRAWER

Solid drawer bottom is beveled at front and side edges.

$\frac{1}{4}$" rad.

Drawer slip is glued to drawer side.

4 **Cut the dovetails joining the sides to the fronts and backs.** I cut these dovetails by hand; half-blind dovetails are in the front and through dovetails are in the back. I will explain the procedure for making the joints, but for a more detailed explanation of cutting dovetails by hand, see "Cutting

Dovetails" on page 164. Perform the same operation for all drawers before going on the next procedure. For example, lay out the tails on all the drawers at the same time before you start sawing. Start by finish sanding the inside surfaces of the drawer parts. Then scribe a line around each end of the drawer sides to mark the length of the tails (or thickness of the pins). With a sharp pencil and your sliding T-bevel set at 12 degrees, lay out the tails on the drawer sides, as shown in *Drawer Detail*. With a square, carry these lines across the end grain on both ends of the drawer sides. Saw and chisel out the small pockets of waste between all the tails. Keep on the waste side of your line as you saw. Then for each drawer, scribe the outline of the tails onto the end grain of the drawer face and back pieces.

With a marking gauge, scribe a line across the inside of the drawer faces and around the ends of the drawer backs to indicate the length of the pins (or thickness of the tails). With a square, carry your pin layout lines down to this pin line. On the drawer backs, you can saw out the pins and chisel the waste between them, but on the front half-blind dovetails, you must basically chisel all of it. Lightly tap the pins into the tails to check the fit of your joints.

5 **Drill the drawer faces for drawer knobs.** On the drill press drill $^{3}/_{8}$-inch-diameter holes through the drawer faces for the knobs. The knobs are centered on the small drawers and centered top to bottom on the large drawers, and they are lined up vertically on each side.

6 **Glue the drawers together.** Glue one drawer at a time, and have everything ready before you begin. You need a small stiff brush, such as one of the inexpensive solder flux brushes, to help spread the glue. I think the best way to glue dovetails is to get all of the joints tapped, just barely together, perhaps for the first $^{1}/_{16}$ inch or so. Apply the glue quickly with the small brush to all the mating surfaces, which are easy to determine with the joints partly together. One or two clamps across the face and back are all you need to pull the dovetails closed. If you place the clamp cauls right over the pins, lay down pieces of wax paper under the cauls. If you place the cauls just behind the pins, set a spacer between the drawer sides to keep the clamp pressure from bowing the sides in. Make certain the drawer is square and flat. Continue in the same manner until you have glued all the drawers together.

7 **Fit and attach the drawer slips to each drawer.** As shown in *Drawer Detail,* each slip has a $\frac{1}{4} \times \frac{1}{4}$-inch groove to accept the drawer bottom. Cut these grooves with a dado blade on the table saw, riding the slips against the rip fence. Ease the top corner of the slip for a more friendly appearance inside the drawer. You can do this with a few passes of a block plane and sandpaper. The bottom of the slip is flush with the bottom of the drawer, so you must notch out the back of the slip where it fits against the drawer back. Position the slip against the drawer side and mark where it hits the drawer back. Make a shallow crosscut with a hand saw, and chisel out the end grain to make the $\frac{3}{16}$-inch-deep notch. In the same way, lay out and cut a $\frac{1}{4}$-inch tenon that will slip into the groove in the drawer front. Glue and clamp a drawer slip to each drawer side.

8 **Fit the drawer bottoms to the drawers.** First cut the drawer bottoms to the final dimensions to fit each drawer. Then bevel the edges of the $\frac{7}{16}$-inch-thick bottoms to fit the $\frac{1}{4} \times \frac{1}{4}$-inch grooves in the drawer faces and slips. Do this just as you did the panels in the case, standing the bottoms on edge on the table saw. Cut the bevels with a combination blade tilted away from the rip fence.

The bottom must be allowed to move with seasonal moisture changes. Where the large drawer bottoms extend under the backs, three screws hold them in place. Two screws are sufficient for the small drawers. For each screw, drill two clearance holes on the drill press for #8 × 1-inch wood screws side by side; then countersink each hole, overlapping the countersinks. Chisel or file the waste between the two holes to make a slotted screw hole. Sand each bottom, and slide it in place, gluing it only along the front edge. Drill slotted pilot holes, and attach each drawer bottom to its back with #8 × 1-inch flathead wood screws.

9 **Turn and attach the drawer knobs.** On a lathe, turn the drawer knobs, as shown in *Knob Detail*. Turn several pulls from one longer blank, sand them on the lathe, and cut them apart after you have removed the turned blank from the lathe. Then chuck the stem gently in the drill press to finish sand the rounded end.

Drill a ³⁄₃₂-inch-diameter hole at the base of the stem, and split the stem down the middle to this hole with a fine back saw. After final sanding the drawer face, glue the pulls into the drilled holes in the drawer faces, turning the stems so the split is vertical. Make a little wedge to fit the split from some hardwood scrap, and glue and tap the wedge in place. Now you can do the final sanding of the drawers.

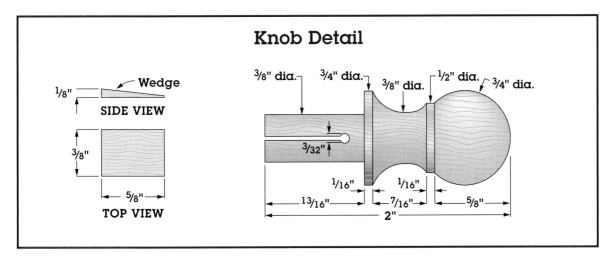

Knob Detail

10 **Apply finish to complete the counter.** The finish you apply is largely individual preference. The original Shaker furniture may have had a shellac or a linseed mixture finish. Modern finishes are more durable. I finished my counter with coat of penetrating oil finish, followed—after it had thoroughly dried—by several coats of sprayed lacquer, which goes on quickly and protects very well. You may want to try a polyurethane finish. One suggestion is to avoid oil finishes in the drawers, as they may later bleed and get on clothes. Shellac works very well as a finish in drawers.

Platform Bed

by Jim Michaud

A marked contrast to the traditional bed is the platform bed. Instead of a decorative frame around the mattress and box spring, you have a huge box that the mattress lies on. (The box spring is eliminated.) Instead of a low gap accessible only to dust bunnies, the space under the mattress becomes a wonderful enclosed space for storage.

Curiously, the first platform bed I ever made was for a client who was interested in relief from an aching back, not storage. But in subsequent versions, I have added drawers and doors to take advantage of the enormous amount of space inside the platform. I recommend that you have the mattress on hand before you begin because exact dimensions vary.

The original platform bed I built was a king size, and the platform was so large that the only hope for getting it into a typical bedroom was to build it in two halves. Each half is identical, and the two cases butt together, back to back, to create the full platform. Even for a queen- or full-size mattress, like that shown in the photo, I would recommend building the platform in halves.

Exploded View

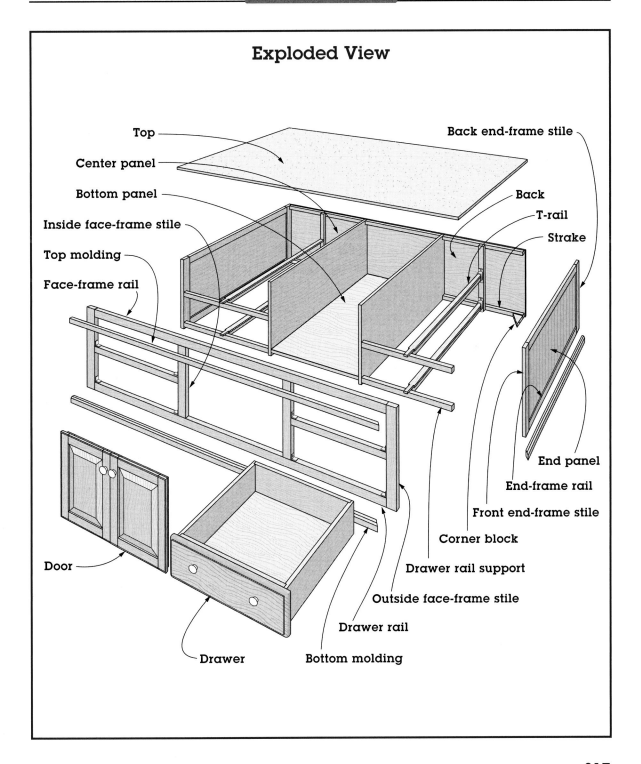

Top

Center panel

Bottom panel

Inside face-frame stile

Top molding

Face-frame rail

Back end-frame stile

Back

T-rail

Strake

End panel

End-frame rail

Front end-frame stile

Corner block

Drawer rail support

Outside face-frame stile

Drawer rail

Bottom molding

Drawer

Door

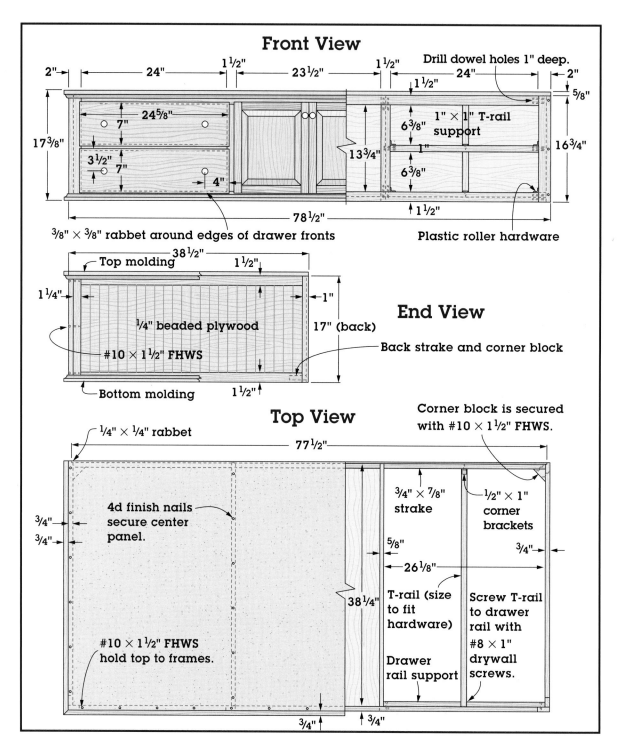

Front View

2"

24"

1 1/2"

23 1/2"

1 1/2"

24"

2"

Drill dowel holes 1" deep.

1 1/2"

5/8"

24 5/8"

7"

1" × 1" T-rail support

6 3/8"

17 3/8"

16 3/4"

3 1/2"

7"

1"

13 3/4"

6 3/8"

4"

1 1/2"

78 1/2"

3/8" × 3/8" rabbet around edges of drawer fronts

Plastic roller hardware

38 1/2"

Top molding

1 1/2"

1 1/4"

1"

End View

1/4" beaded plywood

17" (back)

#10 × 1 1/2" FHWS

Back strake and corner block

Bottom molding

1 1/2"

Top View

Corner block is secured
with #10 × 1 1/2" FHWS.

1/4" × 1/4" rabbet

77 1/2"

3/4" × 7/8" strake

1/2" × 1" corner brackets

4d finish nails
secure center
panel.

3/4"

3/4"

5/8"

3/4"

26 1/8"

38 1/4"

T-rail (size
to fit
hardware)

Screw T-rail
to drawer
rail with
#8 × 1"
drywall
screws.

#10 × 1 1/2" FHWS
hold top to frames.

Drawer
rail support

3/4"

3/4"

Materials List

Part	Dimensions
Platforms (2)	
Tops (2)	$\frac{5}{8}$" × $39\frac{1}{4}$" × $78\frac{1}{2}$"
Backs (2)	$\frac{1}{4}$" × 17" × $77\frac{1}{2}$"
End panels (4)	$\frac{1}{4}$" × $14\frac{1}{2}$" × 37"
Center panels (4)	$\frac{5}{8}$" × $15\frac{1}{4}$" × $38\frac{1}{4}$"
Bottom panels (2)	$\frac{5}{8}$" × $24\frac{3}{4}$" × $38\frac{1}{4}$"
Outside face-frame stiles (4)	$\frac{3}{4}$" × 2" × $16\frac{3}{4}$"
Inside face-frame stiles (4)	$\frac{3}{4}$" × $1\frac{1}{2}$" × $13\frac{3}{4}$"
Top/bottom face-frame rails (4)	$\frac{3}{4}$" × $1\frac{1}{2}$" × $74\frac{1}{2}$"
Dowels (40)	$\frac{5}{16}$"-dia. × $1\frac{7}{8}$"
Drawer rails (4)	$\frac{3}{4}$" × 1" × 24"
Drawer rail supports (8)	$\frac{3}{4}$" × 1" × $26\frac{1}{8}$"
T-rail supports (4)	1" × 1" × $16\frac{3}{4}$"
T-rails (8)	1" × 1" × $37\frac{3}{8}$"
Front end-frame stiles (4)	$\frac{3}{4}$" × $1\frac{1}{4}$" × $16\frac{3}{4}$"
Back end-frame stiles (4)	$\frac{3}{4}$" × 1" × $16\frac{3}{4}$"
End-frame rails (8)	$\frac{3}{4}$" × $1\frac{1}{2}$" × 37"
Strakes (2)	$\frac{3}{4}$" × $\frac{7}{8}$" × 77"
Corner blocks (4)	$\frac{3}{4}$" × 2" × 2"
Top molding faces (2)	$\frac{3}{4}$" × $1\frac{1}{4}$" × 80"
Top molding ends (4)	$\frac{3}{4}$" × $1\frac{1}{4}$" × 40"
Bottom molding faces (2)	$\frac{3}{4}$" × 1" × 80"
Bottom molding ends (4)	$\frac{3}{4}$" × 1" × 40"
Drawers (for 2 platforms)	
Faces (8)	$\frac{3}{4}$" × 7" × $24\frac{5}{8}$"
Fronts (8)	$\frac{1}{2}$" × 6" × $22\frac{15}{16}$"
Sides (16)	$\frac{1}{2}$" × 6" × 35"
Backs (8)	$\frac{1}{2}$" × $5\frac{1}{2}$" × $22\frac{15}{16}$"
Bottoms (8)	$\frac{1}{4}$" × $34\frac{3}{4}$" × $23\frac{3}{16}$"
Doors (for 2 platforms)	
Panels (4)	$\frac{1}{2}$" × $10\frac{3}{8}$" × $12\frac{5}{8}$"
Stiles (8)	$\frac{3}{4}$" × $1\frac{1}{4}$" × $14\frac{3}{8}$"
Rails (8)	$\frac{3}{4}$" × $1\frac{1}{4}$" × $10\frac{3}{8}$"

Hardware

#10 × $1\frac{1}{2}$" flathead wood screws (as needed)

#10 × 1" flathead wood screws (as needed)

#8 × 1" drywall screws (as needed)

#8 × $\frac{3}{4}$" drywall screws (as needed)

4d finish nails (as needed)

4d coated nails (as needed)

$\frac{3}{4}$" brads (as needed)

T-rail glides (8). Available from Rockler Woodworking and Hardware, 21801 Industrial Boulevard, Rodgers, MN 55374-9514; (800) 279-4441; part #28357

$\frac{1}{2}$" × 1" metal corner brackets (8)

Disk rollers (16). Available from Rockler Woodworking and Hardware; part #33381

1" dia. wooden knobs (20)

$\frac{3}{8}$" offset hinges (4 pairs)

Cabinet catches (4)

Customizing Your Bed

The dimensions given in the Materials List are for a king-size bed made from two back-to-back platforms. Queen-size and full-size beds should also be made in two halves, but a twin can be made as a single cabinet. The photo on page 316 shows a full-size bed made by the editor from my design. If you want to make a king-size bed, you are all set, but if you want a smaller bed, you will need to adjust some of the dimensions. Mattress sizes are as follows:

- Queen size: 60 × 80 inches
- Full size: 54 × 75 inches
- Twin size: 39 × 75 inches

As noted, mattress sizes can vary by a few inches, so it may be a good idea to buy and measure your mattress before you build your custom bed.

Make the Subassemblies

Let's get oriented at the start. We typically speak of a bed as having a head and a foot, with sides connecting them. But the platform bed is nontraditional in form, and it's natural to perceive the face with the doors and drawers as the front. The face that abuts the mating platform half is the back. The faces beneath the sleeper's head and feet are the ends.

The platform is constructed from several subassemblies, including the face frame, the ends, the top, the storage cases, and the back. Make these subassemblies first.

1 **Mill the parts for the face and end frames.** Mill the rails and stiles for the face and end frames to the dimensions given in the Materials List. Also mill the wood for the strake and the corner blocks. Although I describe making one platform, remember you must make two platforms, so make the parts for both at the same time. If you have the space, you can assemble both platforms at the same time.

2 **Assemble the face frame.** Dowel joints are used to assemble the framework. Lay out the dowel joints on the face-frame parts, as shown in *Front View.* Guided by a doweling jig, drill two 5/16-inch-diameter × 1-inch holes for each joint.

You must also make a joint between the drawer rails and the frame stiles, since this rail carries the weight of the drawer. Although I make a dowel joint here, I also reinforce this joint with a support rail glued to the back of the drawer rail. After the frame is assembled, you can glue and screw the support rail to the back of the stiles, as shown in *Drawer Rail Support*.

Next, go to the drill press and bore and counterbore three clearance holes for #10 × 1½-inch flathead wood screws in the outside face-frame stiles, as shown in *Front View*. You will screw through these holes to attach the face frame to the end assembly.

Finally, glue and clamp the face frame together. First glue the inside face-frame stiles to the top and bottom rails. Attach the drawer rail to the inside face-frame stiles; then glue and clamp the outside face-frame stiles.

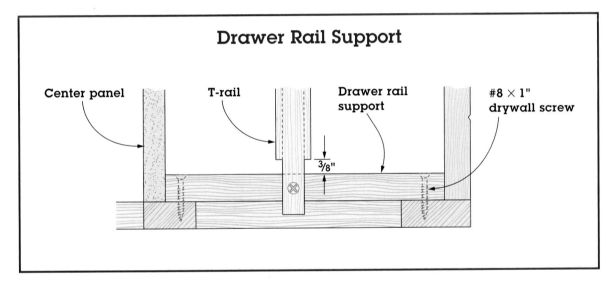

Drawer Rail Support

Center panel   T-rail   Drawer rail support   ⅜"   #8 × 1" drywall screw

3 **Construct the end assemblies.** The ends of the platform are frame-and-panel units with panels made of ¼-inch beaded birch plywood. Building-supply stores and lumberyards sell this plywood for wainscoting. Cut the end panels to the sizes given in the Materials List.

On the long edges of the end-frame stiles and rails cut ¼-inch-wide × ⅜-inch-deep panel grooves on the table saw. You could also cut the grooves with a ¼-inch slot cutter in a table-mounted router. At the same time, cut a ¼ × ¼-inch rabbet on the back inside edge of the back end-frame stiles for the platform back, as shown in *End Frame Detail—Top View*.

Cut the beaded plywood for a snug fit and sand it. Then glue and clamp the rails and stiles around the plywood to create the end frames, making sure they are square and flat. Typically, I don't make a joint between the rails and stiles, letting the glue and plywood hold the pieces together. You may want to make ¼-inch-thick tongues on the rail ends to fit the panel grooves in the stiles. If so, adjust the length of the rails accordingly. (You could also screw the stiles to the rails. If you do this, be sure to drill pilot holes and countersink the screw heads below the surface of the stiles, and make sure they don't line up with the screw holes in the face-frame stiles.)

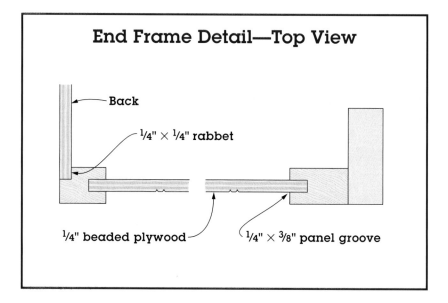

End Frame Detail—Top View

Back

¼" × ¼" rabbet

¼" beaded plywood

¼" × ⅜" panel groove

4 **Make the platform top, center and bottom panels, and back.** Cut the top to the size given in the Materials List (it should be exactly as long as the face frame). With a router, cut a ¼ × ¼-inch rabbet in what will be the back edge to house the platform back.

The top will overlay the face and end frames, and screws will be driven through in into the frame edges. With this in mind, drill and countersink clearance holes for #10 × 1½-inch screws along the front and side edges of the top, spacing them 6 to 8 inches apart and ⅜ inch back from the edge.

The compartment behind the doors is formed by two center panels and a bottom panel together with the top and the platform back. Cut the center and bottom panels to the dimensions given in the Materials List.

Cut the back to the dimensions given in the Materials List.

Assemble the Platform

1 **Attach the frames to the top.** Lay two 6-foot-long hardwood strips across two sawhorses; then place the particleboard top upside down on them.

Glue and clamp the face frame flush with the front edge of the top, also lining it up flush on each end. From below, drill through the countersunk holes in the top to make pilot holes in the frame. Screw the top and face frame together with #10 × 1½" flathead wood screws.

Glue and clamp the end frames flush to the outside edge of the face frame and to the ends of the top. The frames should keep each other square to the top. As before, drill pilot holes into the end frames guided by the previously drilled clearance holes. Screw the top and face frame to the end frames, checking to ensure the assembly is square.

2 **Attach the panels to the top and frame.** Glue the ⅝-inch particleboard center panels to the top, setting them flush with the inside edges of the center stiles on the face frame. Fasten the panels to the face frame with glue and 4d finish nails driven through the stiles into the panel edges.

Glue and nail the bottom panel onto the center panels and to the face-frame rail. Use 4d finish nails. This will help you align the center panels at right angles to the top. After you've done all this, drive 4d finish nails or ringed paneling nails through the top into the edges of the center panels. (You can transfer a pencil line across the top to establish the centerline of each panel before nailing.) Set all nail heads just below the surface, and fill the holes with wood filler. Don't try to attach the panels with screws because screws don't hold well in the edges of particleboard.

3 **Glue and nail the plywood back to the platform.**
Glue the ¼-inch plywood back into the rabbets you
made in the top and the end panels. Also put glue on the back
edges of the storage compartment. Nail the back in place,
checking carefully to make sure the platform is square. If it is not
square, it will not mate well with the other half of the bed frame.

4 **Add the strake and the corner blocks.** The strake
is the piece that runs along the bottom edge of the
back, extending from end frame to end frame. It stiffens and
supports the back panel at this critical location.

Glue and clamp the strake to the plywood back, between the
end assemblies. You can also glue it to the bottom panel of
the storage cavity, which it should butt against. Nail through
the back into the strake with ¾-inch brads.

The corner blocks bridge the back corners of the platform
between the strake and the end panels, as shown in *Strake and
Corner Block Detail.* Drill and countersink clearance holes for
#10 × 1½-inch screws through the corner blocks. Mark and
drill pilot holes into the strake and end assemblies; then glue
and screw the corner blocks in place.

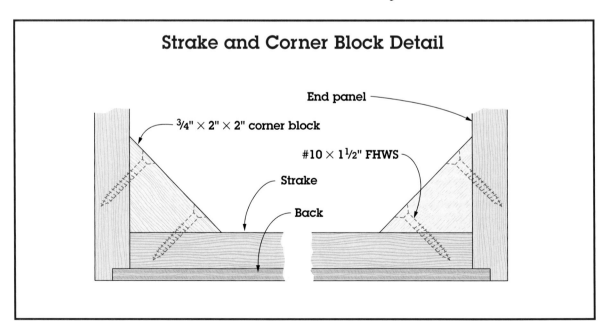

Strake and Corner Block Detail

End panel

¾" × 2" × 2" corner block

#10 × 1½" FHWS

Strake

Back

5 **Attach the drawer runner supports.** The drawers are hung in the platform with a center-mounted wood T-rail and several pieces of inexpensive plastic hardware. *Drawer Runner Detail—End View Cross Section* shows how the system goes together, and the Materials List provides a source for the hardware. The T-rail is attached to the drawer rail at the front and fits into a square plastic housing mounted on the platform back. A plastic molding attached to the drawer back fits onto the wood T-rail to guide the drawer. Small disk rollers, mounted at the bottom corners of the drawer opening, center the drawer.

Getting the drawer hardware installed properly when the platform is upside down is a bit of a mental challenge; but believe me, it's considerably easier than trying to do it with the platform upright.

Cut the T-rail supports to the dimensions given in the Materials List. To fit each support at the back of the platform, the end must be notched where it meets the strake. Drill and countersink a clearance hole for a #8 × 1-inch drywall screws through the support. Glue the supports to the strake, the plywood back panel, and the top. Make certain they are vertical and centered in the drawer opening. Finally, screw the support into the strake, as shown in the photo at right.

6 **Make and attach the T-rail.** Cut eight pieces of stock for the T-rail. Transform this stock into T-rails by cutting wide, shallow rabbets in opposite faces, as shown in *Drawer Runner Detail—End View Cross Section*. Each rabbet can be cut in a single pass on the table saw.

Notch the front of each T-rail where it fits over the drawer rail; then drill and countersink a clearance hole for a #8 × 1-inch screw. Before installing the T-rail, cut back the "ears" of the T-rail where it joins the drawer rail support, as shown in *Drawer Rail Support*. This allows the T-rail glides to drop onto the T-rail. Insert the T-rail into the housing and lower the front end onto the drawer rail. Screw it in place.

Each T-rail is attached to its strake with two metal corner brackets, as shown in the *Drawer Runner Detail*. Screw the

The bottom end of the support for the T-rail must be notched so it will fit around the strake. Drive a screw through the end into the strake to secure it.

Drawer Runner Detail—End View Cross Section

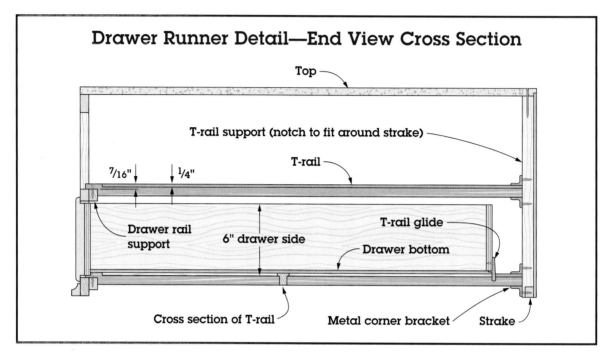

Top

T-rail support (notch to fit around strake)

T-rail

$7/16"$ $1/4"$

Drawer rail support

6" drawer side

T-rail glide

Drawer bottom

Cross section of T-rail

Metal corner bracket

Strake

The plastic roller disks are nailed to the face frame in the corners of the drawer openings. The drawer rests on them, rather than on the wood drawer rail, which makes the drawers very easy to open and close.

bottom corner bracket into the T-rail support, the T-rail to the bracket, and then the second bracket in place above the T-rail with #8 × ¾-inch drywall screws. Finally, screw the T-rail to the drawer rail support.

After the platform has been turned upright, install the plastic roller disks, as shown in the photo at left.

7 **Attach the moldings to the platform.** With the platform upright on the sawhorses, it's time to attach the trim. You can make this molding or you can use stock molding purchased at a home center (particularly if you are going to paint the bed as I have). The profiles of the moldings are given in *Molding Detail*. The top molding is a cove and bead combination, and the base molding is a ½-inch-radius cove.

Cut the long face molding to length with a 45-degree miter at each end. Clamp it in place on the platform, and miter the end moldings to fit. Next, crosscut the back ends of the end moldings to 90 degrees to butt cleanly against the same molding from the other platform. When the moldings fit, glue and clamp them to the platform, as shown. Secure the moldings with 4d finish nails; then set the nails, and fill the holes. Do this for both the top and the bottom moldings.

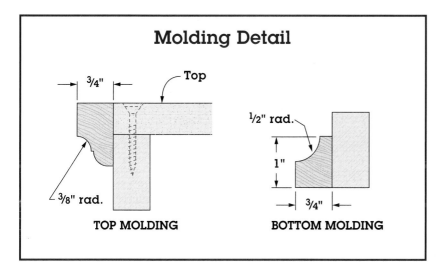

Molding Detail

3/4"   Top

1/2" rad.

1"

3/8" rad.   3/4"

TOP MOLDING   **BOTTOM MOLDING**

Build the Drawers and Doors

1 **Cut the parts to size.** Cut all of the drawer and door parts to the sizes given in the Materials List. I made the drawer boxes from $\frac{1}{2}$-inch Baltic birch plywood with $\frac{1}{4}$-inch birch plywood bottoms. The drawer sizes assume you will take advantage of the entire depth of the platform. You can make the door panels from the beaded plywood you used on the end panels, or make raised panels for a more formal look.

2 **Make the drawer boxes.** On the table saw, crosscut $\frac{1}{8} \times \frac{1}{2}$-inch rabbets in the drawer sides, as shown in *Drawer Joinery Detail.* Adjust the blade height; then slide the drawer sides and front against the rip fence to cut the $\frac{1}{4} \times \frac{1}{4}$-inch bottom groove $\frac{1}{4}$ inch up from the bottom edge. Drill two clearance holes for screws in each front piece to attach the drawer face for #10 × 1-inch flathead wood screws.

Sand the drawer pieces; then glue and clamp the front and back into the rabbets. Note that the back should be positioned in the side rabbets so that its bottom edge is flush with the top of the bottom groove. Nail through the drawer sides into the front and back with three 4d finish nails at each joint. Spread glue in the bottom groove, and slide the bottom in place underneath the drawer back. If the drawer bottom was cut square, it should effectively square up the drawer. Secure the drawer bottom by nailing through it into the drawer back with 4d coated nails.

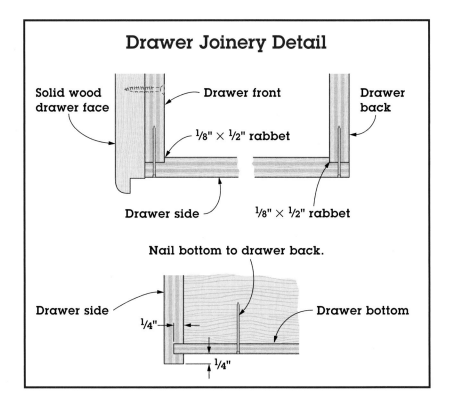

Drawer Joinery Detail

Solid wood drawer face

Drawer front

Drawer back

$1/8" \times 1/2"$ rabbet

Drawer side

$1/8" \times 1/2"$ rabbet

Nail bottom to drawer back.

Drawer side

$1/4"$

Drawer bottom

$1/4"$

3 **Complete the drawers.** Chuck a $3/8$-inch-radius roundover bit in your router and round over all four front edges of each drawer face. With a dado cutter in your table saw, cut a $3/8 \times 3/8$-inch rabbet in all inside edges of the drawer faces. To do this, crosscut the faces for the end rabbets; then slide the faces against the rip fence for the long edges.

Lay out and drill the holes for mounting the drawer knobs; attach the knobs to the drawers, as shown in *Front View*. I like plain round wood knobs. With the drawer box in place in the platform, mark the position of the drawer face on the front of the drawer box. Drill pilot holes for two #10 × 1-inch flathead wood screws into the back of the drawer face. You can attach the drawer faces now, or wait until after you've painted the faces and platform before you screw them in place.

4 **Cut the door joinery.** Construct the doors with tongue-and-groove joints, in which the tenon or tongue fits into the panel groove.

With a dado cutter on the table saw, cut the $\frac{1}{4}$-inch-wide × $\frac{3}{8}$-inch-deep groove for the panel in the inside edges of each of the door stiles and rails.

On the ends of each rail, cut a $\frac{3}{8}$-inch-long tongue to fit the panel groove. You can use the dado cutter to cut the tenons. Reset the cutter height and guide the workpieces over the cutter with the miter gauge. Two passes should cut each tenon cheek.

If you want to make raised-panel doors, you can cut the panels on the table saw or with a panel-raising bit in your table-mounted router, as discussed in "Routing Raised Panels" on page 14. On the table saw, angle a rip blade about 15 degrees away from the rip fence; then stand the panels on edge, and slide them against the fence to cut the raised faces, as shown in *Door Construction Detail*.

5 **Complete the doors.** After you cut the parts, sand them to get them ready for assembly.

Glue and clamp the door rails to the door stiles, capturing the panel as you pull the door together. A plywood panel can be glued into the panel groove, but not a raised panel. A solid wood raised panel needs to be free to expand and contract, or it will eventually break the door. Make sure the door is square and flat.

When the glue is dry, round over the four edges, just as you did with the drawer faces. Then, with the dado cutter in the

Quick tip

Give the panels some room to expand by trimming $\frac{1}{16}$ inch from their long edges on the jointer or with a hand plane. Without this allowance, the panels can actually break the door joinery apart when the humidity is high.

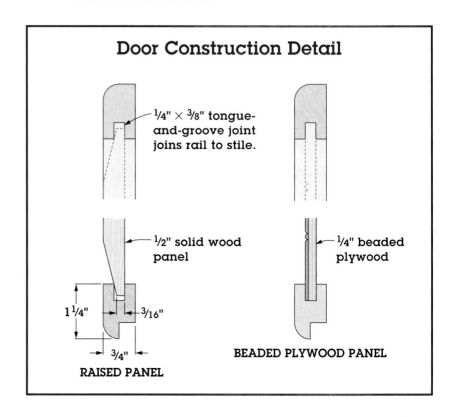

Door Construction Detail

¼" × ⅜" tongue-and-groove joint joins rail to stile.

½" solid wood panel

¼" beaded plywood

1¼"

³/₁₆"

¾"

RAISED PANEL

BEADED PLYWOOD PANEL

table saw, cut a ⅜ × ⅜-inch rabbet on the top, bottom, and outside back edges of the door. *Do not* rabbet the inside edge where the doors meet.

Drill and attach the knobs to the inside stiles. You need ⅜-inch offset hinges for these doors. Mark and drill for the screws; then attach the hinges to the platform to hold the doors. Install a catch of your choice to keep the doors closed. Simple magnetic catches work fine.

6 **Paint the platform bed.** After you have put together both halves of the bed, sand it to final smoothness, and remove all sanding dust. Don't bother about some roughness on the particleboard tops, as it is difficult to avoid and helps keep the mattress in place on the platforms. Paint the bed the color of your choice or, if you have made a hardwood bed, brush it with another finish, such as urethane. Allow the finish to dry thoroughly before you set your mattress on top.

Jewelry Box

by Ben Erickson

Here's a chance to share with that special someone some of the unique wood pieces you've been hoarding. She'll treasure this jewelry box as much as the jewelry she puts in it.

I made this box from walnut, with bird's-eye maple for the raised panel in the lid. The grain of the walnut runs continuously around the box, and a border of walnut string inlay accents the raised top panel. The top is sliced from the box after it has been asembled.

The box is as useful as it is beautiful. Inside, two maple trays are divided into different compartments, which can hold everything from necklaces to earrings.

Exploded View—Box

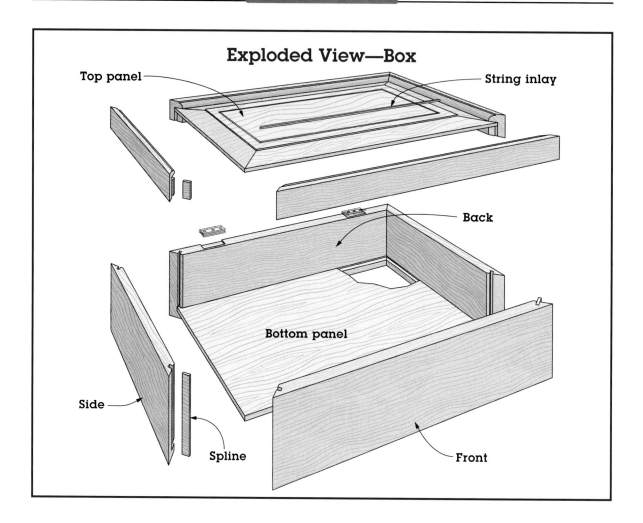

Top panel

String inlay

Back

Bottom panel

Side

Spline

Front

Make the Front, Back, and Sides

1 **Prepare the stock.** Begin by jointing, planing, and ripping a single board to $\frac{1}{2} \times 4\frac{1}{8}$ inches and at least 39 inches long. You'll cut the pieces to final length for the front, back, and sides after routing the bead and cutting the panel grooves. Mark the best side of the board as the outside of the box, and determine which edge will be the top of the box. To help you orient the sides later, draw a continuous arc along one face of the board as a reference mark.

Materials List

Part	Dimension	Part	Dimension
Box		Bottoms (2)	$^3/_{16}$" × $5^{31}/_{32}$" × $10^{31}/_{32}$"
Front	$^1/_2$" × $4^1/_8$" × 12"	Divider	$^3/_{16}$" × $1^1/_6$" × $10^{13}/_{16}$"
Back	$^1/_2$" × $4^1/_8$" × 12"	Dividers (2)	$^3/_{16}$" × $1^1/_6$" × $5^{13}/_{16}$"
Sides (2)	$^1/_2$" × $4^1/_8$" × 7"	Dividers (4)	$^3/_{16}$" × $1^1/_6$" × $3^3/_{16}$"
Top panel	$^7/_{16}$" × $6^1/_2$" × $11^1/_2$"	Splines (16)	$^1/_8$" × $^5/_{16}$" × $^9/_{16}$"
Bottom panel	$^3/_{16}$" × $6^1/_2$" × $11^1/_2$"		
String inlay	$^1/_{16}$" × $^1/_8$" × 24"	**Hardware**	
Splines (4)	$^1/_8$" × 3" × $^3/_8$"	#2 × $^1/_2$" brass flathead wood screws (16)	
		$1^1/_4$" × $^1/_2$" brass box hinges (1 pair). Available from Woodcraft Supply Corp., 210 Wood County Industrial Park, P.O. Box 1686, Parkersburg, WV 26102-1686; (800) 225-1153; part #16K53	
Trays			
Sides (4)	$^3/_{16}$" × $1^1/_6$" × 11"		
Sides (4)	$^3/_{16}$" × $1^1/_6$" × 6"		

2 **Rout the bead, and cut the panel grooves.** Begin by routing a bead on the top edge of the board, as shown in *Top View* and *Front View*, with a $^1/_8$-inch beading bit. Next, make the $^3/_{16}$-inch-wide × $^1/_4$-inch-deep top and bottom panel grooves with a $^3/_{16}$-inch-diameter straight bit in a table-mounted router or by ripping them on the table saw. In either case, run the stock against a fence as you cut the groove. Since most table saw blades are only $^1/_8$ inch thick, you will need to readjust the fence and make a second pass. Space the top panel groove $^1/_4$ inch from the top edge of the board and the bottom panel groove, $^1/_2$ inch from the bottom edge.

3 **Cut the sides to length.** To maintain a continuous grain pattern around the box, cut the sides sequentially from the board. Begin by cutting the back piece, so that the one corner where the grain won't match will be at the rear of the box.

I crosscut the pieces to length on my table saw and mitered all the ends afterward. To ensure that the two sides and the front and back would match exactly in length, I used a stop block clamped to a long fence that was screwed to the miter gauge.

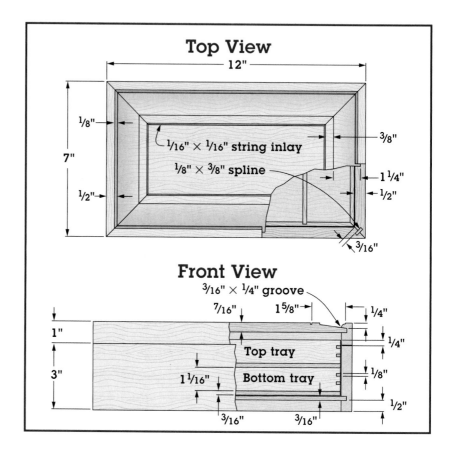

First, using the stop block, cut the back piece to 12 inches long. Next, place a 5-inch-long spacer block against the stop block to cut the first 7-inch-long side. Then remove the spacer block, and cut the front piece to 12 inches. Finally, replace the spacer block, and cut the second 7-inch side.

The ends of all the pieces are then mitered. You can use stop blocks for this also, but place the outside of the box parts up so the tip of the miter doesn't slide under the stop block.

4 **Make the splined miter joints.** First, cut the miters and temporarily hold the box together with band clamps to check for tight joints.

Next, rout the $\frac{3}{16}$-inch-deep spline grooves with a $\frac{1}{8}$-inch-diameter straight bit in a table-mounted router. When routing the grooves, lean the workpiece on a 45-degree ramp, as shown in *Splined Miter Jig*. Then slowly lower the mitered face onto the spinning bit, as shown in the photo top right. Feed the work right to left against the splined miter jig. When the spline grooves have been routed, cut splines to size on the table saw, as shown in the photo bottom right.

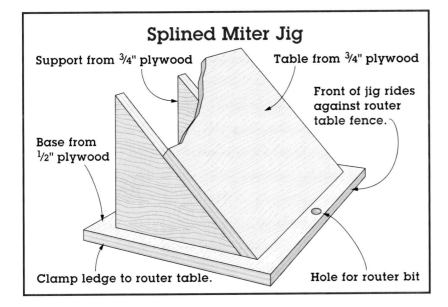

Splined Miter Jig

Support from ³⁄₄" plywood

Table from ³⁄₄" plywood

Front of jig rides against router table fence.

Base from ¹⁄₂" plywood

Clamp ledge to router table.

Hole for router bit

To cut a stopped miter groove, hold the workpiece firmly against the splined miter jig; then slowly lower the workpiece onto the spinning bit. Feed the workpiece from right to left.

Make the Top and Bottom Panels

1 **Cut the pieces to size.** Plane, joint, rip, and crosscut the top and bottom panels to the sizes given in the Materials List. Adjust the thickness of the bottom panel so it will fit snugly in its groove.

2 **Rout the inlay groove.** Lay out the outside corners of the string inlay groove 1⅝ inch from the edges of the panel. Rout a ¹⁄₁₆ × ¹⁄₁₆-inch groove using a router edge guide and a ¹⁄₁₆-inch-diameter bit. Stop short of your corner lines; then use a sharp chisel to square up the groove's corners. Routing both cross-grain grooves before the long-grain grooves will prevent tear-out.

To cut splines on a table saw, first cut them to thickness, as shown. Then use a stop block to cut the splines to width. For strength, orient the grain of the splines perpendicular to the joint line.

3 **Make and fit the string inlay.** Select straight-grained wood for the inlay strips. Rip the stock into $\frac{1}{16} \times \frac{1}{8}$-inch strips on your table saw, aiming for a snug fit in the groove. You'll sand off the projecting $\frac{1}{16}$ inch later. Miter the strips to length using a sharp chisel and a 45-degree guide block. Press all of the pieces into the grooves just far enough to check for tight miters and a snug fit.

Place yellow glue in the groove with a syringe or small-tipped glue bottle, and press the inlay into the groove. Then tap it with a metal hammer to ensure that it seats well. After the glue is dry, use a 120-grit paper in a belt sander to sand the inlay flush with the top panel.

4 **Raise the top panel.** Cut a $1\frac{1}{4}$-inch-wide bevel on the edges of the panel. There should be a step in the panel, as shown in *Front View*. You can cut the bevel with a panel-raising bit in a table-mounted router or by tilting the blade on a table saw and sliding the panel upright against the fence. If you use the table saw, tilt the blade to approximately 11 degrees from vertical.

For more details, see "Routing Raised Panels" on page 14.

5 **Assemble the box.** Assemble the box without glue to check the fit of the panels. Being solid wood, the panels will expand and contract somewhat across the grain with changes in humidity. Each panel can fit without play between the end grooves on the box, but you may need to trim the long panel edges a bit to allow for wood movement. In the humid season, trim off only $\frac{1}{32}$ inch or so. If it's the dry time of year, trim off about $\frac{1}{16}$ inch.

When everything fits well, assemble the box with glue. Clamp it up using band clamps or cauls, as shown in *Clamping Splined Miters*. Check the assembly for square.

6 **Free the lid.** After the glue has dried, use your table saw to rip the 1-inch-high lid free of the box. Set your blade height to slightly more than the thickness of the box sides. Draw a mark across the front of the box for easy realign-

Quick tip

When gluing butt or miter joints, the end grain can absorb glue quickly enough to result in a "starved joint" by the time you assemble your work. To prevent this, first "size" the end grain with a thin coat of glue. After the glue has been absorbed but while it's still tacky, apply a second coat of glue before assembling your work.

ment of the lid later. Cut the short sides of the box first, then the long sides. For stability when making the last rip, you can shim the previous kerfs and tape them shut.

7 **Mortise for the hinges.** I hinged the lid with the brass hinges listed in the Materials List. These quality hinges prop up the open lid at about 100 degrees.

Lay out the mortises for the hinges, setting them in $1\frac{3}{4}$ inches from the ends of the box. To mark each mortise, lay the hinge in place on the box body, and scribe around its outline with a marking knife. Set a straight router bit to a depth just a little less than half the diameter of the hinge barrel, and rout out most of the waste. Guide the cut with the router's fence. Then pare to your knife lines with a chisel.

Install the hinges onto the box body, fold them closed, and carefully align the lid on top of them. Push a sharp knife along the edges of the upper hinge leaf and into the edge of the box lid to transfer the leaf locations. Remove the hinges from the box body, place them on the lid, and mark and mortise them as before.

Attach the hinges to the lid with only one screw each for right now, so you can make slight adjustments later if the lid doesn't line up perfectly.

Make the Trays

The two maple trays fit snugly inside the box. The sides and dividers are all made from $\frac{3}{16}$-inch-thick $\times$ $1\frac{1}{16}$-inch-wide stock. The outside corners are reinforced with mock finger joints, and the dividers fit into dadoes in the sides. The solid maple bottoms are covered with velvet and then screwed to the sides.

1 **Cut the stock to size.** Joint, plane, and rip enough long stock to make the sides and dividers. Cut the bottoms to the dimensions given in the Materials List.

2 **Make the sides.** Cut the sides to length, mitering their corners so that they fit just inside the box.

3 **Make the dividers.** Lay out the $\frac{3}{16}$-inch-wide dadoes in the tray sides, as shown in *Top View—Trays*. I cut the dadoes with a "wobble" dado cutter. (A stack dado cutter won't make slots under $\frac{1}{4}$ inch wide.) But you could rout them or cut them with a couple of passes each over the table saw blade. Then cut the dividers to the lengths given in the Materials List.

4 **Assemble the sides and dividers.** Test assemble the sides and dividers to check for good joint fit and to re-hearse your clamping procedure. Then, with all your clamps at the ready, glue the parts together. Use band clamps to hold the miters together and short bar clamps or C-clamps to hold the dividers in their dadoes.

5 **Make the mock finger joints.** After the glue has dried, cut the slots for the mock finger joints on your table saw. To carry each tray standing on its corner over the blade, use an upright jig with a 45-degree fence. Or you could use a large piece of wood that has a 90-degree V-shaped notch cut into it. Note that the spline's grain should be oriented so that it's perpendicular to the miter seam, as shown in *Exploded View—Trays*.

Cut $\frac{5}{16}$-inch-wide × $\frac{9}{16}$-inch-long splines from $\frac{1}{8}$-inch-thick walnut; then glue them into the slots. After the glue has dried, pare the splines flush with the trays' sides. Then use a belt sander to finish the trays for a snug fit in the box.

Finish the Box

Finish sand the box and trays with 220-grit sandpaper. I sanded all of the edges except the lid joint to create a $\frac{1}{16}$-inch roundover. Then put on your favorite finish.

Cover the tray bottoms with velvet. (I attached it with double-sided tape.) Then drill $\frac{3}{32}$-inch-diameter holes in the tray bottoms, as shown in *Exploded View—Trays*; the oversize holes will allow the wood to move. Attach the tray bottoms to the sides with #2 × $\frac{1}{2}$-inch brass flathead wood screws.

Clamping Splined Miters

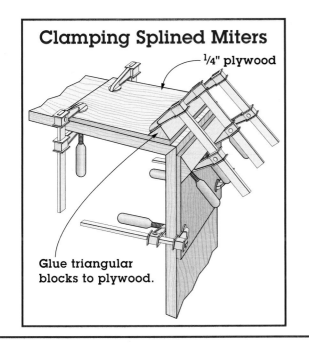

1/4" plywood

Glue triangular
blocks to plywood.

Top View—Trays

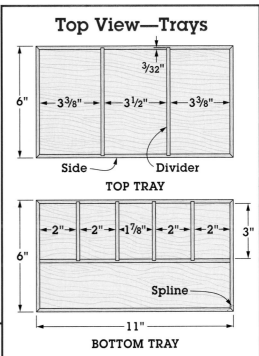

3/32"

6"

3 3/8"   3 1/2"   3 3/8"

Side   Divider

TOP TRAY

2" 2" 1 7/8" 2" 2"

6"   3"

Spline

11"

BOTTOM TRAY

Exploded View—Trays

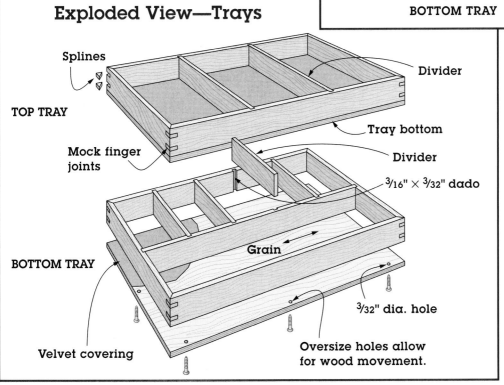

Splines

Divider

TOP TRAY

Mock finger
joints

Tray bottom

Divider

3/16" × 3/32" dado

Grain

BOTTOM TRAY

Velvet covering

3/32" dia. hole

Oversize holes allow
for wood movement.

Sweater Cabinet

by Jim Probst

Sweaters are great pieces of clothing. They can dress up a pair of jeans or make a sport coat seem a little more casual. They're just the thing for those early spring days when you're sick of wearing a coat, and there's nothing like a toasty sweater to kill winter's chill. But sweaters can be a nuisance to store. They're too bulky to fit well in dresser drawers, and it just doesn't make sense to hang them in a closet.

Enter this sweater cabinet, a scaled-down version of an armoire. Its multiple shelves are perfect for holding a multitude of sweaters, and its cedar lining keeps moths at bay. While it isn't small, it isn't terribly large either, so it won't overcrowd whatever room you place it in.

The style of the cabinet is reminiscent of simple, practical Shaker designs. With its clean lines, the cabinet will fit easily into either a contemporary or country-style setting.

The construction is fairly straightforward. The case is dovetailed together at the top, and the bottom and a single fixed shelf are biscuit joined or dadoed into the sides to complete the assembly. A face frame on the front holds two frame-and-panel doors.

The remainder of the shelves rest on pins that fit into a series of holes in the case sides. A little molding and a cedar lining add the finishing touches.

Exploded View

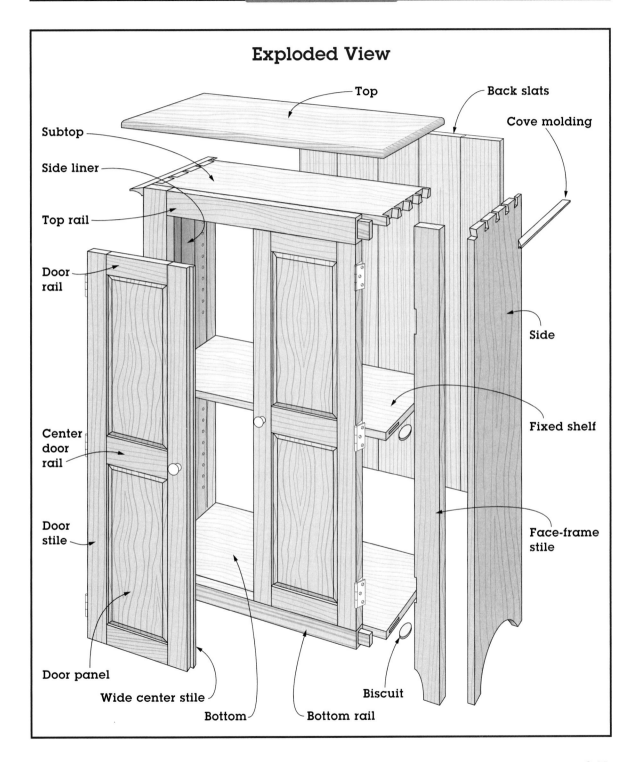

Top

Back slats

Cove molding

Subtop

Side liner

Top rail

Door
rail

Center
door
rail

Door
stile

Side

Fixed shelf

Face-frame
stile

Door panel

Wide center stile

Bottom

Bottom rail

Biscuit

Front View

Side View

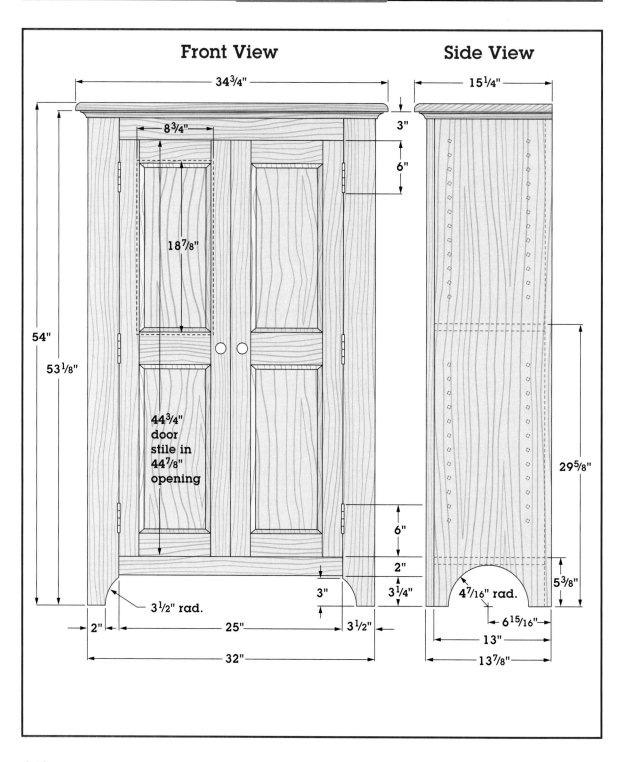

34³/₄"

15¹/₄"

8³/₄"

3"

6"

18⁷/₈"

54"

53¹/₈"

44³/₄"
door
stile in
44⁷/₈"
opening

29⁵/₈"

6"

2"

6"

3¹/₄"

5³/₈"

3"

3¹/₂" rad.

4⁷/₁₆" rad.

2"

25"

3¹/₂"

6¹⁵/₁₆"

32"

13"

13⁷/₈"

Materials List

Part	Dimensions	Part	Dimensions
Case		Center rails (2)	$\frac{7}{8}$" × $3\frac{1}{2}$" × $10\frac{1}{2}$"
Sides (2)	$\frac{7}{8}$" × 13" × $53\frac{1}{8}$"	Panels (4)	$\frac{5}{8}$" × $8\frac{3}{4}$" × $18\frac{7}{8}$"
Subtop	$\frac{7}{8}$" × $12\frac{1}{4}$" × 32"		
Fixed shelf	$\frac{7}{8}$" × $12\frac{1}{4}$" × $30\frac{1}{4}$"	**Hardware**	
Bottom	$\frac{7}{8}$" × $12\frac{1}{4}$" × $30\frac{1}{4}$"	#8 × $1\frac{1}{2}$" drywall screws (4)	
Face-frame stiles (2)	$\frac{7}{8}$" × $3\frac{1}{2}$" × $53\frac{1}{8}$"	#8 × $1\frac{1}{2}$" roundhead wood screws (2)	
Top rail	$\frac{7}{8}$" × 3" × $27\frac{1}{8}$"	3d finish nails (as needed)	
Bottom rail	$\frac{7}{8}$" × 2" × $27\frac{1}{8}$"	1" wire brads (as needed)	
Top	$\frac{7}{8}$" × $15\frac{1}{4}$" × $34\frac{3}{4}$"	#20 biscuits (as needed)	
Back (random-width strips)	$\frac{5}{8}$" × $31\frac{1}{2}$" × $49\frac{5}{8}$"	Shelf pin sleeves (96). Available from Rockler Woodworking and Hardware, 4365 Willow Drive, Medina, MN 55340; (800) 279-4441; part #81836	
Side liners (4)	$\frac{3}{8}$" × $12\frac{1}{4}$" × $23\frac{7}{16}$"	2" × 1" butt hinges (6). Available from Rockler Woodworking and Hardware; part #25726	
Cove molding	$\frac{3}{4}$" × $\frac{7}{8}$" × 68"	$1\frac{1}{8}$" dia. door knobs (2). Available from Rockler Woodworking and Hardware; part #88791	
Adjustable shelves (2)	$\frac{7}{8}$" × $12\frac{1}{8}$" × $29\frac{3}{8}$"	Door catches (2). Available from Rockler Woodworking and Hardware; part #86117	
Doors		Shelf support pins (8). Available from Rockler Woodworking and Hardware; part #30437	
Stiles (3)	$\frac{7}{8}$" × $2\frac{1}{4}$" × $44\frac{7}{8}$"		
Wide center stile	$\frac{7}{8}$" × $2\frac{5}{8}$" × $44\frac{7}{8}$"		
Rails (4)	$\frac{7}{8}$" × $2\frac{1}{2}$" × $10\frac{1}{2}$"		

Make the Case

1 **Cut the pieces to size.** Cut the sides, subtop, fixed shelf, and bottom to the sizes listed in the Materials List. You may need to glue up narrower boards to make up the widths required. Note that the plan calls for the fixed shelf and bottom to be joined to the sides with biscuit joints. They can also be dadoed in place; however, you'll need to add $\frac{3}{4}$ inch to their lengths if you intend to do so.

2 **Rabbet the sides.** Set up a $\frac{3}{4}$-inch-wide dado blade on your table saw, and cut $\frac{3}{4}$-inch-wide × $\frac{3}{8}$-inch-deep rabbets along the back edges of the sides to hold the back. Clamp or screw a wooden auxiliary fence to your table saw fence, and run it right up against the $\frac{3}{4}$-inch-wide dado blade. Slide the sides against this fence to make the cut.

3 **Cut the dovetails in the subtop and sides.** The subtop is attached to the sides with through dovetail joints. (If you're not confident in your dovetailing skills, keep in mind that these joints are eventually covered up with cove molding, so this is a good place to practice.) Lay out the pins on the subtop, as shown in *Dovetail Layout*. Then saw along the layout lines, and chop away the waste with a chisel.

When the pins have been cut, use the subtop as a template to lay out the tails on the sides. Saw along the lines, and chop away the waste as before. For more on making dovetail joints, see "Cutting Dovetails" on page 164.

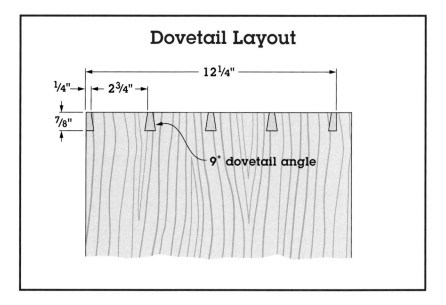

Dovetail Layout

4 **Add the fixed shelf and bottom.** When the dovetails have been cut, trim the fixed shelf and bottom to final length, matching the actual interior dimensions of the dovetailed case. They are attached to the sides with biscuits. Draw lines across the inside of the sides to indicate the top surfaces of the fixed shelf and bottom. Start with the fixed shelf, and clamp it to one of the sides so its end is aligned with the layout line, as shown in the photo on the opposite page. Make three small tick marks along the end of the shelf, as shown. Using them to guide you, cut the biscuit slots. Repeat for the other joints.

If you don't have a biscuit joiner or can't find one to borrow, you can cut ⅜-inch-deep dadoes to hold the fixed shelf and bottom. You will, however, need to add ¾ inch to the length of both the fixed shelf and the bottom.

Biscuit joinery is amazingly fast to lay out and cut. A simple pencil mark is all that is necessary to align the machine. For the slots in the end of the shelf, guide the machine's base right on the surface of the cabinet side. For the slots in the face of the side, guide the machine against the end of the shelf.

5 **Make the face frame.** Cut the stiles and rails for the face frame to the sizes given in the Materials List. Note that the rails are ⅛ inch longer than necessary. This gives the face frame a little extra width, which will make gluing the frame to the case much easier. When the face frame has been glued in place, you can trim the edges of the stiles flush with the case sides.

Lay out the mortises on the stiles, as shown in *Face-Frame Detail*. Rout the mortises with a ⅜-inch straight bit in a plunge router. Guide the router as you cut the mortises with its edge guide, and cut each mortise in several shallow passes. Square the ends of the mortises with a chisel. Lay out the tenons on the ends of the rails, double-checking them against the mortises in the stiles. Make the cheek cuts first on the table saw, holding the rails on end with a tenoning jig. Then make the shoulder cuts, holding the pieces flat on the saw table and guiding them past the blade with the miter gauge.

Make the curved cuts on the bottoms of the stiles on the band saw. Then glue the frame together. Check the frame to make sure it is flat and square before the glue sets.

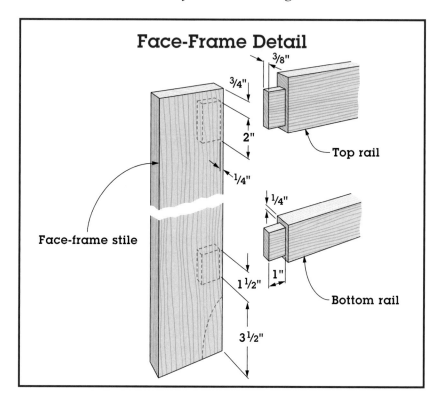

Face-Frame Detail

Face-frame stile

Top rail

Bottom rail

3/8"

3/4"

2"

1/4"

1/4"

1"

1 1/2"

3 1/2"

6 **Cut the curves on the case sides.** Lay out the curves on the bottoms of the case sides, as shown in *Side View*. Make the cuts on the band saw; then clean up the sawed edges with a drum sander.

7 **Assemble the case.** Sand the subtop, fixed shelf, bottom, and the inside surfaces of the sides. Then glue and clamp the pieces together. Measure the diagonals to make sure the case is square. (The diagonals should be equal.)

8 **Attach the face frame.** After the case is glued together, you can glue the face frame in place. With the case on its back, apply glue to the front edge of the case and flop the face frame in place on top. It should be flush with the top and overhang the sides slightly. (The bottom can be trimmed later, if necessary.) Clamp the pieces together. Or you can use 4d finishing nails to supply clamping pressure. Set the heads and fill the holes later.

9 **Attach the top.** While the face-frame glue is drying, cut the top to the size called for in the Materials List. Round-over the front and side edges, as shown in *Front View* and *Side View*, with a ½-inch roundover bit in a handheld router. Once the face frame is dry, attach the top to the subtop with four #8 × 1½-inch drywall screws driven from inside the cabinet near the corners.

10 **Make and attach the back.** The back is made from random-width strips of aromatic red cedar, shiplapped together. First, plane the strips to thickness; then cut them to the length specified in the Materials List.

Next, cut ⅜-inch-wide rabbets in both edges of the strips with a dado blade in the table saw, as shown in *Back Cross Section*. (The first and last strips are rabbeted on only one edge.) Bury the dado blade in an auxiliary fence attached to your table saw fence, exposing ⅜-inch of the blade. Guide the stock against the fence to cut the rabbets.

Attach the strips to the case with 3d finish nails, as shown.

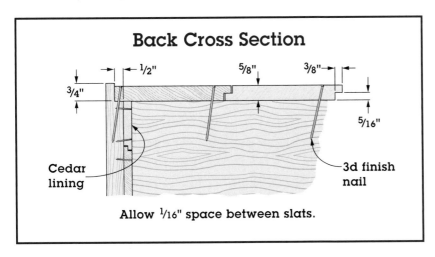

Back Cross Section

½"   ⅝"   ⅜"

¾"

5/16"

Cedar
lining

3d finish
nail

Allow 1/16" space between slats.

Quick tip

If you don't have a depth stop collar for your drill, just stick a masking tape flag to your drill bit to indicate the proper depth. This will not stop the bit but will provide a visual signal to tell you when you have gone deep enough.

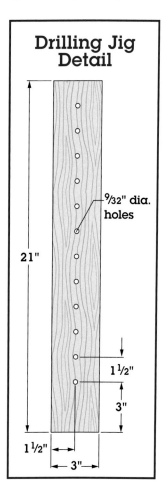

Drilling Jig Detail

21"

9/32" dia. holes

1 1/2"

3"

1 1/2"

3"

11 **Make and insert the side liners.** As shown in *Back Cross Section,* the sides of the case are lined with strips of aromatic red cedar. Plane the strips to thickness, and cut them to length so they fit inside the case. Rabbet the edges of the strips as you did for the back; then nail the strips to the sides of the case with 1-inch wire brads.

12 **Drill the shelf holes.** The adjustable shelves rest on pins that fit into holes drilled in the case sides. However, the cedar liners are a little bit too soft to hold the pins directly, so you'll need to install metal shelf pin sleeves to line the holes and reinforce them. The easiest way to get the holes drilled in the right places is to make up a simple drilling jig from a strip of a durable wood like hard maple. Use the drill press to bore a series of holes through the jig, as shown in *Drilling Jig Detail*. Mark one end of the jig to indicate the bottom.

To use the jig, hold it in the case, first with its edge against the back and then with the other edge against the inside of the face-frame stile; drill the holes with a handheld electric drill. Make sure that the side marked bottom is always down. Put a depth stop collar on the bit to avoid drilling all the way through the case sides. Tap the shelf pin sleeves into the holes.

13 **Make and attach the cove molding.** First, cut the stock for the cove molding to the thickness specified in the Materials List, but leave the stock about 3 inches wide for now. Then rout the profile with a ⅝-inch-diameter cove bit in a table-mounted router. When the molding has been routed to shape, rip it to width and cut the molding to fit around the case under the top, mitering the corners where the pieces meet. Attach the molding to the case with 3d finish nails.

Make the Doors

1 **Cut the pieces to size.** Cut the door parts to the sizes given in the Materials List. You may need to glue up narrower pieces to make up the panels. Note that the length specified for the rails includes a 1¼-inch tenon on either end.

2 Cut the door joinery. Lay out the mortises on the door stiles, as shown in *Door Joinery Detail*. Rout the mortises as you did for the joints in the face frame. Square the ends of the mortises with a chisel. Cut tenons on the door rails to fit the mortises.

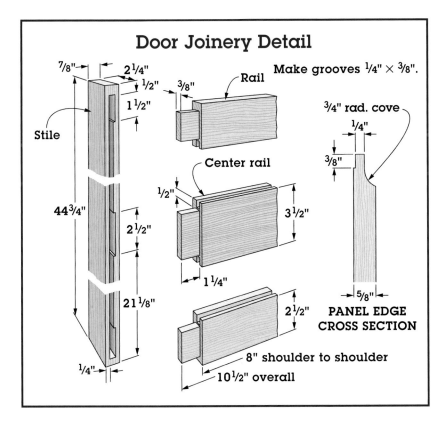

Door Joinery Detail

7/8"   2¼"   ½"   3/8"

Rail   Make grooves ¼" × 3/8".

1½"

¾" rad. cove

¼"

Stile

Center rail

3/8"

½"

44¾"

2½"

3½"

5/8"

PANEL EDGE
CROSS SECTION

1¼"

21⅛"

2½"

¼"

8" shoulder to shoulder

10½" overall

3 Rabbet the center door stiles. The mating edges of the center door stiles are rabbeted so they can overlap when the doors are closed. Cut these 3/8-inch-wide × 7/16-inch-deep rabbets with a rabbeting bit in a table-mounted router. Cut the rabbet in the front, or outside, face of the wide center stile and the back, or inside, face of the narrow stile.

4 Cut the panel grooves. The door panels fit in 3/8-inch-deep grooves cut in the stiles and rails. Cut these grooves in several light passes with a ¼-inch straight bit in a table-mounted router. Clamp a fence to the table, and run the pieces along it on edge. The grooves in the rails should run full length. Those in the stiles should stop in the mortises.

⑤ Shape the door panels. To create the profile on the door panels, I used a ³⁄₄-inch cove bit in a table-mounted router. (If you have one, you could also cut a different profile with a vertical panel-raising bit.) Clamp a fairly tall fence to the table with the bit partially buried behind the fence's face. Hold the panels on edge with their good faces against the fence, and run them past the bit, as shown in the photo below. Cut across the grain first to avoid problems with tear-out. Cut a rabbet around the backs of the panels to create a ¹⁄₄-inch tongue that will fit into the groove in the frame.

⑥ Assemble the doors. Sand the panels and the inside edges of the door frames. You may want to finish the panels before gluing the frames together. This has three benefits: First, finishing the panels separately from the frames is easier than finishing them when assembled. Second, if the panels should shrink after assembly, no raw wood would be exposed. And third, a panel with finish on it is not likely to be glued into its groove, which could keep the panel from expanding and contracting when it needs to.

Quick tip

When you have to make a cut in all the pieces of a frame, such as a groove for a panel, mark one side (either the front or the back) of all the pieces with an X. Then run all the pieces with the X against the fence. This way, the grooves in all the pieces will align, even if they were cut off-center.

To raise panels with a ³⁄₄-inch-radius cove bit or a vertical panel-raising bit, bury the bit partially in a fence, and slide the workpiece against it to raise the panel. Use a tall auxiliary fence to support the panel and keep it from tipping. Rout the end grain first.

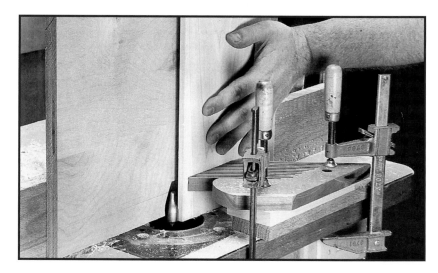

Spread glue on the tenon cheeks and in the mortises with a small paintbrush. Assemble the joints, making sure to slip the panels in place as the frame goes together. Clamp across the joints to draw everything together. Sight across the doors to make sure they are flat, and measure across the diagonals to make sure they are square.

Finish the Cabinet

1 Hang the doors. Mark the hinge locations on the doors and face frame, as shown in *Front View*. Next, lay out the hinge mortises in the doors and at their corresponding positions on the face frame by holding the hinge leaves in place and scribing around them with a marking knife. Chisel out the mortises, and check the fit of the hinge leaves. Screw the hinges into their mortises, using one screw per leaf until you are sure the doors fit well. Adjust the hinge positions slightly, if necessary.

2 Install the knobs and catches. Drill pilot holes for the #8 × 1½" roundhead wood screws that attach the door knobs at the midpoint of the center door stiles, and screw the knobs in place. Locate and install the catches on the backs of the doors and underneath the fixed shelf.

3 Apply the finish. Only the shelves, the bottom, the outside of the cabinet, and the inside of the doors are finished. The rest of the interior is left natural so the aroma of the cedar can work its magic. (A light, periodic sanding of the cedar will renew its distinctive odor and keep the moths at bay.)

The exterior of the cabinet in the photo was finished with Deft Danish oil, which is an oil and varnish mix. It gives the wood a nice thin, transparent finish that really emphasizes the wood's grain. The inside of the top and the adjustable shelves were finished with shellac because cedar fumes can soften varnish.

When the finish is dry, install the shelf support pins and the adjustable shelves.

Quick tip

Furniture hardware (such as hinges) is often installed using brass screws. These screws look great, but they are easily damaged by the process of installation. To keep the screws looking their best, use steel screws to cut the initial threads in the wood. Then, once you are satisfied with the fit of the hardware, replace the steel screws with brass ones.

Philadelphia Highboy

by Lonnie Bird

A Queen Anne highboy is a substantial undertaking, but if you have the time and patience, it need not be intimidating. With the possible exception of shaping the legs, no part of the project is beyond the experience of the typical intermediate woodworker—there are just more parts to the project than there are to most. When you're finally done and move the piece into your home, it will be a source of well-earned and justified pride.

A highboy consists of two parts: The upper case simply parks on top of the lower case, held in position by the waist molding. This eases both the construction and the ability to move it around the house or across the country.

Build it from the bottom up: legs first, then lower case, then upper case, and finally the drawers and moldings. If your shop tends to vary in humidity, avoid preparing the stock or cutting the joinery too far in advance of assembling the parts. This minimizes the danger of parts

failing to assemble properly because they changed shape or dimension.

If you do make mistakes, seriously consider remaking the part rather than patching or hiding the error. By the time you're done, you'll have a substantial amount of time and materials invested in the project. It would be a shame to feel bad about a small area, when most of the highboy reflects much better workmanship.

Exploded View

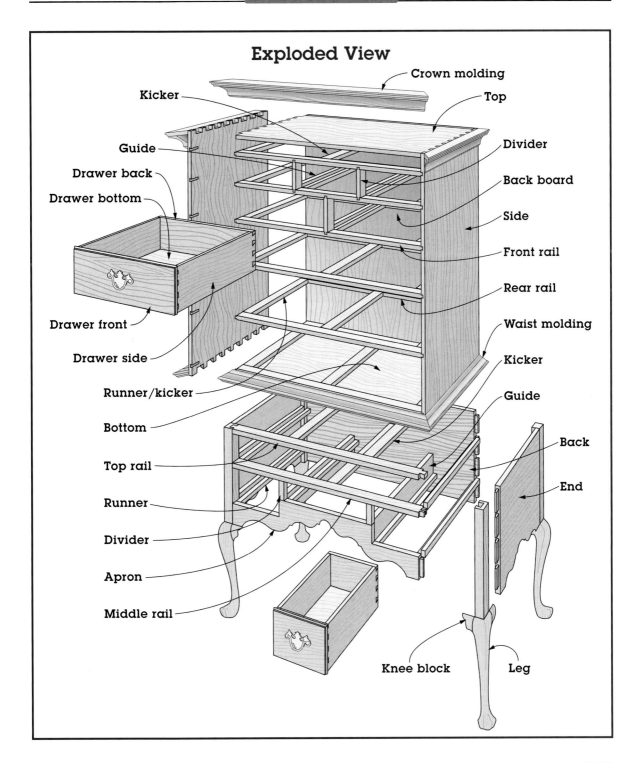

Crown molding

Top

Kicker

Guide

Divider

Drawer back

Back board

Drawer bottom

Side

Front rail

Rear rail

Drawer front

Waist molding

Drawer side

Kicker

Runner/kicker

Guide

Bottom

Back

Top rail

End

Runner

Divider

Apron

Middle rail

Knee block

Leg

Front View

Side View

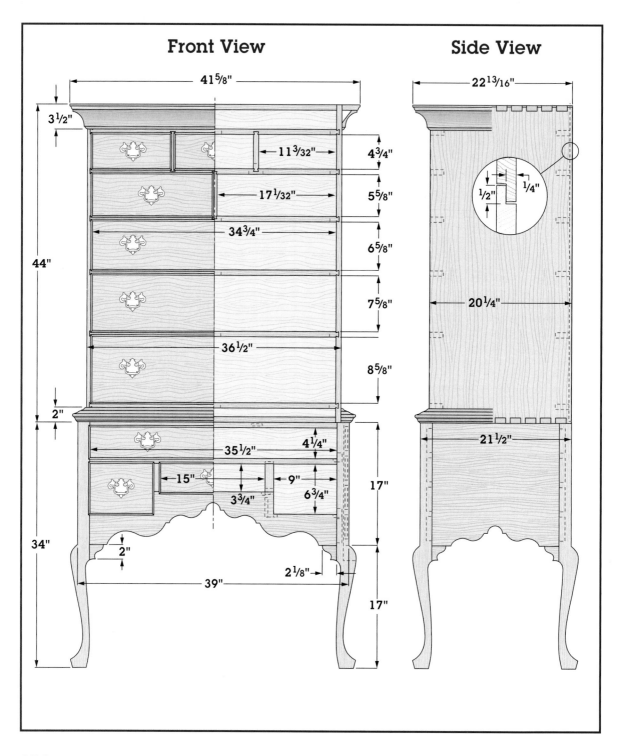

41⁵/₈"

3¹/₂"

44"

11³/₃₂"   4³/₄"

17¹/₃₂"   5⁵/₈"

34³/₄"

6⁵/₈"

7⁵/₈"

36¹/₂"

8⁵/₈"

2"

35¹/₂"   4¹/₄"

15"   9"

3³/₄"   6³/₄"   17"

34"

2"

39"   2¹/₈"

17"

22¹³/₁₆"

¹/₂"   ¹/₄"

20¹/₄"

21¹/₂"

Materials List

Part	Dimensions
Lower Case	
Legs (4)	$2\frac{3}{4}" \times 2\frac{3}{4}" \times 34"$
Knee blocks (6)	$1\frac{7}{8}" \times 2" \times 2\frac{1}{8}"$
Ends (2)	$\frac{7}{8}" \times 17" \times 19\frac{1}{2}"$
Back*	$\frac{7}{8}" \times 17" \times 37"$
Apron	$\frac{7}{8}" \times 7\frac{1}{4}" \times 37"$
Top rail	$\frac{7}{8}" \times 1\frac{3}{4}" \times 38"$
Middle rail	$\frac{7}{8}" \times 1\frac{3}{4}" \times 36\frac{1}{2}"$
Dividers (2)	$\frac{7}{8}" \times 1\frac{1}{4}" \times 4\frac{1}{2}"$
Kickers* (3)	$\frac{3}{4}" \times 2" \times 19\frac{5}{8}"$
Guides* (4)	$\frac{7}{8}" \times 1\frac{1}{4}" \times 18"$
Guides* (2)	$1\frac{1}{4}" \times 4" \times 20\frac{3}{4}"$
Runners* (8)	$\frac{1}{2}" \times \frac{1}{2}" \times 18"$
Upper Case	
Sides (2)	$\frac{7}{8}" \times 20\frac{1}{4}" \times 44"$
Top*	$\frac{7}{8}" \times 19\frac{3}{4}" \times 36\frac{1}{2}"$
Bottom*	$\frac{7}{8}" \times 19\frac{3}{4}" \times 36\frac{1}{2}"$
Back boards* (6)	$\frac{1}{2}" \times 7\frac{3}{4}" \times 35\frac{1}{2}"$
Front rails (6)	$\frac{7}{8}" \times 2" \times 35\frac{1}{2}"$
Rear rails* (6)	$\frac{7}{8}" \times 2" \times 35\frac{1}{2}"$
Dividers (2)	$\frac{7}{8}" \times 2" \times 5\frac{1}{2}"$
Divider	$\frac{7}{8}" \times 2" \times 6\frac{3}{8}"$
Runners/kickers* (19)	$\frac{7}{8}" \times 1\frac{1}{2}" \times 17"$
Guides* (3)	$\frac{7}{8}" \times \frac{7}{8}" \times 17"$
Moldings	
Crown	$2\frac{9}{16}" \times 3\frac{1}{2}" \times 41\frac{5}{8}"$
Crown (2)	$2\frac{9}{16}" \times 3\frac{1}{2}" \times 22\frac{13}{16}"$
Waist	$2" \times 2\frac{1}{16}" \times 40\frac{5}{8}"$
Waist (2)	$2" \times 2\frac{1}{16}" \times 22\frac{5}{16}"$
Drawers	
Upper case drawer fronts (3)	$\frac{3}{4}" \times 4\frac{15}{16}" \times 11\frac{3}{8}"$
Upper case drawer fronts (2)	$\frac{3}{4}" \times 5\frac{13}{16}" \times 17\frac{5}{16}"$
Upper case drawer front	$\frac{3}{4}" \times 6\frac{13}{16}" \times 35\frac{1}{8}"$
Upper case drawer front	$\frac{3}{4}" \times 7\frac{13}{16}" \times 35\frac{1}{8}"$

Part	Dimensions
Upper case drawer front	$\frac{3}{4}" \times 8\frac{13}{16}" \times 35\frac{1}{8}"$
Lower case drawer front	$\frac{3}{4}" \times 4\frac{7}{16}" \times 35\frac{7}{8}"$
Lower case drawer front (2)	$\frac{3}{4}" \times 6\frac{15}{16}" \times 9\frac{3}{8}"$
Lower case drawer front	$\frac{3}{4}" \times 3\frac{15}{16}" \times 15\frac{3}{8}"$
Upper case drawer sides* (6)	$\frac{1}{2}" \times 4\frac{11}{16}" \times 19\frac{1}{2}"$
Upper case drawer sides* (4)	$\frac{1}{2}" \times 5\frac{9}{16}" \times 19\frac{1}{2}"$
Upper case drawer sides* (2)	$\frac{1}{2}" \times 6\frac{9}{16}" \times 19\frac{1}{2}"$
Upper case drawer sides* (2)	$\frac{1}{2}" \times 7\frac{9}{16}" \times 19\frac{1}{2}"$
Upper case drawer sides* (2)	$\frac{1}{2}" \times 8\frac{9}{16}" \times 19\frac{1}{2}"$
Lower case drawer sides* (2)	$\frac{1}{2}" \times 4\frac{3}{16}" \times 20\frac{3}{8}"$
Lower case drawer sides* (4)	$\frac{1}{2}" \times 6\frac{11}{16}" \times 20\frac{3}{8}"$
Lower case drawer sides* (2)	$\frac{1}{2}" \times 3\frac{11}{16}" \times 20\frac{3}{8}"$
Upper case drawer backs* (3)	$\frac{1}{2}" \times 4\frac{3}{16}" \times 10\frac{7}{8}"$
Upper case drawer backs* (2)	$\frac{1}{2}" \times 5\frac{1}{16}" \times 16\frac{13}{16}"$
Upper case drawer backs*	$\frac{1}{2}" \times 6\frac{1}{16}" \times 34\frac{5}{8}"$
Upper case drawer backs*	$\frac{1}{2}" \times 7\frac{1}{16}" \times 34\frac{5}{8}"$
Upper case drawer backs*	$\frac{1}{2}" \times 8\frac{1}{16}" \times 34\frac{5}{8}"$
Lower case drawer backs*	$\frac{1}{2}" \times 3\frac{11}{16}" \times 37\frac{7}{8}"$
Lower case drawer backs* (2)	$\frac{1}{2}" \times 6\frac{3}{16}" \times 8\frac{7}{8}"$
Lower case drawer back*	$\frac{1}{2}" \times 3\frac{3}{16}" \times 14\frac{7}{8}"$
Upper case drawer bottoms (3)	$\frac{1}{2}" \times 19\frac{1}{4}" \times 10\frac{3}{8}"$
Upper case drawer bottoms (2)	$\frac{1}{2}" \times 19\frac{1}{4}" \times 16\frac{5}{16}"$
Upper case drawer bottoms (3)	$\frac{1}{2}" \times 19\frac{1}{4}" \times 34\frac{1}{8}"$
Lower case drawer bottom	$\frac{1}{2}" \times 20\frac{1}{8}" \times 36\frac{7}{8}"$

*Secondary wood

(continued on page 356)

Materials List—Continued

Part	Dimensions	Hardware
Drawers—Continued		#8 × 1½" drywall screws (as needed)
Lower case		#6 × 1" flathead wood screws (12)
drawer bottoms (2)	½" × 20⅛" × 8⅜"	4d finish nails (as needed)
Lower case drawer bottom	½" × 20⅛" × 14⅜"	Queen Anne drawer pulls (16)
		Queen Anne escutcheons (4)

Shape the Legs

1 Dimension the leg stock. Begin with 3-inch-square stock a good 2 inches longer than the final 34 inches listed in the Materials List. Square it up, leaving a piece at least 2¾ inches on side. Select the best two pieces for the front legs; then mark each piece, indicating where it goes in the highboy and the direction each surface faces.

2 Lay out and mortise the legs. Trim the top of each leg blank square; then lay out the cabriole curves on the two outside faces of each leg and the mortises on the inner two faces. The curves are shown in *Apron, Side, and Leg Shapes,* and the mortise layout is shown in *Front Leg Mortises.* Note that both inner faces of the back legs and the side inner faces of the front legs receive four identical mortises, but the front inner faces of the front legs receive only one long mortise for the apron, two smaller mortises for the middle rail, and a dovetail socket for the top rail. Rout or chop the large mortises ¾ inch deep.

3 Saw the cabriole outline. Next, use a band saw to cut the cabriole leg curves. This is straightforward compound-curve cutting: Saw to the lines on one face, tape the off cuts back in place, and saw to the lines on the adjoining face. If you don't have a band saw and plan to cut the curves with a bow saw, you might want to first shape the post blocks to 1¾ inches square on the table saw.

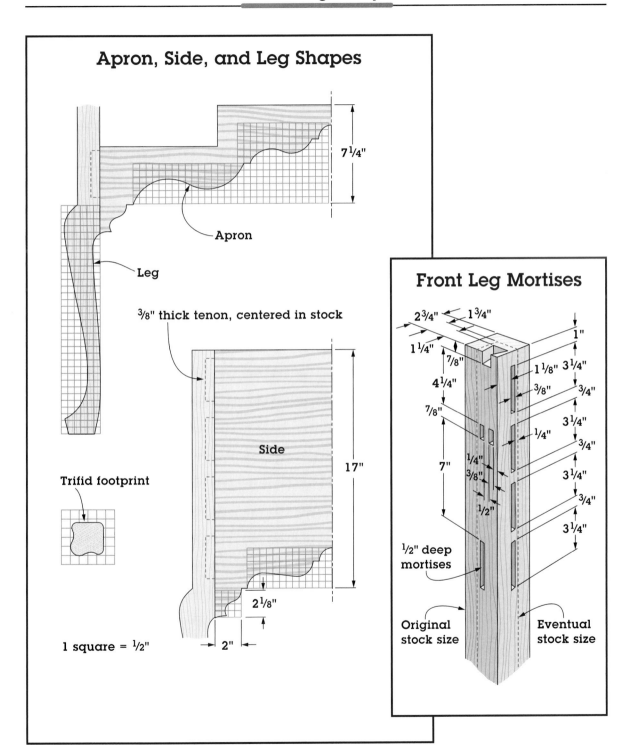

Apron, Side, and Leg Shapes

7 1/4"

Apron

Leg

3/8" thick tenon, centered in stock

Trifid footprint

Side

17"

1 square = 1/2"

2 1/8"

2"

Front Leg Mortises

2 3/4"　1 3/4"

1 1/4"

7/8"

1"

1 1/8"　3 1/4"

4 1/4"

3/8"　3/4"

7/8"

3 1/4"

1/4"

7"

1/4"

3/4"

3/8"

3 1/4"

1/2"

3/4"

3 1/4"

1/2" deep mortises

Original stock size

Eventual stock size

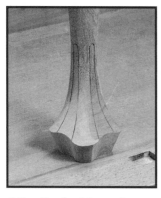

After the feet have been roughly cut to shape on the band saw, lay out the hollows between the toes with a pencil. The hollows extend about 4 inches up the leg to form the "stockings."

Carefully carve the hollows between the toes starting with a ½-inch, #7, spoon-bent gouge. As the hollows narrow as you move up into the stockings, switch to a ¼-inch, #7, spoon-bent gouge. Sand the hollows smooth, but leave a crisp edge between the hollows and the toes.

4 **Shape and smooth the legs.** Shape the legs as described in "Shaping Cabriole Legs" on page 368. The method for carving the trifid feet is shown in the photos at left. Before carving, band saw the feet roughly to shape, as shown in *Apron, Side, and Leg Shapes*.

Build the Lower Case

1 **Dimension the apron, ends, and back.** Prepare your stock for the two ends, the apron, and the back; all should be ⅞ inch thick if possible. Note that the grain in all of these parts runs horizontally.

2 **Saw out the tenons.** Lay out and cut tenons to match the mortises in the legs. They should fit snugly but enter the mortises with only hand force.

3 **Mortise for the drawer supports.** Lay out and rout the mortises shown in *Apron Joinery* and *Back Joinery*. Don't overlook the two mortises in the top edge of the apron.

4 **Cut the drawer openings.** Cut out the openings for the drawers in the two upper corners of the apron. These are best made as stopped cuts on the table saw, finished with a hand saw, and then smoothed with a paring chisel.

5 **Shape the apron and ends.** Finally, lay out the curves on the apron and ends, and cut them on a band saw. Then smooth the cuts with files and/or a suitable sander.

6 **Cut the mortises and tenons for the drawer supports.** You can now dry assemble the legs, apron, back, and ends, holding it all together with a band clamp. Carefully check the actual lengths required for the top and middle rails, dividers, kickers, and runners; then cut the tenons on these pieces to fit their respective mortises. You also need to cut mortises in the rails, as shown in the drawings.

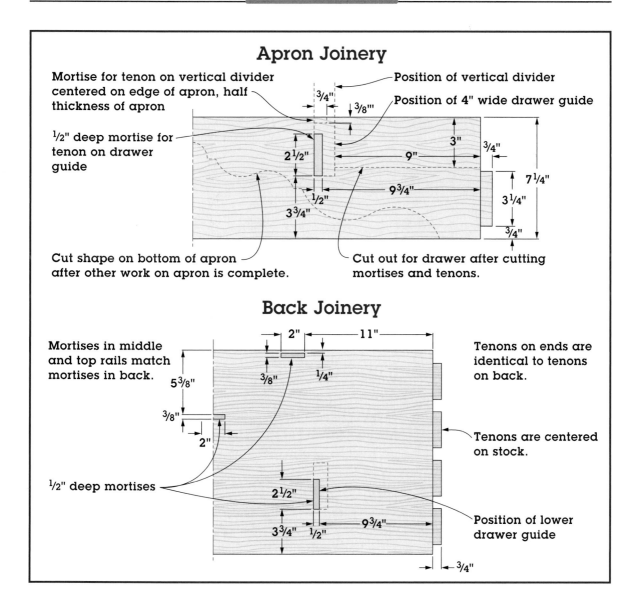

Apron Joinery

Mortise for tenon on vertical divider centered on edge of apron, half thickness of apron

Position of vertical divider

¾"

³⁄₈'''

Position of 4" wide drawer guide

½" deep mortise for tenon on drawer guide

2½"

9"

3"

¾"

7¼"

9¾"

3¼"

½"

3¾"

¾"

Cut shape on bottom of apron after other work on apron is complete.

Cut out for drawer after cutting mortises and tenons.

Back Joinery

2"

11"

Mortises in middle and top rails match mortises in back.

5³⁄₈"

³⁄₈"

¼"

Tenons on ends are identical to tenons on back.

³⁄₈"

2"

Tenons are centered on stock.

½" deep mortises

2½"

3¾"

½"

9¾"

Position of lower drawer guide

¾"

7 **Assemble the back and front.** Reassemble the lower case without glue to check that everything fits properly; then disassemble the case, and glue the back to the two back legs.

Glue the apron to the dividers and middle rail; immediately glue this assembly to the front legs. Finally glue the top rail into the dovetail sockets in the tops of the legs. You can add a wood screw to hold the dovetails in their sockets if you'd like. Make sure the entire assembly is square and lies flat before the glue has a chance to set up.

8 **Smooth out the joints.** When the glue is dry, scrape or plane the post block portion of the legs flush with the apron and back. You may need to pare with a chisel at the tops of the knees.

9 **Install the knee blocks.** Cut the knee blocks to the shape shown in *Apron, Side, and Leg Shapes*. If you like, you can hold two of them in place on the assembled front and trace the leg shape onto them, then cut to just outside the tracing. This will save some hand work in the next step.

Glue the knee blocks in position on the front of the case, slightly proud of the legs. When the glue has cured, pare the blocks flush with the knees, and sand smooth.

10 **Assemble the lower case.** Lay the assembled back flat with the inside facing up; then glue the kickers, drawer guides, and ends in place. Immediately apply glue to the mortises and tenons at the front, and fit the assembled front to the parts that join it. Clamp everything securely, check that all is square, and set the assembly aside for the glue to cure.

Scrape or plane the post blocks flush with the ends; then install the knee blocks on the ends as you did on the front.

Finally, install the remaining drawer guides and runners, as shown in the drawings. These can be glued, screwed, or both.

Build the Upper Case

1 **Size the box parts.** The upper case is a big dovetailed box fitted with traditional wooden drawer supports. Begin by dimensioning the top, bottom, and sides. The dimensions given in the Materials List assume that the box will be assembled with through dovetails, since the ends will be covered with the crown and waist moldings.

2 **Rabbet for the back.** The ½-inch-thick back boards get nailed into rabbets in the sides with 4d finish nails. Rout or saw these rabbets to at least half the thickness of the sides to allow enough stock for the nails.

3 **Cut the corner joints.** Lay out the dovetails on the top and bottom and the pins on the sides. Since they can't be seen, I used equal spacing for simplicity. Rout the joints or chop them by hand, as you prefer.

4 **Fit the rails.** Begin by cutting the rails, runners/kickers, and dividers to the sizes given in the Materials List. Six of the rails should be cut from your primary wood and six from your secondary wood, and all of the runners/kickers can be cut from your secondary wood.

When the parts have been cut to size, lay out the position of the rails on the case sides, as shown in *Front View*. Rout dovetail sockets for the rails by guiding a router with a dovetail bit against a straightedge clamped across the case side. Trim the rails to the precise length, and rout the tails on the ends, as shown in the photo at right. The dovetails on the ends of the rails should fit snugly but easily into the dovetail sockets.

Next, lay out and rout the dovetail joints for the vertical dividers that separate the smaller drawers at the top. Assemble the dividers and the top three rails with glue, making certain that the assembly is precisely square before the glue cures.

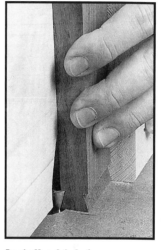

Install a high fence on your router table, and use a push board with an accurately squared corner to rout dovetail tenons on drawer rails and similar parts.

5 **Cut the drawer support joinery.** In the drawer support system used in the upper case, the drawer runners function as kickers for the drawers below. All 19 of them join the front rails with glued mortise-and-tenon joints. To accommodate seasonal expansion and contraction of the upper case sides, the runners/kickers join the rear rails with unglued mortise-and-tenon joints and are cut ¼ inch short, as shown in *Drawer Supports*.

Rout ⅜-inch-wide × ¾-inch-deep mortises in the rails to accept the runner tenons. Three of the mortises will intersect the dovetails where the vertical dividers join the rails.

Drawer Supports

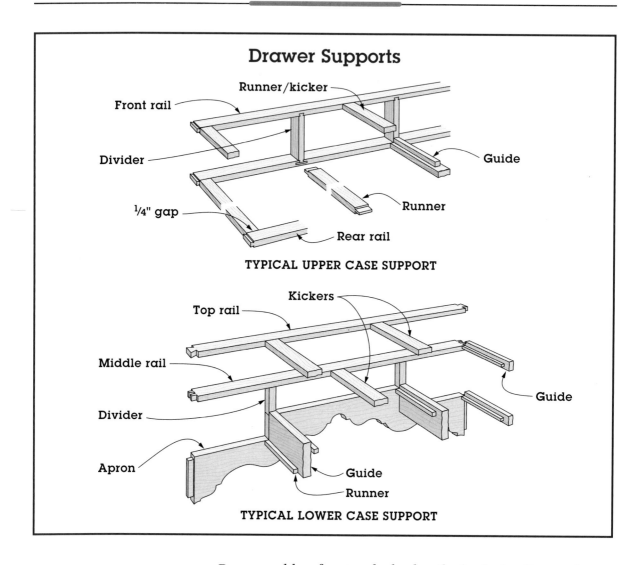

Front rail

Runner/kicker

Divider

Guide

¼" gap

Runner

Rear rail

TYPICAL UPPER CASE SUPPORT

Kickers

Top rail

Middle rail

Divider

Guide

Apron

Guide

Runner

TYPICAL LOWER CASE SUPPORT

Dry assemble a front and a back rail, check the distance between them, add ¾ inch to this distance for each of the tenons, and subtract ¼ inch from the total. Cut the runners/kickers to the resulting length. Cut tenons on both ends of the runners/kickers with a dado blade on the table saw.

6 Assemble the upper case. The upper case assembly requires a lot of careful application of glue to many parts. If you're not careful, you can exceed the allowable open time of the glue, resulting in poor glue joints.

Check the allowable open time of the glue you're using, and keep an eye on the clock. When you run out of time, check that the assembly is square, and allow the glued joints to cure overnight before continuing. The following sequence allows you to stop and let the glue cure at just about any point in the assembly:

- First, glue the top and bottom to the sides.
- Next, glue the front rails into the dovetail sockets in the sides. Be careful not to rack the subassembly of the top three rails and the dividers.
- Turn the assembly face down, check that it is square, and glue the runners/kickers into their mortises.
- Finally, glue the rear rails into their dovetail sockets in the sides. Fit the runner/kicker tenons into their mortises as you go, but do not glue them.

7 **Install the drawer guides.** The full-width drawers in the upper case require no further guides; the sides of the case provide the necessary guidance. Guides are needed, however, atop the runners/kickers behind the vertical dividers. These can extend over the rear rails, but glue them only to the runners/kickers. Glue and clamp them in place; then double-check that the drawer opening alongside the guides is uniform in width from front to back. If it is not, you can unclamp the guides, knock them loose, and reglue them correctly; or you can simply plane the sides of the guides with a rabbet plane as necessary after the glue has cured.

8 **Install the back.** The back of the upper case consists of shiplapped boards nailed into rabbets in the sides. Traditionally, cabinet backs were made from random-width boards, so the boards do not need to be uniform in width but should not be less than 6 or more than 12 inches wide.

Rabbet the edges on opposite sides of the boards ¼ inch deep and ½ inch wide, as shown in *Side View*. (Note that the top and bottom boards will require rabbets on only a single edge.) Trim the boards to fit snugly in the rabbets in the sides of the upper case.

Arrange the boards with $1/16$ inch of expansion room between them and so the rear rails come well within the width of the back boards, not at a joint between boards.

Install them with two nails at each end into the sides and with three nails into the top, bottom, and each rear rail.

Make the Drawers

1 **Prepare the drawer fronts.** Measure all of the drawer openings. Each drawer front should be $3/16$ inch higher and $3/8$ inch wider than its opening. Cut the drawer fronts to size.

Rabbet the top and both ends of the drawer fronts, leaving a $1/4 \times 1/4$-inch lip. This will allow $1/16$ inch of clearance at the top and $1/16$ inch of clearance at each side of the drawers.

2 **Prepare the drawer sides and backs.** Measure the inside dimensions of the drawer fronts at the rabbets. This gives you the height of the drawer sides and the width of the drawer back. The depth of the upper drawer sides is $1/4$ inch less than the depth of the upper case (the lower drawer sides are more than $1/4$ inch less than the depth of the lower case). The height of the drawer backs is $1/2$ inch less than the height of the sides.

Cut the drawer sides and backs to size; then cut the drawer bottom grooves in the drawer sides and fronts. These should be $1/4$ inch wide $\times 1/4$ inch deep and are placed $1/4$ inch from the bottom edges, as shown in *Drawer Construction*.

3 **Dovetail the drawer parts.** The drawers should be joined with half-blind dovetails at the front and through dovetails at the back. Lay them out at 14 degrees using 1-inch tails and $1/4$-inch pins, adjusting the tails as necessary for the specific drawer. Chop out the joints. For more information on cutting dovetails, see "Cutting Dovetails" on page 164. When you're finished, rout the thumbnail shape shown in *Drawer Front Lip* on the front edges of the drawer fronts.

Drawer Construction

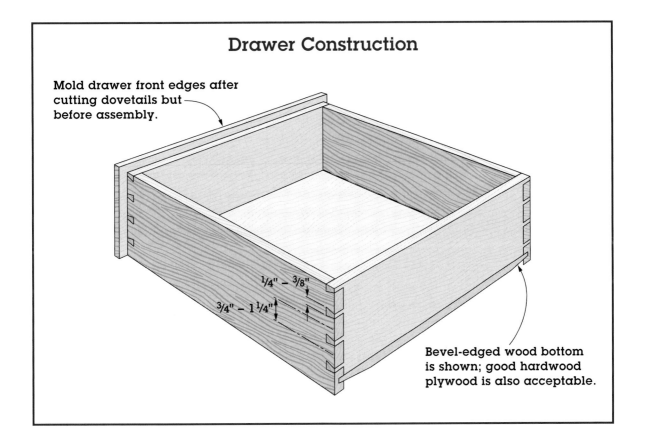

Mold drawer front edges after
cutting dovetails but
before assembly.

$1/4" - 3/8"$

$3/4" - 1 1/4"$

Bevel-edged wood bottom
is shown; good hardwood
plywood is also acceptable.

4 **Prepare the drawer bottoms.** Traditional drawer
bottoms are solid lumber, $1/2$ inch thick, with edges tapered down to $1/4$ inch thick on the lower surface. The grain
runs from side to side. You can make them this way if you
like, or you can substitute a high-quality, no-voids European
birch plywood. In either case, cut the bottoms to size for an
easy-slide fit in the grooves. If you make traditional bottoms,
taper the front and side edges with a hand plane or with a
panel-raising bit or cutter.

5 **Assemble the drawers.** Glue up the drawer fronts,
sides, and backs. Install the bottom (without glue) in
each drawer as you go, checking that the drawer is square.
Then screw the bottom to the center of the back with a single
#6 × 1-inch flathead wood screw.

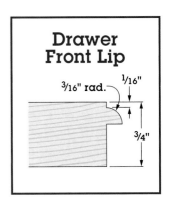

**Drawer
Front Lip**

$3/16"$ rad.

$1/16"$

$3/4"$

Add the Moldings,
Finish, and Hardware

1 **Shape the moldings.** The crown and waist moldings can be built up from smaller stock, as shown in *Crown Molding Detail* and *Waist Molding Detail*.

There is no need to slavishly follow the exact shapes shown in the drawings. Lay out a full-size cross section of the moldings on grid paper, lightly sketching in the shapes shown. Then go over your collection of router bits or shaper cutters, and see how much of the molding you can duplicate or approximate. You may need to buy an additional cutter or two to arrive at a molding that pleases your eye. Pencil in your final selections on the grid paper drawing, and cut the parts. The main central cove of the crown molding is best cut by running the stock diagonally over a saw blade, as described in "Cove Cutting on the Table Saw" on page 24.

2 **Assemble the moldings.** Glue up the waist molding as a stack. Since it is quite difficult to keep five layers accurately lined up while applying clamping pressure, I suggest that you glue only one interface at a time.

Assemble the crown molding, as shown in *Crown Molding Detail*. It is easiest to assemble the crown upside down against a square corner, like that formed by the table saw table and fence. First, put the ogee molding top down on the saw table with its back against the fence. Then glue the cove molding in place with one beveled edge against the bottom of the ogee molding and the other against the table saw fence. The small bead molding can be glued in place now or after the rest of the crown has been installed on the upper case. When the glue has dried, cut small triangular filler blocks out of scrap to fit in the space between the ogee and cove moldings, and glue them in place about every 4 inches. These not only will make the assembled molding stronger and easier to handle but will also give you a place for the wood screws that help hold the molding in place on the upper case, as described in Step 3.

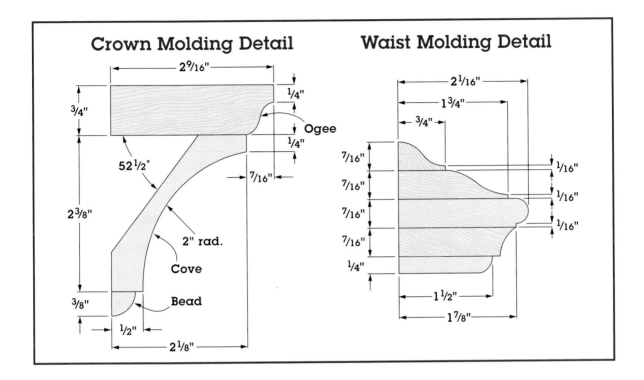

Crown Molding Detail

2⁹/₁₆"
¾"
¼"
Ogee
¼"
52½°
7/₁₆"
2³/₈"
2" rad.
Cove
Bead
³/₈"
½"
2¹/₈"

Waist Molding Detail

2¹/₁₆"
1³/₄"
¾"
⁷/₁₆"
1/₁₆"
⁷/₁₆"
1/₁₆"
⁷/₁₆"
1/₁₆"
⁷/₁₆"
¼"
1½"
1⁷/₈"

3 **Install the crown molding.** Miter one end of the assembled crown molding, and clamp it to the front of
the upper case; then accurately scribe the location of the
second miter. Make the second cut.

Miter an end of a section of the molding for one of the sides,
and clamp it in place but don't cut the molding to length yet.
Do the same for the other side.

When you have all three sections of the crown molding
clamped in place on the case, leave the side sections where
they are and remove the front section. Apply glue to the back
edges of the front section and clamp it to the case.

While the glue takes an initial set, scribe the rear ends of the
side sections at the back of the case. Remove one of the side
sections and trim it to the scribed line. Apply glue to its
mitered end and to the mitered end of the front section that it
will join; then apply glue to the front 4 inches or so of the
back of the molding. (The remainder of the side molding is
not glued.) Check that the glue on the mitered ends has not

(continued on page 370)

Shaping Cabriole Legs

Spokeshaves, rasps, files, and a gouge or two are the only tools you need to shape cabriole legs. And perhaps you'll also need the gumption to try something new. If you think they're extraordinarily difficult, ask yourself why they were so common just a generation or two ago. They're *not* all that difficult.

1 Cut the first leg profile. On the band saw, cut the first side of the leg profile, but don't cut the waste completely off the stock. The "standard" procedure is to cut off the waste and tape it back on with masking tape before cutting the second side of the leg profile. Instead, cut into the profile from each end of the leg, leaving the waste secured by about ½ inch of wood where the grain is the straightest—in this case, at the front of the ankle and at the back of the knee, as shown below. Later, you simply snap the waste off.

2 Cut the second leg profile. Turn the leg to the second profile, and cut away the waste. This time you don't have to worry about keeping the waste attached.

3 Snap off the waste. When both profiles have been cut, snap off the waste that is still connected to the leg stock by prying it with a screwdriver. The straight grain should give way easily, and any indication of the break will be removed in the next step.

4 Shape the foot. An easy way to round and angle the foot is to hold it at an angle against a sanding disk. The photo shows a stationary disc sander, but a sanding disk installed in a table saw would work just as well. This is freeform sanding, using the feel of the wood and shaping by eye. Try to give all of the feet a similar shape, but don't obsess over getting a precisely matched set.

5 Round the leg. Now for the fun part. Sharpen up a good old drawknife with sharpening stones just as you would sharpen a plane iron. With the top of the leg in a bench vise and the foot against your diaphragm, carefully pull the drawknife toward you to cut away the sharp corners of the leg.

6 Smooth the leg. Using a rasp and then a file, remove the marks left by the drawknife; then give the leg its final shape. Carefully round and smooth the leg from the knee down until it is almost round in cross section.

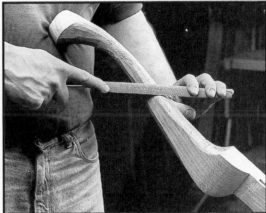

7 Sand away the file marks. Starting with 80-grit paper, remove the marks left by the file. Sand with progressively finer-grit papers until the leg is smooth. To prepare the piece for finishing, 180- or 220-grit paper should be good enough.

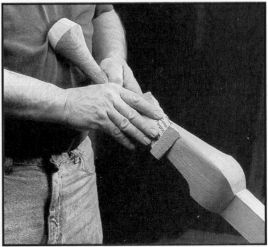

When gluing up awkward parts like assembled moldings, it is often helpful to hold the pieces together with cyanoacrylate, commonly known as Super Glue. To do this, spread wood glue on the mating parts, leaving gaps every few inches for a drop of Super Glue. Put Super Glue in the gaps, quickly position the mating parts, and hold them together for 30 seconds or so. It is often handy to have some cyanoacrylate accelerator on hand, which can be sprayed on the joint to set the Super Glue instantly.

soaked entirely into the end grain; if it has, freshen it up with more glue. Then clamp the section in place on the case. Repeat the routine to install the other side section.

When all of the crown molding glue has fully cured, install #8 × 1½-inch drywall screws through the case sides from inside the case into the filler blocks.

4 **Install the waist molding.** Place the upper case in position on the lower case. Now install the waist molding, following the basic procedure described above for the crown molding, with two exceptions: (1) Glue the waist molding to the lower case, and scrupulously avoid gluing it to the upper case; and (2) glue the side sections along their entire length, not just at the front.

5 **Apply the finish.** Carefully go over the entire cabinet, planing, scraping, and sanding as necessary to ensure that all squeezed-out glue has been fully removed, that all joined pieces that should be flush are truly flush, that all exposed surfaces are smooth, and that sharp corners have been very slightly blunted with fine sandpaper.

Apply a finish, such as 1-pound cut shellac rubbed out with 0000 steel wool between coats and after the final coat. Apply as many coats as required to achieve the finish you prefer; then wax with a brown paste wax and buff. Apply a single coat of shellac on the insides of the drawers.

6 **Install the hardware.** The full-width drawers each receive two pulls and an escutcheon. The remaining drawers each receive a single pull. All the pulls are centered in the height of the drawer front. On the narrow drawers, the single pulls are centered from left to right in the drawer front. The fronts of the full-width drawers are divided into thirds from left to right: For each drawer, the pulls are centered in the right and left thirds, and the escutcheon is centered in the middle third. The escutcheons are flush with the top of the drawer below the lip.

Cherry Vanity

by Kenneth S. Burton Jr.

Commercial bathroom vanities leave me cold—at least those that I can afford do. So when it came time to select a vanity for the house my wife and I were building, we had trouble finding anything acceptable that would fit within our budget.

Rather than settle for something neither of us liked, I decided to design and build a vanity that was more to our taste. By using a combination of solid hardwood and hardwood plywood, I came up with a vanity that looks more like a piece of furniture than a built-in cabinet and that wasn't terribly expensive to build.

The design has a vaguely southwestern flavor, stemming from the frame-and-panel construction and the brackets (or "lookouts") that appear to support the countertop. The frames and panels themselves, with their asymmetrical shapes, are clearly contemporary interpretations of this traditional technique. The overall impression of the piece is one of quiet elegance.

Exploded View

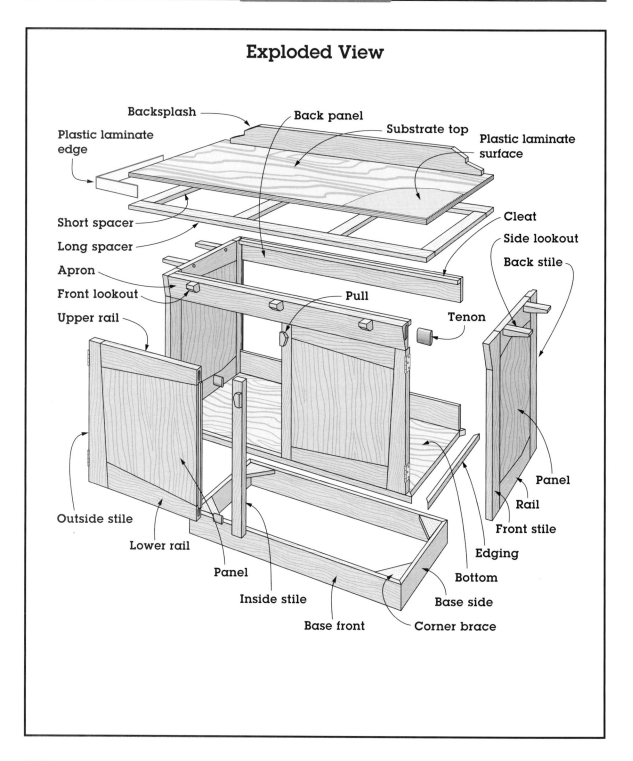

Backsplash

Back panel

Substrate top

Plastic laminate edge

Plastic laminate surface

Short spacer

Long spacer

Apron

Front lookout

Upper rail

Cleat

Side lookout

Back stile

Pull

Tenon

Outside stile

Lower rail

Panel

Inside stile

Base front

Panel

Rail

Front stile

Edging

Bottom

Base side

Corner brace

Materials List

Part	Dimension	Part	Dimension
Case		Upper rails (2)	$1\frac{1}{8}$" × $3\frac{1}{2}$" × $19\frac{1}{4}$"
Back stiles (2)	$1\frac{1}{8}$" × $2\frac{1}{4}$" × 26"	Lower rails (2)	$1\frac{1}{8}$" × $3\frac{7}{8}$" × 18"
Front stiles (2)	$1\frac{1}{8}$" × 3" × 26"	Panels (2)	$\frac{5}{8}$" × $19\frac{3}{4}$" × $18\frac{7}{8}$"
Rails (4)	$1\frac{1}{8}$" × 4" × $14\frac{7}{8}$"	Tenon stock	$\frac{1}{2}$" × $2\frac{1}{4}$" × 20"
Panels (2)	$\frac{5}{8}$" × $15\frac{1}{2}$" × 22"	Pulls (2)	$\frac{5}{8}$" × 1" × $2\frac{3}{4}$"
Tenon stock	$\frac{1}{2}$" × $2\frac{1}{2}$" × 20"		
Bottom	$\frac{3}{4}$" × $18\frac{3}{4}$" × 47"	**Countertop**	
Back edging	$\frac{1}{4}$" × $\frac{3}{4}$" × 47"	Substrate top	$\frac{3}{4}$" × $22\frac{1}{2}$" × $58\frac{1}{4}$"
Front edging	$\frac{3}{4}$" × 1" × $48\frac{1}{2}$"	Long spacers (2)	$\frac{3}{4}$" × 3" × $58\frac{1}{4}$"
Side edging (2)	$\frac{3}{4}$" × 1" × $19\frac{3}{4}$"	Short spacers (4)	$\frac{3}{4}$" × 4" × 17"
Apron	$1\frac{1}{2}$" × $3\frac{5}{8}$" × 46"	Backsplash	$\frac{3}{4}$" × $4\frac{1}{2}$" × $53\frac{1}{4}$"
Apron tenon stock	$\frac{3}{8}$" × $2\frac{5}{8}$" × 12"	Cleats (2)	$\frac{3}{4}$" × $\frac{3}{4}$" × 46"
Back panels (2)	$\frac{1}{2}$" × 6" × $47\frac{1}{2}$"		
Side lookouts (4)	$1\frac{1}{8}$" × $1\frac{1}{2}$" × $3\frac{1}{2}$"	**Hardware**	
Front lookouts (3)	$1\frac{1}{8}$" × $1\frac{1}{2}$" × $1\frac{1}{4}$"	#8 × $2\frac{1}{2}$" drywall screws (as needed)	
Base front/back (2)	$\frac{3}{4}$" × 4" × $42\frac{1}{2}$"	#8 × 2" drywall screws (as needed)	
Base sides (2)	$\frac{3}{4}$" × 4" × $16\frac{1}{4}$"	#8 × $1\frac{5}{8}$" drywall screws (as needed)	
Corner braces (4)	$\frac{3}{4}$" × $1\frac{1}{2}$" × 7"	#8 × $1\frac{1}{4}$" drywall screws (as needed)	
		4d finish nails (as needed)	
Doors		$\frac{3}{4}$" wire brads (as needed)	
Outside stiles (2)	$1\frac{1}{8}$" × $3\frac{1}{2}$" × $22\frac{1}{4}$"	30" × 60" plastic laminate	
Inside stiles (2)	$1\frac{1}{8}$" × $1\frac{3}{4}$" × $22\frac{1}{4}$"	$1\frac{1}{2}$" × 2" brass butt hinges with screws (4)	

Make the Case

1 **Cut the pieces for the sides.** Cut the rails and stiles for the side frames to the sizes given in the Materials List. Edge-glue narrower stock to make up pieces wide enough for the panels.

2 **Cut the side frame joinery.** The frame is assembled with loose tenon joints, wherein both the rail and the stile are mortised and a separate tenon is cut to fit in between. Using a plunge router, rout $\frac{1}{2}$-inch-wide mortises in the pieces, as shown in *Side Frame Joinery Detail*. Make sure you keep the inside surface of all the pieces against the fence as

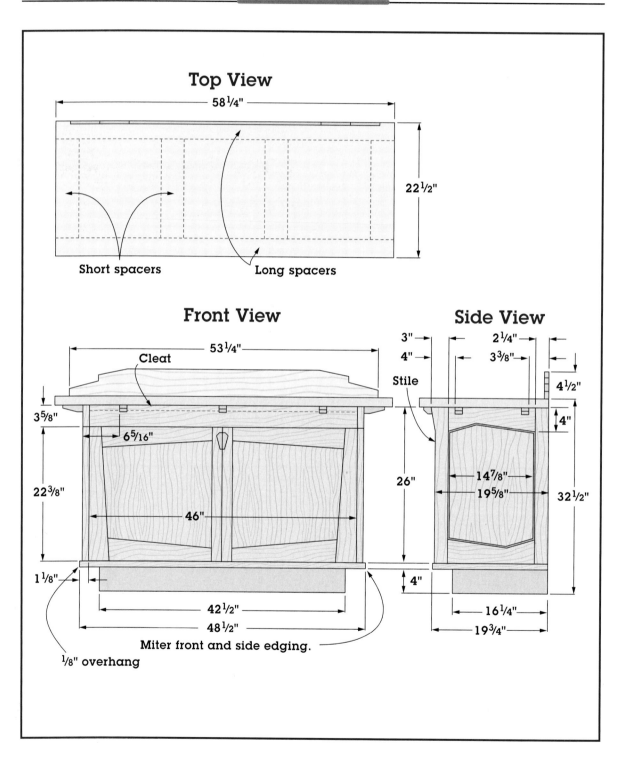

Top View

58 1/4"

22 1/2"

Short spacers

Long spacers

Front View

53 1/4"

Cleat

3 5/8"

6 5/16"

22 3/8"

46"

1 1/8"

42 1/2"

48 1/2"

Miter front and side edging.

1/8" overhang

Side View

3"

4"

Stile

2 1/4"

3 3/8"

4 1/2"

4"

26"

14 7/8"

19 5/8"

32 1/2"

4"

16 1/4"

19 3/4"

you rout, or the surfaces may not be flush when you assemble the frames. Also cut a ⅜-inch-wide mortise near the top end of each front stile to accommodate the apron, as shown in *Apron Joinery Detail*. It is easier to cut this mortise now than after the frames are assembled.

Cut all the tenons from a single piece of wood. Cut the tenon stock to the width and length specified in the Materials List. Then carefully rip it to thickness on the table saw. Round-over the corners with a ¼-inch roundover bit in a table-mounted router. Once the tenon stock is cut to the right size and shape, crosscut it into individual tenons that are slightly shorter (¹⁄₁₆ inch or so) than twice the mortise depth.

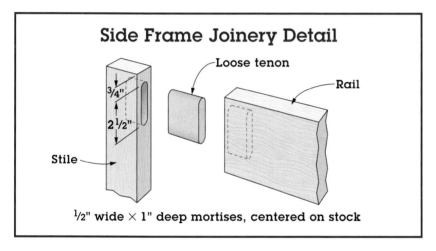

Side Frame Joinery Detail

Loose tenon

Rail

¾"

2½"

Stile

½" wide × 1" deep mortises, centered on stock

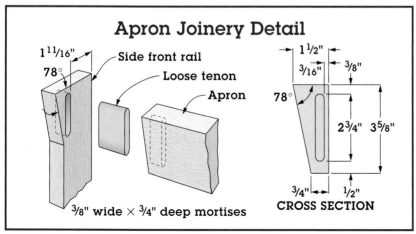

Apron Joinery Detail

1¹¹⁄₁₆"

78°

Side front rail

Loose tenon

Apron

1½"

3/16"   3/8"

78°

2¾"   3⅝"

¾"   ½"

CROSS SECTION

⅜" wide × ¾" deep mortises

3 **Shape the frame rails.** The inside edges of the rails are cut to a V-shape, as shown in *Side View*. The easiest way to make these cuts is to saw them close on the band saw, then clean up the saw marks with a template and a flush-trimming bit in a router.

Make the template from $\frac{1}{2}$-inch plywood, as shown in *Side Rail Template Detail*. Lay out the V-cut as shown, and carefully saw along the layout lines on the band saw. Sand the template to clean up the saw marks and fine-tune the shape. Screw three $\frac{3}{4}$-inch square blocks of scrap to one side of the template to locate the workpieces. Pop the workpieces into the template, and trace the shape on one face. Note that on one frame's pieces, the outside faces of the rails should go against the template, while on the other frame's pieces, the inside faces should be against the template. Cut just outside the layout lines on the band saw.

Once all the rails are cut, chuck a flush-trimming bit in your table-mounted router. Fasten each rail in turn in the template with a strip of double-sided carpet tape, and rout the rails to their final shape, as shown in the photo at left. The bit will leave the point of the V slightly rounded—this will look fine on the finished vanity.

A strip of double-sided carpet tape is all that is necessary to hold the rails in the template as you rout them to shape. Rout from right to left.

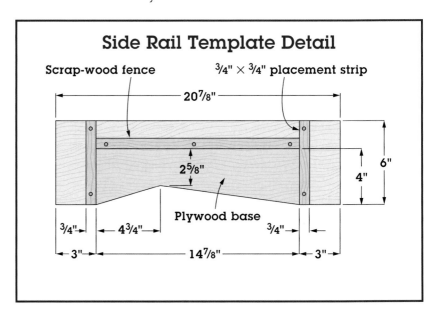

Side Rail Template Detail

Scrap-wood fence

$\frac{3}{4}$" × $\frac{3}{4}$" placement strip

20$\frac{7}{8}$"

2$\frac{5}{8}$"

Plywood base

6"

4"

$\frac{3}{4}$"   4$\frac{3}{4}$" $\frac{3}{4}$"

3"   14$\frac{7}{8}$"   3"

4 **Cut the grooves for the panels.** Assemble the frames without glue, clamping across the joints to keep them tight. Make sure the clamps allow the frames to lie flat. Chuck a ¼-inch wing cutter in your table-mounted router, and rout a ½-inch-deep groove around the inside of each frame, as shown in *Case Cross Section.*

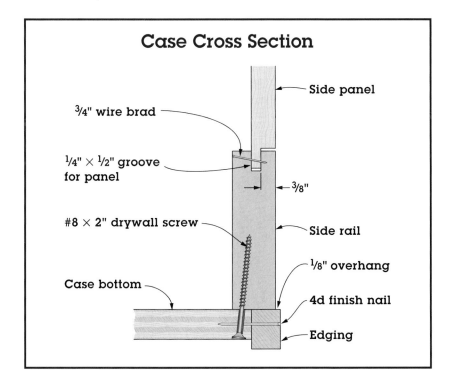

Case Cross Section

Side panel

¾" wire brad

¼" × ½" groove for panel

⅜"

#8 × 2" drywall screw

Side rail

⅛" overhang

Case bottom

4d finish nail

Edging

5 **Shape the side panels.** The side panels must be cut to fit inside the frames. Trace around the inside of one frame onto a piece of ¼-inch plywood. Check the plywood against the other frame to make sure the openings match. If the openings are significantly different (more than ¹⁄₁₆ inch or so), you'll have to make a template for each panel.

Make a second outline on the plywood, ⅜ inch outside the first. This is the shape of the panel you want. Cut the plywood just outside this second layout line, and carefully sand it to shape. Trace the shape onto the wide boards that you edge-glued together for the panels. Carefully cut the panels to shape.

Once the panels are cut to the right shape, they must be rabbeted along their outside edges to fit into the grooves cut in the frames, as shown in *Case Cross Section*. Cut the rabbets with a $\frac{5}{8}$-inch-diameter or larger straight bit chucked in a table-mounted router. Set up the bit so the depth of cut is about $\frac{1}{8}$ inch. Position the fence so part of the bit is buried, leaving $\frac{1}{2}$ inch exposed. Guide the panels along the fence from right to left to make the cuts. Rabbet all the edges of each panel, then raise the bit slightly and make another pass. Continue the process until each panel has a tongue all the way around its edge that slips snugly into the groove in the frame. At the apex of each V, you'll have to round the panel slightly to match the frame. Do this little bit of shaping with a file and sandpaper. You'll also have to round the corners slightly to fit in the groove left by the wing cutter. Check the fit of each panel in its respective frame.

6 **Sand and assemble the sides.** Sand the inside edges of the frames, taking care not to round-over the areas where the rails will abut the stiles. Also sand the panels and give them an initial coat of finish. The finish will help keep the panels from being glued in place should any excess glue find its way into the panel grooves. The panels must be free to expand and contract with changes in humidity.

Brush glue on the insides of the mortises and on the faces of the tenons, and assemble the frames. Be sure to remember to insert the panel before clamping everything together. Check with a straightedge to make sure the frames are flat before letting the glue dry. After the glue dries, center the panels in the openings and pin them in place with two short brads per panel. Drive the brads through the back side of the frame into the panel's tongue at about the center of each rail, as shown in *Case Cross Section*. The brads will hold the panel in place without inhibiting its seasonal movement.

7 **Cut and mortise the apron.** Cut the apron to the size given in the Materials List. It is joined to the side frames with loose tenon joints. (You already cut the mortises in the frame.) With a plunge router, mortise the ends of the apron, as shown in *Apron Joinery Detail,* just as you did with the frame rails. Make tenons to fit the mortises.

8 **Bevel the apron.** Tilt the blade on your table saw over, and bevel the front face of the apron, as shown in *Apron Joinery Detail.* Set your jointer for a light cut, and run the sawed face over the cutter to clean up the saw marks.

9 **Shape the front stiles.** Once the frames are assembled, the front stiles can be cut down in width, leaving a slight flair toward the top, as shown in *Side View.* The angle of this flair should match the bevel on the front of the apron. Fit the apron into the mortises cut in the frames, and trace the bevel onto the front stiles to lay out the angled cut. Set the rip fence on your table saw to cut the stile down to the appropriate width. Make the cut, guiding the back stile along the fence. Stop the cut about 2 inches from the angled layout line as shown in the photo at right. Shut off the saw and allow the blade to quit spinning before backing the frame out of the cut. Finish cutting the frame to width, and make the angled cut on the band saw.

Cutting the flair at the top of the front stiles on the side frames is a two-stage process. Make most of the cut on the table saw, then finish the angled part on the band saw.

10 **Make the case bottom.** The case bottom is made from ¾-inch birch plywood faced with 1-inch-wide edgings to make it appear thicker, as shown in *Case Cross Section.* Cut the plywood case bottom to the size given in the Materials List. Cut the edgings to the listed width and thickness, but leave them an inch or so long for now.

Attach the back edging to the back edge of the case bottom with glue and 4d finish nails. Trim the ends of the edging flush with the ends of the bottom. Cut one end of the front edging and one end of each of the side edgings at a 45-degree angle. Hold the front edging in place, and use it to help position one of the side edgings so the ends meet in a perfect miter. The top surface of the edging should be flush with the top face of the plywood case bottom. Fasten the side edging in place with glue and 4d finish nails. Miter the other end of the front edging and fasten it to the front edge of the bottom with glue and nails; then attach the final side edging the same way. Cut the ends of the side flush with the back edge of the case bottom.

11 **Rabbet the sides for the back panels.** The vanity has two back panels made from $\frac{1}{2}$-inch plywood, one near the top and the other near the bottom. These serve to brace the cabinet and keep it from racking. The space in between the panels is left open for the plumbing.

Set up a dado blade on your table saw, and cut a $\frac{1}{2}$-inch-wide $\times$ $\frac{3}{4}$-inch-deep dado along the back inside edge of each side frame. Cut the back panels to the sizes given in the Materials List.

12 **Assemble the case.** Start assembling the case by screwing the back panels to the side frames with #8 $\times$ $1\frac{1}{4}$-inch drywall screws, two to a joint. Then add the apron. Brush glue in the mortises and on the tenons. There should be enough flex in the back panels to allow the apron to pop into place. Squeeze the joints closed with a clamp. Turn the case upside down and set the bottom in place, centered from side to side and flush with the back. Check to make sure the bottoms of the side frames aren't toed in or out at the front. Screw the bottom to the side frames with #8 $\times$ 2-inch drywall screws, as shown in *Case Cross Section*. When the glue has dried, sand the flair at the top of the frames flush with the front of the apron.

13 **Make and attach the lookouts.** Cut four lengths of stock about 12 inches long to the thickness and width given in the Materials List for the lookouts. Tilt over the blade on your table saw, and chamfer one end of three of the pieces to make the front lookouts, as shown in *Lookout Detail*. Reset the tilt of the blade, and cut the front lookouts to length. The cutoff blade angle should match the apron's bevel angle.

On the remaining lengths of wood, lay out the length and longer bevel of the side lookouts. Cut the pieces to length on the table saw (the blade should be square to the table), then cut the long bevel on the band saw. Sand, plane, and scrape the lookouts to clean up the saw marks. Glue and screw the front lookouts in place with #8 × 2-inch drywall screws, as shown in *Front View* and *Side View*. Drill clearance holes (holes that the screws can pass through without threading) through the apron, and drill pilot holes in the lookouts. Given the angled mating surfaces and the glue, the lookouts will tend to slip around a lot as the screws are tightened. The clearance holes give you a chance to adjust things should the pieces misbehave. Glue and screw the side lookouts to the side frames in the same manner.

Lookout Detail

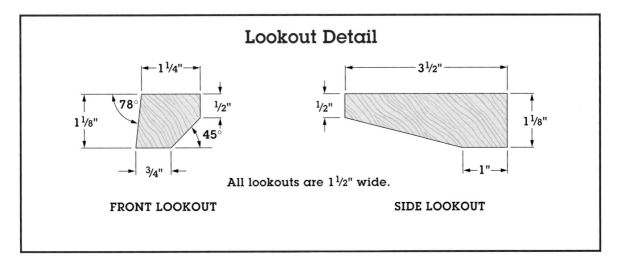

All lookouts are 1 1/2" wide.

FRONT LOOKOUT   SIDE LOOKOUT

14 **Assemble the base.** The vanity sits on a topless plywood plinth, as shown in *Exploded View*. Cut the pieces to the sizes listed in the Materials List. Miter the corners on the table saw, and fasten the base together with 4d finish nails and glue. Cut the corner braces to size, miter the ends, and glue and screw them to the corners of the base with #8 × 2-inch drywall screws for reinforcement.

15 **Attach the base.** Place the case on top of the base, backs flush and centered from side to side. Screw the case in place with #8 × 2-inch drywall screws driven through the case bottom into the top edges of the base.

Make the Doors

The doors are a little bit tricky to make because the outside stiles are tapered. This means the upper and lower rails will be of different lengths. To get the frame to go together properly, each rail must be cut to exactly the right length. The easiest way to accomplish this is to assemble the frame in two stages. First, join the rails to the outside stile. Then run the whole assembly through the table saw, trimming both rails to the proper length at once.

1 **Cut the pieces to size.** Cut the stiles and rails for the door frames to the sizes given in the Materials List, leaving the rails an inch or so long for now. Edge-glue narrower boards to make up pieces wide enough for the door panels.

2 **Taper the outside stiles.** Make a tapering jig from a scrap of ¾-inch plywood, and taper the outside stiles on the table saw, as shown in *Tapering the Stiles and Rails*. Note that you'll be using this jig again when you taper the rails; the only thing that will change is the size of the spacer block.

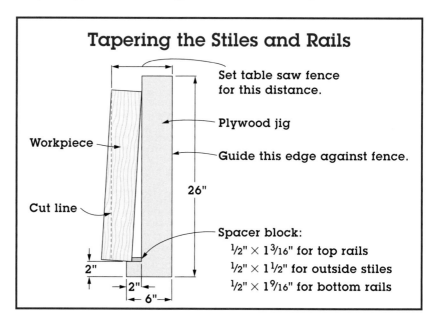

Tapering the Stiles and Rails

Set table saw fence for this distance.

Workpiece

Plywood jig

Guide this edge against fence.

Cut line

26"

Spacer block:
½" × 1³⁄₁₆" for top rails
½" × 1½" for outside stiles
½" × 1⁹⁄₁₆" for bottom rails

2"

2"

6"

3 **Cut the rails roughly to length.** Use a sliding T-bevel to set the miter gauge on your table saw to match the taper of the stiles. Cut one end of each rail at an angle to match the taper so that when the rail is butted against the stile, the pieces' outside edges form a right (90-degree) angle. Hold the pieces in position against the outside stiles, and mark the rails roughly to length with a framing square, as shown in the photo at right. Reset the miter gauge for a square cut, and crosscut the rails at the marks.

4 **Cut the frame joinery.** The door frames are also joined with loose tenon joints. Cut ½-inch-wide mortises in all four pieces of each door frame with a plunge router, as shown in *Door Joinery Detail*. Make tenons to fit the mortises.

Mark the rails about ⅛ inch too long, measuring from the outside edge of the tapered stile.

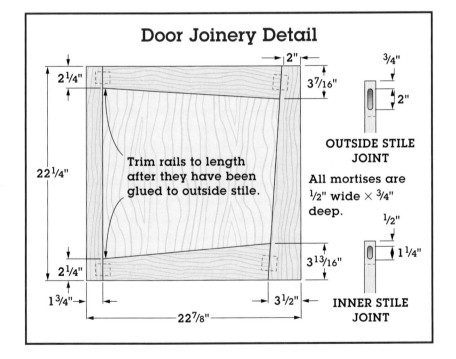

Door Joinery Detail

2¼"

2¼"

22¼"

2¼"

1¾"→

22⅞"

2"

3½"

3⁷⁄₁₆"

Trim rails to length after they have been glued to outside stile.

¾"

2"

OUTSIDE STILE JOINT

All mortises are ½" wide × ¾" deep.

½"

1¼"

3¹³⁄₁₆"

INNER STILE JOINT

5 **Taper the rails.** Using the same tapering jig you used to taper the stiles, taper the rails. You'll have to make a different spacer block for the top and bottom rails and change the position of the rip fence, as noted in *Tapering the Stiles and Rails*.

6 **Cut the rails to final length.** Glue the rails to the outside stiles. Be sure to use a clamping block on the inside ends of the rails so you don't mar them with the clamps. Check to make sure the frames are flat as the glue sets. After the glue dries, set the rip fence on the table saw to cut the partial frames to the right width, as noted in *Door Joinery Detail.* Guide the edge of the outside stiles along the fence to make the cuts. Working this way ensures that the inside ends of the rails will be perfectly aligned.

Note: Cutting the rails to length after you've cut the mortises isn't a problem. You just have to remember to make the tenons slightly shorter to allow for the difference.

7 **Cut the panel grooves.** Fit the inside stiles to the partially assembled frames, and clamp the pieces together. Rout the grooves for the panels with a ¼-inch wing cutter as you did for the case sides.

8 **Make the panels.** Make a pattern from ¼-inch plywood as you did for the side panels. Trace the pattern onto the pieces that you edge-glued for the panels. Cut the panels to shape, and rabbet their edges to form tongues that fit into the frame grooves. Again, the panels should have some clearance to allow for seasonal wood movement.

9 **Sand and assemble the doors.** Sand the inside edges of the frame pieces, and sand and prefinish the door panels. Slip the panels into the grooves in the frames, and glue the inside stiles in place. When the glue dries, pin the panels in place as you did with the case sides.

Make the Counter

1 **Make the substrate.** Make the substrate top and the spacers from hardwood plywood or other sheet material such as medium-density fiberboard (MDF). Cut the spacers to the sizes given in the Materials List. Cut the substrate top $\frac{3}{8}$ inch wider and longer than specified. Glue and screw one long spacer along one long edge of the top with $1\frac{1}{4}$-inch drywall screws. Try to keep the long edges flush, but don't worry about it too much—you'll be trimming them flush in a minute. The ends of the spacer should overhang the ends of the top by about $\frac{1}{4}$ inch.

Trim the long edges dead flush by running the substrate face down through the table saw. Run the edge without the spacer against the fence. Try to remove about $\frac{1}{8}$ inch of material from the overall width of the top. Glue and screw the other long spacer to the second long edge of the top. Set the fence to cut the top to the specified width, and trim the pieces flush. Cut the short spacers to fit in between the long spacers. Glue and screw them in place with #8 × $1\frac{1}{4}$-inch drywall screws. Try to make the outside ones flush with the edge of the top, and try to position the inner ones so they will flank the sink. Trim the substrate to its specified length, trimming the spacers in the process.

2 **Make the sink cutout.** Lay out the shape of the sink cutout on the surface of the substrate. Most sink manufacturers provide a pattern right in the box along with the sink. Keep in mind that the backsplash runs along the back of the counter, so you may want to position the sink slightly forward of dead center. Cut along your layout lines with a saber saw. Test the fit of the sink in the opening.

3 **Apply the plastic laminate.** Rip four strips of laminate to cover the edges of the counter. The strips should be $\frac{1}{2}$ inch or so longer and wider than the surface you want to cover. Start applying the laminate on the back edge of the counter. Coat both the edge of the substrate and the back of the laminate with contact cement. Wait until the contact cement loses its tack, then stick the laminate in place. Take your time aligning the piece so that it overhangs the substrate on all four sides. Apply firm pressure to the laminate with a J-roller or a smooth block of soft wood to set the adhesive. Use a flush-trimming bit in a router to trim the laminate flush with the substrate. Be careful as you're trimming along the bottom

When making a vanity or other cabinet that relies on a sink and/or hardware that must be custom fit, get the fixture and have it on hand before you start. That way you can be sure the item won't be discontinued, and you can take direct measurements if need be.

of the substrate: It is all too easy to have the guide bearing fall into a screw hole, which will allow the bit to cut a "hiccup" in the laminate.

Apply the laminate to the ends of the substrate next. Then do the front edge. Finally, apply the laminate to the top surface. Spread contact cement on both surfaces. When the cement is ready, lay a number of ¼-inch dowels across the substrate surface, and slide the laminate into position. The dowels will hold the two surfaces apart until you are sure you have the laminate where you want it. Once the laminate is in position, start at one end, sliding the dowels out one at a time and sticking the laminate down as you go. Apply firm pressure with a roller or block to set the cement.

Trim the edges of the laminate flush with the edges of the counter. Wipe a little petroleum jelly on the edges of the counter where the bit's bearing will ride; this will keep the bearing from burning the laminate if it should quit spinning. File the edges to make them friendly to the touch.

4 **Make the backsplash.** Cut the backsplash to the size given in the Materials List. Cut the ends to the profile shown in *Backsplash Detail*. Drill holes down through the countertop for the #8 × 2½-inch drywall screws that will secure the backsplash. Five screws should do the trick. Sand the backsplash to get it ready for finishing.

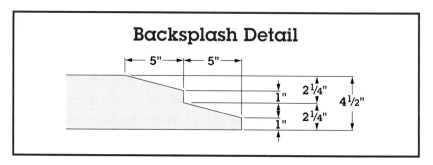

Backsplash Detail

5 **Add the cleats.** Cut the cleats to the size given in the Materials List. Screw them to the inside of the upper back panel and the apron with #8 × 1¼-inch drywall screws.

Finish the Vanity

1 **Hang the doors.** The doors hang from butt hinges screwed to the side frames. Mortise both the side frames and the door frames to accept the hinges. Screw the hinges in place, and check the fit of the doors.

2 **Make and install the pulls.** Cut the pulls to the shape shown in *Pull Detail*. Drill holes through the door frames, and glue and screw the pulls in place.

3 **Apply the finish.** Because of its proximity to water, a vanity needs a very durable, protective finish—polyurethane. Brush on three coats, inside and out, following the directions on the can. Also finish the backsplash, and give the underside of the counter and the edges of the sink cutout a couple of coats for good measure. Finishing the edges of the sink cutout is particularly important because if any water seeps in around the sink's rim, it can cause the plywood to swell, buckling the laminate. Finishing the cutout seals the raw edge of the plywood and helps prevent this problem.

4 **Attach the countertop.** Once the finish is dry, screw the backsplash to the counter with #8 × 2½-inch drywall screws. You may want to apply a bead of caulk to the bottom edge of the backsplash to keep water from seeping underneath. Then set the counter in place on top of the case, flush with the back and centered from side to side. Fasten it to the case with #8 × 1⅝-inch drywall screws driven up through the cleats. Four screws per cleat is plenty.

5 **Install the vanity.** Carry the vanity to its new home, and set it on the floor. Level it, if necessary, by loosening the screws that hold the case to the base and tapping in shims between the two parts. This way any gaps will be up underneath the case, where they will be hidden. Locate the studs in the wall, and screw the vanity in place with four #8 × 2½-inch drywall screws. Hook up the sink, and you're done.

Quick tip

When installing hinges, use only one screw in each leaf at first. This way, if you have to make any adjustments, you'll have only one screw hole to fill. When everything fits the way you want it to, drive in the rest of the screws.

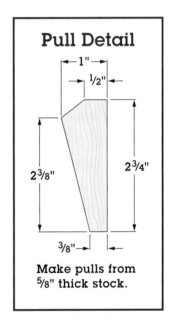

Pull Detail

1"

½"

2⅜"

2¾"

⅜"

Make pulls from ⅝" thick stock.

Index